Social Structure and Testosterone

1

INTRODUCTION

THE confrontation between sociology and biology is not a happy one. Both disciplines are life sciences, and both strive to explain significant aspects of human functioning. Biology begins with the basic cellular, organic, and metabolic processes of the body. Sociology begins with the basic fact of human interdependence and organization into collectivities guided by culture. Neither of these approaches by itself conflicts with the other, but on the margins of each discipline, clarity is lost. A principal point of contact and friction involves the field of ethology, the study of animal behavior in natural settings. Evolutionary and genetic vectors are used to explain mating, fighting, hierarchy, and other forms of social conduct or organization that find parallels among humans and are also the distinct subject matter of sociology. In the ethological tradition it is a short step to the assumption that, if adaptive pressures shaped genetic and social structure among animals, then humans, as evolutionary descendants of earlier forms and facing similar adaptive pressures, also carry genetic infrastructures for their social superstructures. Hence, many human social forms and practices are phylogenetic in origin.

Prima facie this is a plausible argument because humans are biological organisms sharing many anatomical, endocrinological, and structural features with their nonhuman cousins on the tree of evolution. Also, at the infrahuman level, biology appears to shape communal life in a manner that provides us with possible models for human social structure. But to an unwarranted extent, some ethologists (e.g., Lorenz 1966; Morris 1967) have assumed that human affairs must necessarily repeat patterns set down in a phylogenetic template. Otherwise, we would be contradicting Nature. In this they err because, while humans are necessarily as responsive to "bio-logic" as any animal group, unlike other animals we can modify biology through social arrangements, and this becomes increasingly possible as we learn more about the interplay of social and biological parameters.

Where other species are overwhelmingly restricted to *bio*-social limits, we are a *socio*-bio-social species, to a significant extent freed from an immutable biology that lays down social arrangements by genetic fiat. Biological determinist thinkers such as sociobiologists Wilson (1975) and Dawkins (1976) proclaimed in their early work the dominance of the genetic template in determining important social patterns. In response to a firestorm of criticism (e.g., Gould 1980; Lewontin 1977; Montague 1980; and see Freese 1988), they have acknowledged the principle of *coevolution,* in which socially provenanced culture is granted an important causal role along with biology in explaining social patterns (Lumsden and Wilson 1981). Yet, while seemingly backing away from gross biological imperialism (Kaye 1986 says they don't at all), these authors have failed to see that to an extent we may as yet only adumbrate, biology is itself susceptible to social determination. Within broad limits, concrete social arrangements can thus dictate a biology that underwrites specific social consequences. Changing the original social arrangements will change the biological parameters and their social effects as well. Hence, the harmony of body and society that the ethologists have proposed must not omit an account of how social conditions set the course for the body from the beginning.

Although present-day sociologists fiercely object to the sociobiological position, it is a testament to the remarkable power of the biological argument that many nineteenth-century sociologists took their cue from Darwin's evolutionary paradigm. They avidly accepted evolution and the "survival of the fittest" as sociological principles. Although Herbert Spencer ([1862] 1958) developed evolutionary notions even before Darwin published *The Origin of Species* in 1859, Spencer hailed Darwin's work, and Thomas Henry Huxley, one of the age's staunchest Darwinians, was an important intellectual influence on Spencer (see Coser 1971:110). In keeping with Darwin's model of natural selection and environmental adaptation, Spencer argued for the progressive differentiation of social forms. Ludwig Gumplowicz ([1899] 1977) adopted the Darwinian metaphor of "nature red in tooth and claw" (Alfred Lord Tennyson, "In Memoriam A.H.H.," 1850, lvi) and proposed that the basic rule of social life was conflict between separately evolved groups. William Graham Sumner ([1906] 1959), whose fame today rests on his concepts *folkways* and *mores,* argued that those who rose in the hierarchies of power, status, wealth, and distinction did so because they were fit by Nature to do so, while those who lagged behind were also fulfilling Nature's plan. Collectively these ideas came to be known as social Darwinism and were much employed in justifying social inequity, programs of eugenics, and conservative political agendas (see Hofstadter 1955).[1]

All the while, a different intellectual mood was gathering force in the nineteenth century, eventually taking command of the modern sociological stance on evolution and biology. The basic tone was set by Karl Marx, who proposed that particular forms of social conduct were the by-products of historically specific forms of social hierarchy and of possession of the material and social means of production; changes in these forms of social organization changed patterns of social conduct. No particular form of social organization was in fact natural. If it seemed so, it was because humans tend to accept prevailing forms, and because socially and materially advantaged elites use coercion or ideological indoctrination to prevent change.

Emile Durkheim ([1933] 1964) took the argument further, examining the evolution of the human division of labor and the "collective conscience," the normative patterns of belief and commitment that accompanied societal and occupational differentiation. He reasoned that the vast transformation of the division of labor in modern times, and of human consciousness in parallel with it, could not be the result of genetic evolution, since too little time had elapsed for this. Rather, both changes were due to transformed social conditions, namely, the increased density of social interaction and the elaboration of culture in the form of productive technology. In Durkheim's ([1895] 1966: 110) pronouncement, social facts were to be explained only by other social facts.

Rounding out the sociological consensus on the divergent paths of sociology and biology was Max Weber's dictum: "It must be one of the tasks of sociological and historical investigation *first* to analyze all the influences and causal relationships which can satisfactorily be explained in terms of reactions to environmental conditions" ([1904–1905] 1958:31; emphasis added). This despite Weber's assertion in a previous paragraph that hereditary influences in forming character are "very great." It was only, he averred, the insufficiently developed nature of biology as a science that made it imperative to pursue first the sociological and historical paths of analysis. Although biology is today vastly more developed than in Weber's time, the sociological prejudice against biology is only slightly diminished. It is three decades since Wrong (1961:184) admonished sociologists against an "oversocialized" conception of human subjects. Oriented toward a Freudian view, Wrong saw the id as not fully tamable and therefore argued that a raw edge of unpredictability and sometimes savagery must also be factored into social theories. Though much cited, Wrong's plea has gone mainly unheeded, especially by the social constructionist theorists I shall discuss below.

As sociology turned away from the Darwinian model toward a more analytical or socially critical stance after World War I, the ties with biology were sharply severed. The 1930s and World War II saw the completion of the divergence between sociology and biology—a reaction to the horrors of the biologically rooted racism promoted by the Nazis and Fascists. Although the biology was false, the biological approach as a whole was relegated to a penumbra from which it has not yet significantly emerged in sociology.

But the politics of science and the substance of science must be disentangled if possible. What makes bad politics may yet make good science if the two are kept distinct. This is treacherous ground, for, to some, even to suggest that biology may be a useful coign of vantage for sociological analysis is to betray the sociological heritage and promise. In this work, I shall rest my case for a sociological exploration of biology on the most pragmatic grounds: how well the incorporation of biology into sociological analysis fosters the latter. And, not so incidentally, biological analysis too can be enhanced through the examination of the social context of biological processes, as will be shown below.

Today, the sociological sticking point about biological explanations of social patterns is as follows: virtually all agree that while nurture and learning play some role in determining the behavior of nonhumans, the overwhelming influence is genetic. But among humans, the argument goes, learning and nurture and the influence of culture are so powerful that the genetic contribution is but a general one. Human intellect is a new evolutionary condition that negates evolution in the simple sense. Humans are thus capable of levels of collective organization and of conduct that are far removed from simple genetic determination. Indeed, the human potential is to stand evolution on its head. Not the "survival of the fittest," but making all fit to survive is the program of the most advanced societies. This evolutionary capability is not genetic in origin, but is due rather to culture and social organization and to the expression of the power of the weak (in the form of politics) and the conscience of the strong (in the form of normative ethics).

While sociology has observed its recent antibiological strictures more or less canonically, the story of the relations between the two disciplines would be incomplete without observing that sociology, despite its skittishness in biological domains, has nonetheless ventured toward biology in recent years. It has not, as in the days of social Darwinism, sought sources of explanation, but has sought rather to provide them. The emergence of medical sociology as a distinct and popular specialty signifies this development. As imperialistic in its way as ethology, sociology has probed deep into life processes to confront seemingly simple biological verities with amplifying social conclusions. Exemplary in this regard are Dohrenwend's 1967 theoretical analysis of social stress and coronary infarctions and Flood and Scott's 1978 findings on how power and power encroachment among such hospital divisions as administration, nursing, and surgical staff affect both morbidity and mortality among surgical patients.

A most unlikely source of recent sociological interest in biology stems from Marxist sociology and the critical sociology associated with the Frankfurt school. Wilhelm Reich (1976), who presided over an early marriage of Marxism and Freudianism, saw the body as the locus of the deepest incursion of capitalism, particularly involving sexual repression. In the same vein, Marcuse (1955:35) saw Marx and Freud again to the altar, expounding on the notion of "surplus repression," whereby capitalism's early need for disciplined bodies at the anvils of industrial production led to excess repression of instinctual drives, particularly sexuality. His critical assessment was that a body freed of repression could also be a body in the vanguard of social transformation. (Birenbaum 1970 has commented on the fallaciousness of this idea.)

More recently, Turner (1984), taking a leaf from Foucault (1977, 1980), centered attention on the body as the focus of regulation and social control. He read the message of a good deal of social organization as devoted specifically to control of the body, whether through the proscriptions of religion or through the medicalization of deviance and other socially produced bodily conditions. In this same tradition, Freund (1988:839) has addressed the sociophysiological question in perhaps the frankest way yet, exhibiting a willingness to go directly to the physiological literature in order to work out a theoretical pathway to "bring society into the body." He is unusually blunt in his willingness to condemn the "mind-body dualism" that permeates much of cognitively biased present-day sociology. Such a bias leads to a blind social constructionism that exaggerates the prowess of society and mentality without seeing some of the real processes governing the interplay between society and the body.

Indeed, the results of sociological investigation of biological problems provide grounds for sociological optimism in that we have learned that social facts determine not only social facts, but biological ones as well. This is a very powerful argument for sociology, since it implies a causal role in biology when the peril sociologists have feared is just the opposite: that biologists will preempt the explanation of social phenomena.

The typical sociological approach to biology is simply to ignore it or to assert more forcefully and ideologically that biological influence is minimal or nil (Becker 1953; Gagnon and Simon 1973); but to biologists the position taken here may seem to be simply hubris. In essence, I assert that the proper model of the relations between sociology and biology is the socio-bio-social chain. Indeed, according to the new biology (Hamburg 1974), environmental and biological forces mutually influence each other, and, incontrovertibly, the social is today the most important environmental condition. The fundamental premise of this book is that biological processes are, to a significant degree, subject to social influence. The notion of the socio-bio-social chain directs attention to the fact that many biological conditions are themselves nested in social processes, which supervene to shape or potentiate them. These transformed biological conditions then feed forward into social arrangements, to reproduce or change them.

Dominance and Testosterone

The substantive pivot of the work to be presented here is the relationship between dominance or eminence attainment in social encounters and elevations or surges of the male hormone testosterone (T). Dominance is not a property of a person, it is a social relationship. In a dominance relationship one actor is able to compel another to do his or her bidding even when the other is unwilling or would prefer not to comply. The animal literature (see chapter 2) that deals with dominance relationships among conspecifics has established that victory in dominance encounters elevates T, while defeat decreases it. In many animal species T surges appear to be followed by increased access to sexual partners, priority access to food, and greater security from infringement on one's territory.

Among humans, a small but growing number of studies confirm that hormonal responses to victory and defeat are similar to those in animals. Since these studies were initiated only recently, we are not yet fully clear on the benefits of T elevation and the disadvantages of decline. However, studies of T replacement therapy in cases of hypogonadism and with sexually impaired males and females suggest an important role for T in maintaining libido. Other research suggests an important role for T in muscle anabolism, and this is why some athletes have resorted to it and to other androgens. From this we may deduce that T is a distal source of physical power and strength. It has also been found to be related to energy level, an important source of optimism and confidence. Other studies suggest that T is related to concentration and single-mindedness in tackling a task or pursuing a goal. Available data give us reason to believe that, within certain limits, T enhances performance of visuospatial tasks requiring highly abstract intellection.

These correlates of T among humans provide a ground from which to theorize further about the importance of T in human psychic and social affairs. My method is to examine the links of the socio-bio-social chain. In general, dominance or defeat in social encounters, whether as single events or as structured social regularities, is the first link; T elevation or decline is the middle link; and a social or psychosocial consequence is the final link in the chain. I shall apply this approach to a number of questions that previously have not been considered from this comprehensive view. Before turning to these questions, a theoretical-terminological matter must be clarified.

Dominance and Eminence

Because the first investigations of how human social encounters affect T followed directly from the results of the animal studies, they addressed the social side of the question in limited terms. The animal research showed that dominance (often gained in violent encounters) or loss of dominance affected T. Thus, social dominance, or loss of it, among humans was conceived of as the critical independent variable. Indeed, important results were obtained, sufficient to launch a field of inquiry.

But some studies showed that another type of social encounter, though usually not as striking or dramatic, nor as compressed in time as in dominance attainment, could also lead to T elevation. This type of encounter involved recognition by a social group of significant personal attainment or contribution to normatively supported group goals. In this mode of social encounter, opponents did not clash, and no one was defeated. However, individually or collectively, others in the group found reason to grant approval, deference, reward, benefit, rank, and the like. In one study, the attainment was officer status in a military unit, and in another, M.D. status upon graduation from medical school. In both cases, T rose.

While these findings might seem to muddy somewhat the relatively clear waters of the dominance-T relationship, they actually provide a useful and necessary extension of it. Opportunely, the results are compatible with the findings in many studies attempting to identify the fundamental modes of social relations, hence the outcomes are not theoretically embarrassing. In a large number of observational studies of social interaction, two important relational dimensions have been discovered repeatedly (Kemper 1978; Kemper and Collins 1990). One entails actions by one actor toward another that are intended to control, dominate, force, or overcome the other's resistance. The actions taken can range from a simple stare-down to a violent physical attack. Deprivation of accustomed benefits is a frequent tactic. A very large class of behaviors fit this mode of relationship, including strictly verbal assaults such as unflattering comments, criticism, interruption of speech, failure to respond to the other's verbal initiatives, and the like. Collectively, these actions, which are designed to gain social dominance, are termed *power relations*. When they succeed, that is, when they overcome the resistance of the other and the other is compelled to accede, *dominance* is established.

The second dimension discovered in the observational studies entails the accord of voluntary compliance by one actor to another. The reasons for this can be quite diverse: the other conforms to a group standard for performance, beauty, physical stature, worthiness of character, or valued ascriptive attributes; the other is of noble blood, for example. The social response here is to accord benefits, reward, attention, precedence, affection, interest, concern, and, at the ultimate level, love. In contradistinction to power relations in which compliance is gained through coercion, compliance with the wishes and desires of the other in this alternative mode is voluntary and uncoerced. This way of relating has been designated as *status-accord*, or status (Kemper 1978; Kemper and Collins 1990. Taken together, the power and status dimensions comprise an interaction space. Human actors can be located in this space according to the particular mix of power and status behavior they direct toward each other. Thus, each actor has a power and status standing vis-à-vis the other, and this defines the relationship between the actors (Kemper 1978; Kemper and Collins 1990).

Aptly, the power and status dimensions, with a theoretical and empirical literature of their own, allow for an important extension of the understanding of the dominance-T link. I shall use the term *eminence* to refer to attainment in the status mode. Alternatively, then, one may decisively defeat another in a competitive encounter, thus gaining dominance, or one may display striking, status-worthy conduct and gain eminence. Both dominance and eminence are grounds for T elevation. In this book, either dominance or eminence or both will be at issue in specific instances, and this will be reflected in the language that is used.

Theory As Method

This book is a theoretical exploration of the consequences of a body of empirical findings about dominance/eminence and T. I have attempted here to ground the theory in empirical finds and to be faithful to Isaac Newton's: "Hypotheses non fingo" or, roughly, "I do not speculate" (quoted in Shamos 1959:58). Indeed, despite his good intentions, Newton did speculate, as every scientist must. There is virtually no way that theory can limit itself to the available data. Theory is also an outrider, often perilously distant from the empirical findings, yet, when properly inspired, it can direct the flow of research into new and more productive channels. In this sense, theory is a method. Warburton (1983:339), following the approach of Bunge (1968), proposed that "a science increases both by surface growth, i.e., accumulating, generalizing, and systematizing knowledge, or by depth growth, i.e., introducing new concepts, going beyond the available information and explaining it." It is in the latter sense that I see theory leading our knowledge forward.

Given the tridisciplinary focus of this book—sociological, psychological, and biological—the relative standing of theory in these disciplines is pertinent.[2] Considering now only sociology and biology, it is clear that the remarkable attainments of biology in recent years eliminate all dispute over the standing of the two disciplines with respect to eminence. Biology is clearly primary. This does not mean that no confidence can be placed in sociological findings; rather, it means that some areas of sociology are strikingly undeveloped. As a defense against depreciatory and pejorative judgments, sociology has, in some respects, overconformed to the model of science. Sociology deplores speculation (by that name), though, clearly, much speculation appears in sociological work without the label.

Biologists, on the other hand, having so convincingly established the validity of their enterprise, can be much freer in their theoretical roamings in search of elusive explanations. On the frontiers of knowledge, biologists speculate, and they state frankly that they are doing so.[3] The virtue of this method is that it enables a scientist to pose a set of carefully reasoned possibilities that are intellectually plausible, even where no hard data support these surmises directly. To articulate them publicly is to place them in the domain of possible consideration by other scientists working on the same problem. Public speculation is no longer personal, but becomes a collective property—as all science is—and then operates in the collective understanding of the community of scientists. In a science worthy of the name, even such speculations find a yardstick by which they can be evaluated and either accepted or found wanting.

Thus, the canon of scientific purity requires not that we refrain from vaulting across intellectual chasms, but that we subject such leaps of insight to the standard practice of empirical evaluation. Indeed, the only true danger in violating Newton's dictum is to speculate on matters that are not susceptible to scientific demonstration.

Philosophical, ideological, or theological assertions are of this sort (T. Parsons 1951).

At some points, I take the argument further than the data strictly allow. I believe that in no case have I crossed the boundary into a nonscientific domain where propositions cannot, in principle, be tested. I trust that the plausibility of these kinds of assertions will lead to the necessary research that will either establish them or conclusively refute them. Although they are not many, they are necessary for the architectonic structure of the theory I offer here. At worst, they may be considered the equivalent of paleontological filler, which scientists in that field use to sketch out the full figure of an animal form merely from possession of a few fragments from the metatarsal arch, shin, or hip. A case in point is the construction of *Sinanthropus pekinensis* from the discovery of a single fossil tooth (see Hammond 1988:126). The obvious benefit of the speculatively filled-in remainder is that it constitutes a model against which other fragments can be evaluated. In the work that is detailed here, the "fill" is designed to guide empirical excursions along paths that might not otherwise be taken.

Substance

The substance of this book derives from the relationship between dominance/eminence and testosterone. Exemplified in various ways, it links the first two terms of the socio-bio-social chain. The final term is variable. Depending on the problem, different social or psychosocial outcomes are at issue. I explore several questions from the perspective of the socio-bio-social model.

The first deals with male sexuality, focusing first on an unresolved question from the Kinsey data in which it was found that lower-class males have higher rates of sexual activity than higher-class males up to about age forty, but after that the higher-class males have the higher rates. Other studies generally confirm this pattern. Kinsey and his colleagues explained the difference between classes strictly as a matter of culture; that is, different values attach to sexuality and masculinity in different classes. This approach fails to consider either social structural or biological vectors as possible determinants of the age-class interaction effect. I will examine the question in light of differential opportunity for dominance or eminence, hence surges of T, at different stages of the life cycle in different social classes.

A second issue pertains to male sexual infidelity. Although this pattern is clearly under normative control—permissive norms can, theoretically, lead to 100 percent infidelity—the interesting question is how to explain infidelity when social norms are clearly against it. It is possible to invoke such explanations as inadequate socialization or subcultural norms that tolerate infidelity, but these are likely to account for only a portion of the conduct. Here I again invoke the dominance/eminence–T link to examine possible sources of drives or motives for infidelity.

A third consideration of male sexuality leads to a general theory of how dominance/eminence, mediated by T, affects sexual incentives and satisfactions. My effort is to understand the link between dominance/eminence and the quality of intimacy with sexual partners. I shall argue that sexual occasions are themselves importantly dominance or eminence encounters and thus share all the consequential emotional and behavioral effects of these for both self and other.

In a fourth inquiry, I will consider the possible effects of the recent transformation in women's roles, and, therefore, in opportunities for dominance/eminence, on women's T-estrogen balance. This socioendocrinological change may have important effects on the performance of abstract visuospatial tasks, as required in occupations such as engineering, mathematics, architecture, and the like. I seek to pin down the social and historical validity of what is known as the Broverman hypothesis, which argues for women's relative deficiency in such tasks due to their sex-linked T-estrogen balance.

Finally, I will consider the possibility of vicarious dominance/eminence as a mechanism of social control. Given that dominance/eminence, underwritten by T, can assure a comfortable adjustment to the environment, and given that not all can be dominant or eminent in society, the question arises about how to maintain motivation in important cadres of actors whose commitment is deemed necessary in a modern society. The classic solution to the problem of motivating relatively deprived strata has been the idea of false consciousness, whereby those who are disadvantaged are pacified through getting them to identify their interests with those who are depriving them. While this idea has indubitable merit, I believe it rests too much on cognitive grounds. I will offer here an alternative that is rooted in the body; namely, false potency, a possible result of vicarious dominance/eminence.

Sociologists and Physiological Knowledge

Although sociologists may be attracted by the topics covered in this book, some may resist the specifics that involve physiological processes, hence lose an opportunity to become acquainted with the dynamics of the socio-bio-social chain. To forestall this, I wish to provide a definition of the situation that may be helpful. It stems from my own experience when I first encountered psychophysiological data in my study of emotions (Kemper 1978). As a sociologist, I initially resisted reading materials about the physiological sites, structures, or processes of emotion. This meant that the brain, autonomic nervous system, and neurotransmitters were terra incognita for me for a time, because I would either avoid reading the materials, even in otherwise interesting and pertinent articles or books, or read with such a glazed state of attention that later I could not call on what I had read. It was simply that I did not care. As I defined my situation, I did not need to deal with biological questions when my professional identity was that of sociologist.

Ultimately, sense overcame nonsense and I allowed myself to be persuaded. I found it very helpful to read an account of the bodily loci and processes of emotions in a book by sociologist Gordon Moss (1973). I copied the relevant pages, read and underlined copiously, and, after a third reading, recognized that a systematic body of knowledge was covered there. More important, coming that far enabled me to see that certain findings at the psychophysiological level resonated with our knowledge about certain structures and processes at the sociological level. At that moment, my know-nothing attitude toward a specialized knowledge that lay outside the boundaries of my professional commitment was transformed into an avid interest. Indeed, from that point I steeped myself in the physiological literature because I saw how important a sociological advantage it afforded. Only by coming to terms with the language and questions of physiology and psychophysiology could I pursue a truly adequate sociological theory of emotions. Indeed, I could thereby demonstrate the power of sociological analysis in a domain ordinarily considered distant from it. Once perceived as a possibility, this was not a prize I intended to shun because of mere academic bias, spurious notions of specialization, or discreditable laziness. Sociologist readers can thus take heart. Also, in what follows, technical details about T are few, and what is necessary is handled briefly and with the sociologist in mind.

Biologists and Sociological Knowledge

Having addressed the fears of sociologists about biological knowledge, it is imperative to address the possible disdain of biologists for sociological understanding. It is a common experience among sociologists who meet physicians, physiologists, psychoneurologists, or endocrinologists that a dominance encounter takes place, and most often members of the biological groups act as if they have won it. It then can take enormous effort to bring the biological scientist to the point of admitting any pertinence or relevance to the sociologist's point of view. First, the dominant partner in social encounters ordinarily sets the agenda of topics and how they will be discussed. This means that the issue is often automatically phrased in biological terms, most often at a level that the sociologist cannot understand. This immediately provides the biologist with a self-fulfilling prophecy: the sociologist is an inferior scientist, and his or her ignorance of the biological details confirms it. Second, the biologist frequently begins with the prejudice that sociology is not a science. In the rank order of the professions and occupations in Western societies, science has high honorific status. And justly so. It is a noble calling—both as a warrant of the powers of the mind and as a frequent source of the most humane contributions to the human lot. But it is also a potential source of unwarranted snobbery, in which the ranking of the disciplines according to their "scientificness" is also a social device to claim attention, resources, and authority. If biologist readers remark that this is commonplace knowledge, they should also recognize that it is sociological knowledge that is being held so cheap.[4] Indeed, it is the sociologist's work to study the social organization of groups and the structure of intergroup relations, the sources and consequences of dominance among groups, and the way in which linguistic devices, such as the label "science," become not merely descriptors, but honorifics that may obscure much more than they honor.

The peril of the biologist reader of this book is that he or she may regard the sociological stance as scientifically lacking, hence not worthy of serious attention. This would be to fail to appreciate, not sociology, but modern biology, which is a science of life, not merely biochemical reactions in cells or organic processes. This means that where biological processes occur in the context of social relations, the latter are significant in guiding the biological process, that in different social circumstances the process would not occur in the way that it does or would not occur at all, and that the way to understand the biological fully is to incorporate a view of it from the seemingly distal stance of the social.

A case in point is that in the study of sexuality and intimacy, biologists have sought to understand physiological processes that have nonetheless eluded their understanding. The argument of this book is that sexuality and intimacy—even at the animal level—are so crucially social as well as biological that neither perspective can give an adequate account without the other. In another instance of the inseparable mix of the biological and the social, I consider here the effect of the transformation of women's social roles on their biological processes. Women's biological template in one social structural setting may be very different in another setting. This can almost never be discovered by looking at the biological parameters of females only at one point in time. Instead, we must find out how their biology changes at different points in time as the social structural position of women changes.

The biologist reader must accept that there are some biological problems that cannot be settled without knowledge of the social setting of the tissues, organs, or secretions at stake. This requires acknowledgment that, at least in some domains of biological analysis, the social can be decisive. This book deals with questions of that sort, where biology and sociology assemble into a socio-bio-social chain to explain what neither discipline can explain alone.

I turn now to a final, regrettably polemical, but necessary preliminary consideration, dealing once again with the sociology-biology debate, but this time as an intradisciplinary struggle among sociologists for the right to define sociological reality. The focus of the debate is sexuality, but as sociologists are well aware, the implications extend radially to cover the entire field. Although at this point biologist readers may conclude that the debate does not concern them and that the next section may be skipped, in fact it concerns them deeply. What kind of sociological theory they have to confront and build bridges toward does make a difference to biology. In one kind they face an implacable foe, in another is the opportunity for complementary theories that illuminate the pathways toward each other.

The Social and Biological Construction of Sexuality

Currently the dominant sociological perspective in explanations of sexuality is social constructionism (Gagnon and Simon 1973; DeLamater 1981; Reed and Weinberg 1984; Tiefer 1987). This view, which relies heavily on the "social script" approach of Gagnon and Simon (1973), holds that there is no essential, biologically driven sexual nature that determines sexual conduct. According to Tiefer, who was describing Michel Foucault's compatible stance, rather than sexuality being grounded in biology (an understandably common view), "there is a human potential for [sexual] consciousness, behavior, and physical experience able to be developed ('incited') by social forces" (1987:72–73). These forces are cultural and historical (Gagnon 1973) and they become available to individuals in the form of "scripts" that underlie the "learning [of] the meaning of internal states, organizing the sequences of specifically sexual acts, decoding novel situations, setting limits on sexual responses, and linking meanings from nonsexual aspects of life to specifically sexual experience" (Gagnon and Simon 1973:19).

Scripts for sexual conduct are presumed to be like scripts for any other behavior. They organize and determine in a general way both conduct and the meaning of the conduct, without which the behavior, even sexual behavior, presumably would not occur. Gagnon and Simon note: "It is only because they are embedded in social scripts that the physical acts themselves become possible" (1973:9). For example, to explain differences in sexual behavior in different social classes (as I will do below), one would look at the different class scripts for such behavior. Indeed, in their landmark study of sexual conduct, Kinsey, Pomeroy, and Martin (1948) more or less took this view. No independent incentive value is attributed to hormonal or biological vectors or to other sociological conditions. According to Gagnon and Simon, "with reference to socioeconomic status (SES) differences, the link to the biological level appears even more tenuous, unless one is willing to invoke the relatively unfashionable conceptual equipment of social Darwinism" (1973:18). Indeed, social Darwinism is not only out of fashion, but is also heartily condemned by present-day sociologists, as we have seen above. Gagnon and Simon do not contemplate that there may be biological pathways into the analysis of socioeconomic status differences in sexuality that have nothing at all to do with outmoded doctrines of social class superiority and inferiority derived from Darwinian theory. Their stance resonates with Durkheim's rejection of any biological explanation of social facts, a position that perhaps made sense in 1895 when Durkheim was trying to gain acceptance for sociology as an autonomous form of explanation.[5] Sociology today is far from needing to defend its flanks againt the incursion of other disciplines. Indeed, its forte is that it can explain some problems in other disciplines, including biology, that those disciplines cannot themselves explain.

Notwithstanding that social intervention in the form of cultural prescriptions indubitably shapes, directs, and constrains sexual behavior just as it does eating, sleeping, working, and so forth, we must recognize that it can do this with either a light or a heavy hand. If light, then the more individual, spontaneous, impulsive, and biological elements have greater play; if heavy, then the more personal, unsocialized, and biological elements are suppressed (even repressed), but, it seems reasonable to conclude, higher amounts of deviance inevitably result. As theorists of the Labeling school claim, deviance is in some part a product of the degree and type of social control (Becker 1963; Troyer and Markle 1982).

We must recognize, too, that every formal social constraint—law, rule, or moral principle—is directed against practices that would prevail to a significant degree were the constraint not articulated and enforced. For example, Judaic and Christian norms that have restricted sex behavior to procreation in constituted families were promulgated to oppose pagan practice of a less restrictive sexuality, or what moralists have called "license." Social constructionists might argue that license itself is a normative form, simply social constraint in the other direction. This suggests an appealing thought experiment that may test the validity of some of the more extreme assertions of the social constructionist argument on sexuality.

Let us consider two societies, one with rigorously constraining sex norms and the other with relatively little restriction. We might compare rates of sexual deviance in the two groups: to what extent in the restrictive society sexuality is practiced in opposition to the social constraints against it, and to what extent in the unrestricted society sexuality is left fallow and unpracticed, again in opposition to the social constraint. I do not consider here whether the unrestrictive society actively fosters sexuality or simply permits it. A society that actively fosters sexuality—where norms specifically prescribe conduct, with sanctions for nonfeasance—would provide a more stringent test. In the simply permissive society, the unrestricted sexual conduct is simply a "social current" (Durkheim [1895] 1966:4), which is what members of the society observe most others to be doing. To understand the ratio of the social and biological contributions to sexual conduct in the restrictive and the unrestrictive society, we must consider the relative costs, consequences, and sources of deviance in the two settings.

In the restrictive society, to oppose the norms by one's sexual conduct requires a proactive role: finding a potential partner; engaging in seduction, persuasion, or purchase to obtain the partner's consent; avoiding surveillance from agents of social control; managing one's own or one's partner's guilt, shame, anxiety, or depression that may follow the prohibited sexual behavior. All this takes daring or compulsion. In addition, there are the penalties for violation both to contemplate and to undergo if deviance is detected; for example, parental rage and other family sanctions, social ostracism, perhaps imprisonment, and sometimes physical punishment and death. By contrast, in the permissive society of our thought experiment, deviance, that is, not engaging in relatively free sexuality, would seem to be cost-free; there are no penalties, and no arduous proactive efforts are required. One simply refrains.

Yet, despite moral opprobrium and other perils, sexual deviance is common enough in restrictive societies: masturbation, incest, homosexuality, forbidden coital positions and orifices, fellatio, cunnilingus, premarital sex (and the out-of-wedlock pregnancy that is its frequent sign), extramarital sex, and prostitution. Even in the relatively puritanical period prior to our recent sexual revolution, Kinsey, Pomeroy, and Martin (1948; and Gebhard and Johnson 1979, using the Kinsey data) reported the following frequencies for various sexual deviances among males: masturbation, over 90 percent by age seventeen; premarital sex, over 80 percent by age nineteen; extramarital sex, about 40 percent; coitus with prostitutes, more than 65 percent by age thirty; homosexual experience, more than 35 percent by age twenty-five. (I cite the Kinsey data since they derive from a time when sexual codes were stricter than they are today, when deviance was more of a violation of social norms and scripts for sexual conduct.)

For some of these practices, particularly premarital and extramarital sex, there is undeniably a second sexual code—the double standard—which permits these behaviors by males while restricting them for females. Setting aside for the moment the female case, it seems plain that the second sexual code for males is somewhat after the fact, not before it. Male power in society has been such as to enable it to sanction its own deviance, overriding the culture's broader precepts for sexual conduct. That women have not been able to do the same is due at least in part to patriarchal power and possession and to women's consequently more suppressed (and repressed) sexuality. But as a more egalitarian social structure dethrones patriarchy, female sexuality emerges in every way as determined and fierce as that of males (Miller and Fowlkes 1980; Vance 1984). It is not social scripting that does this, but the opportunities afforded by increased power and status to satisfy one's desires.

In considering the two societies of our thought experiment, their sexual codes and respective types of deviance, we have little difficulty understanding why there is deviance in the restrictive society. Sexual libido or desire presses against the barriers to its expression. For this to occur on a social scale does not require that every individual's libido be equally strong and urgent. For various biological and social reasons individuals differ in libido strength. But we may also suppose an average strength—indexed in part by the rates of sexual deviance.

However, abstinence, which is sexual deviance in the permissive society, would be more difficult to explain. This is because sexual activity is pleasurable for most people—and, again, it is not social construction that makes it so. In the permissive society, excluding those below the normal range of libido (hypogonadal males, for example), those who are deviant by refraining from sexual opportunity might have religious, philosophical, or ideological scruples. These would oppose whatever biological drive underlies the active pursuit of sexual satisfaction. But it is implausible to think that many would refrain. There is just too much evidence for what it costs the mind and will to win against the flesh to provide an easy social script answer as the key to sexual conduct. Despite the logical and empirical arguments afforded by our thought experiment against a simple social constructionist view of sexuality, we can recognize that culture—the script writ large—decrees what is and what is not "sexual." For example, some groups find women's breasts arousing, some others apparently do not. (Whether they truly do not, or whether the ethnographic report merely notes a normative proscription that is much contravened in private is not easy to determine, but may have to be considered in the same light as normative proscriptions in our own society against masturbation, which are violated at exceedingly high rates [Kinsey, Pomeroy, and Martin 1948; Kinsey et al. 1953].) Notwithstanding cultural particularism with respect to the erotic, for most males there is something about females that is arousing. In dealing with somewhat similar issues, Perper (1985) has very sensibly made this point. Crucially, no society could or would proscribe all sexual behavior between men and women. This is not because it is inconceivable, but rather because it is impracticable without a degree of social control that would in time self-destruct from the biological frustrations of those whose task it was to enforce the unenforceable. Partial efforts of this kind over the centuries by religious orders have frequently foundered. No script or prescription urging violation of the stern sexual code was necessary for this to happen.

In the restrictive society of our thought experiment, deviance might stem from more or less conscious resistance to the authorities of social control (state, church, family); from philosophical and moral considerations about what constitutes human freedom; or from *biology*, namely, plain sexual desire aroused by the myriad ways in which desire is aroused in any given individual. For social constructionists, this motif of desire cannot exist because there is no essentialist biological sex drive. As Simon argued, "It is an 'illusion' that the body is a source of compelling sexual messages, controls sexual conduct, or is universal in its sexual expressions" (1974; quoted in Tiefer 1988:74). Hence, from a constructionist perspective, deviant sexual conduct can have no biological origin.

Contrary to the constructionist position, our thought experiment suggests, as Freud ([1927] 1961) did, that while society and sexuality can exist in various states of tension, from repressive hegemony to openness at the level of culture, practice presses hard for satisfaction of libidinal interests regardless of cultural controls. (G. Becker 1984 has provided a useful model of how the sex-inhibiting and sex-promoting tendencies may supplement each other in a given society.) Indeed, for Freud, societal stability requires some amount of control over sexuality. How much control is a question that some have posed

(Marcuse 1955; Brown 1959). The point here is that it is as foolish to eliminate biologically driven libido as a determinant of sexual conduct as it would be to eliminate appetite for food from discussions of what people do when they are hungry. Though culinary, gustatory, and other alimentary factors are to a great extent culturally determined, that is, socially constructed (Elias [1939] 1978), beneath them is a drive that does not brook nonsatisfaction except under the most stringent intellectual or emotional constructions, for example, a hunger strike on behalf of a political cause or the warped psychic resolve of an anorexic. Although no one, to our knowledge (as Beach 1957 pointed out), has ever died specifically from sexual deprivation, this means only that the sex drive is more amenable to social shaping, not that it has no autonomous strength or direction.

Some sense of the delicate balance that prevails in the relations between biological and social knowledge may be gleaned from Beach's culturological assertion about male sexuality and from the biosocial findings of Udry and his colleagues a generation later (Udry 1988; Udry and Billy 1987; Udry et al. 1985). Beach asserted that "the adolescent boy's periodic preoccupation with sexual matters is traceable to psychological stimuli, external or phantasied, and is not dependent upon his recently matured reproductive glands. His erotic urges stem more from sociocultural factors than from those of a strictly physiological nature" (1957:4–5). This statement is perfectly compatible with the current social constructionist view and is echoed in Gagnon and Simon (1973:18).

However, in a pioneering set of studies designed to ascertain the relative contributions of social and biological factors to sexual behavior among adolescents, Udry and his colleagues (1985) have shown that for males the central explanatory variables for sexual intercourse and other components of sexuality are androgenic hormones (mainly testosterone). In another study (Udry and Billy 1987), the basis for transition to sexual intercourse for young males is mainly hormonal. Social factors such as age (reflecting changes in age-graded norms for sexual conduct) and attractiveness (reflecting social norms for this attribute) drop out of the prediction equations once the hormones are entered, although an individual attitudinal factor (permissiveness about sexual conduct) remains. For females, social factors determine intercourse, but androgens (sex hormones) determine what might be called libido effects, such as desire for intercourse (Udry, Talbert, and Morris 1986). As Udry and his colleagues put it, "There can be no doubt that the effects of androgens on sexual behavior must operate through execution of learned patterns of social behavior as described by Gagnon and Simon. . . . Boys who progress to more intimate levels of sexual behavior follow a socially learned sequence (kissing, then increasingly intimate petting, then coitus). But our data strongly suggest that the degree of involvement in these socially determined patterns of sexual behavior is heavily influenced by serum androgenic hormones" (1985: 94). The point is clear: social scripts may construct what one may do and what it is legitimate to do in a given society to satisfy a libidinal interest. But this is not the whole story. Whether or not, other things equal, there is libidinal interest in the first place and thus pressure to take the steps the script provides—or even proscribes—is biological. Sexual deviance flourishes not so much because of ignorance of the script, or because there is a countercultural script, but rather because the script itself cannot fully regulate the conduct it seeks to direct. A separate, hormonal factor determines whether and when one chooses to engage in or deviate from script behavior. This makes sexual behavior biosocial, and a comprehensive theory needs to contain both the social and the biological elements. Indeed, the theory of the succeeding chapters is socio-bio-social. The social receives its full due, as social constructionists require, but not quite in the same way they would have it. To appreciate this, we must touch on another mode in which this work differs from the conventional social constructionist approach.

Culture versus Social Structure

Coupled with its abiological approach, social constructionism also emphasizes culture rather than social structure as an explanatory priority. In part this is because social constructionism derives from such cognitive and cultural approaches as symbolic interactionism, symbolic anthropology, ethnomethodology, literary deconstructionism, existentialism, and phenomenology (Tiefer 1987). It focuses on mental and symbolic operations and on their major tool, language. As the principal vehicle of culture, language becomes the overarching framer and framework of reality.

Notwithstanding their useful exposition of the role of culture in the determination of sexual conduct—and this is not denied here—social constructionists' virtually exclusive commitment to the cognitive, linguistic, and cultural approach has deterred appreciation of another form of social construction: the direct action of social structure. For present purposes, social structure is the arrangement of individuals and groups in a series of hierarchies in which some have more power and resources (i.e., are dominant) and/or receive more status or deference (i.e., are eminent). Like culture, social structures construct social conduct, but differently from the culture-linked normative processes that are widely understood to be the meaning of present-day social constructionism. Social structures socially construct either indirectly through determination of culture content, or directly.

In the matter of determining culture content, those who have power and resources or who can mobilize deference (or status) control the means of cultural production, enforce certain cultural definitions, and socialize others according to the cultural dictates they espouse. Ordinarily, the elites of power and status or deference foster cultural definitions in accord with their own interested version of reality (frequently called *ideology*), although sometimes they espouse segregated and specialized cultures—one style for themselves and another for the remainer of society (see, e.g., Elias [1939] 1978). Social constructionist sociologists fully recognize this indirect effect of social structure, and their work consists mainly of an elaboration of its implications (Gagnon 1973; Tiefer 1987).

What social constructionists typically ignore about social structure, despite some lip service to the importance of power in society, is its direct effect. At the macro level, the powerful not only enforce socialization codes and define reality through culture, they also beat, arrest, and imprison opponents; they enforce deference routines by painful sanctions; they compel conformity by inducing fear of punishment; they overcome opponents in direct confrontations in courts of law and in election contests; and they impose their will through legislative and judicial fiats, business and governmental executive decrees, and by direct exclusion from education, jobs, housing, recreation, and other opportunities.

At the micro level, the powerful control their interpersonal environments through verbal and physical violence, preemptive decisions, reducing others to dependency, and forming coalitions with the weak in order to defend against potential rivals (Simmel 1950; Ridgeway and Diekema 1989). By these actions, a social structure thrives at the micro level that is no less authentic than at the macro level where social roles are formalized and reflect society's social organization.

In the foregoing examples, it can be seen that social structure as used here encompasses the entire range of relations that issue directly in hierarchy, from the most fixed, as in class divisions, to the most fluid, as in the shifting fortunes of interpersonal interaction between intimates—or anyone, for that matter. Social structure is to an important extent independent of culture because it does not rely exclusively on expectations for behavior, or norms, and is less subject to intervening interpretation through language and symbols. For example, a punch in the mouth is a punch in the mouth, and usually it hurts.[6] A high-decibel vocalization in an argument is oppressive physiologically. Undeniably, these may also have symbolic, hence cultural, significance, but when they occur, it is also a direct injury over and above any cultural interpretation as insult or impropriety. By extension, any loss or deprivation, for example, of money, power, or status (when taken in Weber's 1946 sense as the ability to achieve one's will in a communal action) is similarly noxious in a direct way. Likewise, any gain of money, power, or status, whether as a result of a contested microinteraction or as a feature of position in the macrostructure of society, is a real, as opposed to symbolic, victory. Not that symbolic victories and defeats are unimportant; but they gain meaning only because there are real ones. Collins (1975, 1981, 1990) has proposed that direct structural effects tend also to have a cumulative effect. Victory in one microinteraction generates energy and confidence and these angur well for success in future interactions. Among losers, there is a corresponding loss of energy and confidence that bodes ill for the outcomes of future interactions.

The advantage of the direct social structural approach taken here is that it ties in both theoretically and empirically more closely with biological states and attributes of the actor than does conventional social constructionism. For example, Collins (1975, 1981, 1990) has formulated the outcomes of his social structural theory in organismic and emotion terms—energy and confidence. I have hypothesized connections between power/status interactional outcomes, the raw materials of social structure, and emotions and their physiological substrates (Kemper 1978; 1987). Mazur (1985) has formulated a biosocial theory in which success and failure act through enhanced or depressed T to augment further success or failure. Although it is not impossible in principle to build similar links between culture and physiological outcomes, this has been shunned by social constructionists for various reasons (see Tiefer 1987 for a review), so no progress on this question can be expected from that quarter for the present.

There is a good deal that is as yet unplumbed in the confrontation between social constructionist and nonconstructionist approaches. No sociologist will deny the validity of constructionism as commonly understood. But sociologists who deny there is anything else block the development of a more complex sociology that meshes fruitfully with other sources of explanation rather than merely dismissing them.

To conclude, some of the data and the argument I will present here belong to a different context from that of the dominant paradigm in present-day sociological considerations of sexuality. I examine not culture, but social structure, and look to biological as well as social vectors of sexuality. The sociologically unremarkable conclusion will be that the social determines the biological, which then feeds forward to determine the social, not only for sexual conduct, but for domains well beyond it.

2

SOCIAL STRUCTURE, TESTOSTERONE, AND MALE SEXUALITY

IN a remarkable study, Mazur and Lamb (1980) discovered elevated levels of the hormone testosterone (T) in young adult men who scored decisive victories in tennis matches, while T declined in the losers. Booth and his colleagues 1989 have replicated this finding. Mazur and Lamb also found that mere victory (when tennis winners were not sharply distinguished from losers) or gain without effort (winning a one-hundred dollar lottery that was totally determined by chance) had no effect on T. Finally, they found a rise in T in medical students within a day of their graduation; that is, when they achieved significant social elevation. Earlier, Kreuz, Rose, and Jennings (1972) found that during the difficult early stages of officer candidate school, T level and sexual interest declined in the trainees. By the end of the course, T level, along with sexual interest, had returned to normal. In accord with these results, Elias (1981) discovered greater elevation of T in winners of college wrestling matches than in losers. Ellertsen, Johnsen, and Ursin (1978) found that military trainee parachutists who executed good jumps in the final stage of schooling showed elevated T, and Davidson, Smith, and Levine (1978) found that T fell significantly among the same group of trainees after their initial, frightening jump from a training tower. Dabbs (1988) also reported elevated T for forty-eight hours in one parachutist after a successful skydiving experience. Jeffcoate and colleagues (1986) found that after two weeks aboard the circumscribed environment of a small sailing vessel, the two most dominant men showed the highest elevation of T from baseline.

In each of the studies reported above, human males displayed higher levels of T after social interactions or socially valued experiences in which they emerged dominant over competitors or attained significant elevations of social status; also, in a number of cases, they displayed reduction (or lesser rise) in T after losing a direct competitive struggle or confronting a serious status-threatening experience.

My purpose in this chapter is to extend the implications of this work by examining the relationship between location in societal social structure—the main arena of dominance and status attainment—and T, especially as this affects male sexual behavior. The argument here is that social structure affects T level in males, and that this ramifies for sexual practice through the relationship between T and both sexual appetite (libido) and performance (potency and ejaculation). In pursuing the analysis, some nonobvious conclusions will emerge in relation to the variable association between social structure and male sexuality over the life span.

This venture into sociopsychoendocrinology proceeds through relatively uncharted waters. There is little tradition in scholarship, and there are only a few empirical studies that reflect the approach taken here. Only very recently have any efforts in this direction been initiated (see Barchas 1984; Barchas and Mendoza 1984; Ellis 1986; Ellis and Ames 1987). In the scant research in sociophysiology (Kaplan and Bloom 1960; Barchas 1976), the main approach has been to measure physical properties with external indicators, such as heart rate, skin temperature, blood pressure, and electroencephalograph (EEG) waves. In research experience with T, several methodological epochs can be noted. Until recently, studies of T level in humans were also conducted mainly in a noninvasive way, through urine analysis. However, the development of radioimmunoassay techniques (discussed in Doering et al. 1974; see also Strand 1983) made possible highly accurate determination of T in blood plasma, where T level is more nearly like what reaches target organs than is true for urinary T (Nieschlag 1979). A substantial amount of our current knowledge is based on studies of this type. Even more recently, a method to detect T in saliva has been perfected (Wang et al. 1981). This technique, which provides a very good approximation of the amount of effective T (known as *free T*) that actually binds with receptor cells, has rapidly become the method of choice (Booth et al. 1989; Dabbs et al. 1987). Although saliva sampling is not as invasive as venipuncture, it does require a few minutes to collect enough saliva to assay, and, like other methods, the interruption of ongoing activity may, depending on the research interest, impose some constraint on the behavior that is at issue. To what degree this is the case is presently unknown. Notwithstanding the different methods for T analysis used by the investigators whose work is reviewed here, the findings discussed in this book do not vary by method.

First, to provide some endocrinological orientation I will briefly discuss the known properties of T from the perspective of a social interest. Next I will turn to the main topic of this chapter: the relationship between social structure, T, and male sexual behavior. In chapter 3 I will explore two additional aspects of male sexuality—infidelity and the social components of sexual conduct in the course of emotional intimacy—from the same social and biological perspectives.

Testosterone

The human endocrine system consists of glands (e.g., adrenal, thyroid, pituitary, pancreas, testes, ovaries) that manufacture and release hormones into the bloodstream. Hormones are chemical messengers that instruct various target organs to perform or to cease to perform certain actions that are more or less vital to life, for example, normal growth, proper metabolism, spermatogenesis in males, and periodic ovum release in females.

Androgens are a class of hormones, found mainly in males (although females also possess these), of which T is possibly the most important. Manufactured mainly in the testes in males (and in the adrenal cortex and ovaries in females), T is responsible for the differentiation of male and female primary sex characteristics at about the seven week of fetal life. Without the gonadal release of testosterone (and possibly other androgens), which is diffused to the brain through the bloodstream by the male fetus, even a genetic male will not develop male external genital organs. T is responsible for differentiation of the central nervous system (mainly the hypothalamus) into male and female types with respect to differentiated reproductive cycles and functions (Vander, Sherman, and Luciano 1975; Martin 1985). Males also receive major surges of T at puberty so that the task of sexual differentiation can be completed (estrogen surges in females at that time). T is responsible for the development of secondary sex characteristics in males, such as pubic and facial hair, deepening of the voice, and ability to ejaculate sperm-laden semen. Insight into the role of T in this process has been gained through the investigation of those rare individuals who become sexual anomalies—genetic males who develop female genitalia or genetic females who possess male genitalia at birth (Money and Ehrhardt 1972; Ehrhardt and Meyer-Bahlburg 1979).

In normal males, T is found in blood plasma in amounts ranging between about 3.5 and 8.5 billionths of a gram per milliliter. T secretion into the bloodstream follows a circadian rhythm, with highest levels reached during the early morning hours (DeLacerda, Kowarski, and Johanson 1973). There is also rapid temporal variation in T level, with secretions occurring six or seven times a day in short spikes (Nieschlag 1979; Schwartz, Kolodny, and Masters 1980). T sharply increases with REM (rapid eye movement) sleep or with tumescence during sleep, and morning erections occur when T is at its highest (Nieschlag 1979; Schiavi et al. 1982). T level generally begins to decline at about age fifty to fifty-five (Vander, Sherman, and Luciano 1975; Nieschlag 1979). However, this has not been found to be universally true (see Baier, Biro, and Weinger 1974; Harman and Tsitouras 1982), and this issue will be discussed further below. Regardless of T level in blood plasma, a good deal of T is physiologically inactive because it is bound by sex hormone binding globulin (SHBG). Only unbound, or free, T is available to act on target organs or receptors (Nieschlag 1979). It is estimated that between 2 and 8 percent of T is unbound (Dai et al. 1981; Hammond et al. 1986).

Frequent sampling of T is a recent development, and the usual practice has been to rely on single samples. Researchers estimate that there is a fairly high correlation between single samples taken on different days (Monti, Brown, and Corriveau 1977; Olweus et al. 1980). Single samples of T are estimated to lie within 20 percent of mean T level at the 68 percent level of confidence (Bradford and McLean 1984; Schwartz, Kolodny, and Masters 1980). This large error of estimate appears to be a function of the rapid oscillations that are possible in T level. For example, Doering et al. (1974) report "random peaks" with an amplitude of 50 percent of mean T level within a period of several hours.

In concluding this discussion on a point of variability in T, it is necessary to consider the sources of this variability. First, T level is argued to be under biological, perhaps genetic, control (Dai et al. 1981). However, were this the only source of variation, any investigation of the matter would be restricted to the endocrine and other biological systems. A principal assumption here is that, to an important degree, T level is under psychological and social control. The latter, especially, will be examined for its effect on T and on certain putative precursors or sequelae of T, namely, dominance/eminence, aggression, and sexual conduct, and how these vary by position in the social structure of society.

Social Structure and Male Sexual Behavior

My purpose now is to examine the relationship between social structure and sexual conduct as mediated by T. But the path is not direct. Dominance and aggression are also implicated, mainly because they

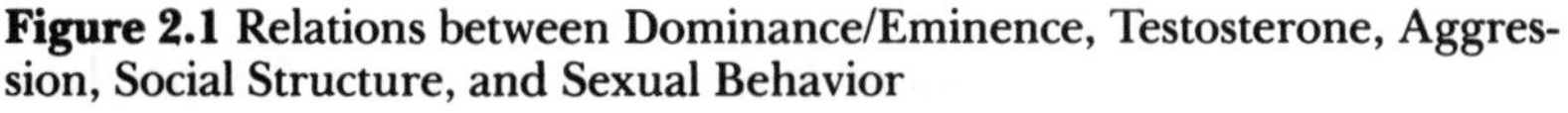

Figure 2.1 Relations between Dominance/Eminence, Testosterone, Aggression, Social Structure, and Sexual Behavior

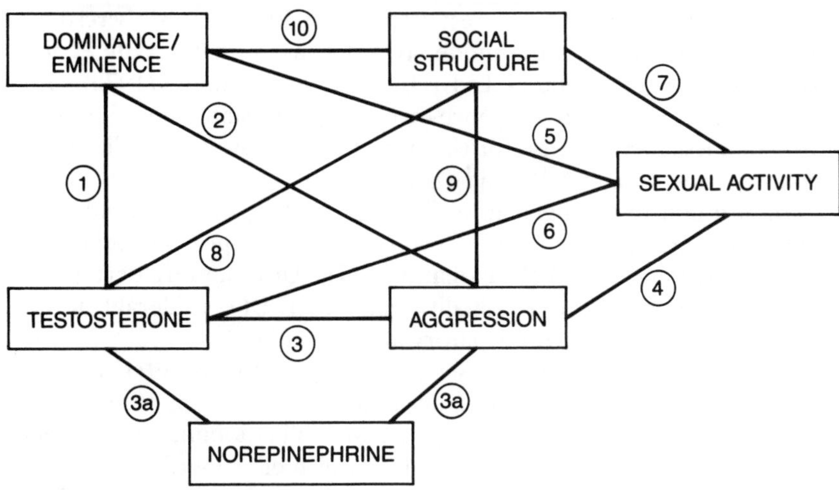

have been linked both to T and to sexuality. In addition, they are related to social structure. Taken together, there are five variables, and it is useful to examine the relations among them. Figure 2.1 depicts the five variables connected in the manner of a completely saturated causal or path diagram. It is not intended to be taken literally as a causal model because the data do not permit a clear delineation of causal direction. This is indicated by the absence of the arrowheads that are found in path models. It is likely that many of the links are reciprocal, as will emerge in the discussion below. To afford greater clarity in connecting discussion to model, paths are numbered and will be discussed in numerical order. (An additional pair of paths, both labeled 3a, which connect only with T and aggression, is also shown in figure 2.1 and will be discussed below.) The argument will both unfold and cumulate as we move from path to path.

Testosterone and Dominance/Eminence

At the outset of this chapter I cited research in which T was elevated in winners or among those who achieved an unwonted level of recognition or status through their own effort. As discussed in chapter 1, *dominance* refers to elevated social rank that is achieved by overcoming others in a competitive confrontation, and *eminence* is where the elevated social rank is earned through socially valued and approved accomplishment. Both dominance and eminence are described by Mazur and Lamb (1980) and Booth et al. (1989), via tennis victories and medical school graduation, respectively. In Elias's (1981) wrestling matches, dominance is the mode, as is the case with Jeffcoate et al.'s (1986) nautical competitors. In Kreuz, Rose, and Jennings (1972), officer candidates attained eminence through formal status elevation, as is true in a less formal sense for the parachutists in studies by Ellertsen, Johnsen, and Ursin (1978) and Dabbs (1989).

In addition to the behavioral findings relating human social rank elevation and T, there are now two confirming paper and pencil results (Christiansen and Knussmann 1987a; Udry and Talbert 1988) linking dominance as a personality trait and T. Of considerable interest, too, are the many confirmatory animal studies.[1]

In a long-term analysis, Rose, Bernstein, and Gordon (1975) followed the vicissitudes of dominance and T in two groups of monkeys. In an initial group of four males, when an alpha (dominant) emerged, his T level rose, while the T level of the most subordinate of the remaining three dropped 80 percent. When this group was subsequently introduced into a larger established group, the initial four contested for dominance and lost. Their T level fell. But the alpha animal of the established group experienced a 238 percent rise in T after he successfully maintained his dominant position.

Keverne (1979) found that the dominant monkey in a social group had higher T in the presence of females than the most subordinate animal. But if the alpha monkey was removed, the T level of the subordinate rose. Even a beta (second most dominant) monkey had insufficient T to ejaculate when the alpha was present. But in the absence of the alpha, his T level rose sufficiently to enable him to ejaculate.

Confirming the results of the studies with humans, Mendoza and her colleagues (1979) found that when dominance hierarchies were established in various groups of male monkeys (as is normal in these species), the dominant animals showed a marked increase of T, while the subordinates showed a marked decrease.[2] What is most compelling is that the T level of the animals prior to interaction did not predict subsequent dominance status. According to Mendoza, "Relationships between males, therefore, influence each individual's physiological state rather than the individual's physiological state determining the nature of the relationship to be formed" (1984:20–21). This is fully in accord with the fundamental hypothesis about the relationship between social structure and T that is being examined here.

The animal results permit us to suppose, as Mendoza et al. (1979) suggest, that it is not dominance per se that leads to elevated T, but the acquisition (and possibly reaffirmation) of dominance. In fact, in well-established groups of monkeys, dominance status and T levels are not correlated (Mendoza 1984). T levels are particularly susceptible to change when dominance relations change, but in stable social-rank orders, T levels regress to a mean and are apparently responsive to other influences (Rose et al. 1974). In this respect, Mendoza (1984) noted that secretions or infusions of T do not increase dominance status, nor does reduction or elimination of T (by castration) change dominance status (but see Keverne 1979:294) or prevent one from attaining it.

Two noteworthy effects linking T level to dominance have been found: rise in T with attainment of dominance and decline in T with loss or submission. Henry (1980) included both effects in his comprehensive integration of hormonal with emotional and interactional outcomes. They also are vitally involved in the connection between social structure and sexuality over the life span (discussed below).

Dominance/Eminence and Aggression

There is no special literature on the relationship between dominance and aggression, though it is clear that the two overlap: some, but not all, dominance, is achieved and maintained by threat of aggressive action (Keverne 1979). At least some aggression that is intended to achieve dominance fails to do so, leading instead to defeat. Although the aggressive basis of dominance is implicit in virtually all animal studies, there are species in which aggressive relations do not emerge (Chance and Jolly 1970; Jolly 1972; Mendoza 1984). Among humans, it is clear that elevated social rank can be founded on either an aggressive or a nonaggressive basis—the power (dominance) and status (eminence) modes. Mazur distinguished between dominance (elevated social rank) and aggression (behavior with intent to harm another), and proposed that, at least among humans, "testosterone affects dominance behavior but not aggressive behavior" (1983:564). Hinde (1979) also conceptually disjoined aggression and dominance. However, not all investigators do this, and both data and discussion of them are sometimes contaminated by the obscuring of the difference. This is one of the many cautions that the discussion in this chapter must observe. The dominance-aggression nexus will be considered again below in relation to sexual activity. But first it will be useful to examine the relationship of T to aggression. Any evidence of this connection can at least partially confirm the separate results linking dominance to T, because on some occasions dominance is attained through aggression.

Testosterone and Aggression

There is consistent evidence that males are more physically aggressive than females (Maccoby and Jacklin 1974). Some aggression may be due to males' larger average physical stature and muscle mass. Since both physical stature and muscular development are related to testosterone (Strand 1983; Martin 1985)—and this is the reason for the widespread use of testosterone-related steroids by athletes (Haupt and Rovere 1984)—there has been a natural interest in the relationship between T and aggression. Animal studies show a relationship between T and aggression (Beach 1977), but the relationship is unclear because aggression often occurs in the presence of females, when T levels may be especially elevated (Keverne 1979). Furthermore, when females are present, the dominant male, whose T level is relatively elevated by virtue of his dominance activities, initiates the aggression (Keverne 1979).

Among humans, investigators have pursued a possible three-way link between T, aggression, and sexual conduct by focusing on T and aggression among sex offenders. Rada, Laws, and Kellner (1976) found that child molesters and rapists in general were not significantly different from normals in T, but violent rapists had significantly higher T levels than other sex offenders or normals. Although Bradford and McLean (1984) found no relationship between sexual violence and T in their study of sex offenders, and Langevin et al. (1988) could not discriminate between sexual sadists and normals by T level, Bradford (1988) reported T differences according to the violence of the acts committed by sex criminals.[3]

Studying ordinary criminals in prison, Kreuz and Rose (1972) found that those who had committed violent crimes in adolescence had higher T, although there was no connection between T and fighting while in prison. Kreuz and Rose reasoned that early physical maturity, stimulated by rapidly rising T, had placed these men at greater risk of committing aggressive acts in adolescence. In another prison study, Ehrenkranz, Bliss, and Sheard (1974) found that men who had committed violent crimes (murder, assault) did not have higher T than men who were socially eminent in the prison (they held prestigious jobs). But both these groups had higher T than other types of prisoners. Dabbs and his colleagues (1987) also found higher T levels among convicts who had committed violent crimes. Inmates with higher T level were also rated as tougher by other inmates. (See also Schiavi et al. 1984, who found the T-violence connection among a group of genetically abnormal XYY convicts).

Several other studies offer additional, modest confirmation of the T-aggression relationship. Scaramella and Brown (1978) found that T level in competitive hockey players was positively correlated with six of seven ratings of aggressiveness provided by the players' coaches, although only one of the correlations was statistically significant. Among adolescent boys, Olweus et al. (1980, 1988) found a relationship between T and several self-descriptive items indicating low frustration tolerance and high willingness to respond aggressively to aggression directed toward them. Susman and colleagues (1987) found a relationship between T and personality measures of aggression and display of aggressive emotions among adolescent boys.

There are also some rejections of the link between T and aggression in humans. Although Persky, Smith, and Basu (1971) found a positive relationship between T and scores on the Buss-Durkee hostility scale, other investigators found no relationship (Meyer-Bahlburg, Nat, and Boon 1974; Monti, Brown, and Corriveau 1977) or only a weak one (Doering et al. 1975). In a laboratory study examining the effects of gonadotropin-releasing hormone (this stimulates secretion of T), no relationship was found between elevated T and anger, irritability, or aggressive behavior (McAdoo et al. 1978). Nor did Huesman and his colleagues (1984) find a relationship between T and aggressive acts in a longitudinal study of thirty-year-old males.

In sum, while there appears to be some involvement of T with aggression, the relationship is not clear-cut. Ordinarily, T is assumed to be a precursor of aggression rather than a sequel, and aggression and dominance are not always distinguished. Some of the ambiguity of the T-aggression relationship may be clarified by viewing aggression as a contest for dominance, as Mazur (1983) has argued. Another channel into the T-dominance-aggression relationship is through the links between T, norepinephrine, anger, and aggression.

Testosterone, Norepinephrine, and Aggression

Figure 2.1 shows one factor that does not have universal connections, norepinephrine (NE), which is linked only to T and to aggression. NE is a chemical neurotransmitter; that is, it carries nerve impulses across the synaptic gap between neurons of the sympathetic branch (SNS) of the autonomic nervous system (ANS) to arouse various organs. Because of the relationship between NE and anger, which is a frequent precursor of aggression, it is useful to examine the relationship between T and NE. A series of studies found that anger was differentially characterized by physiological signs indicating elevated secretion of NE (see, e.g., Funkenstein 1955; Funkenstein, King, and Drolette 1957; Elmadjian,

Hope, and Lamson 1958; and Graham, Cohen, and Shmavonian 1967. Although this has been disputed (Frankenhaeuser 1976; Levi 1972), the so-called Funkenstein hypothesis persists and can be seen to organize the evidence no less systematically than the explanation espoused by its opponents (see Kemper 1978 for an extensive treatment of this issue). The interest here is in whether T is related to NE. If so, there would be additional ground for supporting the T-aggression link, and through it the T-dominance nexus.

There are several bodies of work that make the T-NE connection, though none is conclusive. In a comprehensive theory based largely on empirical results from comparative studies, Henry (1980) proposed that aggression as a response to challenge-to-control is accompanied by activation of the sympathetic adrenal-medullary system (as detailed by Mason 1968), with concomitant elevations of both T and NE. By contrast, escape behavior or defeat and submission do not elevate NE and more likely decrease T (see also Berkenbosch 1983). Hence, T and NE are in a somewhat covarying relationship.

Another line of inquiry into the T-NE link is by investigators of how type A and type B personalities affect susceptibility to coronary artery disease. Both elevated NE and elevated T are found in type A persons as contrasted with type B persons (Jenkins, Rosenman, and Zyzanski 1974; Zumoff et al. 1984; Williams et al. 1982). One of the distinguishing characteristics of type As is their greater likelihood of response to threat and frustration with aggressive coping, mainly hostility and irritation (Carver and Glass 1978). These may be efforts to gain dominance or to prevent losing it.

To this point, I have been dealing with NE in the peripheral sector of the ANS; that is, where neurons connect with the major body organs modulated by ANS activity—heart, lungs, skin, pupils, and so forth. Now I turn to the central nervous system (CNS), or brain, where NE also performs neurotransmitter functions. Here, too, there is some evidence of a T-NE relationship. Some researchers have found a possible T-NE connection via studies of monoamine oxidase (MAO) in rhesus monkeys (Redmond et al. 1976; Redmond, Murphy, and Baulu 1979). In the brain, MAO metabolizes NE, thereby reducing its availability at receptor sites. A low level of brain NE means that it is not available for emotional activation. MAO inhibitors are used pharmacologically to elevate NE levels in the brain when this is considered desirable, as in depression, where NE levels are unusually low. Indeed, because low libido is a classic symptom of depression, there is a basis for assuming that a concomitant depression of T occurs at such times, thus preserving the covarying character of T and NE. Although Sachar's research team (1973) did not find lower T levels in depressed patients, several subsequent studies have found this effect (Vogel, Klaiber, and Broverman 1978; R. T. Rubin et al. 1981; and Yesavage et al. 1985). Also, Redmond and his colleagues found a negative relationship between blood-platelet MAO and T in monkeys, precisely what one would predict to support a pattern of T-NE covariation (Redmond et al. 1976; Redmond, Murphy, and Baulu 1979).

Additional support for the T-NE link via MAO comes from Daitzman and his colleagues (1978), who examined gonadal hormones in relation to the psychological trait "sensation seeking." Zuckerman (1984) proposed that sensation seeking reflected a disposition to require a variety of novel and complex experiences to maintain optimal levels of arousal. This orientation is presumably enhanced by high levels of brain NE, which in turn is fostered by low levels of MAO. The higher NE level should also lead to higher T, which Daitzman et al. (1978) indeed found.

In yet another approach to the T-NE link, Sinyor et al. (1983) found that NE levels were higher in trained aerobic runners than in untrained runners. This result takes on meaning in light of the finding by Young and Ismail (1978) that the aerobically fit also have higher T levels. Dai et al. (1981) also found higher T in men aged thirty-nine to forty-five who did vigorous exercise on a regular basis.

Finally, in a rare study of human sexual behavior (others will be discussed below), Wiedeking's research team (1977) investigated NE in relation to sexual conduct. (Regrettably, T was not examined.) A single male subject was monitored while he engaged in sexual relations on three occasions. Both sexual arousal and erection were strongly related to NE (r = +.56 and +.76, respectively; $p < .001$ in both cases). This conforms with the elevated T pattern at the same points found by Fox et al. (1972), discussed below. During one of the sessions the subject unexpectedly received a telephone call, which resulted in "unsuppressible anger" (Wiedeking et al. 1977:143). NE level at this point increased fourfold over resting level, as the Funkenstein (1955) hypothesis would predict, and was even higher than NE level at orgasm later in that session. The subject's highest NE level was attained in a session in which, having achieved orgasm in coition, he failed to achieve orgasm in another coition thirty minutes later and instead masturbated to orgasm. NE level rose 1,200 percent at this point. Again, the failure to obtain T readings is regrettable, but the close correspondence between NE elevation, anger (aggression), and sexual arousal and erection is what is wanted to sustain the T-NE-aggression link. Although T-NE-aggression covariation is of interest in its own right, its value here is to reinforce the link between T and dominance via the link between T and anger or aggression that may lead to dominance, and this has been done.

Aggression and Sexual Activity

A number of authors have proposed that anger/aggression and sexuality are related (Freud 1933; Storr 1968; Stoller 1976; Barclay 1969), and Schenk and Pfrang (1986) found a positive correlation in single (though not among married) men between aggressive personality and frequency of sexual activity, low age at first sexual encounter and number of sex partners. However, others have attempted to discriminate between dominance and anger/aggression in the relationship with sexuality. Malamuth, Feshbach, and Jaffe (1977) have argued that sexual arousal is inhibited by hostility. This is sustained by Rubin (1976), who found that the decline of sexual contact between working-class husbands and wives in the middle years was at least partly due to unresolved resentments of the men against their spouses. Physiologically, too, there may be some grounds for the inhibitory effects of anger on sexual performance. The sympathetic nervous system, which is activated in anger, would inhibit activation of the parasympathetic nervous system, which is mainly responsible for erection (Strand 1983). Bozman and Beck (1988) proposed another solution here, based on the separation of the physiological mechanisms involved in desire (libido) and arousal (erection); for example, T appears to operate on desire, but not on arousal. They suggested that anger may cause a decline in desire, but not in arousal. Fear, on the other hand, may lead to a decline in arousal, while desire remains constant (see also Beck et al. 1987).

Lest these results appear to contradict what we have established earlier in relating anger and aggression to T (possibly through their link to dominance), we must be careful to distinguish the target of the aggressive and hostile feelings from the potential source of the sexual feelings. The results from marital pairs obtained by Rubin (1976), Hunt (1974), and Pietropinto and Simenauer (1977) strongly suggest that sexual activity will be curtailed if the two are the same, possibly due to the mechanism of depressed desire, as detailed by Bozman and Beck (1988). On the other hand, aggressive arousal in one context, possibly entailing increased T if dominance is attained, may enhance sexual arousal in another context.

There is a difference, too, between aggression that ends in dominance and aggression that does not. In a specifically sexual context, the former can turn out to be rape, and the latter might reflect the withdrawal pattern of angry husbands described by Rubin (1976).

This would support the view that aggression is not inherently linked to sexual arousal or activity except insofar as dominance, which then elevates T, is a result of the aggression.

Dominance/Eminence and Sexual Activity

Elevated social rank, whether through dominance or eminence, ordinarily disposes toward precedence in, and higher frequency of, sexual relations.[4] Laboratory studies of animals are incontrovertibly clear on this. Coe and Rosenblum (1984) report that Bonnet male monkeys, like most other monkeys, establish dominance relations immediately upon contact. However, unlike some others, they are then friendly and affiliative until a female is introduced into their setting. The dominant animal then acts aggressively toward the subordinate and monopolizes the female, while the subordinate hangs back. Even if the dominant animal is caged behind glass and the subordinate is alone with the female, the subordinate will not mount. If the dominant is out of sight, the subordinate animal will proceed to have sexual relations. Yet, after this, if the dominant animal is returned to the cage, the subordinate appears to act guilty, as if it expected punishment or were acknowledging "violation of the social code" governing its subordinate position (Coe and Rosenblum 1984:51).

Keverne (1979), working with talapoin monkeys, reported similar patterns, as did Phoenix (1980), who found that when a group of rhesus monkeys who had been socially deprived in infancy were released into a corral with accessible females, the initial copulators were the four most dominant animals. Only when the four were removed did some of the remaining monkeys engage in sexual relations. Keverne explained this pattern of dominance and sexual precedence as a function not only of the usual aggression of the dominant animal against subordinates, but also possibly as a result of the greater attractiveness of the dominant animal to the female. Keverne found that females look more at the dominant animal and invite him more for intercourse than they do subordinates (280).

In contrast to the results from laboratory studies, data obtained on captive animals in large settings more nearly like natural habitats suggest that subordinate status does not preclude animals from successful coitus (Eaton 1978). Keverne (1979) also acknowledged that in natural settings territories are too large for dominant animals to be able to monitor their entire troop, hence even nondominants can escape the oversight of their superiors.

Sociobiologists (e.g., Wilson 1975) argue that the propensity for sexual linkage between male animals who are dominant and females who are more attracted to them than to subordinates is an evolutionary device that guarantees reproductive success. According to this view, dominant animals will be more likely to assure the survival of their offspring, and somehow the females 'know' this. Whether this explanation, which seems plausible for animals, applies to humans is conjecturable, although sociobiologists insist that it does (see Remoff 1985; and Buss 1989, whose work is discussed below).

Among humans, the relationship between interpersonal social rank and sexuality is less clearly established, although the evidence points in this direction. Several North American studies investigating the qualities that females prefer in males include clear indices of attributes that foster social eminence: ambition-industriousness (Hudson and Henze (1969); ambition, energy, and enjoyment of work (Langhorne and Secord 1955); achievement and mastery (Centers 1971); ambitious and hardworking (Kemper and Bologh 1980). Buss (1989) has extended this work to encompass thirty-seven different cultures, in at least thirty-four of which females preferred males who were good financial prospects, ambitious, and industrious. These attributes reflect eminence potential. Competence as a surrogate for eminence was also found to be associated with greater likelihood of coitus for men (Kallen and Doughty 1984).[5]

In studies of human judgment, Miller and Byrne (1981) and Kelley et al. (1983) found that males and females who were described as dominant were also more likely to be described as more sexually active and more masculine. The effect was particularly strong for females evaluating males. In another study, Keller, Elliott, and Gunberg (1982) compared the personalities of young adult males and females who had and had not engaged in coitus. They found that dominance was a more prominent feature in the personality of men who had had sex than among women who had. But among women who had had sex, dominance was a more important personality trait than among female virgins. (The last findings will be considered again in chapter 4.) Sprecher, McKinney, and Orbuch (1987) obtained similar results about males: a male was perceived to be more dominant if his first experience of coitus was in a casual, rather than a close or steady, dating relationship. Komarovsky's (1976) intensive study of a small sample of college men found that those with low scores on a scale of dominance also had the lowest mean scores on another scale labeled heterosexuality. Indeed, these men were the most likely to be virgins.

Although not qualifying as scientific data, an observation by Gustav Flaubert ([1857] 1977:90) in his novel *Madame Bovary* also helps us to understand the intimate connection between dominance and sexuality. Emma Bovary attends a ball at the chateau of the local marquis. Flaubert turns his literary loupe on

> a few men (some fifteen or so), of ages varying from twenty-five to forty, who were scattered about among the dancers or standing chatting in the doorways [who] were distinguished from the general run by a sort of family likeness which one could not help observing despite the disparities of age, dress and feature. . . . They had the sort of complexion rich people nearly always have—the clear, pale tint that dainty white china, shimmering satin, and beautifully polished furniture, bring into stronger relief. . . . Their air of calm indifference betokened the serenity of passions that daily found appeasement; yet all their fine and gentle ways did not hide that sort of autocratic manner that comes of dealing with things spirited but not too intractable, things that provoke one's prowess or titillate one's vanity—the handling of a thoroughbred, or the conquest of a beautiful wanton.

Further supporting the social rank–sexuality link, Kreuz, Rose, and Jennings (1972), as reported above, found increased sexual interest among officer candidates as their stressful training period reached its conclusion. It was also the time when they attained a new status level, clearly an eminent one.

A final perspective on dominance and sexuality is gained from Luria's analysis of pornography: "Explicit in much pornography is power over women—helpless, weak, and exquisitely available women. Even the chains on women seem redundant. If the male gender curriculum teaches boys to attend to dominance cues and information, the pornographic literature surely shows men as dominant" (1982:403). Luria broached here the role of dominance, even in fantasy, as a stimulus to sexual relations for males. Person (1980) elevated the dominance theme to a general principle underlying male sexuality, which, in her psychoanalytic view, represents domination. In line with this, Garcia and colleagues (1984) discovered that males were more aroused by heterosexual erotic scenes in which their own sex was dominant in the encounter. However, contrary to Person, Garcia et al. also found that the same was true for females. The implications of this will be considered in chapter 4. Indeed, this darker side of the dominance-sexuality relationship was found by Lisak and Roth (1988), whose sample of sexually aggressive males tended to respond with high sexual arousal to rape depictions (see also Malamuth and Check 1983) if domination was part of their motivation for sexual activity in the first place. They found, too, that personality measures of dominance correlated positively with self-reported sexual aggression. Aggressive themes are also prevalent in sexual fantasies (Hariton and Singer 1974; Stoller 1976; Hunt 1974; Pietropinto and Simenauer 1977; Hite 1981). Analyzed closely, these are often, in fact, themes of dominance. Indeed, Stewart and Rubin (1976) reported that males with higher need for power (a personality measure) also tended to view more pornography.

The line of argument thus far has pointed to three conclusions: first, dominance/eminence attainment is accompanied by elevated levels of T; second, the link between aggression and T can be understood via the substantial overlap between aggression and dominance; and third, dominance/eminence means precedence in or greater opportunity for sexual interaction. In order to establish the last point more firmly, evidence of a relationship between T and sexual activity—especially prior levels of T—would be helpful. I turn to this now.

T and Sexual Activity

We enter here upon a lengthy analysis in which some pivotal relations of the socio-bio-social theory in the sexual domain are deduced. To begin with, the facts are relatively few, sometimes conflicting, and open to various interpretations. Precisely here an integrative theory may serve a useful purpose. To achieve this requires examination of sexual behavior and sexual intimacy as forms of social relationship. Only when the sexual and the relational are seen to be meaningfully connected can we gain insight into the sometimes puzzling results of the research on the relationship between T and sexual activity.

Although the data are not entirely consistent, there are several bodies of research that support the idea of a connection between T and sexual activity. There is a gross sense in which the association is conclusive: castration removes the main source of T in males. Subsequent to such loss, sexual activity inevitably declines (Goy 1968; Michael 1972; Phoenix, Slob, and Goy 1973), most likely through loss of both desire (libido) and the ability to ejaculate (which are related to T, as discussed below). Necessarily, the experimental work in this area has been done with nonhuman species. But human reports confirm this general finding (Bremer 1959; Beach 1977).

The importance of T for sexual behavior is revealed also in animals with seasonal mating patterns. T level rises with the approach of the time when females will be in estrus (Mendoza 1984). But efforts to induce sexual behavior by T injections contrary to normal seasonal variation have failed (Keverne 1979), possibly due to failure to modify other triggering mechanisms of seasonal sexual variability, for example, levels of light, which affect hormonal release via the hypothalamus (Strand 1983:563). Interestingly, human male T is at its highest in the autumn (Dai et al. 1981), leading to speculation that autumn is optimum for the survival of offspring born nine months later in the spring and summer, assuming that T enhances sexual activity in the first place.

Further evidence of the effect of T on sexual behavior is found in cases of sexual dysfunction, which can occur in several ways: failure of sexual interest or desire (loss of libido), of erection (impotence), and of ability to ejaculate. T level seems more definitely tied to libido and to ejaculatory competence than to erectile function (Keverne 1979); Nieschlag 1979; Bancroft and Wu 1983; Schwartz et al. 1980; Davidson, Kwan, and Greenleaf 1982; Schiavi et al. 1988). Therapy with supplementary T is often successful for these problems. According to Beach (1977) and Salmimies et al. (1982), T may also affect potency; but Schiavi et al. (1988) suggest that this may be a secondary disorder contingent on anxiety about failure of desire. Human hypogonadism, a condition that involves abnormally low levels of T, is strongly associated with disturbances of sexual behavior. In many cases administration of replacement T initiates libido and sexual activity (Bancroft and Skakkebaek 1979; Salmimies et al. 1982: Bancroft and Wu 1983; Davidson 1980).

Further supporting the link between T and sexual arousal, there is evidence that T level in human males often increases in response to psychosexual stimulation, as in viewing sexually explicit materials (Pirke, Kockott, and Dittmar 1974; Laye 1981; Bancroft and Wu 1983; Hellhammer, Hubert, and Schurmeyer 1985); in response to a sexually oriented interview (LaFerla, Anderson, and Schlach 1978); and in mere conversation with a friendly young woman (Dabbs, Ruback, and Besch 1987).

Another body of evidence for the association between T and sexual activity comes from cross-sectional studies in which level of circulating T is correlated with sexual behavior. One or two samples of blood plasma, for example, are taken to provide a reading on circulating T. Subjects also tell about their past and/or current sexual behaviors. Among the clearest demonstrations of the connection between T and sexual behavior using this method are the findings of Udry and his colleagues (Udry and Billy 1987; Udry et al. 1985) discussed above. Because Udry's sample (youths just past the threshold of puberty) was somewhat special he (1988) warned against generalizing the results to another age group, but the evidence is compelling that the dominant factor in determining coitus and other sexual conduct, including masturbation and desire for future sex, is T.

In several other cross-sectional studies of either younger or older males, T was found to be related to a sexual behavior criterion. Monti, Brown, and Corriveau (1977) found no relationship between T and and coitus, but did find a significant positive correlation between T and masturbation in their sample of university students. Dabbs and Morris (1989), analyzing data from a 1988 Centers for Disease Control study of Vietnam veterans, found that high T level was associated with having many sex partners, although the relationship held mainly among lower socioeconomic status veterans. In a study of married, older males, Persson, Nilsson, and Svanborg (1983) found that those with higher T level had significantly more coitus per month. In several other studies of middle-aged and older males, where the criterion of sexual activity included masturbation, the relation of T to sexual behavior was also confirmed. In a group of males ages forty to over ninety, Davidson et al. (1983) found a decline over the years in both T and orgasms, but a significant relationship between T and sexual activity remained. Yesavage et al. (1985) also found a positive relationship between sexual activity and T in a sample of depressed males, although this was reduced to nonsignificance when age and depression level were controlled. And in a sample of healthy elderly men, which must be accounted special because of its high educational level—74 percent with B.A.'s and 45 percent with M.A.'s or Ph.D.'s—Tsitouras, Martin, and Harman (1982) found that the highest rates of sexual activity were associated with highest level of T.

Another research strategy in the effort to link T to sexual behavior is to obtain blood plasma samples daily or several times a week over a period of several weeks or months and examine the relationship between T and reported sexual activity. Several research groups used some variant of the longitudinal method, and each found a positive relationship between T level and sexual activity intraindividually; that is, as T varied over time within the individual, there was either greater or lesser sexual activity—the higher the T, the higher the activity (Doering et al. 1974; Kraemer et al. 1976; and Knussman, Christiansen, and Couwenbergs 1986). But even here some variation was noted. Doering et al. (1974) and Knussman, Christiansen, and Couwenbergs (1986) found that the higher T level tended to precede sexual activity, but Kraemer et al. (1976) found that the sexual behavior preceded the higher T. Supporting the presex higher T position, Harris Rubin et al. (1984) reported longer latency to erection and lower T in men who had recently experienced more orgasms.[6]

On the other hand, interindividually, these investigators obtained results that differed from the intraindividual analyses. Although Knussman, Christiansen, and Couwenbergs found a positive relationship between T and sexual activity interindividually, Doering et al. and Kraemer et al. found a negative relation. This anomaly, found also by Pirke, Kockott, and Dittmar (1974), suggested the possibility that sexual activity occurs not so much because of T, but as "the body's method of elevating testosterone level" (Kraemer et al. 1976:131). This is an interesting speculation, but it may err in attributing the mechanism simply to "the body," hence to a strictly biological mechanism. As will be developed below, psychological and social instigators may also move the body to actions that elevate T. All in all, the evidence reviewed to this point suggests that a normal level of T is incontrovertibly related to sexual competence and that sexual activity varies to some extent with the amount of T.

But this is not all. The T–sexual activity relationship is more elusive than what has been suggested thus far. T seems to be a necessary, but not a sufficient, basis for sexual conduct. For example, neither Schwartz, Kolodny, and Masters (1980) nor Schiavi et al. (1982) found T differences between their samples of sexually dysfunctional and normally functioning males, indicating that the presence of normal amounts of T does not assure normal sexual activity. Furthermore, in human males, variation in coital frequency is found for men with the same levels of T, and similar coital frequency is found with different (even marginally normal) levels of T (Fox et al. 1972; Raboch and Starka 1972, 1973; Raboch, Mellan, and Starka 1975).[7] According to Nieschlag (1979:197), there may simply be a threshold "above which sexual activity is independent of the absolute level of the hormone."

If, as suggested above, erection is independent of T, the threshold effect is understandable in the case of coitus, since a partner is involved. She may be unwilling or unavailable when his T is elevated and he is aroused, or she may initiate activity and bring him to erection when his T level is low and he is not aroused. In somewhat astonishing data, Muelenhard and Cook (1988) found that more men than women reported that they had experienced unwanted coitus. The most frequently given reason for this was enticement by the partner. This can be understood as coitus in a possibly low state of T, but high partner facilitation or initiation.

In what may appear to be another negative finding concerning T and coitus, Persky et al. (1978) found in a small sample of married university students (or their spouses), that while the husbands' sexual initiation behavior was unrelated to their T level, a more complex variable was related to T level: responsiveness to a sexual overture, regardless of which spouse initiated it. If husband's T level was high and wife initiated sexual contact, he responded to it, but did not if his T level was low. If his T level was high and he initiated sexual contact, his wife responded to it, but not if his T level was low. If these findings can be relied upon, they reveal a high degree of biosocial subtlety in the sexual interplay between partners. Intuitively, this result seems to be more veridical with our suppositions about how spouses might manage their only partially covarying sexual appetites and satisfactions. Raboch and Starka (1973), who found that men with only marginally normal levels of T maintained coitus schedules very much like men with normal T levels, suggested that a socially facilitative environment, by which we must assume a cooperative partner, can compensate for the deficit in T. Although lacking a physiological incentive from T, a male still might initiate sexual activity because other cues invite him to do so and he feels constrained to comply. The social constructionist understanding of sexual conduct as serving not only libidinal interests is very valuable in this regard (Simon 1974).

Some of the ambiguity in the data relating circulating level of T to sexual activity also may be due in part to the population used in data collection. Some studies have sampled populations of married or otherwise steadily partnered males. For research purposes, when coitus is the criterion, these populations are more likely to produce a sufficient number of data points within the time frame of the study and also give evidence of a more regular pattern of sociosexual activity, due to greater access to a partner. Single men, not regularly partnered, are more likely to have a more erratic coital pattern, perhaps with unusual peaks and lows of activity spread over a longer time period.

Although the research logistical preference for the married or otherwise partnered is understandable, the physiomechanics of T in relation to different components of sexual competence may actually lead to distorted results when only this group is investigated. The weight of opinion is that T is related to desire (libido) and to ejaculation, but not to arousal (erection). Married or partnered males differ from unpartnered males in their sociosexual circumstances, and this bears on the kind of results that can be obtained when the intent is to examine the relationship between T and sexual activity, especially coitus.

First and foremost, a single male (unlike a married or partnered male) does not usually have a partner who is available for coitus when he is. This requires that he find one. Ordinarily, this should be keyed to desire, hence to T. Assuming that a partner is found, erection and ejaculation should ensue. On the other hand, the married or partnered male may feel desire (due to T) and initiate a sexual overture, but his overture may not succeed (though it more often does). Indeed, one of the standard complaints of husbands is that their desire for coitus exceeds their opportunity for it because of their wife's lesser desire for whatever reason (Goleman 1989a). On the other hand, if his T is low and he feels no desire, but his spouse does, he may become the target of her sexual initiation. Here, his path and the single man's path diverge. The single man's coitus (requiring both erection and ejaculation) depend fundamentally on his desire, since without desire he is unlikely to initiate any movement toward coitus. But the married man can be brought to erection—except if he has a motive to resist this—and ejaculation by his partner even if his desire initially was low or nonexistent. Clearly, we must proceed very cautiously in drawing conclusions from the existing studies, because of their failure to distinguish between married or partnered and unpartnered men in their opportunities for sex as mediated by desire which would be linked strongly to T.

A different research strategy might be thought able to settle the outstanding issues about the T–sexual activity relationship once and for all: testing T immediately before and immediately after coitus or masturbation. This would avoid to a great extent the problem of whether the subject were married/partnered or unpartnered. According to a number of investigators who have used this method to examine T and sexual activity patterns in rhesus monkeys, T rises only after tactile contact, perhaps including intromission with receptive females (Rose, Bernstein, and Gordon 1972; Vandenburgh 1973; Bernstein, Rose, and Gordon 1977). Keverne (1979) found that for talapoin monkeys, simply viewing females was not sufficient to elevate T; actual contact and initiation of intercourse was necessary. From a comparative perspective, these results are somewhat limited inasmuch as we would be hard put to identify anticipation or desire in infrahuman forms. Hence, results with humans are required.

Relatively close-up studies of humans engaged in sexual activity are rare. Although Western cultural values are relatively restrictive with respect to sexual behavior, most cultures create a wall of privacy around the act of coitus (Ford and Beach 1951), presumably because there is high vulnerability to failure when privacy is violated. Understandably, then, researchers in this area are most often affiliated with hospitals, and their subjects are recruited from among hospital personnel. Presumably, hospital personnel are more conditioned to lack of privacy of the body and bodily functions.[8] The added requirement of taking blood or saliva samples before and after coitus creates further possible distortion. There is a general problem here that touches on whether or not body-intrusive and/or mood-interrupting observations can capture an entirely normal response in matters of sexual conduct. However, Masters and Johnson (1966) have shown how far the matter can be taken. Yet, we do not know to what extent the techniques of measurement and the very experience of performing highly charged behaviors as part of a scientific investigation change the psychological and biological processes from what might otherwise prevail. Any conclusions we draw must be tempered by acknowledgment of this ignorance. Three studies with humans can be cited.

Testing one married male over a period of three months, Fox et al. (1972) found that eighteen events of coitus occurred in a pattern unrelated to daily readings of T level. This means that especially high levels of T did not necessarily lead to coitus. However, levels of T immediately before and immediately after orgasm were higher than a control level obtained at another time on the same day. Though, on average, T level was higher after orgasm than before, the difference was not significant; in fact, T level was higher after orgasm in only seven of sixteen occasions of coitus for which there were complete data.

Unfortunately, the timing of the preorgasmic blood sample—"from 5 to 35 minutes (generally less than 15 minutes) before orgasm" (Fox et al. 1972:57)—along with absence of information on whether, and to what extent, sexual contact had begun, leave us in the dark on the question of whether T level rose in anticipation of, or desire for, sexual activity or only after it had begun. Nor is there any information as to whether the subject or his spouse had initiated the intercourse occasion.

The complexity of the T-sex relationship is compounded by the results of another study with humans (Stearns, Winter, and Faiman 1973). Using six couples, the investigators arranged to have blood plasma samples drawn from the males about sixty and thirty minutes before coitus and ten, thirty, and sixty minutes after coitus. There was no significant difference between T levels before and after coitus. These results conform with what Fox et al. (1972) found with their subject, but leave intact their finding that T was elevated over a control level on the same day as coitus.

The timing of the first precoital blood sample in Stearns, Winter, and Faiman's study (sixty minutes earlier) leaves us in doubt about whether sexual contact had been initiated. We can assume that it had not, though certainly the idea that it would was present. Nor is the first sample necessarily sixty minutes prior to orgasm, which might have come even later unless programmed to occur at a certain time. This cannot be determined from the published report. In any case, the results obtained would seem to argue against any relationship between T and sexual activity.

In a third study, Lee, Jaffe, and Midgley (1974) examined T level in a group of eight married males as early as sixteen hours and as late as thirty minutes prior to coitus, immediately after coitus, and twenty-four and forty-eight hours later. Subjects had been instructed to abstain from coitus for two days before the test occasion. As in the Fox et al. (1972) and Stearns, Winter, and Faiman (1973) studies, no significant before-after difference in T level was found.

T level in masturbation has also been studied in before-after fashion. Although the culmination in orgasm may be the same as in coitus, the social and psychological dimensions of masturbation would seem to be radically different, and some difference in outcomes can be expected if social and psychological parameters are significant in sexual behavior. Fox et al. (1972) obtained blood samples both five to ten minutes before and five minutes after ejaculation from eight men, ages twenty to thirty-eight. Although T increased in five of the eight, the difference was not significant for the whole group; hence, ejaculation per se could not be considered causally responsible for increase in T. Regrettably, Fox and his colleagues did not obtain control values of T at another time of day, as they had in their research on coitus. Therefore, we do not know whether or not there was a rise in T in anticipation of masturbation. However, masturbation in the laboratory for the purpose of fertility analysis also did not lead to increase in T (John Bancroft, cited in Nieschlag 1979).

On the other hand, Purvis and his colleagues (1976) obtained significant differences in T before and after masturbation, using a sample of thirty-four males, eighteen to twenty years old. They explain the difference between their result and that of Fox et al. (1972) as due possibly to a difference in sample size. Indeed, in a subsample of eleven subjects who volunteered for an additional experiment, no difference appeared in their before-after T level. Purvis et al. also reported that T increase was negatively related to masturbation time, which ranged from nine to forty minutes. The maximum increase in T appeared at about twenty minutes of masturbation duration.

In a second study of what they called "sham" masturbation, with the eleven volunteers mentioned above, Purvis et al. (1976:442) examined whether merely anticipating masturbation would increase T level. Subjects were led to believe that once again they would masturbate, but after providing a "before" blood sample, they were simply allowed to wait the same length of time that they had individually taken to masturbate in the first study. The "after" blood sample was then taken. No before-after difference was found merely from anticipation, and in this respect the results for this small group did not differ from the results for this same group in the first study, when they actually masturbated. However, although Purvis et al. did not analyze the data, there was a remarkably elevated level of T (for both the before and after measures) during the sham study compared with the before-after T levels of the eleven subjects when they participated in the original study. It could be argued that T did in fact rise in anticipation of masturbation, given that the subjects had had an experience of sexual arousal and orgasm that they now could anticipate. Thus, it appears that ejaculation, whether in coitus or masturbation, may, but does not necessarily, affect T level. The available data do not permit a firm conclusion on this issue.

Taking stock once again, the data we have on humans agree that sexual desire depends to some extent on T. Sexual activity (coitus or masturbation) also depends on T, but perhaps to a lesser extent. Coitus, at least, can occur when T level is either high or low, and individual differences in T, except perhaps in the very young (just past puberty) and the elderly—their free T levels are somewhat comparable—do not correlate very well with amount of sexual activity. Indeed, this does not astonish, since there are many personal and social concomitants to sexual behavior that operate independently of T level. However, sexual activity does seem to depend to some extent on within-individual variation in T level.

At this point, we may judge that the role of T in sexual activity is problematic. In such cases, methodological conjectures abound. Consider Schiavi et al. on the possible reasons for differences in findings about T: "Inadequate matching of controls, lack of standardization of blood sampling conditions, and lack of consideration of diurnal or episodic variations in circulating testosterone may also play an important role in the dissimilar findings" (1984a:240). Rubin et al. also suggested that "inconsistent or confusing results . . . may be due to . . . variables under environmental or social control (e.g., availability and/or attractiveness of a partner, attitudes and expectations regarding acceptable rates and modes of sexual expression, religious and legal interpretations of appropriate conduct, etc. These factors are highly variable across individuals and difficult to control experimentally" (1984:306). However, divergence among empirical results also encourages new surmises and prompts a readjustment of theoretical vision. Something of this kind will be attempted now.

The principal ambiguity in the putative connection between elevated social rank, T, and sexual activity is that although T surges after dominance or eminence acquisition, it may or may not be elevated before sexual activity and only sometimes does it appear to be elevated after it. Given this confused picture, we may wonder whether T has anything to do with sexual activity (if T level is within the normal range) or in linking dominance/eminence to sexual behavior.

A second area of ambiguity in the link between T and sexual activity is the matter of causal direction. Given the relationships between dominance/eminence and T and dominance/eminence and sexual activity, we would assume that T would intervene and be elevated prior to sexual activity. But neither Kraemer et al. (1976) nor Fox et al.

(1972) found such a correlation. Indeed, sexual activity may lead to increased T, but again the data are not clear.

I wish now to propose a view of the social and biological connections in sexuality that can clarify the ambiguities and lead us to an understanding of how T is related to dominance/eminence and to sexual activity. The firmest data we have in this puzzle show the link between dominance/eminence and T. I shall assume the validity of this result. I shall also assume that T enhances sexual desire. The data from studies of successful T therapy in cases of sexual dysfunction and the findings of Udry and Billy (1987), Udry et al. (1985) and Knussman, Christiansen, and Couwenbergs (1986) provide a basis for this view as a heuristic hypothesis.

If dominance/eminence-released T enhances sexual desire, it could do so in two ways: first, it could lead to more active pursuit of a sex partner. This is what one would normally expect of a sexually aroused male. Second, the higher T level could make the male more attractive to females. Keverne and others (see discussion in Keverne 1979) have argued that T makes the dominant male animal perform better sexually: more mounts and more ejaculations; it may also help the aroused male to focus more persistently on the female. (According to animal studies by Andrew 1978, one effect of T is enhancement of the ability to concentrate one's attention on a task. This is largely confirmed in humans by Broverman et al. 1968; Klaiber, Broverman, and Vogel 1971; and Waber 1977a.) The male's better performance and his greater attention in turn may lead to the female's greater interest and receptivity to the male with higher T. Pheromones may help in the process, but there is no evidence of this as yet (Keverne 1979).

The female may also be more attracted because the dominant male is likely to be a better protector of any offspring that result from the sexual union or because the dominant male will sire offspring more likely to survive (Alexander 1979). Whether this strictly sociobiological hypothesis can be applied to humans is highly conjecturable, but perhaps it can be accepted pro tem simply to provide an additional basis for interpreting the phenomena in question. With these elements in place we can provisionally say the following: When a male has achieved a significant victory or gained significant social status, he experiences a surge of T that enhances sexual desire and, perhaps, in females, a receptivity that makes coitus more likely.

If these links are in fact operative and causal as specified, we must still explain why the available data do not clearly show elevated T prior to sex behavior, and why T is only sometimes found to be elevated after sex.

I shall offer now five heuristic propositions to organize the rather ambiguous data. These will guide the discussion that follows. First, within the normal range, T is not related to the physiological aspects of sexual activity per se, with or without a partner. It does not rise in anticipation of or desire for such activity, nor does it rise afterward because of sexual activity. Second, T is related to dominance/eminence. When elevated social rank is attained to a significant degree, T rises; when it is lost, T declines. Third, surges of T after the attainment of dominance/eminence enhance libido and perhaps attractiveness to potential sexual partners. In this way, rise in T can precede sexual activity. Fourth, when the sexual activity itself constitutes an attainment of dominance or eminence, T will rise, which often leads to more sexual activity until exhaustion of self or partner. In this way, T rise can follow sexual activity. Fifth, fantasy attainment of dominance/eminence can also produce T elevation, but probably to a lesser degree than real attainment of the same level of elevated social rank. Fantasies may work physiologically because they are so often of such egregious magnitude. A realistic fantasy would probably flop as an enhancer of T.

We must now reexamine some of the previous materials more closely in light of these contentions. Keverne's (1979) report of dominance and sexual interaction among talapoin monkeys is a good place to begin. His investigation is perhaps the only one to pursue the several issues that face us in almost the detail that is required, and I shall examine his findings closely. There may be some demurrer to relying so heavily at this point on comparative data, and Benton (1983) has raised specific objections about the value of such a procedure when, considering the importance of culture and advanced human cognition, the phylogenetic distance between human and infrahuman species is so great. Yet, lacking an adequate set of studies on humans, animal models of sexuality give us at least some ground for elaborating hypothese about humans, as Davidson (1980:278) pointed out, so I shall proceed along this course (see also Goodfoot and Neff 1987). The reader who remains dubious should judge the method by its results.

Keverne treats several points of interest to us. First, during a period of isolation, "when no males had access to females, both the putative dominant and subordinate males had low levels of plasma testosterone which were not significantly different from each other" (1979: 274). This establishes that when the animals were segregated both from females and from each other, and neither dominance nor sexual interactions were at issue, T levels were undifferentiated.

Second, when the males were allowed contact with females—all males together with all females—a dominance order emerged among the males. But this was unrelated to sexual interaction because the females had been ovariectomized and hence did not display the swelling of the sexual skin that indicates receptivity and arouses the sexual interest of the males. During this period, "none of the males, dominant or subordinate, showed many mounts or ejaculations and inspections of the females' perineum were rare" (Keverne 1979:273). What is crucially missing from Keverne's report is whether at this point the dominant and subordinate monkeys differed in T. We would expect differences from the results reported by Rose, Bernstein, and Gordon (1975) and the review by Mendoza (1984). (In a later report, which accumulates additional observations in Keverne's laboratory, Eberhart, Yodyingyuad, and Keverne (1985) do not present information on this phase of the experiment, namely, when the ovariectomized females are not sexually attractive to the males.)

Third, after the females had been given replacement implants of estrogen, thus producing the normal swelling of sexual skin and indicating their readiness for coition, sexual interactions sharply increased. "But this was the prerogative of the dominant male with the [most] subordinate still showing few mounts or ejaculations. All males showed some interest in the females and inspected their perineal regions, the dominant male showing the greatest number of inspections and the most subordinate male very few. Masturbation increased in the lower ranking males . . . but decreased in the dominant male" (Keverne 1979:273). Dominance thus preempts the sexual field, just as it does the field of interaction between males alone.

Fourth, "with oestrogenized females there was a significant increase in plasma testosterone in the dominant males [in two different groups studied] . . . but not in the subordinates" (Keverne 1979:274). Two issues are crucial here: one is the T effect; another is the implied effect of masturbation. With respect to T, it appears that when sexual interaction begins, T level rises. Keverne was particularly concerned with whether T rises in anticipation of sexual interaction or after it begins. He argued for the latter on two grounds. One is that other researchers have found that sexual interactions can continue for a lengthy period in castrated monkeys (see Wilson and Vessey 1968; Phoenix, Slob, and Goy 1973), although they will eventually decline (Beach 1977). Since castrates lack testes, the major source of T, their sexual behavior is clearly not T-driven, although some T is also produced in the adrenal cortex (Strand 1983).

A second reason Keverne argues for postsex T is that "when we have males alone in a cage and introduce females either with or without oestrogen but prevent male access to them, we don't see an increase in plasma testosterone. Only when the males have access to the females does the testosterone level rise" (1979:293). Thus, there appears to be strong evidence that, at least in this sepcies, T does not rise before sexual interaction, but sexual interaction produces T.

Now we must consider more closely the character of sexual interaction. It involves tactile-motor-physiological and, to some degree, cortical (psychological) experiences on the one hand, and, at least potentially, social interactional experience on the other. The crucial question is, which of these is producing the rise in T? To answer this, the T effect of masturbation is relevant.

Among the subordinate monkeys, masturbation increased when the females were sexually available, yet their T levels did not increase. Hence, it is not the tactile-motor-physiological components of sexual behavior that instigate T. This result confirms several reports (Fox et al. 1972; and Bancroft, cited in Nieschlag 1979:198; Purvis et al. 1976 is an exception and will be discussed below) that masturbation produces no rise in T. If we can draw an inference here it is that T rise is a function of the social interactional properties of sexual interaction and not its strictly biological properties. More specifically, as proposed heuristically above, T elevation results from dominance (or alternatively eminence, when dealing with humans) in the sexual interaction. How can this be? We must recognize that as in every other type of interaction where dominance/eminence produces T, sexual interaction that results in elevated social ranking does also. If this were not the case, social interaction with a sexual content would be an anomaly and this is not likely to be the case.

There are several ways in which sexual interaction is social interaction, with the possibility of a dominance/eminence denouement. First, except in rape, prostitution, or frank promiscuity, sexual interaction ordinarily takes place within an ongoing social relationship, one that has a past and is most often certain to have a future. In virtually all cultures, except where custom ordains specifically who will bond with whom or where such bonding is arranged without the personal will of the main parties, the relationship ordinarily came into existence because the male courted the female. This might even mean that he caught her eye first, before he knew that he was interested in her. Notwithstanding, whether she knew his qualities beforehand or he had to make a case for them, the relationship could not proceed unless he had something to offer by way of personal appearance, physical strength, courage, boldness, sensitivity, material possessions, tastes and sensibilities, prestige and power in the community, and so on.

The display or promise of these qualities is a warrant by a man to a woman that he is worthy. If she accedes to his self-presentation, she confirms his worth. In terms employed above, she confers status upon him by conferring herself. This means, generally, that she accepts him for a partner in an ongoing relationship, one which will more than likely include sexual interaction, but is broader than this intimacy alone. By gaining her acceptance, he has attained a sweet success: eminence as I call it.

In a variant scenario, she resists his blandishments, enticements, and claims of worthiness, either preferring another, or no one, or acting capricious and teasing, according to culturally programed courting ritual. For many men, this only inflames passion and the desire to win her, and may, foolishly, become the principal motive of the pursuit, her true qualities obscured. If she at last accedes, it is a victory of some proportion for him, and the emotion attendant on success is even more acute than in the case where acceptance came more easily; this is true where so complete a gain is hard-won and perhaps even the victory comes as a surprise. It is a yet stronger claim to eminence, with a dominance motif included by virtue of the struggle and its victorious outcome.

In yet another and darker variant, his invitation and self-presentation are met with blanket and immutable refusal and rejection, perhaps even with contempt. If he does not abandon the pursuit, rape is possible. Domination and control are carried to an ultimate point. In terms previously elaborated, it is strictly a power relationship, where compliance is involuntary.

These three versions of possible contexts for sexual interactions, from culturally most approved to most violent and disapproved, share one quality in common. This is that each involves social interaction in which a male gains a female, either by getting her to confer high status willingly on him (eminence), or through overcoming her resistance through force and threat (dominance). In sum, the sexual interaction takes place within the context of a social encounter in which it is possible to attain dominance or eminence or some combination of these. Under such circumstances T should rise, just as it does in dominance/eminence encounters outside the sexual domain.

With this in view, we can look more closely at the immediate intimate interaction itself. How can we conceive of the social interactional properties of intimacy? Though the content may be highly charged, the relational form must partake of the same basic properties as all other interactions, regardless of content. These basic properties are power and status. By touch, movement, and word, humans enact, employ, and convey to each other expressions of power and status—they control and force (power) or they voluntarily gratify and give (accord status). Every sexual interaction is some mix of these elements.

Though, in what we suppose to be ideal sexual interaction, the status component outweighs the power component, sometimes pseudopower elements such as biting, scratching, and drawing blood are included (Ford and Beach 1951). These possibly serve to create a simulacrum of "struggle," half-play, half-serious, in which the male must vanquish his prize. Thus, there can be a dominance encounter even at the core of intimate interaction. The benefits of dominance can also be attained through eminence, as has been discussed, and this is better fostered by tenderness, even in the midst of passion. (This will be discussed in chapter 3.)

It follows from the fundamental understanding that T is known to surge after dominance/eminence acquisition that, if either is attained in the sexual interaction, T will rise. It should be evident that dominance/eminence are not inevitable or necessary outcomes of sexual interaction, hence, T will not always surge as a consequent. This may explain why Fox et al. (1972) sometimes found elevated levels of T after sexual interaction and sometimes not, and why Stearns, Winter, and Faiman (1973) and Lee, Jaffe, and Midgley (1974) did not. Below I will consider some reasons why dominance/eminence may not ensue from a sexual interaction and why T is not elevated afterward.

To return to the examination of the Keverne (1979) study, we may assume that the alpha monkey's exploration and mounting of the receptive females was a significant benefit of his dominance. Hence the T level of the already dominant male was given a further boost. We can obtain some idea of how this might operate from another observation by Keverne. Successful sexual interaction appears to require a T surge. Keverne reported

> on two dominant males, one intact and one castrated and receiving a testosterone implant. The intact dominant can and does show an increase in testosterone levels whereas the castrate doesn't, being on constant testosterone replacement. If we compare mounts and ejaculations, 75% of mounts result in ejaculation in the intact male *who experienced a testosterone increase*. . . . With the *same* females, the castrated dominant (who didn't stay dominant for long) mounts the females but doesn't achieve ejaculation. (1979:293–294, emphasis added)

According to Keverne, it was precisely because the castrated male did not experience the surge in T from his mounts that he was not able to consummate his attempt at sexual interaction: "What the castrated male doesn't get is the surge or increase in testosterone which the intact male's testes produce" (1979:295). The castrate's dominance in the sexual encounter did not lead to the normal hormonal sequel—a T surge—therefore, the encounter failed through lack of ejaculation, and ultimately, this animal's relative dominance in the social group itself failed.

With some modification, I propose the same for human males as for Keverne's monkeys. Dominance or eminence display or acquisition provides the T surge that underlies an enhanced sexual appetite or sexual competence, which in turn leads to greater appetite and better performance, as manifested, for example, by firmer, longer-lasting erections or capacity for more orgasms. This is underscored for human males by Knussman et al., who found that "individuals who are more stimulated and whose erection times are on the average longer, possess higher T levels" (1986:442). This also confirms the earlier report by Rubin et al. (1984), who found that T concentration was positively correlated with maximum size of erection as well as average strength of erectile response to an erotic film. Notwithstanding these results, a substantial dominance/eminence attainment may not be necessary; there must only be enough of either to reinforce T at the critical point in a sexual interaction.

A fifth point of interest is that Keverne tried to ascertain whether rise in T resulted from the sexual behavior or from the aggression by dominants toward subordinates. This is a complex issue, as indicated earlier, involving the confused relation between dominance and aggression. Keverne's answer is only partially satisfactory. He examined interactions in an all-male group. There

> the dominant male is attacking and threatening others . . . but it is only when females are introduced that sexual behavior occurs and plasma testosterone levels increase. *At this time, the aggressive behavior of the dominant male does increase* and one cannot rule out that aggression given in the context of sexual activity may contribute in some way to the increase in male plasma testosterone. Likewise, the increased aggressive behavior received by the subordinate may also have been instrumental in preventing both sexual behavior and increased plasma testosterone. (1979:275–276, emphasis added)

Several issues emerge here. First, Keverne does not report that the dominant male has elevated T in the all-male group. (The later report by Eberhart, Yodyingyuad, and Keverne 1985, which accumulates results from four groups, also does not mention this all-male phase.) We must recall that once the hierarchy is established, T levels are not particularly differentiated, even if aggressive and threatening behaviors occasionally occur (Mendoza 1984; Rose et al. 1974). However, in the later report (Eberhart, Yodyingyuad, and Keverne 1985), the T level of dominants is significantly higher than that of subordinates, even after the hierarchy has stabilized. Despite relatively infrequent aggression, dominant males apparently attacked and threatened other monkeys (Eberhart, Yodyingyuad, and Keverne 1985).

Second, there is the usual difficulty of disentangling dominance from aggression. However, we may suppose that increase in aggression when the females were introduced could serve no other purpose than to establish conclusively who would have access to them. The already dominant animal was simply reestablishing his dominance in the new situation. Whether or not this action alone led to the increase in T cannot be ascertained on the basis of Keverne's methods. But we can be sure that the failure of T to rise in subordinates was due to the renewed enforcement of their subordination. Though not conclusive, this shows that at least some of the T effect is dominance-driven, even when sexual opportunity is present.

Another issue is that it is not clear, though it is not likely to be the case, that there was a perfect temporal separation of the dominance-related aggression toward other males and the sexual approaches to females made by the dominant male. Doubtless, these actions were intermixed, providing additional room for conjecture as to exactly which behavior—the dominance-related aggression or the dominance-related sexual interaction—was responsible for the rise in T. In fact, I assume it was both because sexual interaction can be as much of a dominance interaction as interaction between males.

As if to anticipate this question, Keverne does have additional observations. When the dominant and the most subordinate monkeys were each separately allowed to be alone with the females, "both males showed significant increase in plasma testosterone" (1979:277). Thus, it appears that when dominance among males is not at issue, sexual interaction alone is capable of elevating T; but, as I have reasoned above, it is not the physiological-sexual, but the sociosexual interaction that leads to a rise in T. Human data also follow this path, albeit they are of a different order. Dabbs, Ruback, and Besch (1987) found that T rose in males after they engaged in a ten-minute conversation with a confederate of the experimenters' who had been instructed to be warm and friendly, ask questions, and show interest; that is, to confer status, or eminence. T rose after such encounters with both male and female confederates, but more after conversation with a female. With respect to a subordinate animal given free rein with females, without a dominant animal to hamper or hinder him, it is perhaps not anthropomorphic to suppose that the opportunity is as much one of dominance as it is of simple sexual accessibility.

Eberhart, Yodyingyuad, and Keverne (1985) found that after monkeys had been in the subordinate position over a lengthy period (up to seven months), they failed to take advantage of sexual opportunity when housed with receptive females, even in the absence of other males. The experience of subordination thus carried over. (This pattern of depressed sexual behavior among long-term subordinates will emerge again when we consider the relationship between social structure and human male sexual behavior). Even the exceptional subordinate who did engage in sexual interaction, as reported above, did not initiate much sociosexual behavior, but was the beneficiary of the many presentations that were made to him by the females (Eberhart, Yodyingyuad, and Keverne 1985). Nevertheless, his T level rose, and I believe that it is heuristically valuable to suppose that, even if attenuated, dominance still accompanied this animal's sexual interaction. Perhaps it would even be accurate to refer to this animal as having attained eminence.

A final, and perhaps conclusive, point from Keverne's report is that the increase in T in the dominant male was not simply due to increased testicular blood flow; that is, elevated sexual activity passing more blood through the area where T is manufactured, hence clearing more of it into the bloodstream (Lincoln 1974 suggested this is a possible explanation of higher plasma T after sexual arousal.) The alternative would be that the sexual behavior acts upon the central nervous system (CNS), which in turn releases more T; and this was indeed found. More specifically, dominant males showed higher levels of luteinizing hormone (LH), which is a hormonal precursor of T release in the CNS (Strand 1983). A subordinate, by contrast, showed no increase in LH (or T, as reported above) until he was the sole male in the presence of females.

This result is of paramount importance, since it points again to a behavioral rather than a strictly physiological mechanism as the source of the increased level of T. Sexual activity per se (e.g., the subordinates' masturbation) did not elevate T. Social interactional behaviors in which a relational outcome of dominance was obtained did. Admittedly, there is a loose end here, since the dominant male's aggressions against the subordinate and the sexual interactions were closely linked in time and were probably interwoven. But we can tie up this loose end by recalling that the subordinate also showed elevated T when he was alone with the females and thus allowed to be dominant.

We can return now from this lengthy exploration of the Keverne study. At this juncture we may consider again the few studies of human sexual activity, which did not appear to find that sexual activity was higher at peak points of T. First, Stearns, Winter, and Faiman (1973) and Lee, Jaffe, and Midgley (1974) could not find this connection because their six couples were having sex apparently for the sake of science, sex unrelated to what was going on in their lives otherwise. Second, Kraemer et al.'s procedure may have precluded finding a relationship between T surge and sexual activity. They reported that a blood sample was drawn "every other day between 8 and 9 a.m." and that "for each subject, testosterone readings were separated according to whether there was or was not any orgasm reported in the period extending from midnight 32 hours before the time of blood drawing to midnight 16 hours after the time of blood drawing to midnight 16 hours after that time" (1976:127, 128).

Given the known rapidity with which T level oscillates (Schwartz, Kolodny, and Masters 1980; Murray and Corker 1973; Schiavi et al. 1982), the time frame of Kraemer et al.'s investigation may simply have been too broad to capture how the T surge is related to sexual ativity. They did find that T was higher after, rather than before, sexual activity and assume that it was the sexual, qua physiological, activity that accounted for it. Alternatively, I propose that it was the dominance/eminence components of the sexual interaction that led to the elevated T. This is as plausible a hypothesis as that of bodily need offered by Kraemer et al. (1976) and stands on firmer ground: the well-supported link between dominance/eminence and T.

The study of a single individual by Fox et al. (1972) comes closest to being able to detect T rises in relation to sexual conduct. Yet they found that coitus was not related to peaks of T. This finding is contrary to what is proposed here, but closer examination is required. It will be recalled that Fox et al. found that both preorgasmic and postorgasmic T were elevated over a control level of T in a blood sample obtained at another time on the same day. This was true for each of the eighteen occasions of coitus in the study period. Given our assumption that T is strictly related to dominance/eminence, this would mean that the dominance/eminence features of sexual interaction can be initiated prior to orgasm. It is not hard to see how this can happen.

A certain responsiveness by the partner and her willing compliance with the message of his sexual signals would clearly mark the beginning of such a dominance/eminence experience. T should then rise. If the sexual invitation was declined but the rejection not taken too seriously, T level would probably be unaffected. If the rejection was taken seriously, it might lead to anger. But if the anger did not result in overcoming the partner's resistance (I do not speak of rape here) and attaining dominance, T level would be likely to fall, since the rejection has turned into defeat. In case of rape, T level would probably surge in a major way.

In fact, we have no way of knowing from the report by Fox et al.

(1972) how many sexual invitations offered by the male subject to his spouse during the research period were declined and in what manner. From the social relational perspective on T, dominance/eminence, and sexual activity, such information is as important as charting T in relation to orgasm. Interestingly, postorgasmic T was elevated over preorgasmic T on only seven of sixteen occasions of coitus (two occasions lacked complete data). According to what I propose here, this would mean that although the sexual interaction was initiated in a dominance/eminence frame of mind, it did not always end that way. How might this occur?

Clearly, dominance/eminence in sexual interaction is not a necessary outcome. One can, in fact, suffer loss. One may fail to win the female's interest, specifically, her arousal. She may be tired, angry, distracted. She may be physically unwell. For whatever reason, she is not receptive. She may comply out of a sense of duty, but in the acutely nuanced unfolding of the sexual minuet, something is lacking—a keenness, a passion, a giving of self, which is what can be conferred in sexual intimacy. Here is where "faking it" comes in. In such cases he may believe he has succeeded in winning her, but some ingredient of authenticity may be missing, thus robbing the experience of its highest possibilities.

Another condition that makes loss probable is poor performance. Though gaining the initial arousal of the female and her willing involvement in the sexual interaction, the ability to continue satisfactorily may deteriorate. He may be too rough or too hurried, or he may offend her sensibilities. The social character of the sexual interaction can thus change; she may become resistant or detached, and what promised to be, and was until then, victory can turn into defeat. A buildup of such emotions as anger, guilt, and depression can accentuate the decline.

Also in the performance domain, premature ejaculation is the most prevalent male sexual problem (Masters and Johnson 1970; Munjack and Kanno 1979). In a study designed to establish a baseline for normal male sexual behavior, Reading and Wiest (1984) found that 38 percent of men in their sample indicated premature ejaculation was a distinct problem for them or wanted to be able to delay orgasm longer. It is not hard to see that this difficulty alone can contribute significantly to a male's sense of failure in a sexual interaction. I need not elaborate the details of how a partner might respond, in word or gesture, if the prematurity left her unsatisfied.

In addition to loss or well-defined defeat, sexual interaction may not bring any sense of social elevation because there is neither the feel of conquest, nor of attaining great status conferral. Here is where ennui comes in. Sexual interactions that have become routinized and perfunctory may satisfy all of the male's physiological requirements of the situation—erection and ejaculation—without in effect engaging any but the most tepid social components. One may simply be physically present and psychologically unmoved. Kinsey, Pomeroy, and Martin's attribution of boredom by virtue of many reptitions of a "relatively uniform sort of experience" (1948:257) is fully comprehended here (see also Gagnon and Simon 1973). The excitement is gone, and it might appear that this is due to the lack of novelty. I believe this has been misunderstood.

Assuming one does not switch partners, one approach to novelty is through new positions in coitus or new times or places for it. Although some positions in intercourse may be more physiologically arousing than others, especially for the female (because of improved clitoral stimulation), I contend that the success of novelty in this regard is not due to the improvement of physiological sensations. Rather, positional novelty is potentially of value because it entails a social relational change either between the partners or between them and the community that sets the boundaries of legitimate sexual practice. Otherwise it will not succeed in reanimating the sexual interaction.

For example, in the case of female-above, her greater control over the pace and timing of the physiological means her greater arousal, and this is a tribute to his ability to arouse her, although some men apparently do not appreciate this (B. Sadock and V. Sadock 1976). In the case of rear vaginal entry, by its similitude to the pattern of virtually all infrahuman species, there is a mimic of the undisputed dominance of the male over the female (B. Sadock and V. Sadock 1976). In general, violating conventions of position, time, or place requires a boldness to carry off that may not be far from that which accompanies the kinds of victories that often lead to dominance. Though novelty per se is stimulating (Berlyne 1971), in sexual interaction novelty may work because it reinstitutes the possibility of a social outcome of dominance or eminence. Zillman (1986) reviewed various options employed in the effort to overcome sexual boredom, but saw them only as potential excitatory stimulants of the sympathetic nervous system, rather than as relational contributors to T.

Another device used to revive failed sexual interaction is fantasy. Bored mates apparently resort to fantasies of sexual encounters with desirable partners even as they engage in tactile-motor-physiological interaction with a partner who only mildly excites them (Pietropinto and Simenauer 1979). Here again we see that the revitalized capacity for sexual arousal and enjoyment depends more on the social—even if only imagined—than on the physical.

Although these kinds of fantasies, often of dominance or eminence, may play some role in sexual interactions with a partner, hence improving on reality, probably the largest role for fantasy is in masturbation. The evidence is strong that masturbation by males is often accompanied by fantasies of a sexual drama in which the masturbator exercises violent control over his coparticipant(s), or they find him irresistible and want to be ravished by him (see Hite 1981, for masturbation fantasies of rape or of multiple partners). These, of course, are dominance and eminence themes, respectively.

In the several negative results obtained in the relation between T and masturbation (Fox et al. 1972; Bancroft, cited in Nieschlag 1979), there was no control for fantasy, specifically fantasies of dominance/eminence. Under laboratory conditions, masturbation is not likely to be accompanied by fantasy, although the evidence is strong that otherwise it is (Kinsey, Pomeroy, and Martin 1948; Hite 1981). Since monkeys are not known to be able to fantasize, their T level also does not rise before or after masturbation. As indicated above, Keverne (1979) found reduced T in subordinates, despite increased frequency of masturbation.

However, the Purvis et al. (1976) study of masturbation departs from the pattern of no T effect. I frankly speculate that fantasy was a more likely accompaniment of masturbation in this sample than in the samples obtained by Fox et al. and Bancroft. In Bancroft's study (cited in Nieschlag 1979), males had come to a fertility clinic for sperm testing. There is reason to surmise that these probably older males with a serious, specific purpose—and perhaps fearful of a threatening discovery about their potency, their potential for fatherhood, and other such real and symbolic threats—would have shunned converting the occasion into something inappropriately hedonic. Fox et al. (1972) used eight males, ages twenty to thirty-eight (more than likely medical or hospital personnel). They ejaculated five to ten minutes after the "before" blood sample was drawn. (By contrast, the subjects of Purvis et al. 1976 took from nine to forty minutes.) It is possible that Fox et al.'s volunteers were also known to the researchers, hence were also under some constraint not to dwell on the hedonic aspects of the experience.

On the other hand, the thirty-four volunteers in the Purvis et al. (1976) study were eighteen-to-twenty-year-old conscripts serving in the Swedish army. We may assume that masturbation was a larger part of their total sexual outlet than among the older subjects in the other studies of masturbation (Kinsey, Pomeroy, and Martin 1948). Notwithstanding, they took considerably longer to ejaculate. Indeed, Gebhard and Johnson (1979:223, table 174) reported that less than 5 percent of the Kinsey sample did not reach orgasm by nine minutes—the minimum time taken by the Purvis et al. volunteers. What prolonged the activity? We may assume that, despite the relative anonymity, some element of embarrassment among these doubtless unsophisticated young men may have caused them to delay an activity that would otherwise be entirely private. But, I wish to propose, fantasy too may have entered the experience, one of institutionally sanctioned hedonism—a truly rare event. Purvis et al. (1976) reported that T was highest in those who took about twenty minutes to masturbate. Longer sessions than that led to lesser increase in T. This suggests a possible optimum fantasy self-stimulation time—at least in the population sampled.

While there is no evidence that fantasies of dominance can increase testosterone level (no research has been done), there is evidence that sexually explicit materials can (Pirke, Kockott, and Dittmar 1974). Of course, fantasies can lead to sexual arousal (Bancroft and Wu 1983: 65), and T is related to arousal; hence, the link may exist between fantasies of dominance/eminence and T. Indeed, Bancroft and Wu maintain that the main mechanism of T in sexual desire may be to change cognitive accessibility to images of sexual content. If there is a central (brain) effect, perhaps it is not strictly a matter of sexual content, but concerns content that carries a dominance or eminence theme into a sexual context.

Yet, even when fantasy accompanies masturbation, this can only be a pale copy of reality. Pornographic materials may come closer to producing a T surge because they frequently depict explicit dominance or eminence. Bancroft and Wu (1983) found that among those who were deficient in T, arousal was greater to a pornographic film than to own-fantasy. It may be that pornography is a form of highly simplified and crystallized dominance or eminence relations (Luria 1982). Males who are bereft of the opportunity for these in real life can identify unmistakably with the illustrated dominator. Since pornography apparently soon exhausts its capacity to arouse (Money 1973), it must represent ever new possibilities of dominance in the sexual context. For some, only the starkest and most violent depictions of dominance can arouse powers of identification and give them the possibility of a T surge. One thinks here of the Marquis de Sade's *One Hundred Days of Sodom and Gomorrah* or *The Story of "O"* in which there is increasingly violent resolution of sexual and presexual interaction. It is as if, clinically, the pursuit and conquest of a willing female has so little capacity by itself to arouse one sexually that only with the superaddition of violence is there sufficient, or augmented, T to allow the sexual act to go forward.

Crucially, no studies of human sexual behavior have considered dominance/eminence as possible precursors either of T or of sexual appetite. The matter is not simple, principally because three contexts of possible dominance/eminence are involved. First is the communal setting, entailing all of the roles and relationships that give a male much of his general social standing. It involves such matters as occupational prestige, income, breadth and scope of networks of support, reputation as an exemplar of community values, and the like. These sum to a dominance/eminence standing—and associated opportunities for attaining yet higher levels of social rank—that existed prior to the sexual encounter.

Importantly, in gender-differentiated social structures, a substantial part of a male's community standing can come at the expense of females, who are excluded or discriminated against in the competition for dominance/eminence.[9] As modern social structures become oriented to a more egalitarian view, some part of males' community-based dominance/eminence will necessarily be relinquished. If males resist this, it may be related in part to the threat to this source of T surges. Some women have argued that many men are less interested in women now that women have entered the competition for dominance/eminence in increasing numbers (Gittelson 1979; Ehrenreich 1983). If this explanation of supposed lesser interest in women is true, the mechanism may be that less dominance or eminence in men produces fewer rises in T, hence less desire. If so—and the issue is very complex—the answer clearly cannot reside in retraditionalizing the social structure by excluding women from community dominance/eminence competition, but by exploring whether community dominance/eminence in women enhances their potential for sexual arousal (there is some evidence for this in Purifoy and Koopmans 1979; Schindler 1979), and how this in turn may reignite the sexual fire between men and women, albeit with a new source of fuel. Chapter 4 deals with some of these issues.

The second context of male dominance/eminence involves the sexual partner, whether wife, lover, casual acquaintance, or prostitute. Regardless of community ranking, the specific relationship with the partner also generates a dominance/eminence standing. Although we would expect a positive correlation between community and partner-relationship standing, it need not be high. Community rank is relatively stable, slowly acquired and generally maintained over a long period; but partner-relationship dominance/eminence can fluctuate widely on a daily, or hourly, basis as quarrels and endearments punctuate the vicissitudes of the interaction, sometimes elevating dominance/eminence standing sharply and sometimes leaving it shattered. It can be seen that every argument or conflict is a challenge to the existing pattern of dominance/eminence. Even if a male ordinarily dominates in a traditional marriage or intimate relationship, a quarrel, until decisively won, negates the dominance for endocrinological purposes.

The third context of dominance/eminence emerges in the intimacy of the sexual interaction itself, the specific moves of touch and word that are directed to the other to rouse passion and gain assent to sexual culmination. (This does not preclude a proactive female.) Here, finally the nested quality of the three contexts of dominance/eminence has its denouement.

Research into sexual interaction has only barely considered these social and relational sources of dominance as they bear specifically on the pattern of sexual interaction. Epidemiological surveys of sexual behavior, such as that by Kinsey, Pomeroy, and Martin (1948) have touched on community standing. Clinically oriented materials (Masters and Johnson 1970; V. Sadock and B. Sadock 1976) and works such as Rubin's (1976) have dealt with the partner-relation issue. And to an extent perhaps not fully understood, Masters and Johnson (1970, 1976) and the host of how-to manuals have dealt with the relational conditions of the intimate interaction itself. Clearly, each of these social components is pertinent to the unfolding of motives and acts that result in, and interact with, endocrinological events.

A final point here concerns the precise function T serves in the dominance/eminence-T-sex equation. T has been associated with reduced anxiety and with increased energy (McAdoo et al. 1978), persistence (Andrew 1978), physical strength (Nieschlag 1979), and stamina (Young and Ismail 1978). Are these of any relevance to the issue at hand?

T can serve physiologically, psychologically, and, when properly translated, behaviorally to augment the sense of well-being and maintenance of an adaptive, satisfaction-oriented encounter with the environment. Physiologically, apart from the direct sexual functions of T elaborated above, T is also an agonist of erythrocyte (red blood cell) production. As such it may counteract possible loss of hemoglobin and resulting anemia (Strand 1983). In this mode T may provide its most effective contribution to physical energy.

Physical energy is the basic steam upon which human effort proceeds toward its goals (Collins 1981, 1990). Higher energy means greater capacity to work and to endure over long periods until goals are attained. Andrew (1978) has linked T to persistence of effort. This is not always functional, as, for example, when it would be adaptive to shift attention from one sphere of behavioral or cognitive commitment to another (see Waber 1977a and discussion in chapter 4). However, in many enterprises, persistence added to relatively high energy is likely to lead to success.

As the common expression has it, success feeds upon itself, Indeed, psychologically the attainment of victory or acclaim is a powerful cortical catalyst, enticing one to take on bigger projects where even greater success can be attained. Mazur proposed a reciprocal link between T and dominance (and we may add eminence as well).

> High or rising testosterone facilitates erect posture, strutting, assertive gestures, and the like; while depressed or falling testosterone inhibits these and produces instead the stooped posture and other deferent gestures of low status. The positive feedback between dominance behavior and testosterone helps to explain the stability of status hierarchies as well as the momentum often associated with strings of triumphs or defeats. Each triumph elevates testosterone, enhancing both the formidable demeanor of the the victor and the probability of further triumphs; each defeat depresses testosterone, reinforcing both the stooped posture of the vanquished and the likelihood of subsequent defeats. (1985:339)

In their replication of Mazur and Lamb's (1980) tennis study findings, Booth et al. (1989) confirmed Mazur's observations at least in part. They found that winners had higher T not only after their matches, but also just prior to their next match. Data were insufficient to test the remainder of Mazur's hypothesis. Indeed, it would seem right that cortical, endocrinal, and skeletal components of the organism should be in harmony in large undertakings.

Among the normal projects of adult males is sexual satisfaction. This is true for both higher- and lower-ranked males. With strong phylogenetic continuity, the social encounter of sexuality in the natural course leads to a sense of dominance/eminence. This is so because to court a female, to garner her attention to oneself, to have her, in fact, choose oneself over others, to make her sexually eager for oneself and to justify that eagerness by satisfying her are potent inspiriters. Each sexual encounter that follows this paradigm is an attainment that produces T. As argued above, sexual attainments produce T in much the same way that other social interactions do, and for the same reason.

For Freud ([1905] 1959), sexual confidence was the key to all other confidence. We need not accept the unidirectional thrust of Freud's proposition, but that sexual confidence supports general self-confidence cannot be disputed. Plainly, what has been argued above is that confidence derived from the dominance/eminence that produces T can flow in the other direction as well.

To dally once again with evolutionary teleology, one might say that those males who achieve frequent victories and dominance/eminence in the hunt, on the battlefield, on the playing field, on the street corner, in the counting house, courtroom, or boardroom, or in the scientific laboratory, and who, consequently, achieve more frequent elevations of T, are better prepared to pass along their genes. T, in this view, serves as both a general and a specifically sexual energizer. Tracking this view further, we can see that general energy and sexual energy must be linked to each other, for, over the long course of human history, we may suppose that once a male had sired offspring he would have needed the means to protect and support them and their mother. If the sexuality of the reproductive process were not importantly refreshing and renewing, it would deplete energy for the next task, namely, providing for the products of that sexuality. Hence, T serves to integrate the activities and energies required for successful transmission of genes.

Finally, the specific mechanism for T as an agonist of sexual desire and the pursuit of sexual goals may simply be that a surge of T provides pleasure. According to Davidson et al., who take a very broad view of the possible effects of T, there may be a "direct effect of T to lower the threshold of genital sensation in receptors whose activation stimulates sexual desire as well as erection. . . . The behavior-reinforcing properties of sexual pleasure could suffice to explain all the effects of androgen on sexuality through a 'domino' process involving increased sexual thoughts or fantasies, spontaneous erections (including nocturnal ones), coitus or masturbation, satisfaction and even ejaculation" (1983:618–619). If Davidson and his colleagues have got it right (O'Carroll, Shapiro, and Bancroft 1985 do not think so), T serves sexual conduct by facilitating the "pleasurable awareness of both sexual thoughts and activity," even in the rising tension of the arousal stage, but certainly before then as well. The "initial awareness" of pleasure need not even be fully conscious (Davidson et al. 1983: 618). We may tentatively surmise from this model that the surges of T that follow dominance/eminence attainment do induce a heightened accessibility to sexual thought and action. This mechanism will be central to the next step in our analysis of how the socio-bio-social chain helps to explain the relations between social structure and sexual conduct.[10]

This lengthy consideration of T and sexual activity is now concluded. What I have sought to do is to show in the face of complex and ambiguous results that T enhances desire, and under certain conditions this is reflected in the frequency of sexual behavior. Sexual activity itself has been analyzed as a social encounter (real in the case of coitus, fantasy in the case of masturbation) that has dominance/eminence opportunities.

One result of applying this understanding was to explain why T sometimes rose after sexual activity and sometimes did not.

If the undeniably labyrinthine analysis of this section is valid, it provides a view of sexual activity that is as much anchored in social and behavioral logic as in endocrino-logic. Indeed, without such a translation of the empirical results accumulated thus far, they would constitute a highly incoherent account of the behavioral and hormonal pattern.

We can now proceed to the analysis of how the macrostructure of society affects levels of sexual activity in different social groups. The relations among dominance, aggression, sexuality, and T discussed to this point provide a basis for understanding the workings of the larger social structure in the sexual sphere.

Social Structure and Sexual Activity

Social structure was defined above as the arrangement of individuals and groups according to their power and status or deference. These elements approximate how we define stratification systems, so we may use social structure in the macro sense to refer to the distribution of social class position in society. Different theories of social class designate different indicators of class position (Collins 1975; Matras 1975). For present purposes, education, occupational prestige, and income will indicate class standing. They are known to be correlated variables (Matras 1975), and they are widely used as class indicators. They also imply such further distinctions as level of authority and autonomy in work, community standing via style of life afforded by income and by offices and memberships, and both present comforts and prospects for postretirement security (Collins 1975). The issue now is social class and sexual behavior.

It is remarkable that the most complete and most thoroughly analyzed set of data on sexual conduct among males in the United States was published more than forty years ago (Kinsey, Pomeroy, and Martin 1948). In analytical scope the Kinsey investigation far exceeds anything done either previously or since, despite the serious methodological flaws of that study, which were mainly defects of sampling (Cochran, Mosteller, and Tukey 1955).[11] Major subsequent surveys of sexual conduct (Hunt 1974; Pietropinto and Simenauer 1977, 1979) are as deficient methodologically as Kinsey's—the researchers failed to obtain an adequate sample of a defined population. Yet, other than the results of write-in surveys, of which there are several and which are even more badly flawed, this is all that is available to us for purposes of analyzing the relationship between sexual conduct and social class across the life span. Westoff and Ryder (1977) obtained some pertinent data on frequency of sexual intercourse in marriage from the National Fertility Study, but these have been analyzed in only scant detail for our purposes (see Trussell and Westoff 1980).

Under the circumstances, it is fortunate that the available studies report somewhat similar findings with respect to the influence of social class on sexual activity. The comparability is somewhat compromised by the failure of Hunt and of Pietropinto and Simenauer to provide rigorous breakdowns of social class practices by age. This will emerge as an important consideration below.

In general, Kinsey, Pomeroy, and Martin; Hunt; Pietropinto and Simenauer; and Trussell and Westoff find lower rates of sexual activity among those with higher education and occupational levels and among white-collar workers than among those with lower educational and occupational levels and among blue-collar workers. The convergence of four studies on this finding gives us some confidence that the results are not only valid, but also stable over at least a thirty-five-year period in which very large transformations in the American social class structure and in specific sexual practices have been recorded. Using profile analysis, Clement (1989) confirmed the relative stability of male sexual practices over this period. In a relatively small sample, Weinberg and Williams (1980:33) found that, despite some convergence of sexual practices, "sexual embourgeoisement" had not occurred since Kinsey's data were collected. Indeed, though there is evidence that lower-class sex practices have moved closer to higher-class practices in such areas as masturbation and amount and type of foreplay and that a similar convergence by higher- to lower-class practice has occurred in the area of premarital coitus, the major quantitative difference between the classes appears to hold: lower-class males have more total sexual activity than higher-class males.

However, when age is introduced into the analysis, a somewhat different picture emerges—one that is crucial for the central hypothesis of this section. Kinsey, Pomeroy, and Martin (1948:336, table 81) provided the most detailed results: until age thirty, males with zero to eight years of education exceed those with a high school or college education in total sexual outlet. Between ages thirty and forty, the high school educated exceed those with zero to eight years of education and the college educated. After age forty, the college educated rise to first place over the zero-to-eight group. No data are provided for the high school educated after age forty.

When nonmarital sexual outlet is examined (this includes premarital sex, extramarital sex, and sex with prostitutes), approximately the same pattern is found: before age thirty, males with a high school education or less have higher rates; after age thirty, rates are highest for the college educated (Kinsey, Pomeroy, and Martin 1948:348, table 85). When marital sex alone is considered, a complementary pattern is found: at the lower-class levels, marital sex is less of total sexual outlet among younger married men than among such men at an older age. The reverse is true for high-class levels: by age thirty, marital sex is a lesser proportion of total outlet than when they were younger (Kinsey, Pomeroy, and Martin 1948:382, table 97). Kinsey, Pomeroy, and Martin 1948:357) also report that professionals, the highest class level for which they had data, had less marital sex as a proportion of total sexual outlet than upper white-collar workers, the next lower group in the Kinsey class hierarchy. Only in total marital and extramarital coitus (Kinsey, Pomeroy, and Martin 1948: 358, table 89) does the age by social class reversal fail to occur. This requires some further consideration.

The Kinsey data on which the argument here centrally pivots are replete with methodological problems, notwithstanding that they are the best we have to date. This was fully recognized in a remarkably candid admission by Kinsey's own collaborators (Gebhard and Johnson 1979:8–9) concerning the frustrations encountered in using the results of the first Kinsey volume (Kinsey, Pomeroy, and Martin 1948), "one of the most difficult books to work with ever written." In order to mitigate some of the defects of sampling, of data aggregation, and of mixing disparate populations, Gebhard and Johnson provided a "clean" version of at least some of Kinsey's original data set. An important revision was the removal from the sample of homosexuals, mental hospital patients, and incarcerated prisoners (see Gebhard et al. 1965 for the analysis of the prisoners' sexual practices, some of which will be examined below).

Kinsey, Pomeroy, and Martin presented the mean frequency of total marital and extramarital coitus for the whole sample, including prisoners (1948:358, table 89). In those data, at all age levels, those with college education or higher had lower coital frequencies. These results directly negate the hypothesis proposed here: the interaction between age and social class.

However, when we examine the clean data (Gebhard and Johnson 1979:375, 399, 402; tables 326, 350, 353), we see that the hypothesis is supported: at younger ages, those with less than a college education have higher coital frequencies; by ages forty-one to forty-five, those with a college education or more have higher frequencies. The main difference in the two data sets is the exclusion of the prisoners' data from the clean results. The effect of this removal on the original

Kinsey table, in which the coital hypothesis is refuted, can be seen when the prison population is compared with a control group of nonprisoners matched for age.

In both the marital and extramarital coitus categories, at approximately the age when, according to the hypothesis here, lower-class males would begin to lag behind middle-class males in coital frequency, the prisoners have higher rates than the control group of nonprisoners (Gebhard et al. 1965:598, 616; tables 71, 77). Gebhard and Johnson (1979:4) acknowledged that the prisoners constitute a sexually distinct population. Thus, including the prisoners distorts the conditions under which the hypothesis can be tested.

Although other surveys of sexual behavior do not, unfortunately, provide exactly comparable data, their results generally confirm the age-related reversal in sexual practice among the class levels found in Kinsey, Pomeroy, and Martin (1948) and Gebhard and Johnson (1979). Pietropinto and Simenauer (1977) found that, over time, better-educated males find sex more enjoyable than do those who did not finish high school. They also found that in choosing an "ideal" sex life, "desire for marriage *with outside sexual activity* climbed steadily with earning power, from 12% under $10,000 to 27% at $25,000. Professional men topped the occupational ranks with 26% choosing marriage *plus*" (Pietropinto and Simenauer 1977:89–90; emphasis added). These results resonate perfectly with Kinsey, Pomeroy, and Martin's (1948:357) finding about professionals, discussed above. (I assume that higher income and occupational level are positively correlated with age for a working population.) In response to a question dealing with conditions under which sex might be avoided, better-educated and higher-income respondents were found least likely to avoid sex. Hunt (1974) was also in accord with the Kinsey and the Pietropinto and Simenauer patterns, reporting that extramarital sex is more prevalent among less-educated men before age thirty-five, but that the difference narrows after that age.

Trussell and Westoff (1980) found that, controlling for other variables, white-collar workers had marital sex less often than blue-collar workers. This confirms the general pattern. While the study seems to refute the age-related reversal, it must be understood that the National Fertility Study, from which the Trussell and Westoff data were derived, was mainly concerned with contraceptive use and sampled married women aged fifteen to forty-four. Only about 25 percent of the husbands were older men, for whom the age-class reversal is noted in other studies.

Three studies of sexual practice among aged populations also contain some relevant data. Pfeiffer and Davis (1972) found that either income or a direct social class measure was correlated positively with enjoyment, interest, and frequency of sexual relations in a sample of married men ages forty-five to sixty-nine. In a study of married men ages sixty to seventy-nine, Clyde Martin (1981) found that when sexual activity was graded into high, medium, and low categories there was a clear linear trend showing that males at the professional and technical levels exceeded proprietors and those in managerial posts, who exceeded lower levels. A similar rank order was found for education: postgraduates had higher levels than those with a bachelor's degree, whose levels were higher than those with less than a bachelor's degree. The one study to find no relationship between sex conduct and social class among an aged population was by Persson, Nilsson, and Svanborg (1980), who collected data from a Swedish sample of married men seventy years of age. This study aside, an empirical generalization appears to emerge: The lower the social class level, the higher the sexual activity in younger years; the higher the social class level, the higher the sexual activity in older years. My intention is to explain this in a manner consistent with the earlier analysis of the relationship between dominance, sexuality, and T.

At the outset, it is clear that older age per se, which is related to lower levels of sexual activity in all classes (Kinsey, Pomeroy, and Martin 1948; Hunt 1974; Pietropinto and Simenauer 1977), is not in itself at issue, since obviously all individuals age regardless of social class.

Although aging, the physiological processes of bodily decline over the years, may vary with social class due to differences in the arduousness of labor, the quality of nutrition, and the quality of health and medical care (Mechanic 1978), aging in this sense is not likely to account for the variation in sexual activity we are seeking to explain. Differential aging cannot be excluded entirely, but it fails as a comprehensive explanation (see Kinsey, Pomeroy, and Martin 1948:587) because it cannot explain the lower rates of sexual activity by men in the higher class in the earlier years unless we assume that their health is poorer at that time than the health of members of the lower class.

It is well known that social class membership differentially disposes one's life chances. It is also known from the Kinsey data that higher-class sexual practice overtakes that of the lower classes in mid-adulthood. One possible reason for this could be that by that stage lower-class health is poorer, hence there may be an inhibition with respect to engaging in sexual behavior, whether for reasons directly related to health, or indirectly via esthetic concerns about weight, complexion, and the like. Gebhard and Johnson do show that the "current health" of males without a college education is poorer than that of college-educated males (1979:110, table 63). Since there is no breakdown by age, we cannot evaluate the possible effects of health on the age–social class interaction in sex behavior shown in the Kinsey, Pomeroy, and Martin (1948) data.

To evaluate the effects of health we must examine other data, where we see that, even if health is an issue at later ages—and it is not being precluded here entirely—it cannot be used to explain the differences in sexual behavior in younger years. Even in the younger years, the health of lower-class males is more impaired than that of higher-class males (National Center for Health Statistics 1983:12). In fact, at different age levels, the ratios of those with one to eight years of education to those with sixteen or more years of education who have fair or poor health are as follows: ages seventeen to twenty-four, 9.6 to one; ages twenty-five to thirty-four, 7.5; ages thirty-five to forty-four, 6.6; ages forty-five to fifty-four, 5.4; ages fifty-five to sixty-four; 3.4; and sixty-five years and over, 2.3.

The ratios constitute a declining series, which shows that in the earlier years lower-class males are much more likely to be in ill health than higher-class makes. Yet they are more active sexually. In the later years, higher-class males catch up considerably in poor health, but at the same time emerge as the sexually more active group. These results should lay to rest any supposition that health is a decisive factor in explaining the reversal in sexual practice.

Furthermore, several studies of sexual activity in healthy older men show the differential pattern of greater activity in those with higher class standing (Pfeiffer and Davis 1972; Martin 1981). As will be seen below, aging does explain some of the variation, not because it is related to poor health, but because it reduces the ability of lower-class men to obtain surges of T.

Duration of marriage is another possible explanation of class difference in sexual activity. Controlling for age, men of higher social class are married fewer years than men of lower social class. This is simply due to the earlier age of marriage at the lower-class level. There is also evidence that frequency of marital coitus declines with duration of marriage (Kinsey, Pomeroy, and Martin 1948; Udry, Deven, and Coleman 1982; James 1983; Jasso 1985). Putting these two together, it might be that male motivation for intercourse declines with familiarity. Since males in the lower social classes generally commence heterosexual relations earlier than higher-class males (Kinsey, Pomeroy, and Martin 1948; Hunt 1974), they may simply become tired or bored sooner—as Kinsey, Pomeroy, and Martin (1948:257) contend.

Although there are data that show higher rates when there is a novel partner (Kinsey, Pomeroy, and Martin 1948) or when one is not in continuous contact with one's steady partner (Linnankoski 1981, in a study done with monkeys), the fatigue or boredom hypothesis is wanting as a major explanation. For one thing, earlier entry into sexual activity is associated with higher rather than lower rates in later years (Kinsey, Pomeroy, and Martin 1948). Hence, lower-class males, who initiate coitus earlier (Gebhard and Johnson 1979:267, table 218), should have these higher frequencies, yet do not. Furthermore, Martin (1981) found that older men (sixty to seventy-nine) with higher rates were more likely to have had more than one marriage. This is exactly the case of the lower-class males in Kinsey, Pomeroy, and Martin's sample. They are more likely to be in a second or third marriage (Gebhard and Johnson 1979:337, table 288), which may help to explain the continuing superiority of this group in marital coitus across the life span (Kinsey, Pomeroy, and Martin 1948:356, table 88).

Another possible explanation for the differential rates of sexual activity by social class involves T. If T surges differed by social class, and these differences reversed with age, we would have another way to explain the data. I turn to this possibility now.

Social Structure and Testosterone

There has been virtually no interest in determining T levels by social class. Bradford and McLean (1984) found no relationship between T and social class indicators among a group of fifty males arrested for sexual offenses. It is not known whether this sample adequately represented the social-class spectrum. The one major epidemiological study of T (Dai et al. 1981) omitted social class as a control variable, but subsequent analysis showed no differences in T level by either education or income (personal communication). Dabbs and Morris (1989) found higher T in males with lower SES compared with higher-SES males sampled from the population of Vietnam veterans.

Although there is no conclusive evidence of mean differences in circulating T by social class, there may be a difference in the frequency with which T surges occur, as well as the possibility of an age-class interaction that affects these. To find out we must examine the link between social structure and aggression.

Social Structure and Aggression

To the degree that T is linked to aggression—in effect to dominance that may result from aggression, as reviewed above—there may be more T surges at lower social class levels because physical aggression is a much more likely coping solution in times of interpersonal conflict for lower-class males.

Social class as a topic is fraught with some of the same conflictfulness as social class as a fact of social life. No one with eyes to see can deny the existence of differential advantage, privilege, opportunity, and power—some of the more deleterious effects of these class differences. Indeed, even race is dismissed as a causal factor in favor of class to explain some of the most devastating deprivations in American society (Wilson 1978). The differences cumulate on account of inherited wealth and differential opportunities for income due to education, occupational standing, socialization advantages, "cultural capital" (consisting of resources of language and taste [Bourdieu (1979) 1984:12]), and other conditions of advantage. To varying degrees, with the emergence of the welfare state, virtually all developed societies recognize the importance, need, and desirability of providing a basic floor of citizenship benefits beneath the least fortunate so that they do not sink into an unredeemable state (Marshall 1973). Notwithstanding such remedies, the social organization of work and the reward system of capitalism, which is based on the principle of differential reward for what is regarded as differential contribution, as well as the sheer power of some to control the distribution of benefits, mean that a lower class continues to exist. Some necessarily have less.

Stereotypes of social class are as prevalent as stereotypes of any other social category; for example, the decadence and sexual licentiousness of the upper class, the rigid, moralistic conformity of the middle class, and the brutality and violence of the lower class. By definition, stereotypes assign as true to an entire group what is true only about some of its members. Social scientists can justly take pride in their efforts to combat stereotypes about Jews, blacks, Italians, Asians, women, and other sociologically defined minorities. Countless numbers of students in introductory courses in sociology, psychology, and anthropology have been enlightened about the nature and danger of stereotyping.

However, in their effort to combat stereotypes, social scientists have sometimes become susceptible to a social ailment that, while nowhere as dangerous as the stereotypes they have fought, is nonetheless counterfactual and, finally, unproductive for scientific understanding. I wish to label this flaw as *sentimentalization* of the very groups who are otherwise stereotyped. No group is immune to being sentimentalized—perhaps the classic case is the idea of the Nobel Savage in the eighteenth century—but some are subjected to it more than others. At present, for a host of reasons having to do with the serious drive to create a more egalitarian society, among the most sentimentalized groups is probably the lower class.

Since the lower class is a disadvantaged group, some of the less appealing (from a middle-class perspective, which includes most of the readers of this book) aspects of lower-class life are ignored, distorted, or otherwise distanced from awareness; that is, they are sentimentalized as opposed to being stereotyped. One reason for this is that the less appealing attributes of lower-class life may be the product of the very social processes that created the initial disadvantage. To shed obloquy on others for what is not their fault, is, in the telling phrase of Ryan (1971) to "blame the victim." Rather than do this, people of conscience may bend over backward, shut their eyes and sentimentalize through denial. There is some danger of this in examining lower-class patterns of violence.

A careful examination of the social science literature supports the view that the lower class is physically more aggressive and more violent in its social relations than the middle class, whether one looks at childrearing, adolescent and young adult peer groups, street encounters, domestic relations, conflict resolution, or crime.[12] Thus, as a general proposition, I argue that lower-class life, compared with middle-class life, is more violent, more given to direct, immediate, emotion-guided physical confrontations, and that status challenges are more frequently entertained and resolved in a direct and speedy manner.

Lower-class anger is more likely to be expressed in physical action than middle-class anger. Harburg, Blakelock, and Roeper (1979) found "anger-out" to be the dominant lower-class mode. Also, blue-collar workers and/or high school dropouts were more likely to harm their partners physically in cases of infidelity and were more likely to report an exchange of physical blows when there was disagreement (Pietropinto and Simenauer 1979). Explosive violence in response to frustration is more prevalent in the working class (Rubin 1976). Acting-out personality disorders manifesting aggressive outbursts are also, in general, more prevalent in the working class (Dohrenwend and Dohrenwend 1969). Lower-class culture is more predicated on the maintenance of one's status by physical means (Cohen 1955; Miller 1958).

Family violence toward spouses and children is more frequent in the lower class (Gelles and Straus 1988). Some have suggested that this may only appear to be the case due to middle-class reticence to admit violence and to police reluctance to recognize and arrest for it. If true, it could be only partially true. That is, norms for reticence concerning admission of violence can be assumed to have some effect on reducing the actual commission of it. Therefore, even middle-class reticence to admit violence would lead us to suspect that, other things being equal, there is simply less of it to admit. But other data also support the stronger likelihood of domestic violence in the lower class. In the matter of fatal child abuse, Sullivan and Thompson (1988:89) point out that this would be difficult even for the affluent to conceal, and existing studies show the clear relationship of abuse and of fatal abuse with economic disadvantage, or lower-class status (U.S. Department of Health and Human Services 1982; Garbarion 1981).

Erlanger (1974) has attempted to dismiss the evidence for higher endorsement by the lower class of physical punishment in childrearing. Despite a strenuous effort to do so through the examination of a number of major studies, Erlanger is left to conclude that "there is indeed some correlation, but that it is probably not strong enough to be of great theoretical or practical significance" (1974:81). The reports on fatally injured children (see above) do not support this interpretation.

In the matter of spousal violence, Hornung, McCullough, and Sugimoto (1981) have specified further the conditions in which a husband may abuse his wife. They found that men in lower educational or occupational niches who have higher-status wives are more likely to be violent. Indeed, in such cases, life-threatening acts occur more than six times more often than when the occupational positions of the spouses are about the same.

We may add to this the greater lower-class cultural interest in boxing and other violent sports and in films and television shows that contain violent content (Frank and Greenberg 1980; Gallop 1986). In addition, ethnographic accounts of lower-class communities provide evidence of a more or less persistent undercurrent of violence or potential for violence (Gans 1962; Whyte 1943; LeMasters 1975).

Finally, while there is growing agreement that law violation is pandemic through the social class structure (Tittle, Villemez, and Smith 1978; Hindelang, Hirschi, and Weis 1979), when crimes are differentiated into violent and nonviolent, a disproportionately high number are committed by those of lower educational and socioeconomic status (Tittle, Villemez, and Smith 1978; Wolfgang, Figlio, and Sellin 1972; Thornberry and Farnworth 1982).

For present purposes, the more immediate expression of anger in the lower class and the aggression that ensues can be associated with concomitant or successor rates of increased T. Each occasion of relatively violent anger produces a winner and a loser. Sometimes the loser is not only defeated, but dead. I propose that there are more occasions in the lower class when a decisive engagement follows the arousal of anger. Often, the advanced mechanisms of social control—police, courts, and laws—are not invoked; justice is done according to the strengths of the contending parties, and often, their allies, as seen in gang combats.

It may be objected, that if there are decisive victors, there are also losers. But at lower social class levels, losers can more easily convert their losing status into that of victor. This is because the pecking order of lower-class life is more definite. A loser in one contest can less inhibitedly find someone else to dominate, frequently a spouse, a girlfriend, a child, a sibling. Family violence, while pandemic in the social structure, is more prevalent at lower social class levels (Straus, Gelles, and Steinmetz 1980). Hence, even losers have the opportunity to retrieve their status and emerge winners. Such devices, involving the greater clarity of the pecking order, are simply less available to the higher class.

By contrast, higher-class members are caught in a net of relatively suppressed affect woven by social organization. A more effective socialization, a greater access to secondary means of anger enactment (e.g., the legal suit), a greater vulnerability to the undesirable consequences of direct acting out of anger that goes hand in hand with a greater investment in maintaining a smooth and equable facade interpersonally and in the community all contribute to the management of anger—not so much whether there is anger, but rather steering it away from direct expression. "Anger-in" is the major middle-class mode (Funkenstein, King, and Drolette 1957), or "reflection" when provoked (Harburg, Blakelock, and Roeper 1979). Middle-class socialization focuses earlier on control of anger (Miller and Swanson 1960) and on self-control in general (Kohn 1969). The consequence is that even if anger occurs as frequently in higher-class as in lower-class life—although this is unknown—the resolution of anger is far slower in the higher class. The egregiously slow pace of the legal system with its cases that drag on for months and years serves to dampen the emotional fires and to draw out the process of victory until the keen edge of it is dulled. Surely it is not like the direct resolution of anger through immediate aggression.

Taking these results as representative of a pattern of greater propensity to aggression in the lower class, we can deduce that T surges on these grounds are more prevalent in the lower class. I continue to assume that the link between aggression and T is mediated by the connection between aggression and dominance, which is more closely linked to T. Yet, these results on aggression differences between social classes, which have been marshaled to explain sexual behavior differences, do not yet explain the age-related reversal that has been noted above. If the T hypothesis here, via aggression and dominance, is to have any validity, it must be capable of reversal with age. I wish to propose how this may occur.

The differences between lower-class and higher-class life in the expression of anger and the direct, decisive outcomes it generates ought to narrow with age, reducing the lower-class edge. It takes a younger man to throw himself thoughtlessly into a physical fray, or a foolish one to risk a pounding from someone younger and stronger than himself. The father who beat his nine-year-old son is not likely to beat his son of nineteen, regardless of how much the father believes his son deserves it.[13] All in all, the battlefronts of lower-class life turn over to cadres of the young. Street gang warfare is not a pastime of thirty year olds. As men at working-class levels age, they are less and less frequently able to enter the lists for direct hand-to-hand combat. Less combat means less opportunity for quick, telling victories, hence less dominance and less frequent surges of T. With less T, there is less frequent sexual arousal, and this is precisely what the data, detailed above, show. Lower-class sexual activity rates decline relative to higher-class levels.

This still does not explain the emergence with age of the higher-status group as the most sexually active class. For this we must consider another aspect of the difference between lower and higher classes as this relates to victory, to dominance/eminence, and to T. We can do this by examining the last of the paths shown in figure 2.1

Social Structure and Dominance/Eminence

It is clear that social class, our signifier of social structure, contains elements that pertain to dominance. For example, those who have authority are dominant, while those who do not are subordinate. Those who lack autonomy in work are subordinate, not dominant. Those who have financial resources are dominant relative to those who do not. Occupational prestige also lends eminence, since it entails deference from those with lower prestige.

In this essay, however, dominance and eminence are broader concepts than social class. They pertain to all interactions in which power or status is differentiated between actors. Thus, even at the lowest social class levels, as we have just seen, there are many who are dominant within their class at the micro level with spouses, siblings, coevals, older persons, children, and others. At the highest social class levels there are subordinates in their social relations at the micro level with siblings, coevals, older persons, and others. Dominance/eminence refers to the direct outcomes of social interaction, while class position means one's location in hierarchies created indirectly and ordered according to criteria—prestige, income, power of office—that are impersonal. Collins (1981:984) identified these two and linked them as the "microfoundations" (dominance) "of macrosociology" (social class).

On the face of it, those in higher social classes are clearly winners, hence dominant or eminent, when compared with those at lower-class levels. Control, autonomy, longevity, health, ease, comfort, material possessions (obviously)—"life chances," as Weber (1947) put it—are more favorable at higher class levels (Matras 1975; Collins 1975; Mechanic 1978).

Yet, in the area of sexual outlet and pleasure (life's "greatest gratification," according to Freud 1951:69), the higher class does not clearly emerge until relatively late—indeed, not until well past the prime of male sexual potency, as measured by total sexual outlet, which is understood to occur at about age twenty (Kinsey, Pomeroy, and Martin 1948:220, table 44; Strand 1983). Barring any congenital biological difference between the upper and lower classes, the differences in rates and in peaks of sexual pleasure must have a social origin. I contend that, quite apart from any cultural differences between classes, the difference relates to the timing and frequency of T surges in the different social classes: At lower social class levels, the most frequent T surges occur in earlier years, while in later years the most frequent surges occur in higher-class groups.

In the previous section I provided some grounds for the view that in early years, lower-class behavior patterns linked mainly to direct aggression result in frequent experiences of dominance, hence T surge, hence higher rates of sexual activity. Here the problem is to explain the emergence of the higher class in later years as the more sexually active. As with the lower class, higher-class sexuality is dependent on the type and timing of its dominance/eminence, and T surges. How this may work will now be detailed.

According to Kinsey, Pomeroy, and Martin (1948), the basic pattern of sexual conduct is laid down by the late teens. Remarkably, even if there is future social mobility, the teenage sex pattern supposedly conforms to the pattern of the class of destination, rather than the class of origin. Miller and Simon (1974), Vener and Stewart (1974), and Coles and Stokes (1985) found this was so. This requires explanation.[14]

First, there may be a transmission of family values, particularly where parents are fostering higher-class status for their son. Just as they urge the imitation of higher-class orientations to education, occupational goals, and deportment, they also may instill a moral perspective about intimate relations between the sexes. Indeed, in one sense, social mobility may not be confirmed until one has acquired a spouse of the class one aims for. It is thus reasonable to assume some influence of parental values, whether they are transmitting the values of their own community or of a higher-level community.

Second, there are the practices of one's peers. Kinsey, Pomeroy, and Martin (1948) pointed out that these often override parental interests. Peer and same-sex older companions are central as models and in transmitting information and value ratings of sexual conduct. One's status in the peer group depends on one's ability to meet, or to appear to meet, the sexual norms of the group (Reiss 1967; Carns 1973). This holds for both lower- and higher-class youths.

Third, there is the complex interplay between class values with respect to education and occupation, on the one hand, and the kinds of conduct that become associated with a more open sexual nature in the teen years on the other. Specifically, in those years a certain bravado, physical daring and prowess, and sensation-seeking conduct—in a word, "ballsiness"—produce attitudes of sexual receptivity in many young women of one's cohort. Such activities include athletics, feats of strength, competition in contests of a nonintellectual sort such as car racing, and sustained masculine pursuits such as heavy drinking. Again, high rates of winning are possible. The winners gain not only status, but surges of T. They are not only more attractive, but they are more energized for sexual encounters. It is mainly at the lower end of the social spectrum that these "manly" practices are pursued, with their greater opportunities for winning and for T.

By contrast, in those years, higher-status youths would be more likely to shun those activities that lead to the more frequent surges of T in their lower-status counterparts. Yes, there is tennis (see Mazur and Lamb 1980.)[15] But, on average, higher-status activities are more likely to be intellectual, involving books, talk, concern with philosophies of life, with politics, and with cultural symbols. These are not only not physical, they are also not as clearly competitive, nor as likely to produce decisive victories. Not that cerebral victories count for nothing. They are simply not as likely to be decisive (as Mazur and Lamb 1980 show is necessary for the testosterone surge) nor as frequent. It has been suggested that conversation is a significant arena for dominance/eminence attainment and thus that higher-status males' conversational encounters are fraught with opportunities for T elevation. Undeniably, the swift rejoinder, the telling point, or acute witticism can gain a social advantage in conversation. But higher-class conversational codes appear to have no equivalent to the lower-class, mainly black, practice called "playing the dozens" (Abrahams 1962:209) in which personal status in a group depends to a great extent on how well one replies to rounds of taunting, calculated insults, and put-downs from other members, and how smartly one can turn the tables of denigration on others. Higher-class conversations appear to be governed more by the kind of collaboration to preserve and protect each other's esteem that Goffman

(1967) noted was a paramount feature of talk, at least in the social locations in which he observed it. Even when competition is strenuous—to get a place in the best schools, to make law review (Turow 1977)—the time spans are much longer than for the competitions of the lower class. Higher-class projects often take a long time. Attaining a law or medical degree or a Ph.D. is a lengthy process, with "victory," or status attainment, culminating years of depressed, anxious lack of victories (see, e.g., Mazur and Lamb's 1980 study of medical school graduates).

Inevitably, however, the preponderance of victories turns in favor of the higher groups. Not only are the lower groups losing their physical strength and potency to engage in combat and pursuits of the type that produced many of their T surges in early years—this is the aging effect—but the upper groups come to reap the benefit of the long investment they have made, beginning very young, by taking control of the social structure. They come to be in charge of the dominant institutions and of the myriad organizations that make up these institutions. As such they are now frequent competitors and winners—in business, in the courts, in legislative and executive bodies, both public and private—and their decisions are enforceable over the resistance of others (hence their "power," as Weber 1946 put it). They come ultimately to reign, to govern, and to judge. They assume the dominant places in society, and their daily lives are exercises in dominance and eminence. This should lead to frequent surges of T, more sexual arousal, and more sexual activity.

The Kinsey and other data reported above point to the higher levels of sexual outlet sought by the professional and technical elite in comparison even with other upper white-collar occupations. For one thing, this can be due to greater opportunity afforded by positions that allow for more travel and contact with new women, or by the availability of more money with which to stimulate romantic impulses in themselves or their partners, or to afford the financial obligations of an affair (see, e.g., Gagnon and Simon 1973). But the professional and technical elite is also more involved in tasks that lead to more frequent decisive victories and to the high incomes that symbolize their preeminent status, not merely underwrite it materially. The legal and medical professions are cases in point. But the sciences, which often confer high status in organizations and mid- to upper-level management, also conform to this pattern.

Indeed, we may expand this analysis by considering all occupations from the perspective of whether or not they foster or permit autonomy or self-direction in their practitioners (Kohn 1983). While self-direction does not signify dominance per se, it does signify the obverse, namely, that one is not weakly subordinate. According to the materials presented earlier, while victory initiates higher T flow, defeat, or even subordination, inhibits or reduces T (Mazur and Lamb 1980; Keverne 1979; M. Elias 1981; Mendoza 1984). Occupations and occupational levels that deny autonomy and place one under the direct and frequent supervision of others reflect one's subordinate status.[16] Here, too, the fate of lower- and higher-class workers differs as they grow older: lower-level jobs are most frequently subordinate with low autonomy, while upper-level jobs are more frequently self-directed. This is indeed crucial for the difference in lower- and middle-class socialization (Kohn 1969).

In sum, then, the data on sexual activity show that, relatively, the lower class begins high and ends low, while the higher class begins low and ends high (there is, of course, a decline with age for males in both classes). Kinsey, Pomeroy, and Martin took note of the differences and attributed them to "differences in sexual adjustment in marriages at the different levels, as well as the force of the mores which lie at the base of most of these class differences" (1948:356–357). To this extent, despite his training as a zoologist, Kinsey was a social constructionist, as described earlier.

Certainly mores come into it, but the social structure also acts directly upon sexual conduct by producing greater or less arousal by virtue of the opportunities it generates for personal victories that give dominance or eminence and provide for a surge of T. As seen here, these opportunities vary by age in the different classes. Mores, such as their power may be, may simply ratify what is already well entrenched in social structural practice. In this regard, as Durkheim pointed out, "There are certain ways of mutual reaction which, finding themselves very conformable to the nature of things, are repeated very often and become habits. Then these habits, becoming forceful, are transformed into rules of conduct. The past determines the future. In other words there is a certain sorting of rights and duties which is established by usage and becomes obligatory. The rule then . . . only expresses in clear-cut fashion the result of a given situation" ([1933] 1964:366). Hence, social structure, with its differential opportunities for dominance/eminence and consequent T surges, helps us to understand the sexual pattern of different social classes at different life stages. To conclude, it is not that culture plays no role in determining sexual conduct. Rather, the point here has been to show that sexual conduct is constructed by more than culture and that an appreciation of the hormonal consequences of social structural outcomes helps us better to understand the patterns of social conduct we find.

Discussion

This chapter began with the empirical generalization that dominance/eminence attainment elevates testosterone in males. On the basis of plausible, though not conclusive, evidence, I assumed also that T is a libido agonist that leads to sexual interaction. The three elements—dominance/eminence, T, and sexual interaction—comprise a socio-bio-social chain. I have tried to demonstrate here that patterns of sexual interaction, an important type of social conduct with a significant biological precursor, can be understood better by considering all links in the chain: the social precursors that affect the biological precursors that affect the social outcomes. Indeed, without a full socio-bio-social address to the question, certain data on the biology of human sexual interaction may be uninterpretable. In fact, this ambiguity may account for the paucity of efforts to collect such data since the mid-1970s.

By definition, the social includes all instances of human behavior that are influenced by the real or imagined response of other human beings, from the micro processes of one-to-one interaction to the macro processes of global blocs confronting each other. An important social process is dominance/eminence attainment, with both social and biological effects. But while dominance/eminence attainment is the socially proximate cause of T elevation in males, a larger social context, namely, social class, allocates opportunities for dominance/eminence by age. This helps to explain the reversal in frequency of sexual activity in different classes at a certain age.

A sense of the social that has perhaps not been offered before is found in the analysis of sexual interaction itself as an opportunity for dominance/eminence attainment. The major failure of the researchers who undertook to study T and human sexual interaction is that they saw such interaction only in biological or physiological terms. In this regard, the researchers of animal sexual interactions have been advanced, recognizing the social nature of the sexual encounters under their inspection.

What animal researchers can do we can also do when we treat human sexual interaction. Viewing sexual intimacy itself as a potential dominance/eminence encounter may be the missing link in understanding the often puzzling and inconsistent results of investigations of human sexual behavior and T.

I want to conclude now with two research-oriented issues that derive from the soci-bio-social framework. First, the considerable effort to link T to sexual activity has had very mixed success. Some investigators find a link; others do not. My contention has been that what links T to sex is not T level, but T surge. Without the extra quantity of T, sexual activity is not likely to depart from some average amount for the particular group the individual is a part of.

I mean here a biosocial group comprising persons with particular biological and social features. An example can be found in the work of Meuser and Nieschlag (reported in Nieschlag 1979), who studied sexual activity and T among male singers. They found that basses had higher T level than tenors across the life span and higher sexual activity in the age period of twenty to forty years. Significantly, the basses fell below the tenors in sexual activity in the succeeding years, between ages forty-one and seventy.

To understand these results, it would be necessary to pursue the dominance experiences of these two groups over the biosocial life cycle. This would entail an investigation of relative timetables for the maturation and decay of different vocal types; the numbers of each type in relation to the number of roles for which they are needed (in opera, for example); the stratification of operatic roles according to the appeal of the character (for example, heroes are usually tenors; villains, baritones or basses); the interaction between these several elements and body type (basses are larger and heavier, according to Meuser and Nieschlag) and how this conforms to cultural ideals for good looks at different ages. It may be seen that these details focus on the possibilities of dominance and eminence, hence T surge. To clarify the confusion about the relationship between T and sexual activity, the social determinants of T surge may be among the most productive routes.

A second point that bears on research into these questions involves what might be termed "laboratory sex," whether coitus or masturbation. Masters and Johnson (1966) did a signal service for this kind of study, but their results are interpretable largely within a physiological framework. Yet, normally, in the sense of what is most often desired, sexual conduct is a social act, with or without a partner. Sexual conduct implies relationship and usually occurs within the context of a relationship. The strictly biological aspects are strongly susceptible to the conditions of the ongoing relationship, both surrounding and in the context of the sexual activity itself.

Placing the sexual activity in the laboratory (or at home under laboratory conditions, which regulate timing via need for blood sampling) introduces new social factors that may override the existing ones or constrain their normal emergence. For example, it is not too much to suppose that in the studies by Stearns, Winter, and Faiman

(1973) and Lee, Jaffe, and Midgley (1974) the couples engaged in a considerable amount of humorous banter about "doing it" for the sake of science. (If they did not treat their experience somewhat humorously, then they were altogether too grim and mechanical to be normal.) The consequence of these couples' research focus would have been suspension of the normal ebb and flow of social relations between the partners. Indeed, their most salient social relationship at the peak of sexual interaction may have been with the absent researchers. While a strictly biological approach to sexuality may be content to exclude the elements of relationships, precisely such exclusion may confound the pattern of presently available data.

The issue here is that the laboratory approach may preclude, via a sociosexual indeterminacy principle, our ever measuring both sexual and social components as they would normally be without the additional constraint of observation (blood or saliva sampling, for example). Certainly, single coital events are most likely to fall prey to this distortion.

In this regard, Fox et al. (1972), who followed their single case for three months and eighteen coital occasions, probably came closer to obtaining a more veridical sociosexual set of observations. Yet, of course, they failed to consider the relevance of the social. Notwithstanding, even future investigations accounting for the social must seek their data over a long period (as did Fox et al.) in order to preclude as much as possible the social relational artificiality induced by laboratory conditions (see also Heiman 1980 and Heiman and Rowland 1983 on the artificiality of the laboratory investigation of sex-related responses). Obviously, similar considerations apply to studies of masturbation.

3

INFIDELITY AND SEXUAL INTIMACY: REFLECTIONS OF THE DOMINANCE/EMINENCE–TESTOSTERONE RELATIONSHIP

THE dominance/eminence–testosterone (T) nexus affords additional insights into male sexuality, which will be explored in this chapter. The first concerns infidelity, a behavior pattern that is often proscribed in normative codes, though frequently endorsed for males by the alternate code of the double standard. Male infidelity has been variously attributed to the existence of this second code (the social constructionist explanation), to simple arrogation of privilege based on power over females (the direct social structural explanation), and to the overweening compulsion of male gonadal stimulation (the biological explanation). All these may be involved. Here I shall examine infidelity from the perspective of the socio-bio-social chain.

A second focus of this chapter is an effort to synthesize a comprehensive theory of sociosexual relations, with attention to how the dominance/eminence–T relationship might influence the type of sexual outlet as well as the quality of intimacy with a partner. I shall rely heavily on the insights of the previous chapter about the dominance/eminence aspects of sexual interaction itself. These aspects have largely been omitted as an explicit consideration in previous accounts of sexual intimacy.

INFIDELITY

Infidelity is considered a strong breach of the marriage bond in most, though not all, societies (Ford and Beach 1951). The proscription against infidelity has much to do with patriarchal dominance and the treatment of women as chattel, and often there is a double standard that is considerably more punitive toward unfaithful wives than toward unfaithful husbands. Whether partially sanctioned for men or not, infidelity is sexual conduct that violates an existing standard: exclusive commitment to a spouse. Barring specific proscriptions (perhaps of a religious nature), under ordinary circumstances one's spouse is supposedly available for as much sexual enjoyment as time and energy can support. Both to give sex and to accept it are, in fact, conjugal duties. Yet, some proportion of men and women in all societies find reason to seek sexual satisfaction outside the sanctioned domain.

Although the percentages of unfaithful male spouses in American society are not exactly compatible as one moves from Kinsey, Pomeroy, and Martin (1948) through Hunt (1974) and on to Pietropinto and Simenauer (1977, 1979) and Yablonsky (1979), due both to methodological and cohort variation, it is clear that a substantial proportion of men (and, increasingly, women) are unfaithful to their spouses or their steady intimate partners. Botwin (1988:9) cited Kinsey collaborators Paul Gebhard and Wardell Pomeroy as offering estimates as high as 65 percent. Investigators of male sexual practices offer varying explanations. Kinsey, Pomeroy, and Martin observe: "It is still not clear how often the conditions of marriage itself are responsible for . . . decline in marital intercourse. Long-time marriage provides the maximum opportunity for repetition of a relatively uniform sort of experience. It is not surprising that there should be some loss of interest in the activity among the older males, even if there were no aging process to accelerate it" (1948:257). They further note that "among married males, the rise in importance of extra-marital intercourse is chiefly at the expense of marital intercourse which contributes less and less to the total picture" (1948:259). The monotony hypothesis was augmented considerably by later investigators, in part because they directed specific questions about infidelity to their respondents. According to Hunt, "The intense pleasure some people experience during extra-marital acts may, for instance, owe less to the sexual acts being performed than to the revenge being taken against their mates, or to the excitement of doing something forbidden and dangerous, or to the feelings of personal desirability and success engendered by those acts, or even to the rediscovery of a lost capacity for romantic love" (1974:265). Pietropinto and Simenauer (1977) explicitly asked what lay behind infidelity. Among men who were unfaithful, poor sex or fighting with the partner were often cited. Other reasons included "an exceptionally attractive woman," "a woman who understands me better," an "available woman at work," and "being in love."

In this section I wish to present a theory of infidelity that encompasses the variety of analytical and phenomenological explanations presented by Kinsey and others, but also takes account of the materials on dominance/eminence, testosterone, and sexuality discussed above. I propose that a significant amount of infidelity among males stems from two major relational sources. The first is dominance/eminence–T related. I call it *overflow* infidelity. In this type, the acquisition and exercise of significant power and/or status, that is, dominance or eminence, produces a surge of T, which leads (in a manner to be described) to illicit sexual involvement.

The second type of infidelity, which I call *compensatory* infidelity, is also relationally based. It has two subtypes. In the first, a man seeks to regain lost status through involvement with a new sex partner, thus making possible a dominance/eminence encounter and a T surge. The quest is essentially for the usual, expected, or deserved gratification that one is being denied. In subtype two, the interest is not in sexual gratification per se, but rather in causing hurt to another, as in revenge. Here, sex is used as a weapon of power. The issue is not dominance/eminence in the sexual interaction, but dominance over a third party, usually one's spouse or other steady intimate partner. Clearly, both subtypes of compensatory infidelity can operate simultaneously. A third type of unfaithfulness, *underflow* infidelity, blends elements of the social structure, which is the source of overflow infidelity, with elements of compensatory need. This type will be discussed at the end.

Overflow Infidelity

The overflow hypothesis is predicated on the assumption that males who are frequent winners, hence dominant or eminent, frequently experience a T surge. More often gonadally aroused (as discussed in chapter 2), they more often have a lower threshold of sexual accessibility. Either they seek sexual encounters voluntarily, or they are sought after for them by females who respond to the enhanced dominance/eminence–T aura these males exude (Botwin 1988:14). One thinks here of social and political "stars" and their cadres of enthusiastically willing sex partners—groupies. The biographies of John F. Kennedy and Martin Luther King, Jr., attest notoriously to this effect.

However much dominance/eminence attainment stimulates T, infidelity breaks a bond and violates a trust. Unless there was never any intention or requirement to remain faithful (as in open marriage; see O'Neill and O'Neill 1972), a commitment or scruple of some kind must be overcome or some revision of understanding must take place to allow the infidelity to occur. Overflow infidelity indeed has a rationale.

Dominance/eminence attainment that produces T comes at the price of effort (Mazur and Lamb 1980; Elias 1981; Kreuz, Rose, and Jennings 1972); hence, it is often a source of elevated pride and self-esteem, as well as providing a sense of energized well-being. Although self-esteem is accounted good in general, too much of it carries a burden: it can easily disrupt existing social arrangements that were entered into to fit a lower level of self-adequacy. On a small scale, repeated victories lead to a state that Durkheim ([1897] 1951) depicted for societies in the condition he called "anomie."

Anomie is a state in which the rules and standards that determine how much is enough have broken down, leaving people adrift in a sea of unsatisfiable desire. Durkheim's great insight was that what we deem sufficient for our satisfaction is, beyond certain minimum levels, relative to our station in life. The groups that locate us in social space provide us with necessary horizons of aspiration and desire. Within these horizons we can be content. Should we begin to desire beyond them, the realities of social life, as defined by our station, would leave our desire unfulfilled, and ourself discontented. Ordinarily, under stable social conditions, we accommodate our desires and aspirations to our location in social space and are relatively content. But if the tempo of social change should quicken and the groups we belong to disintegrate, the horizons of desire they set for us become fluid or ill-defined. We lose our bearings and we no longer have a standard against which to test our surfeit.

Frequent dominance/eminence attainment may create a state of anomie on a small scale. There may seem, then, to be no limit to how much one deserves. Since one is so often surpassing existing boundaries, one loses a sense that there are any limits. One's appetites are unleashed. In Marcuse's view, sexual appetites in Western societies have long been hemmed in by what he called "surplus repression" (1955:35). This is the condition of unecessarily stringent control over sexual behavior that Marcuse attributed to the need of capitalism for workers who are not overly distracted by sexual interests and pursuits. Given such surplus repression, the frequent attainment of dominance/eminence can serve to derepress desire and its expression.

The reality of the social boundaries that contain our appetites is reflected in social norms and standards that prescribe our conduct. For the married, the boundary laid down by Western culture is summarized by the injunction, Thous shalt not commit adultery. But marriages are not isolated from the rest of society. They are contained within the community where the members of the marriage also have a location and a standing.

When one's standing changes upward or is marked by frequent collisions with the upper limits of the community's ranking system, then the standards of the community become attenuated, and how they apply to one's marriage is also affected. One's self becomes larger than the self the community and the marriage can contain. The standards of the community, which are usually the standards of the marriage, lose their hold. Shakespeare captured this very well in *Henry V.* When Katherine of France protests a certain modesty in a matter relating to the progress of her courtship by the English king, Henry—interestingly, fresh from his great victory at Agincourt—remarks:

> O Kate, nice customs court'sy to great kings. Dear Kate, you and I cannot be confined within the weak list of a country's fashion: we are the makers of manners, Kate; and the liberty that follows our places stops the mouth of all find-faults,—as I will do yours for upholding the nice fashion of your country in denying me a kiss: therefore patiently and yielding. [*Kissing her*] You have witchcraft in your lips, Kate. (act 5, scene 2)

In overflow infidelity, the social norms that bar infidelity lose their force because they apply to a social place and a social pattern the frequently dominant or eminent individual has transcended.

There is also a hubris that attends frequent dominance/eminence attainment and goes hand in hand with anomie to break the mold of existing social controls and limitations. This hubris—the sense that one is preternaturally endowed and hence above the rules—stems from repeated confirmations of the importance of the self as opposed to the importance of the collectivity.[1] The hyperimportance of self facilitates an easier, conscienceless satisfaction of one's appetites and desires, including the sexual.

Given that we are speaking of infidelity, there is obviously a spouse or steady intimate partner. Why can she not satisfy the somewhat hyperlibidinal state of her partner? Her state, both social and sexual, is also important. Unless he is indifferent to her feelings, which are not always compatible with his, he must refrain from forcing sexual attention on her. She is not always ready or willing when he is. His unusually aroused sexuality is not necessarily in tune with her own, which is as much contingent on the social dimensions of her life as his is on his life.

The overflow hypothesis predicts a heightened sexuality among those males who are victors or who achieve high status in work and/or community roles. Seidenberg (1973) suggested that it is common knowledge that one of the standard rewards of high corporate status is the privilege of maintaining a mistress. It would, of course, follow from this that the different social class levels would be differentially active in extramarital sex. I have already discussed the general case above. Here the interest is specifically in infidelity. As Kinsey, Pomeroy, and Martin (1948) report, there is greater infidelity among lower-class males when young and greater infidelity among higher-class males when older, exactly the pattern we would expect from class- and age-based differences in the distribution of victories and the attainment of eminence.

The overflow hypothesis also predicts greater infidelity among men in some occupations than in others. I do not mean here occupations with greater opportunity, for example, the traveling salesman of anecdotal notoriety. (LaRue and Dabbs 1989 found that salesmen were not especially high in T.) Sexuality depends on more than opportunity, and people appear to find a way to circumvent barriers even when opportunity seems to be entirely absent. Occupations that may be more disposed toward infidelity are those that have relatively high frequencies of victories, where decisive encounters occur relatively often, and where winning can mean winning big. Paradigmatic occupations of this sort are the major professions, such as law, medicine, entrepreneurial business, and high finance, where crucial decisions of life and death or great wealth turn on one's actions. Money is a blatant symbol not only of the victories of the past, but also of the potential for victories in the future. For some women money may be an aphrodisiac, and it gives men who are actively acquiring it frequent surges of T. Greene, Lee, and Lustig (1974; cited in Botwin 1988), estimated that the incidence of infidelity rises to 70 percent among those with incomes above sixty-thousand dollars. (Obviously an inflation moderator must be factored in; and though the 70 percent figure is not much higher than Gebhard's and Pomeroy's general estimates (also cited in Botwin 1988:14) it must be seen in the light of Greene et al.'s substantially lower figures for those with incomes closer to the median.) Botwin reasons that high income allows a male to feel less guilt over an affair because its cost is less likely to deprive his spouse and children. This is plausible, and, if true, would impart additional status through this further symbolic meaning of money.

Creative professions should also be high in infidelity because the creative epiphany is a moment of exceedingly high victory. Unlike professions where victory is confirmed more or less immediately because it is pursued in a social environment (the courtroom, the operating theater, the stock market) or in the entrepreneurial realm, where money is palpable and the products of money tangible, the validation of creative victory is often delayed. A public must pass judgment on the work of art, the scientific theory, the philosophical treatise. Hence, the overflow hypothesis will account for somewhat less of the infidelity in the creative occupations, except when we are dealing with stars whose attainments are both frequent and large.

Military victors are another category in which there must be extremely powerful T surges. The terrible pattern of rape that has historically attended the winning of battles can be explained only in part by hatred of the enemy or by opportunity after a period of sexual deprivation. A substantial part would seem to depend on the flow of victory- and dominance-based T. Mutatis mutandis, sports victors, who are further aggrandized by often deliriously cheering fans (the implications for the fans are explored extensively in chapter 5), must also experience a heightened sexual energizing and desire fueled by T. In general, any occupation that involves public appearances, in which public approbation is sought and frequently obtained, also shares in the victory-T syndrome. This would include both the performing arts and politics.

Compensatory Infidelity

Whereas overflow infidelity is the product of an abundance of T, compensatory infidelity by contrast seeks T. This can be seen in terms of two patterns of social relations. Just as victory is the social relation of T surge, what may be conjectured as a quest for a T surge proceeds also out of one or both of two types of failed social relations.

As detailed in chapter 1, social relations can be understood as the standing of two actors in relation to each other on the dimensions of power and status. It is possible in this model for an actor to lose status; that is, actor A reduces the amount of reward he or she voluntarily gives to actor B. This can happen in any number of ways, but usually it involves a reduction in the level of benefits previously given by A and taken for granted by B. In Kemper (1978) I have presented a detailed analysis of what B's resulting emotions are likely to be. When, by virtue of his or her own incapacities or defects, B sees the situation as virtually hopeless or irremediable, with little chance of getting A to change his or her behavior, the resulting emotion is likely to be depression. This does not necessarily mean all-out clinical depression. But it is depression, and it is caused by the loss of some real or symbolic sustenance or reward that was previously available. The depression expresses a hunger for that sustenance. When the lost status consists of intimacy and closeness, whether sexual and/or emotional, there is a ground for one type of compensatory infidelity. What is no longer being given by A must be sought from another source. Husbands and wives who deny each other emotional or sexual intimacy are most likely to separate; but if they do not, infidelity is one recourse to satisfy what is an "existential" need (Kemper 1978:334).

This form of compensatory infidelity proceeds largely out of a sadness and longing for what cannot be gotten from one's partner. It would include those men whose partners are simply less giving or sexually needful. It would also include those men who have been abandoned emotionally or sexually by partners they still love, though the formal relationship is maintained. Classically, it is the type of infidelity that women with cold, unappealing husbands may resort to or allow themselves to fall into; Anna Karenina and Emma Bovary are literary archetypes.

The second mode of compensatory infidelity also begins with status loss, but the attribution of cause is to A, the party who withdrew the status in the first place. There must be some amour propre, a feeling that the other has not only violated the terms of the relationship, but has also violated the very self of the deprived partner. The hypothesized emotion here is rage or anger (Kemper 1978). The compensatory infidelity is motivated by revenge, the desire to inflict on the other the same degree (not necessarily type) of hurt that the other inflicted on oneself. Jealousy, which centrally turns on the anger generated by real or imagined loss to a third party of an intimacy that is exclusive, is a prime source of compensatory infidelity of the second type. Botwin reported that infidelity is more likely to be a male coping mechanism in jealousy (1988:44). Beyond revenge, the intended effect of compensatory infidelity is victory dominance, especially in a context where one has been denied eminence by virtue of the status loss.

Although overflow infidelity is akin to the pervasive pattern of animal sexuality in that it simply follows a T surge after dominance/eminence attainment, revenge-based infidelity does not follow the pattern of animal sexuality. It takes a particular cortical development to foresee what the emotional sequel of infidelity is likely to be, both for oneself (a hoped-for retrieved sense of self-esteem) and for the other (possible hurt and pain because of the implied loss).

Viewed as a retrieval process, the endocrinological outcome of both types of compensatory infidelity may be T, which energizes and reenergizes so that one can undertake one's work and community roles with the passion that can bring them to fruition and to a new surge of T, perhaps even a sufficiency of such surges so that one is in the overflow condition. Dominance thus displayed may gain its final triumph by reanimating in the spouse or steady partner the desire to be intimate and giving.

It is tempting to speculate that compensatory infidelity, qua sexual experience, is less satisfying than overflow infidelity. In the latter, there are no extraneous motives. Simple gonadal arousal leads to behavior that leads to sex. By contrast, compensatory infidelity is diluted by emotions of depression and/or resentment and, perhaps, fear. These activate the sympathetic nervous system in ways that conflict with sexual arousal (Zuckerman 1971; Bozman and Beck 1988). Although guilt—which may be the primary extraneous emotion in overflow infidelity—also detracts from arousal, it may be a less activating emotion autonomically (Kemper 1987) and is also likely to be counteracted by the strong surge of T.

Underflow Infidelity

A final type of infidelity includes both compensatory and social structural elements. Though different social class-age groups have different timing of victory and success (see chapter 2), many men at precisely the period of their own class and age group's highest success rates are themselves not successful.

There is an instructive example of this from a World War II survey of attitudes in the American military (Stouffer et al. 1949). Though promotion rates were higher in the air force than in the military police, overall discontent with promotion policy was greater in the air force than among the police. The explanation was "relative deprivation." When many in one's group are being promoted, a person who is not promoted is likely to have a stronger feeling of discontent. Among the working class when young and the higher class when older, there are also losers. Not everyone can lead the street corner gang, nor can everyone be chief executive of the company. Those who are left out or defeated at these times are likely to feel their loss more keenly than they would have at another time, and their principal emotion is most likely to be envy. Botwin claimed envy is a prime instigator of infidelity (1988:277). A career setback is taken as an attack on masculine pride, and a sexual conquest is pursued to counter this feeling, since sexual success is also a victory. Whitehurst (1969) found that a large proportion of the unfaithful men in his sample felt alienated, estranged, and powerless. Their infidelity was compensatory, but the compensation sought was not for deprivations experienced in sexual relationships, but for those in the social structure. In this respect their situation was the converse of that of winners. For this reason their infidelity may be labeled *underflow.*

Social Relations and Sexual Intimacy

That sexual conduct is importantly social conduct is fundamental to the approach taken here. Even solo sexual activity, as in masturbation, is a reflection of the social—for the most part the unavailability of a partner, but it may also signify fear, inflamed desire, or even hatred for another. Isolation or solitariness must not be interpreted simply as nonsocial. Simmel (1950) made this point compellingly in his consideration of the role of numbers in social life. Two is not the minimum number for social life; one can serve as well, since one always carries others in memory and his or her actions are undertaken in reference to them. Simmel's point is no less well taken in the present context. The inclusion of fantasy relations, often of dominance/eminence, emphasizes the social character even of masturbation.

If sexual oneness is social, how much more so when there is twoness, as in coitus. If the error about solo sex is to think that it is not social, the common error in sex à deux is to think that it is strictly biological. Researchers into human sexuality have investigated T, age, body fat, alcohol consumption, amount of exercise, age of partner, timing of menses, time of coition, phases of excitation and resolution, and the like (Masters and Johnson 1966; Tsitouras, Martin, and Harman 1982; Dai et al. 1981). These are by and large biological conditions. Remarkably, only animal researchers have examined some of the social parameters of the sexual situation; for example, dominance and submission, rank order of the female, and quality of interaction, as in aggression, invitation, resistance to intromission, and so on (Rose, Bernstein, and Gordon 1975; Rose et al. 1978; Keverne 1979; Mendoza 1984). Parenthetically, we may note the crucial contribution made by animal investigators to the understanding of human sexual conduct.

Though the sexual interaction of humans is at least as much contingent on cognitive and interactional factors as the sexual interaction of animals, researchers have explored this aspect of sexuality very little. There are virtually no data, and there is little theory that deals with the matters of sexual practice that will be considered here. The purpose of this section is to offer a tentative appraisal from a theoretical perspective of how sexual practice and sexual feeling depend on social relations.

The analysis begins with the phenomenological observation that sex can have a tonic effect: sometimes one feels very good after sex—buoyant, energized, keen-sensed, high. But sometimes one feels fatigued, depressed, deflated. Though sexual activity carried to consummation, as has often been remarked, is good even when bad, there has been a failure to observe that some occasions of sexual intimacy make one feel very, very good, and others do not. If the difference is recognized, there is as yet no clearly defined set of terms by which to formulate the difference. Hence, variability in the satisfaction one can derive from sex has remained largely unspecified and unanalyzed.

Certainly physical state may contribute to the postsex feeling. One may be well rested or fatigued to begin with; the body may be in a high or low state of fitness, thus variably able to mediate sexual exertion; one may be in a good or declining state of health, and so on. However, these conditions do not capture other essential elements that determine the outcome of sexual activity; namely, the social context and its accompanying emotions. These must, I believe, be considered equally with biological factors in understanding how one feels after a sexual episode.

Two qualifications inform the analysis. First, it comprehends the relational and emotional conditions that are brought to the sexual situation. The analysis does not include the vital interactional and relational outcomes that occur with the sexual partner, if there is one. The omission is intentional. It will enable me to deal first with a relatively simple model of the social preconditions of sexual experience. It will be seen by the end of the discussion that this basic model will apply in most respects to interaction with the sexual partner. In reality, the two patterns will interact to produce the actual result. At the outset, the interaction with the sexual partner is kept constant, so to speak. This allows for ease of presentation. I assume nothing about the partner at this point, but more will be said on this below.

The second restriction on this analysis is that it presents the case from a male viewpoint. This is clearly only half the matter. The limitation stems from the fact that in this unresearched domain, what little data there are pertain to males. This has not gone unnoted, and in recent years feminist thinkers have upbraided theorists and investigators for seeing sexual conduct only from a male perspective (see Rossi 1973; Tiefer 1978; Miller and Fowlkes 1980). Notwithstanding the defect of a one-sided analysis, I believe something can yet be gained for an understanding of all sexuality by more clearly focusing on the male experience.

In addition, the author is male. Although there ought not to be such variants as male science or female science, we are now sophisticated enough to know that science in large measure is social (what is counted as knowledge, what methods to use, what problems to investigate, what audiences to seek, and so forth) and that we cannot help but bring a social vantage point to our theory and our practice (Blume 1974). This is not necessarily bad if we know we are doing so and are conscious of the social standpoint of our productions. Clearly, each social division will consciously or unconsciously espouse and support a somewhat different scientific enterprise, and one may not cumulate the same body of knowledge as the other. Yet, if society comprises a heterogeneity of social perspectives, it will necessarily have to acquire knowledge through the lens of each of them. At this point in societal history, for reasons I need not expatiate on here, most knowledge is organized from a male point of view, no less what is contained here. But there is one final reason for the male orientation of this presentation. Given the state of the art, at times it becomes necessary to use oneself as an instrument of both discovery and of verification (Kaplan 1964). The subjective elements of sexuality, or any other human practice, cannot be conveyed to any other person, whether in scientific or common discourse. Yet it is precisely toward that subjective experience of feeling good or not feeling good that the present analysis is devoted.

With respect to the issue of how to measure feeling good, verbal measures of satisfaction, though they suffer from the problem of the basic incommensurability of human feelings, would suffice for the purposes of this analysis were they sufficiently focused on physical and psychic satisfaction in particular sexual episodes. Such measures would allow the investigation of the specific precursors of sexual satisfaction and whether one would or would not feel good in particular sexual interactions, rather than merely whether one is satisfied with the sexual relationship overall. Given the remoteness of existing measures and the close focus of this analysis, there is perhaps some virtue in allowing in the subjective stance of the author. (There is no question that the reader will do the same.) Since the author is male, male readers will obtain a somewhat better reading on the author's subjective interventions than will females. But females, too, may gain from having at least one male data point with which to contrast or compare their own subjective experience.

We must refer back now to the model of social relations presented in chapter 1, the well-established notion that social relations can be usefully described for analytic purposes by two dimensions, power and status. Power means the ability to achieve one's own ends even over the resistance of others. When others comply, they do so involuntarily.

Figure 3.1 Social Relations and Sexuality

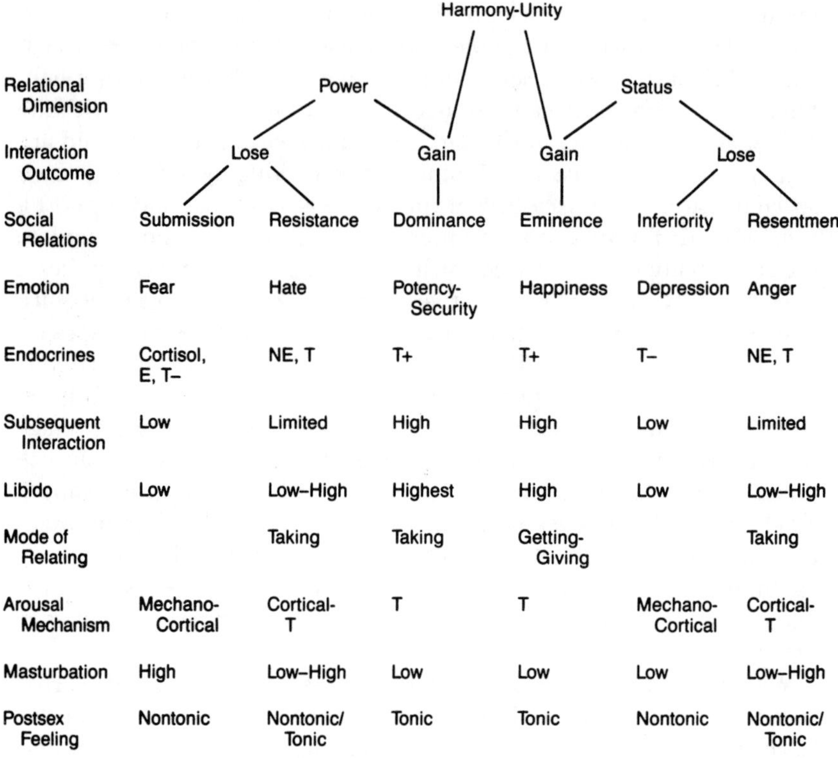

Social Relations	Submission	Resistance	Dominance	Eminence	Inferiority	Resentment
Emotion	Fear	Hate	Potency-Security	Happiness	Depression	Anger
Endocrines	Cortisol, E, T–	NE, T	T+	T+	T–	NE, T
Subsequent Interaction	Low	Limited	High	High	Low	Limited
Libido	Low	Low–High	Highest	High	Low	Low–High
Mode of Relating		Taking	Taking	Getting-Giving		Taking
Arousal Mechanism	Mechano-Cortical	Cortical-T	T	T	Mechano-Cortical	Cortical-T
Masturbation	High	Low–High	Low	Low	Low	Low–High
Postsex Feeling	Nontonic	Nontonic/Tonic	Tonic	Tonic	Nontonic	Nontonic/Tonic

Status accord involves voluntary compliance with the wishes and desires of another. One genuinely wants to please the other, as in wanting to gratify a friend or other person one likes, and the efforts entailed in doing so are satisfying in themselves. Each actor in a relationship has a power and status position via-à-vis the other. My overall hypothesis is that power and status relations and their associated emotions organize the framework of interaction, endocrine substrate, and style and type of sexual practice that leads to the endpoint of feeling good or not. The whole formulation is depicted in figure 3.1, and will be referred to in the following presentation.

Interaction Outcome

In order to activate the model, we must consider how to represent outcomes of interaction between two human actors in power and status terms. In fact, a very simple schedule of outcomes will suffice. At the conclusion of an interaction episode, which may be a split second or years in duration, there are two main possibilities for each relational dimension. Each actor can gain or lose power and can gain or lose status. The category of no change in power and/or status can be excluded by reasoning that if social relations are deemed satisfactory initially, a lack of change can be considered equivalent to gain; if they are unsatisfactory, a lack of change can be considered equivalent to loss. Although there is both a power outcome and a status outcome for each actor from each interaction episode, I will consider the power and the status outcomes as if they were discrete. This is unproblematic except where the power and status outcomes for a given actor are directionally different. I relegate this case to a residual category for the present.

Social Relations

To gain or lose power and/or status simply records the outcomes of the interaction. Ensuing from these are further patterns of social relations and their associated emotions. In power loss, one is now less able to impose one's will on the other or to offer resistance to the other's will. Depending on how much cost one is able or willing to absorb, one may either submit to the other or continue to resist. When status has been lost, there are also alternatives. These depend to a large degree on the assignment of responsibility or agency for the loss. If one feels one is oneself the agent—through some failure of nerve or competence—one must accept one's inferiority. This entails a self that is not only less than it was before, but also one that may be less than that of the other who is able to deprive one of status. Contrariwise, where agency for the status loss is assigned to the other, we have the classic case of resentment at unjust treatment.

When power and/or status are gained, the relational consequences are simpler. In power gain, there is dominance. In status gain, there is a similar elevation, which I have labeled eminence. We must consider now what it means to have or gain power and to have or gain status. Though differences between them have been noted, they share an important feature in common: each is a route to obtaining compliance from the social environment. Status entails compliance that others give voluntarily; power enforces compliance from others, but in one essential sense the result is the same. In each case the world is brought into harmony with one's self and one's needs or desires. In this respect, the subjective feeling may be akin to the sense of harmony and unity when one is in love. Indeed, love and status are related; love is the ultimate in status accord (see Kemper 1978 for discussion of the relation of status, harmony, and love). It may well be that the subjective experience of power is, essentially, little different from that of love; namely, a sense that the world is fully responsive to oneself. In power, the self is a fixed point, and the world has been coerced to accommodate it. Infantile omnipotence is thus realized.

Emotions

Each of the social relations that result from interaction is accompanied by a primary emotion. Drawing on extensive earlier work (Kemper 1978, 1987), I assign the emotions as follows: submission—fear; resistance—hate; dominance—potency/security; eminence—happiness; inferiority—depression; resentment—anger. Since there is both a power outcome and a status outcome, the subject has two emotions, and these will frequently reinforce each other; for example, fear and depression, hate and anger, potency/security and happiness. Sometimes, an interaction will result in a mixed outcome; for example, loss of power and gain of status. The emotional resultant may engender inner conflict or necessitate driving out one emotion in preference to another, or the emotions may be experienced in alternating fashion. The issue is complex and important in emotion theory (see Plutchik 1980; Izard 1977; Ekman 1984), but it need not detain us here. As indicated above, I will treat each relational outcome separately.

Endocrinological Outcome

There is a physiological side to every emotion, and this is represented in the autonomic nervous system (ANS) by changes of heart rate, blood pressure, skin temperature, lung capacity, size of pupils, and the like. These enable the body to adapt to the demands of the situation that instigated the emotion. The demands may be for calmness and contentment; hence, excitation or arousal is not a necessary result in emotion, only a frequent one. The activation or damping of the ANS is carried out by various hormones and neurotransmitters, the most prominent of which are epinephrine, norepinephrine, and acetylcholine. There are others, but these three have been linked differentially to specific emotional states (Funkenstein 1955; Gellhorn 1967; Kemper 1978) and hence have a special status. Among the other hormones which are involved in emotional arousal in a more general way are adrenocorticotropic hormone (ACTH), which is a messenger from the pituitary to the adrenal cortex to release corticosteroids under conditions of stress (which may attach to different emotions). One of these is cortisol, which is elevated in stress reactions (Mason 1968). In addition, there is T. A differential picture of T secretion emerges in the different social relational–emotional contexts, and it is on this that I wish to focus.

When power is lost and one must submit, there is evidence that cortisol is elevated and T is depressed (Henry and Stephens 1977; Henry 1980; Berkenbosch 1983). When fear accompanies submission, epinephrine is elevated as well (Funkenstein 1955). The resistance alternative to power loss has not been explored, so the endocrinological sequel is not clear. Yet, we may surmise that continuing resistance should conserve T. The losers of hard-won matches in Mazur and Lamb's (1980) research showed no decrement of T. In addition to T, the continuing aggressive response to the other should also see elevated NE, as argued by Henry and Stephens (1977) and as discussed in chapter 2. Since there has been some loss, epinephrine and cortisol should also be somewhat elevated, although probably not as high as in the case of submission.

When status is lost and the relational-emotional pattern is inferiority and depression, the evidence is for elevated cortisol and reduced T (Kreuz, Rose, and Jennings 1972; Henry and Stephens 1977; Davidson, Smith, and Levine 1978) and, possibly, reduced brain NE as well (Kety 1972). In the resentment alternative, anger is accompanied by NE and the T level should remain stable. At least there should be little drop, since the issue is still being contested.

Power gain and dominance are accompanied, according to many reports, by elevated T and reduced cortisol (Mendoza 1984; Keverne 1979; Mazur and Lamb 1980). However, Elias (1981) reported a positive relationship between T and cortisol in winners of wrestling matches, but not in losers. The reason for this unusual finding is not clear. Status gain and eminence are also marked by increased levels of T. In what follows, the main concern will be with the effects of T.

Subsequent Interaction

Interaction patterns subsequent to gain or loss of power and/or status will be responsive to the gains and losses incurred. These bear on sexual interaction by enhancing or decreasing opportunity for contact with potential sexual partners. Submission in power loss should lead to low levels of interaction, essentially, keeping one's head down. Resistance, too, should impose some limits on interaction, inasmuch as there is still a conflict to be resolved. Loss of status associated with depression is most clearly associated with low levels of interaction, essentially apathy or withdrawal. On the resentment side of status loss, there ought again to be some limitation on interaction. We may think here of energy bound up in anger and thus not available for other endeavors. In each of these outcomes, compensatory sexual activity, as in compensatory infidelity, is also a possibility. Whether or not this is sought, the overall pattern of interaction in cases of power and status loss should be relatively reduced compared with ascendance in these two relational dimensions. In both power gain and status gain, interaction levels should be high, with access to others being within one's power or being the natural consequence of the high regard of others. There is also both the confidence and the lack of anxiety that would keep such gainers from shunning further interaction where new triumphs might be gained (Collins 1981; Mazur 1985).

Libido

Like Freud [(1910] 1957:214) I consider libido to be sexual desire and its press for resolution. One of the central assumptions here is that libido is enhanced by a surge of T. For present purposes, libido is the proclivity to sexual arousal and to seeking a resolution of that arousal. In accordance with this view, submission to power loss entails reduced T, hence low libido. Although T level may reequilibrate in time (Mendoza 1984), submission means that there will be few opportunities for T surge. Hence, libido will not often flare. In the contrary case of resistance to power loss, T is not reduced. Also, as long as resistance continues there are occasional victories, hence occasional surges of T. This suggests that libido ought to fluctuate widely in this condition from low to high.

Status loss entailing inferiority and depression appears to be accompanied by low libido in company with reduced levels of T according to the current weight of clinical evidence (Vogel, Klaiber, and Broverman 1978; Rubin et al. 1981; Yesavage et al. 1985), though this latter point has been disputed (Sachar et al. 1973). Like resistance in power loss, resentment and anger in status loss do not concede the relational outcome. T is not reduced, and there may be occasions when some recapture of status is possible. Like resistance, this would permit a wide range of libido from low to high.

In power gain, libido ought to be at its highest level, supported by the increase in T and by the opportunities to exercise dominance and hence derive new surges of T. Status gain also entails high T, but libido may not be quite as high as in power gain. The difference may reside in the greater bonding opportunities that the eminent enjoy, as compared with the dominant. By definition, status is voluntarily granted by others, who choose to be in the presence of the person whose status they are enhancing. The solidarity, loyalty, and affection that result can satisfy a need for connection with others that might otherwise seek expression more exclusively in libidinal form. In the case of the dominant, holding aside any status considerations, others are present and available only involuntarily, hence the libidinal may have a freer rein.[2]

Mode of Sexual Relating

In the usual case, libidinal satisfaction is wrought in a direct sexual encounter with another; but, in fact, another may be present only in fantasy. Where libido is low, as in submission in power loss and inferiority in status loss, the chances are least that there will be a sexual partner. According to the conditions elaborated above, arousal is likely to be less frequent. Nonetheless, when it occurs, there may be neither sufficient drive to acquire a partner nor sufficient verve to attract one. (Here is where low T is critical.) Hence, these are cases where libidinal satisfaction will be most often served by masturbation, that is, partnerless sex. (Of course, if there is a facilitative partner who is sexually desirous or kind, coitus may take place even when libido is low (see, e.g., Raboch and Starka 1973; Muelenhard and Cook 1988).

Those who are at the resistance and resentment poles of power loss and status loss respectively have the potential for wide variability in libido; therefore, they are on occasion sexually aroused and seeking satisfaction. Since they have not abandoned themselves to surrender and helplessness, they can still attract sexual partners and gain their consent. I propose that, when aroused, their sexual mode of relating is like that of the dominant: taking. Some explanation of this type of relating is required.

To take is active and/or self-oriented, by contrast with more passive and/or other-oriented behavior. In the sexual context, taking means that self is the subject who acts, while the other is an object who is acted upon. This can be said despite any "proceptive" (Beach 1976) or soliciting behavior on the part of the other. In fact these behaviors are invitations to the male to be "taken," as the word is used occasionally in quasi-pornographic or parodic literary descriptions of sexual encounters. A fully aroused female character in such stories often indicates her readiness by crying out, "Take me!" The connection between taking and dominance should be clear. Ordinarily, only the dominant can take. Hence, the maximum of taking occurs in the relational mode of dominance. The self-oriented character of power is also evident. It has emerged through conquest and, underwritten by the high testosterone surge, is simply carried forward to further conquest. Indeed, the sexual partner provides yet another occasion for victory.

By contrast, the eminence mode allows for a different stance, that of giving and getting. By definition, to receive status is to receive voluntarily conferred benefits from others. Sexual access is one form of such a voluntary compliance. Instead of need to take, the stature of eminence is effective through its ability to evoke benefits from the giving of others. This enables the subject to be more passive, to accept arousal from the other, or to allow the other to take a more active and giving role in the sexual encounter. Accompanying the ability to get in this way, there can be, paradoxically, the greater capacity to give in return.[3] Whereas taking is self-oriented, giving is other-oriented. Pleasure can be dedicated as a gift to the other rather than as a prize for the self. This should allow for a degree of tenderness that is absent from the taking mode. It should also be possible to achieve a merging of self and other more easily.

The capacity to give oneself to another appears to be founded on a felt adequacy of having received—in the course of socialization and in one's recent social interactions (Pearce and Newton 1963; Isen and Levin 1972). This penetrates the sexual encounter itself. In a sexual interaction in which one has the sense of.having been truly given to, strong urgings of reciprocity move one to want to give in return. Initially, this has to do more with the qualities of intimacy and trust that are conferred than with the physiosexual aspects. Out of such moments of felt high estimation in the eyes of the other there may emerge a profound sexual desire for the other that is rooted in a gratitude that has no other aim than to merge, to become one with the other. This is to give oneself wholly to the other, body and soul, as it were.

I propose that in both the resistance and resentment conditions, the sexual model would be that of taking. In both these patterns of relating, the aroused emotions are premised on deprivation and one's own neediness. From this perspective a sexual encounter is an opportunity to recoup, whether actually or vicariously, some of what was lost, as in compensatory or underflow infidelity. There is also the possibility, once the sexual interaction is underway, for the hate and anger that underlie these types to leak out.

Although the notions of giving and taking, of getting and being taken, are hardly more than surmises, they may be among the most important in terms of the tone that is imparted to the sexual interaction. In a broad way, to take is to exercise power over the other; to give is to accord status. The partner's emotions, whether of fear and anger or security and satisfaction, will be engendered by giving and taking and will flow back into the interaction to condition its later stages.

Arousal Mechanism

There are three possible ways to generate male arousal: through direct or physically proximal stimulation of the mechanoreceptors in the penis, a "reflexogenic" mode, as Weiss (1972) calls it; through cortical excitation as in fantasy or sexual thoughts (Bancroft and Wu 1983); and by action of T on genital loci to produce pleasure (Davison, Kwan, and Greenleaf 1982). Each of these must lead to activation of the parasympathetic nervous system (PNS), which controls tumescence. Although these channels for arousal are distinct, they may come into play as secondary modes of arousal on any given occasion.

There is reason to believe that the different relational outcome modes are associated with different channels of sexual arousal. Prima facie, the dominance and eminence modes are accompanied by T surges, which ought to be their fundamental arousal mechanism. Whether T surges lead to greater capacity for concentration on sexual fantasy, as Bancroft and Wu (1983) imply, or to greater responsiveness when there is also contact with mechanoreceptors in the penis is not clear. Astonishingly, social constructionists John Gagnon and William Simon (1973) proposed increased penile sensitivity as an explanation of why male puberty leads to enhanced sexual interest.

In the case of both submission and inferiority, T is depressed and libido is low, hence there will be a generally low likelihood of arousal. If arousal does occur, I propose that it is most often via mechanoreceptor contact. If not simply a matter of accidental contact and stimulation, this is a willed arousal, and in that sense is cortically controlled. But this is not cortical arousal as described above, where fantasy itself leads directly to arousal. The depressed state of persons in the inferiority category, with its very low libido, may make them even more remote from arousal than the submission category. Stated otherwise, persons in the submission category may be more capable of cortical arousal (perhaps via pornography) as well as arousal through mechanoreceptors.

The resistance and resentment types are endowed with T, and although surges are not frequent, this mode is available to them. Yet T is not so plentiful that it can constitute the major source of sexual impetus. It may be conjectured that individuals in the resistance and resentment conditions are susceptible to vivid recapitulation of both their past losses and possible future success through fantasy. If this is true, the cortical path to arousal is a well-traveled one for them.

Masturbation

It took the research of Kinsey, Pomeroy, and Martin (1948) to establish the almost universal pattern of masturbation among males. What they also showed was that masturbation varied as a social outlet by social class (middle-and upper-class males were more prone to masturbate in youth), and that masturbation was not absent among those with steady sexual partners. This last finding is the most compelling from a social relational perspective. While one can understand masturbation when there is no partner, what possible reasons could there be for masturbation when there is an available sexual partner? A man may be so highly sexed that his partner cannot be available as often as he would like. Yet this is to suggest that a partner is not available. A man may desire to control premature ejaculation and masturbate prior to coitus on the theory that later ejaculations are likely to be delayed (Kaplan 1974:296). This may be kind both to one's partner and to one's self-esteem, in that one can perform more satisfactorily. Another ground for masturbation would be where the partner is alienated from him or he from her, as during a long-enduring quarrel (see Reading and Wiest 1984).

Here the interest in masturbation is in connection with the social relational and sexual interactional contexts. I propose that in the two most sexually aroused types, the dominant and the eminent, masturbation is likely to be low. This is because there is in each case the resource for obtaining or for attracting a sexual partner. Given that sexual behavior with a partner is the culturally preferred mode, these types are able to obtain such partners with relative ease. Recall from the discussion in chapter 2 Keverne's (1979) observation that dominant monkeys ceased masturbating once females were available.

The inferiority-depression type, with reduced libido, is also likely to be low in masturbation because there is simply very little arousal. Further, among the depressed, pleasure taken from the self may increase depression, since it may be considered a warrant of one's social deficit.

Masturbation is more likely among those who engage in fantasy. Kinsey, Pomeroy, and Martin (1948:363) found that sexual fantasy was more prevalent among higher-class youths due to their greater involvement in symbolic materials—books, pictures, and the like. These youths also had higher rates of nocturnal emission and masturbation; both are sexual outlets without partners. The social relational types involving resistance and resentment are also cortically oriented, which ought to lead to relatively high rates of masturbation. The cortical mode of arousal is particularly disposed toward masturbation because once there is sexual arousal through cortical means, if a partner is not at hand or soon in prospect, masturbation is the quickest and easiest method of discharging the excitation. In the relational mode of submission, with cortical arousal a distinct possibility, masturbation is likely to be even higher than among the resistance or resentment groups because there is lesser opportunity for sexual interaction with a partner.

Postsexual Feeling

There is little doubt that sexual satisfaction is one of life's highest pleasures (Freud 1951:69), yet there are degrees of feeling good, and, as indicated by the possibility that sex can be bad, there are times when it is better. This has clearly to do with many things, including anatomical fit, degree of arousal, aesthetics of the setting, conflicting emotions, as in guilt over infidelity, and so on. There are also the precursor relational conditions, including where self and other stand in the power and status interactional space, along with the ensuing emotions, patterns of relating, source of arousal, and the like. Finally, with a partner, there is the power and status configuration in that dyad (Schenk, Pfrang, and Rausche 1983; Reading and Wiest 1984) with its accompanying emotions and facilitations or hindrances of arousal, including the degree of receptivity and proceptivity of the partner and the dominance/eminence opportunities of the sexual interaction itself (see chapter 2). Clearly, the complexity of the sexual situation is such that we have hardly begun to appreciate all its parameters.

Yet, following the line taken here thus far, I wish to venture some surmises about what kinds of relational-emotional conditions are most promising for good sex. By good sex I mean sexual activity that leaves one with a tonic feeling: buoyant, energized, prepared for more sex. The opposite is also possible. I propose that T sex is best, that is, sex ignited by a T surge. Dominance and eminence are the two relational types for which T is the major source of arousal. The arousal is unthinking, unwilled, and phylogenetically the most natural. To discharge sexual tension in those circumstances must be as direct and unproblematic as drinking water when one is thirsty or eating when one is hungry. Just as these natural functions and responses are satisfying and refreshing in and of themselves, so is T sex.

However, I wish to remark on a distinction between the two Testosterone-sex modes. In the dominance mode the approach is that of taking, in the eminence mode it is giving and getting. I wish to extract the giving for special attention and label it *tender sex*. Tender sex differs from ordinary T sex in that it is most likely to evoke giving from the partner. This means that in the ongoing sexual interaction, there is further mutual status enhancement, a continuous feeding of eminence and follow-through from that. Here we may note a possible distinction between dominance and eminence that affects the ultimate level of satisfaction. As among infrahuman forms, among humans there is frequently more than a single coition. It may be that the satisfaction of the first coition is greater in the case of dominance. Libido is judged to be highest, there is an active mastering of the partner in the taking mode, and the resolution of this highest tension is thus likely to be very satisfying.

Yet, while the first coition may have been extremely satisfying for the dominant male, his partner may be less than satisfied and may now be more resistant to being overpowered.[4] She may now be in the resistance mode, and the immediate interactional context is one in which the earlier dominance no longer operates. Indeed, if there is a sexual interaction victory, it may come at some cost. In initiating the second coition that cost will be higher than in the first. Though there was great satisfaction in the first coition and there is a new T surge, something has been aroused in the partner that changes the relational condition. By contrast, the second coition in tender sex feeds upon its own success. Its T surge comes from status gain, a gift by the partner in the interaction that takes place in the interval after the first coition. Hence, tender sex may be more satisfying at later stages in the sexual interaction.

Cortically instigated arousal is likely to be less satisfying than either T-inspired taking sex or tender sex. I propose this as the major mode of arousal of the resistance and resentment types. Only scant evidence exists to support this surmise, but it crucially connects fantasy inversely to T. In an experiment designed to compare arousal among hypogonadal and normal males, Bancroft and Wu (1983) found that while the two groups were equally aroused by an erotic film, the hypogonadal males were less aroused than normal males by their own fantasies. When T replacement was administered to the hypogonadal males, their arousal to own fantasy was equal to that of the normal males. According to Bancroft and Wu, "The simplest explanation is that erotic fantasy is a weaker stimulus [than the erotic film, ergo] more sensitive to . . . androgen withdrawal" (1983:65).

Bancroft and Wu conjecture that the active mental work of fantasy, as contrasted with the passive condition of simply watching the erotic film, is enhanced by androgens, either by permitting concentration of attention (as described by Andrew 1978) or by enhancing visuospatial imagery ability. The latter is found to be superior in males (Maccoby and Jacklin 1974) and has been linked specifically to T by Broverman et al. (1968). This will be extensively explore in chapter 4.

Although an erotic film also arouses via cortical paths, it clearly allows for easier identification and self-placement into the erotic encounter. To the extent that the scenes represent dominance, this is explicit and available for self-reference, hence more easily linked with the possibility of a T surge. Though low in T, even hypogonadal males may conceivably experience a modest T surge in such facilitative conditions. By contrast, own fantasies may not so directly or vividly create a dominance scenario. Indeed, extraneous and self-defeating images may intrude, however unwelcome. Obviously, own fantasies cannot be scripted in advance with the definitive conclusiveness of a film.

Apparently, T makes a difference in the degree to which fantasies can stimulate arousal. In the resistance and resentment types, T is less than maximal, so there should be some deficit in arousal. Though slight, this deficit signifies that what is brought to the sexual interaction is not wholehearted sexual interest. This cannot but reduce the satisfaction of the encounter.

The submission category is heavily dependent on masturbation. It has been reported that masturbation can provide more intense orgasms than coitus (Hunt 1974; Hite 1981). Intensity is a subjective notion as discussed here, but some evidence for an endocrinological substrate is provided by Wiedeking et al.'s (1977) finding that NE level rose 1,200 percent after masturbation, which was even higher than after coitus. Yet, intensity may not correlate perfectly with the mood of feeling good. Indeed, the extremely high NE elevation may leave a dysphoric residue. This would depend, apparently, on the rapidity of recovery from such extreme activation of the SNS (Forsman 1980; Rauste-von Wright, von Wright, and Frankenhaeuser 1981), and no data on this are reported in Wiedeking et al. (1977). Although there is no definitive knowledge here, the available data do not support the conclusion that a more intense orgasm leaves one more satisfied. Indeed, it may do the opposite. Masturbation has another deficit with respect to satisfaction. Though it usually culminates in the pleasure of orgasm, pleasure is bought at the price of violating a prevailing social attitude concerning the lesser desirability (if not, still, depravity) of bringing oneself to sexual climax (Jensen 1976). Adult males who resort to masturbation are prone to think of it as an adolescent activity; hence, many depreciate themselves for it

(McCarthy 1984). It is possible to conclude that masturbation carries with it a surplus of negative concerns. It is not likely that these enhance the positive quality of postsexual feeling.

The final category of social outcome types is the inferiority-depressed. The classical syndrome of depression includes loss of sexual appetite and loss of ability to take pleasure in what ordinarily gives pleasure (MacPhillamy and Lewinsohn 1974). There is no reason to think that the inferiority-depressed type feels very good in the aftermath of sexual interaction, whether the sexual mode is coitus or masturbation (though the latter is likely to be more frequent). Indeed, this would violate an essential condition of the social relational and emotional state he is in.

Discussion

I have contended above that the most pleasurable sexual outcome may, in the first coitus, result from the T surge of dominance. There is something odious about this. Our vanity is that we have transcended our primate roots and are sensible to a qualitatively different level of experience. Hence, the purely animalistic implication of the dominance hypothesis here runs counter to cherished anthropocentric suppositions. Indeed, I have no evidence for the hypothesis; it is more of an informed speculation, which relies, obviously, on Freud's (1951) argument in *Civilization and Its Discontents*. There, Freud considered the antinomian character of civility and desire. On the one hand, there is the need for accommodation to the cooperative venture that is society; on the other, there is the pressing need for resolution of sexual and aggressive tensions. The two confound each other and pose the human dilemma that Freud uniquely understood.

Whether or not with "surplus repression," as Marcuse (1955) has suggested, society has necessarily imposed limits on sexual expression and aggression so that its own needs can be met. Freud averred that the price in the sexual domain is neurotic inhibition. Although current, relatively liberal sexual practices would seem to belie the notion of inhibition, it is not clear that recent sexual liberation in modern societies has in fact truly freed individuals of sexual hang-ups. Indeed, the failure to find true freedom can be attributed in part to the continuing aura of societal disapproval for unrestrained sexual practice—the polymorphous perverse original state according to Freud, and worthy, according to Marcuse, of revival. However, acquired immune deficiency syndrome (AIDS) is a new peril on the sexual landscape, which is bending morality back to an earlier, more restrictive position.

The free individual in the sexual and aggressive domains would be the one who is least concerned with societal sanctions or disapproval. At perhaps its most extreme, such would be a Nietzschean character who chooses his own way regardless of societal judgment. Within the terms of the social relational model proposed here, this would most nearly be approximated by the person who has attained dominance, who has overcome the resistance of others and has the confidence that he can do so again in any future encounter. This is the person most liberated from social constraint. (I offer no judgment on this type here). I say most liberated because, unlike the eminent, who achieve status elevation and who may also break the boundaries of social control (as discussed above in the section on infidelity), the dominant are not dependent for their sense of well-being on the voluntary responses of others. The dominant simply take what they want.

The dominant disposition concentrates concern on the self. The other in the social relationship is of less moment. In the sexual domain, the partner simply counts for less. The dominant male's satisfaction is the issue, and it determines the timing and the tactile and verbal features of the sexual encounter. Disturbingly, this leads to a more unalloyed and unhampered drive to please the self. One need not wait, one need not take the other into account. At its worst it is rape, and this is the maximum of power and dominance in a sexual interaction. But even at lesser levels, the focus on self to the exclusion of the other is central to the sexual release.

Something about this strikes us as unacceptable. Our ideology about ourselves as "but a little lower than the angels" does not favor power and dominance, at least not in theory. Hence, we pay lip service to love and to the forms of social relations—mutual giving and getting—that underlie love. Yet, in reality, power is attractive, for despite its costs it has some aspects that draw people to get it and use it. One of those aspects, hardly before perceived but logically an accompaniment of power, is that by being heedless of others one's satisfactions may be the greater. At least in the first instance.

In the sexual domain, the first instance is the first coitus. Tender sex, the mode of the eminent, may be just a bit too other-serving at this point in what is fundamentally a process by which nature demands its due for reproductive purposes without a whit of concern for who loves or overpowers whom. But after the first coitus, I have suggested, the odds on satisfaction run in opposite directions for the dominant and the eminent.

For the dominant, the sequel is that the costs of power become more apparent. There is more likely to be partner resistance (though submission is also possible), and more power must be brought to bear to attain the same compliance the second time. This increase of cost is doubtless most often manageable, but in the calculus of pleasure may diminish the benefit on the second occastion.[5] For the eminent, the perhaps overconcern of the first coitus is recompensed with a flow of care and concern from the partner who has experienced loving—the sociosexual giving that is possible in the encounter between a man and a woman. Hence, the reward is gained through a heightened openness of both self and other that leads to the denouement of tender sex. It is perhaps this that poets have striven to describe in the union of the body and spirit that sexual interaction makes possible. Such union must produce a tonic feeling that beggars our ability to describe.

Yet, in order to attain this state, the social must have its due. In order to gain this ecstasy, one must forbear immediate pleasure, as the dominant are wont to demand. The lesson once again, and it is an old one, is that by giving, one gets. Clearly, laboratory studies of sexual interaction are far from having attended to these nuances and refinements of sexual life. Yet, just as clearly, this is our need if we are to comprehend more fully how the sexual plays its social as well as its biological role in the socio-bio-social chain.

4

SOCIAL STRUCTURE, TESTOSTERONE, AND WOMEN'S SPATIAL ABILITY: REVISITING THE BROVERMAN HYPOTHESIS

A potential field of scientific inquiry that lies fallow may reflect the understandable time lag between a fruitful discovery and its exploitation by what is called "normal science" (Kuhn 1962). I suspect there is something more, namely, gender bias (not unknown in science, as Tiefer 1978 and Bleier 1979 have pointed out), behind the underdevelopment of studies of testosterone (T) in females.

Since T is the major male sex hormone, it has been investigated more in males, just as estrogen (E), the major class of female sex hormones, has been investigated more in females. But T is also part of the female endocrinological profile—manufactured in the ovaries and in the adrenal cortex. Given the provocative findings associated with T in males, as described in chapter 2, it is of prime interest to know whether this hormone operates in the same way in females, whether it is responsive to the same social stimuli and incentives, and, if so, whether it produces the same social effects as in males. Little of this is known. At present, we have only tantalizing bits of data hinting at enormously important social effects on T levels in females, parallel in many ways to the effects on males. But this is still a frontier on which there is much to be discovered.

Notwithstanding the deficit of hard detail and replicated studies, some useful insights have emerged, along with some interesting theories, showing that T is importantly related to female sexuality, aggression, dominance, and certain forms of intellect, particularly in the domain of spatial relations. The data allow at least a mild conjecture that T performs some similar functions in females and males. Yet it is perhaps of even greater interest to examine these effects in females because, if they are confirmed, they operate in an important sense opposite to what traditional social structures command. In males, T is clearly related to the experience of dominance/eminence, and this is consonant with the traditional social structural position of males, who are expected to be dominant or eminent. Yet, if T in females is also related to dominance/eminence, this is biosocially anomalous given the usually subordinate position of females in traditional social structures. It would mean bodies pulling in one direction and societal prescriptions for conduct in another. If one views all social life as struggle, then a socioendocrinological conflict is merely another front in a pandemic war. On the other hand, given a better understanding of biological processes, it may be possible to create a more reasoned social structure based on the realities of bodily processes.

Status quo ideologists often defend unequal social arrangements from behind biological ramparts because biology has seemed to be an immutable barrier against which reformist social hopes must crash in vain.[1] Yet, these efforts to employ a biological argument in the service of social rhetoric are doubly vulnerable. First, the argument depends on the state of current knowledge, which is often incomplete. For example, the cranial-weight explanation of sex differences in intelligence seemed plausible enough until it was shown to be false. The second pitfall of biological explanations is that they may not take into account the social factors that determine the operative biological conditions, that is, the full socio-bio-social chain. Hamburg (1974) has acknowledged that in the new biology the social and the biological exert a mutual influence.

Here I take up the biological questions once again from a social perspective, seeking to understand variations in T in females, how social arrangements may determine these variations, and what the social consequences of variation in female T may be. I will examine here the issue of sex differences in *spatial ability*, a form of reasoning that involves the ability to think abstractly about the location of objects in space or their transformation in space as they turn on one or more axes. This ability has been related to skills in advanced mathematics and abstract reasoning, as in science (Meehan 1984), and also to artistic, engineering, architectural, and musical abilities (see Geschwind and Galaburda 1985, pt. 1). Apart from the strictly factual aspects of the matter, there are political and ideological dimensions. While there is general agreement that, on average, males are superior to females in at least some tasks requiring spatial ability (Linn and Petersen 1985), beyond this consensus breaks down. One view is that the sex difference in spatial ability is due to genetic or endocrinological differences between the sexes; the strongly opposed view is that the difference is due to differential socialization and encouragement, and is a consequence of the larger structure of hierarchical relations between the sexes.

There is indeed evidence to show that socialization variables explain at least part of the imbalance in mathematical and spatial skills by sex. For example, mathematics performance differences decline when number of courses in advanced mathematics is controlled (Linn and Petersen 1986). Also, training females in spatial tasks improves their skills in performing these tasks (Goldstein and Chance 1965; Brinkmann 1966; Connor, Serbin, and Schackman 1977), although, apparently, not universally so (Liben and Golbeck 1980). But socialization may not explain the entire difference between the sexes (Benbow 1988). There may yet be biological differences between males and females that lead to unlike abilities in the spatial domain. But it must not be assumed, a priori, that the biological difference is frozen in genetic amber, so to speak, preserved as an adaptive mutation that remains our ineluctable fate.

I entertain here a complex hypothesis, namely, that there is a biological difference between males and females that affects their average performance in certain types of abstract problem-solving requiring spatial ability, and that the specific biological element involved is T, which males ordinarily possess to a greater degree than females. However, this describes only part of the phenomenon. I hypothesize further that, even if T is responsible for spatial ability differences between the sexes, a historical transformation in the social roles of women is significantly changing their testosterone titers, hence also changing the biological effects. In this analysis I give full due to biology, once it is seen as itself susceptible to alteration by social arrangements. In entertaining these hypotheses, I do not thereby accept as true the putative link between T and spatial ability. Rather, I take that link as a working hypothesis that must be examined within a larger socio-bio-social framework. Only then can we rest assured that we have not accepted as a biological verity what is true, not absolutely, but only historically, and is susceptible to changed social arrangements in a different time.

Spatial Ability

In their widely cited review of studies comparing males and females on a broad spectrum of traits, Maccoby and Jacklin (1974) reported strong evidence for the superior skills of males in tasks involving spatial relations. No studies since that time have negated the finding, although some have qualified it by showing specific areas of spatial abilities in which male-female differences are more likely to be found, and others have reported that male-female differences are declining (Linn and Petersen 1986; Kolata 1989). Spatial ability has been usefully divided into three dimensions by Linn and Petersen (1985): mental rotation, spatial perception, and spatial visualization. *Mental rotation* is the ability to rotate a two- or three-dimensional figure around one or more of its axes and accurately represent it in its new orientation(s); for example, which faces would a marked cube display after being rotated ninety degrees through one or more of its axes. Ordinarily, speed of accurate solution is measured. *Spatial perception* involves the ability to determine the spatial location of objects with respect to the orientation of one's own body, despite distracting information. One of the most widely known spatial perception tasks involves the "rod and frame" test, in which a person must establish the true vertical for a rod located in a frame tiled more than twenty degrees from the vertical. Another test requires locating a true horizontal line for fluid in a tilted bottle. Tasks that test *spatial visualization* include finding simple figures that are embedded in complex visual patterns and determining how a folded piece of paper with specific markings would appear when unfolded.[2]

In a comprehensive metaanalysis of 172 results assessing sex differences in spatial ability published after the Maccoby and Jacklin (1974) review, Linn and Petersen (1985) arrived at several important conclusions about the three dimensions of spatial ability. Males exceed females in mental rotation ability by anywhere from a quarter to a whole standard deviation, depending on the task. But, Linn and Petersen note, in one of the more complete studies of this ability (Kail, Carter, and Pellegrino 1979), females produced a bimodal distribution in speed of rotation: some 30 percent of females were slower than all males, while some females performed just as well as males.

In spatial perception, males are again superior, by anywhere from a third of a standard deviation for those under eighteen years of age to two-thirds of a standard deviation for those older than eighteen, with the difference between males and females detectable as early as age seven in some research (Block and Block 1982). The meaning of the increasing difference in ability over age groups is not clear. Linn and Petersen suggest that there could be a developmental change in the magnitude of the difference in ability, or the result could reflect either a difference in cohorts or in populations sampled at the different times or ages. With respect to the third spatial ability component, spatial visualization, Linn and Petersen's metaanalysis uncovered neither sex nor age effects.

In sum, males exceed females in some aspects of spatial ability, some of the difference originating well before puberty and perhaps increasing after puberty. Each element of these findings has been subject to intense scrutiny, mainly with the object of disentangling the objective from the ideological threads of explanation. Some investigators (as will be detailed below) propose that male-female differences in spatial ability stem from the same genetic or endocrinological sources that account for the basic reproductive differentiation of the sexes. Countering this, Newcombe (1982) proposed that since spatial ability differences appear earlier than puberty, when males and females are very much alike in their hormonal profile, the differences must result from the early socialization of boys and girls into different tasks that engender and train spatial ability. Hence, she regards the widening difference after puberty as simply the effect of longer differential socialization.

If, indeed, male-female differences in spatial abilities can be explained by differential socialization and encouragement, the problem resolves itself in a relatively straightforward manner. As with numerous other socialized differences, this one would give way as socialization practices changed. Socialization includes both direct tuition in the relevant skills and encouragement to undertake training to master them. In recent years both have been tried in fields requiring spatial ability. For example, more female high school students are taking more courses in mathematics and in mechanical drawing (*New York Times*, August 15, 1985, sec. C, 1). These courses provide the kinds of skills and mastery that boys have traditionally received in preparation for technical careers.

However, there are socializing practices apart from direct tuition or encouragement to undertake certain kinds of training, or to pursue certain kinds of careers, that also bear on whether particular skills are developed. For example, it has been suggested that differential childrearing with respect to such matters as geographical space may ramify into later career choices. Boys are allowed to wander farther from home, so must learn earlier to locate themselves spatially (Harper and Sanders 1978). Dating and courting patterns are still traditionally based; hence, the male will usually drive the car, deciding where to go and figuring out how to get there. In this respect, cars are still part of a masculine culture, and males may gain more territorial and spatial acumen through wider experience of travel. The geographic-territorial socialization hypothesis fits also into a genetic explanation of male-female differences in spatial ability. It has been conjectured that it was adaptive for males to hunt while females stayed close to camp with children. Over time, those hunters who could wander far and find their way back to camp gained an evolutionary advantage (Hamburg 1974). Notwithstanding the plausibility of this argument, Bleier (1979:61) cited evidence that among early hunter-gatherers women, too, roamed from camp as much as ten miles to gather their provender.

Petersen and Hood (1988) present evidence for several other possible socialization-based differences between males and females that might account for sex differences in spatial ability. First, females appear to choose problem-solving strategies that are more conservative than those of males, thus curtailing their spatial ability score through slowness or through reluctance to risk error by guessing when in doubt. Second, females may have lower motivation to perform on gender-typed tests that stress male-oriented problems and examples. Third, parents and teachers have generally expected less of female children in the mathematics and science domain than they have of males. Linn and Petersen (1986) also report on the lower level of confidence exhibited by females about their mathematics skills, despite achieving higher grades, on average, than male students. These differences between males and females reflect more or less direct effects of socialization.

Yet another socialization-based hypothesis explaining sex differences in spatial ability reflects some possible indirect effects of socialization. Lynn (1966) proposed that males and females ordinarily have learned their respective gender roles in somewhat different family contexts, at least until recently. Even in relatively nontraditional households, mothers are still primarily responsible for child care in the early years. This may require temporarily deactivating a career or working part time. Or it may involve providing another (usually female) caretaker, whether familial or hired, for periods when the mother is unavailable. The net effect, then, is for young children from infancy until schooling begins to spend overwhelmingly more time with the mother or other females than with the father or other males.

The socialization context this presents for gender role acquisition differs for boys and girls. For girls, it is a matter of what Lynn calls "lesson learning": observing one's role model (mother) and acquiring her repertoire of knowledge, ability, and motives (Brim 1960). However, boys face a different problem. They must learn through verbal instruction. In a gender-differentiated culture, it will not do for them to acquire the mother's role repertoire, since this would not suit their male role requirements (assuming traditional gender-role differentiation). But the father is ordinarily absent for most of the day in families of the type discussed here. He leaves for work early and returns home at or past the young child's bedtime. Hence, the father is not available for the most part as a role model to provide lesson learning. Instead, the boy is instructed verbally what to do and what not to do to satisfy gender-role requirements. Much of this tuition is abstract in that usually there are no male exemplars physically present to demonstrate concrete instances of the desired behavior. Thus, he must figure out and learn his gender identity and its role requirements from a somewhat abstract mental exercise rather early in life.

Lynn (1969) cited evidence that these notions can be fitted into a general concept of "distance," whether physical or emotional, from the same-sex parent. He postulated that there is an optimum distance for satisfactory gender-role learning. But he also found that optimum distance correlated positively with mathematical and spatial ability. Boys in households where the father is away at work all day during the child's early years and who is not emotionally distant when he is present have an optimum context for acquiring the ability to perform abstract thought as is required in the advanced sciences and mathematics. Importantly, the same formula holds for girls. If mothers are not always present and are not emotionally distant, girls, too, acquire not only a female gender identity, but also the ability to perform well in mathematics and science. While Lynn's hypotheses have not been much investigated, they offer an interesting perspective on how socialization itself must be understood as implying more than simply direct tuition and role encouragement.

On the biological side of potential explanations of the sex difference in spatial ability, the most fundamental is that there is a specific, sex-linked gene for the ability (Bock and Kolakowski 1973). Notwithstanding that there may be an evolutionary adaptive advantage to spatial skills in males, the research results have been conflicting on this question (Linn and Petersen 1985), and, to date, no gene for spatial ability has been discovered. However, according to Yen (1975; see also McGee 1979), greater heritability has been found for spatial perception, in which male-female differences have been shown, than for spatial visualization, where they have not.[3] This clearly suggests a biological involvement over and above any socialization effects. There are also biological approaches that depend on hormonal differences between the sexes. I will examine these in greater detail after the next section.

Consequences of Spatial Ability Differences

Although it is of interest for descriptive and theoretical reasons to understand the degree of and grounds for male-female differences in spatial abilities, there are also practical consequences, particularly in modern societies. To the extent that such differences exist and play a role in science achievement (see Linn and Petersen 1986), they tend to preclude women from entering professions and occupations where spatial ability, or its correlates in abstract reasoning, is especially required. These professions include mathematics, theoretical physics and chemistry, architecture, engineering, and music composition—pathways to some of the highest societal achievements and rewards (Harris 1981:117). To be excluded because of a skill deficit is somehow regarded as not only to be different—as are male and female roles in reproduction—but also inferior. Since the most advanced social and political ethos of our time does not countenance inferiority for any categorical group, the issue has deep ramifications for matters of social organization and hierarchy between the sexes. It is thus important to determine the precise amount and basis of the difference between males and females in spatial ability. Noteworthy also is that regardless of any real sex difference in spatial ability, estimated by Linn and Petersen (1985) to be about one standard deviation at maximum in the most extremely divergent of the spatial ability components between the sexes, differential recruitment into scientific and engineering professions far exceeds what might be expected strictly on the basis of the spatial ability difference. Eccles (1987) has examined this issue closely by comparing male-female ratios of high scorers in mathematics with male-female ratios in occupations requiring mathematical and spatial ability skills.

The shaping function of spatial ability with respect to occupation and career is reported to be strong. Witkin and Goodenough (1977) studied the relationship between a measure of spatial perception they call "field independence" and a variety of educational and occupational choices. Those who are field independent, that is, demonstrate relatively high spatial ability, tend to choose college majors that lead to careers in more impersonal, abstract, theoretic, cognitive, and artistic areas, while those who are more field dependent tend to choose person-oriented careers in the humanities or social sciences. The effect is demonstrated even in the manner in which students change fields of study over the course of the college career so as to achieve greater compatibility between their career trajectories and their cognitive abilites.

Yet, incontrovertibly, there is also evidence of growth in women's spatial ability in recent years and in their pursuit of occupations that require spatial ability. Rosenthal and Rubin (1982) and Becker and Hedges (1984) have demonstrated that male-female differences in spatial ability have significantly declined in recent years. On average, somewhat less than 60 percent of males and somewhat more than 40 percent of females would now pass a given criterion. Although this still indicates a substantial male advantage, it is narrower than was previously the case. The declining difference could be obtained in two ways: an absolute increase in skill by females, or a decline in skill by males. Both seem to have occurred according to the Educational Testing Service's (ETS) analysis of its spatial ability examination results since 1960 (*New York Times,* August 15, 1985, sec. C, 1). While females have improved, males have declined. Results from a Massachusetts Department of Education testing program also indicate improved female standing (*New York Times,* March 21, 1986, sec. B, 5). In standardized skills tests—some of which, such as mathematics, are related to spatial ability—at the third, sixth, and ninth grades, females outperformed males. Despite the improvement by females, ETS noted a general decline in spatial abilities among both male and female adolescents in the United States. In this regard, Stanley and Benbow (1982) and Benbow (1988) reported a decline in the number of females scoring in the extremely high ranges of the quantitative portions of the widely used Scholastic Aptitude Test (SAT). With contrary results such as these, it would appear that there are multiple forces at work both to augment and the depress performance, particularly among females.

These ambiguities aside, in the last two decades parents, educators, government, industry, and the media have socialized and encouraged women far more than previously to participate equally with men in the full spectrum of work and community roles, particularly in those high-prestige and high-income occupations where women have been least present. Marked changes have occurred in the proportions of women in the advanced professions (law, medicine, the sciences) and in political life (Beller and Han 1984). For example, in law, females advanced from 4 percent in 1972 to 18 percent in 1986. In medicine, the proportion of females increased from 10 percent in 1972 to 17 percent in 1986 (*New York Times,* March 19, 1986, sec. C, 1). However, in engineering and the sciences, where spatial ability is most pertinent, the starting proportions were much lower and the increases, while proportionally great, still leave women with very low involvement. In chemical engineering, the advance from 1972 to 1981 was from less than one percent to 6 percent, and in electrical and electronic engineering, the advance was from one to 4 percent. Other technical disciplines do not fare even this well in increasing female participation: females in architecture increased from 3 to 4 percent from 1972 to 1981; in mechanical, aerospace, and civil engineering, the maximum percentage of females in 1981 was less than 3 percent (Beller and Han 1984). Overall, in figures collected by the National Science Foundation (1982), about 10 percent of physical scientists, 20 percent of mathematicians, and 5 percent of engineers are women. Doubtless these figures will show a continuing upward trajectory as later data become available.

There is no dearth of explanation for this relative lack of occupational development in the spatial ability fields at a time when certain legal and social constraints have ostensibly been removed. It may be argued that these occupations are particularly resistant bastions of male domination, or that a full effort has not yet been made to attract women to them, or that a lingering tradition of "femininity" somehow discourages involvement in technical or abstract occupations (*New York Times,* August 15, 1985, sec. C, 1). In regard to the last notion, law and medicine deal mainly with people, while most of the spatial ability fields deal either with things or with symbols. Whatever the explanation, women have not moved as rapidly into careers that are apparently the most dependent on spatial abilities.

However, if we examine the choice of college major among women, the outlook for a more desegregated occupational structure improves, even though women are traditionally less able to translate a college or professional degree into a stable career in the field of the major (Bielby 1978; Marini 1980). In some of the main spatial ability fields, enrollments of women have increased significantly: in architecture and environmental design, from about 4 percent in 1969 to 24 percent in 1978; in mathematics and statistics, from 37 percent in 1969 to 41 percent in 1978; and in engineering, from less than one percent in 1969 to 7 percent in 1978 (Beller and Han 1984:112). Thus, we see some remarkable advances, with even more striking ones in the offing if current projections are realized.

It behooves us to understand the grounds for the accelerating, albeit slow and uneven, improvements noted here. How does this pattern of slow growth in women's involvement in certain technical careers conform to what we understand about spatial ability? There are alternative paths here. First, we might assign the present growth to the removal of formal and informal professional barriers, which previously kept women out of certain fields. Earlier, in the face of these bars to employment, and advancement, many women simply did not try. More recently, equal opportunity laws, affirmative action, and a change in male consciousness about the fairness, wisdom, or legality of the previous policy have cleared the way for women's entry into these occupations. This would allow those women with high spatial ability to practice in the fields for which they are qualified. However, since, according to some accounts, they are relatively few in number, this would explain the present slow growth of women's participation in the professions of interest.

A second possibility, augmenting the first, is that although in the past women were socialized to avoid occupations where professional barriers were strong, socialization practices more recently have encouraged women to enter those fields now that the barriers have been breached. Hence, women are now being taught to see these fields as possible for themselves and are being trained to participate in them. This would explain the striking increase in selection of these fields as college majors.

A third possibility, and the one I will explore here, is that in addition to the reduction of professional barriers and the enhancing efforts of a more active socialization and encouragement to enter fields previously low in women's participation, the recent transformation of women's social structural position, which both accompanied and produced the changes noted, has also affected women's biological readiness to participate in those fields requiring spatial ability. This assumes that there is a biological factor in aptitude for certain kinds of occupations, but that the factor itself can be socially determined to a significant extent. My point of entry into the biological sources of spatial ability is the Broverman hypothesis.

The Broverman Hypothesis

Although differential socialization is a powerful argument and clearly explains many differences noted between males and females, it is a relative latecomer. Earlier, biological hypotheses located the differences in genetic or physiological differences between the sexes. Here I will examine one such hypothesis, propounded by Broverman et al. (1968), and I will refer to it as the Broverman hypothesis. I do not assert that it is true. There is evidence both for and against it. Rather, my purpose, is to examine it as if it were true, but to question its sociological and historical applicability. That is, even if it were true at a certain point in time, social changes that also change biological processes may be invalidating the grounds for the hypothesis at present.

In an earlier paper, Broverman et al. (1964) presented the concept of "automatization cognitive style." This referred to whether individuals perform better in "simple, perceptual-motor tasks (strong automatizers)" or in "tasks requiring initial inhibition of response so as to facilitate perceptual restructuring (weak automatizers)" (1344). To be a strong automatizer implies the ability to be aroused quickly, with a corresponding inability to withhold a perceptual rush to judgment. By contrast, weak automatizers are less immediately aroused and thus have, or are able to take, the time to restructure the perceptual problem so as to obtain a more accurate solution.

Broverman et al. extended this notion to provide a comprehensive explanation of what had been noted in many studies: the superiority of females in the performance of many tasks requiring "relatively simple perceptual-motor association"; for example, reading accuracy, speed of identifying and naming stimuli such as colors, tasks that demand "rapid perception of details and frequent shifts of attention," tasks of manual dexterity, and others in which prior learning produces an advantage (1968:24).

By contrast, males had demonstrated superiority in what Broverman et al. called "inhibitory perceptual restructuring tasks" (1968:24), where the individual must "separate certain stimulus attributes from the field in which they are embedded" (1968:25) or resist the influence of a pattern in order to be able to reorganize a set of stimuli into a new pattern, as for example, in the rod and frame test, which is one of the principal ways in which spatial ability is measured (see Linn and Petersen 1985). Clearly Broverman et al. (1968) were dealing with what we have identified here as spatial abilities, and they accepted as valid the collection of evidence that showed these to be, on average, stronger skills among males than among females.

Broverman et al. (1968) considered, as one must, the socialization hypothesis, but rejected it as a complete solution because of two types of evidence. First, there was evidence of female superiority in a culture-free tasks, unaffected by socialization, that reflected simple perceptual-motor activity, namely, eyelid conditioning. This involves training the eye to blink at the presentation of a conditioned stimulus, such as a light or a sound, that has previously been paired with an unconditioned stimulus, such as a puff of air, which would usually cause an eye-blink. Broverman et al. (1968) reported female superiority in eighteen of nineteen studies of this phenomenon, with the differences significant in eight of the investigations. Second, Studies of infrahuman forms (rats and chickens) revealed similar patterns of differences between the sexes: females do better in performance of previously trained skills (e.g., in running wheels in preferences to straight runways), while males do better at novel tasks requiring inhibition of initial responses (e.g., in learning mazes). (For opposing views, see Juraska, Henderson, and Muller 1984; Beatty 1979).

Rejecting the socialization hypothesis, Broverman et al. (1968) turned to a biological explanation. Considering that the phenomenon in question was a sex difference, they entertained the hypothesis that the differences in cognitive abilities could be explained by differences in the potential of male and female hormones to activate the central nervous system (CNS), or brain and spinal cord. The Broverman hypothesis is that females do less well on tasks requiring inhibition and perceptual restructuring because female sex horhomes, principally E, produce more arousal in the CNS than male sex hormones, principally T. Higher, faster arousal somehow facilitates firing of neurons that are already programmed to execute previously trained skills, but when inhibition of previously trained responses is required, E defeats this. T, on the other hand, is less catalytic for neuronal firing; thus, it is superior to E for tasks requiring perceptual inhibition.

The process is presumed to work as follows: the autonomic nervous system (ANS), which regulates the major organs of the body (heart, lungs, stomach, genitals, skin, and so on) so that they may cope adequately with both environmental and internal demands, is divided into two branches, the sympathetic nervous system (SNS) and the parasympathetic nervous system (PNS). These operate in more or less reciprocal fashion, each providing negative feedback to the other in order to maintain a kind of homeostatic balance. Norepinephrine (NE), the neurochemical transmitter of the SNS arouses or activates target organs, while acetylcholine (ACh), the PNS transmitter, tends to damp down these same organs.

While the manifest work of the ANS occurs in the body's end organs—we become aware of rapid heartbeat, facial flush, sweating hands, churning stomach, and the like—the fundamental executive operations of this system take place in the CNS. There the hypothalamus and the pituitary gland release the neurochemical commands that ultimately travel to the peripheral organs of the sympathetic and parasympathetic systems. The two branches of the ANS, including their CNS loci, have been designated as adrenergic and cholinergic for the sympathetic and parasympathetic branches respectively: adrenergic because it was once thought that the major neurotransmitter of the SNS was an adrenalinelike substance (called sympathin), although, in fact, it is the related substance norepinephrine (see Burn 1975:33–34); and cholinergic because the major transmitter of the PNS is acetylcholine (ACh). Other terms have been used: ergotropic for the adrenergic system, since it energizes the organism for a variety of tasks or work (Greek root: *erg*); and trophotropic for the chloingeric system, since it orients the organism toward reduction of effort, conservation of energy, and nutrition (Greek root: *tropho*) (Hess 1954; Murphy and Gellhorn 1968:54).

Broverman et al. proposed that the main effects of E and T in connection with spatial ability occur in the central loci of the adrenergic and cholinergic systems. In their words, "The human sex differences in cognitive abilities . . . are reflections of the balance between the activating influence of central adrenergic processes and the inhibitory influence of central cholinergic processes, which, in turn, are influenced by gonadal steroid 'sex' hormones" (1968:27). Thus, activation of the adrenergic system will lead to arousal, rapidity of response, and the accurate performance of well-learned tasks; and activation of the cholinergic system will lead to a slowing down of response and, presumably, the ability to explore possible alternative responses in complex situations, especially those involving spatial relations.

Both of the main gonadal steroid sex hormones, E in females and T in males, activate the adrenergic system. But E is a stronger activator than T. It increases synthesis of NE, which is not only the neurotransmitter of the SNS at the point where it is in contact with target organs, but is also a neurotransmitter in the brain that is related to alertness and motor activity. Depression has been associated with inadequate presence of a class of neurotransmitters (including NE and serotonin) known as monoamines, and some antidepressant drugs operate mainly by reducing metabolism of monoamines (Kety 1972). As a consequence, these drugs are known as monoamine oxidase (MAO) inhibitors. Both E and T act as MAO inhibitors, thus providing for more brain NE; but, according to Broverman et al. (1968), E is a more potent MAO inhibitor, allowing for more adrenergic activation than T.

Presumably, E also inhibits ACh synthesis. ACh is a major neurotransmitter associated with the peripheral nodes of the PNS (where nerve endings join the target organs), and it is also a neurotransmitter in the CNS (in a manner Broverman et al, 1968 apparently did not consider, and which will be discussed below). In the peripheral (as opposed to central) portion of the ANS, where neurotransmitters directly affect body organs, ACh has different effects from NE. Whereas the latter is associated with activation, the former is associated with deactivation. Broverman et al. (1968) reasoned that the inhibiting effects of E would reduce ACh, thereby reducing deactivation. The net result for females would be a more roused CNS. In short, the Broverman hypothesis locates the difference between males and females in spatial abilities in brain processes that are affected differentially by male and female hormones.

Much of the evidence cited by Broverman et al. (1968) was collected on infrahuman species, and there is always the danger that cross-species generalization may be false (Bleier 1979; Benton 1983). Hence, they proposed a variety of human studies to test their hypothesis. Among the easiest to pursue is testing women at different stages of the menstrual cycle, which consists of several phases, each with a characteristic endocrinological profile. The first phase after menstruation is called the follicular phase, after follicle-stimulating hormone (FSH), which acts to prepare an ovum for release. In the second phase, which occurs at about the midpoint of the cycle, an E surge produces ovulation. The last part of the cycle is called the luteal phase, after luteinizing hormone (LH), which prepares the uterus for implantation of a fertilized ovum. During this period, progresterone, a mild androgen, is also present in relatively high amounts (Strand 1983).

According to the Broverman hypothesis, at the time of the E surge, just prior to ovulation, women should do relatively well on previously learned perceptual motor tasks and less well on tasks requiring cognitive inhibition and perceptual restructuring. The results of studies investigating this consequence of the Broverman hypotheses have been mixed. Kommenich et al. (1978) and Broverman et al. (1981) did find that women in the ovulatory phase of their menstrual cycle, when E is highest, are most "automatized." On the other hand, neither Hutt et al. (1980) nor Gordon, Corbin, and Lee (1986) found that any phase of the menstrual cycle had an effect on task efficiency. Other studies, too, provided mixed evidence for the Broverman hypothesis (Majeres 1977; Provost 1981; Forte, Mandato, and Kayson 1981). Broverman et al. (1981) contended that some of the negative results may be explained by the failure of investigators to eliminate annovulatory women from their samples. Anovulatory women may make up between 20 and 35 percent of samples according to some estimates (see DeAllende 1956). In their 1981 investigation, Broverman et al. found that 24 percent of women in the samples were anovulatory. They suggested other methodological improvements, including locating more precisely the time of research subjects' estrogen and progesterone peaks.

One of the more provocative reports that tests the Broverman hypothesis, at least indirectly, is by Hampson and Kimura (1988) and Kimura and Hampson (1988). The results of the latter study were so startling that the press took immediate note (Blakeslee 1988; *Newsweek,* November 28, 1988, 61). (The immediacy and possible inaccuracy of the press response was severely criticized from a feminist perspective by Benderley 1989.) Kimura and Hampson reported that in a relatively large sample (N = 200) for this kind of work, the women performed better on spatial relations problems on days in the menstrual cycle when their E was low, and better on automatized tasks when their E level was high—precisely as Broverman et al. (1968, 1981) hypothesized. The sample consisted of 150 young adult women and 50 postmenopausal women on E-replacement therapy. In E-replacement regimens, women take E for approximately twenty-five days of the monthly cycle, thus making for sets of high- and low-E days. The improvement in spatial ability on low-E days closed about half the average gap between males and females in this ability. A distinction between the younger and the older groups was that the older women's spatial ability was not as depressed as that of the younger women. According to Diamond (1984), older female rats show improved visual and spatial ability. A comparable result in humans could be due to the loss of E after menopause and a consequent change in the T/E balance.

Some studies of the variable properties of the SNS and PNS are also moderately supportive of the Broverman hypothesis. In the 1940s Wenger (reported in Wenger and Cullen 1972) proposed the concept of "autonomic balance," which refers to the relative dominance of each of the autonomic systems. Wenger found that children in whom the PNS was dominant displayed more patience and were less easily distracted than SNS-dominant children. Porges (1976) proposed that maturation entails a general shift from SNS-dominance to PNS-dominance, so that reactivity is reduced and cognitive control increased. Boyle, Dykman, and Ackerman (1965) found that boys whose autonomic responses were relatively labile had faster reaction times, but committed more errors in simple tasks. They proposed that this was due to a difference in "inhibitory capacity." These results provide some support for the different contributions of the SNS and the PNS to the accomplishment of tasks possibly requiring different degrees of cognitive inhibition. On the other hand, Schmock (1971) found that SNS-dominant girls (ages five to eleven) were superior in math and reading and were more conforming and tenacious than PNS-dominant girls, who were more aggressive. No effects of autonomic balance were found in a group of five- to eleven-year-old boys. Although the results obtained with the notion of autonomic balance are not uniformly favorable to the Broverman hypothesis, they do provide some evidence for it.

In a more recent development, Nyborg (1984) offered a theoretical approach that cut across that of Broverman et al. (1968). Nyborg proposed an extensive model of male-female differences, including spatial ability, based on the T/E ratio. Called the general covariance model, it "assigns to sex hormones the ultimate biochemical responsibility for producing not only gender-related differences in sensory modality priorities, but also in interests, cognitive style, gender role differences, physical energy expenditure, androgenization of muscles and fat distribution, and in other gender-related somatic characteristics. All these traits would depend on whether or not sex hormones were present at the right place, and at the right time, and in the right amount" (Nyborg 1984:501). From a review of the intellectual and spatial ability of various endocrinologically anomalous groups—males and females whose genetic and/or hormonal profiles differ from normal or are in conflict with each other; for example, congenital adrenal hyperplasia (CAH) girls, XYY males, and the like—Nyborg concluded that spatial ability varies curvilinearly with the presence of estrogen.

Lest this seem simply contrary to the Broverman hypothesis, which relies on T as the main agonist of spatial ability, it should be noted that according to some investigators (see Goy and McEwen 1981), a major share of T in the brain is aromatized (chemically converted) to E before it binds to neuronal receptors. This would make E, not T, the major operative sex hormone in the CNS. Thus, for males the following would be expected to hold: males low in T are low in spatial ability because they have an insufficient amount for conversion to an optimal level of E; males high in T are also low in spatial ability because they have too much T for conversion to an optimal level of E; males with moderate amounts of T produce an optimal amount of E through chemical conversion and thus, according to Nyborg, have a peak level of spatial ability. Most females are ordinarily high in E and thus above the optimal level for peak competence in spatial relations. A low level of E or even a transient drop, as during certain phases of the menstrual cycle, would bring females closer to optimal spatial relations performance.

In Nyborg's formulation, T plays a somewhat different physiological role than it does in Broverman et al.'s (1968) analysis, although the net results of the two approaches are the same with respect to stages of the menstrual cycle. To reconcile the approaches, it may be conjectured that transient increases in T for females can move females toward an optimal level of E for spatial relations by deactivating some of the E. Vogel, Klaiber, and Broverman (1985) found that synthetic T reduced the level of E. Since my concern in this chapter is with female spatial ability, and since Broverman's and Nyborg's predictions for females coincide, I will continue the analysis within the Broverman framework. Furthermore, this will permit me to apply to females some of the materials developed about males in chapter 2.

Critiques of the Broverman Hypothesis

As might be expected, Broverman et al.'s very bold hypothesis (1968), has been criticized both on ideological and neurophysiological grounds. The former is easy to understand, since the Broverman hypothesis implies that, on average, females are permanently barred by their endocrine status from certain creative activities and leading occupations. Parlee (1972) scorned this idea with unwonted irony (for a paper in a scientific journal). Fausto-Sterling (1985) also rejected hormonal arguments as blatantly sexist.

The neurophysiological critiques (Singer and Montgomery 1969; Parlee 1972) attacked the biological status of the hypothesis. Broverman et al. (1968) contended that the effects of activation and inhibition are accomplished in the brain via the adrenergic and cholinergic systems, respectively. The argument is basically about neurochemistry, specifically that the predominantly male and predominantly female sex hormones interact with and either facilitate or interfere with NE and ACh, putatively the neurotransmitters of the adrenergic and cholinergic systems in the brain.

According to both Singer and Montgomery (1969) and Parlee (1972), Broverman et al. (1968) mistakenly attributed to central adrenergic and cholinergic activity the same neurochemical specificity (NE and ACh respectively) that is observed at the synapses of the target organs of the peripheral systems. Hence, Broverman et al.'s (1968) citation of data showing the interaction of the sex hormones with NE and ACh may be beside the point if these neurotransmitters do not function at the central level as they supposed.

What is known is that the hypothalamus is the central site regulating the ergotropic (adrenergic) and trophotropic (cholinergic) systems. According to Gellhorn (1968), the ergotropic system is activated at the posterior end of the hypothalamus, while the trophotropic is activated at the anterior and medial portions of the this organ. It is also known that NE, one of the crucial neurotransmitters in the Broverman model, is most heavily concentrated in the hypothalamic area of the brain (Strand 1983:1168). But it is not clear that ACh, the other important neurotransmitter in the Broverman model, is also present in the relevant hypothalamic sites, nor, even if it is present, that it works specifically on the trophotropic system as intimated.

A useful clue in this direction has been provided, and it nudges us a bit closer to the Broverman et al. (1968) version of what transpires in the neurochemistry of the CNS. Nadi, Nurnberger, and Gershon (1984) discovered that the psychological state of depression is marked by an abnormal affinity of skin cells for ACh. These researchers conjectured (though they have not established) that there is a similar affinity for ACh in the brain cells of those who suffer from depression. The basis for this supposition is that according to Roth et al., "receptors for hormones and neurotransmitters evolutionarily predate the development of the central nervous system" (1982:225). Thus, Nadi, Nurnberger, and Gershon (1984) suppose that the same genetically determined results obtained at the skin surface would also obtain at the brain level for the same ACh receptors.

Depression, which according to one hypothesis is marked by an insufficiency of NE (Kety 1972), is also associated with excess activation of the trophotropic (cholinergic) system (Gellhorn 1968:148) in the brain, leading to excess inhibition. Hence, Nadi, Nurnberger and Gershon (1984) contribute to the Broverman hypothesis by providing at least indirect evidence that the same neurotransmitter Broverman et al. (1968) argue is involved in inhibition of perceptual responses is, in fact, involved when inhibition is carried to the excessive lengths that mark depression.

Two additional findings from the Nadi, Nurnberger, and Gershon (1984) study do not fit so neatly into the Broverman model. First, the dermal affinity for ACh is also present in those who suffer from mania, the opposite pole of depression and arguably associated with excess adrenergic stimulation. It is possible that this result is due to what Gellhorn and Loofbourrow (1963) have called "tuning"—a state of the ANS in which, owing to excess stimulation of one branch, either SNS or PNS, stimuli that ordinarily activate the other branch operate instead to augment activation of the first branch. Under such conditions, the usual relations between neurotransmitters and their effects may break down. Another possibility here is that, since mania and depression often go together, the potential for excess activation by ACh and excess activation by NE may coexist. A second result found by Nadi, Nurnberger, and Gershon (1984), which is not so easily explained, offers something of a puzzle for the Broverman hypothesis. It is that females display higher levels of the ACh effect than males. This is clearly contrary to the Broverman position.

Perhaps in light of the critiques and the results of investigations both by themselves and others, Broverman, Klaiber, and Vogel (1980) reformulated the analysis of the postulated brain mechanisms and sex hormone–neurotransmitter interactions involved in spatial ability differences between the sexes. The main victim of the second look was ACh, which was dropped from the revised version of the theory. The main burden of the analysis now rests on the effects of sex hormones on MAO and, through it, on NE. Broverman, Klaiber, and Vogel explicitly hypothesized that "the gonadal hormones E and T achieve their effects on the CNS via their regulatory influence on the enzyme MAO. MAO is found predominantly within the adrenergic neurons of the body where it metabolizes various monamines thought to be neurotransmitters for adrenergic nerves" (1980:65). Furthermore, "NE is believed to be a primary neurotransmitter of the central adrenergic nervous system [and] levels of NE are controlled in part by the intraneuronal metabolic activity of MAO" (Broverman, Klaiber, and Vogel 1980:66). The hormones E and T now come into the picture by affecting the level of MAO.

To support this new view, Broverman, Klaiber, and Vogel (1980), cited a number of animal and human studies. A 1963 study by Wurtman and Axelrod showed that female rats have lower MAO activity levels than male rats, that giving E to male rats lowered their MAO level to that of females, and that giving T to female rats elevated their MAO to the male level. This would appear to confirm a role for E and T in modulating MAO level differentially by sex. A 1966 study by Kobayashi et al. found that female rats whose ovaries (the principal source of E) had been surgically removed had higher MAO levels than intact females, but that administration of E lowered MAO activity to the normal female range. And in a series of studies (see Broverman, Klaiber, and Vogel (1980:67), researchers found that E and T had a significant effect on motor activity in rats because they provided differential stimulation of the central adrenergic system through their effect on MAO level. Broverman, Klaiber, and Vogel (1980) offered not only comparative data, but also human studies to establish their hypothesis. In 1971 Klaiber et al. showed that women in the premenstrual phase, when both E and progesterone (an antagonist of E) were high, had about twice the level of MAO activity as in the preovulatory phase, when only E was high. Further, they found that the normally high rate of MAO activity in amenorrheic and postmenopausal women was significantly reduced when E was administered.

At present, the Broverman hypothesis relies only on the action of E and T on the rate of MAO. E causes a decline, thus leaving a larger residue of NE to activate and arouse the CNS adrenergic system. T also diminishes MAO activity, but less so than E. The net effect is that compared with E, T leaves less NE to arouse and activate the central adrenergic system. The differential effects of the gonadal sex hormones thus explain the sex differences in MAO activity, central arousal, and, ultimately, at the end of this route, spatial ability.

Regrettably for the 1980 Broverman position, some more recent results remain mixed on the MAO version as well. Contrary to the hypothesis, Klinteberg et al. (1987) obtained results suggesting that low MAO activity (the normal female pattern according to Broverman et al. 1980) was associated with high spatial ability in both males and females. Also, Arque, Unzeta, and Torrubia (1988) and Klinteberg et al. (1987) found that males had lower MAO activity than females (the opposite of Broverman et al.'s claim). Nor is the issue entirely settled as to whether NE, the operative adrenergic-system stimulant, whose excess presence presumably prevents perceptual restructuring, varies by phase of the menstrual cycle, especially by level of E. Wasilewska, Kobus, and Bargiel (1980) found that it did, but Collins, Eneroth, and Landgren (1985) did not.

A Heuristic View of the Broverman Hypothesis

As can be seen, although there is evidence that favors the Broverman hypothesis, it is neither entirely satisfactory nor conclusive. But the lack of definitive status is less important than the opportunity the hypothesis offers for an exploration of the effects of social transformations on biological processes. I shall assume the validity of the Broverman hypothesis and examine whether or not it would be sustained today, not so much on the basis of its neurochemical mechanisms, but on the implicit social ones that may affect the neurochemistry of spatial ability. Broverman and his colleagues took this aspect of the biology of spatial relations entirely for granted.

My point of entry into the debate is T. If women's T levels, either tonic (baseline) or phasic (in response to stimuli), have changed in the years since Broverman et al. (1968) proposed their explanation of male-female differences in spatial ability, then even if their depiction of the operations of the adrenergic and cholinergic mechanisms were entirely correct, the hypothesis would no longer appear to be applicable. Although, in principle, neurochemically valid, it would no longer have a phenomenal world for it to explain.

I believe that the years since the original statement of the Broverman hypothesis in 1968 have seen more extensive changes in the social structural position of women in the United States than any other historical period. In education, occupation, sexuality, political and community standing, women have moved significantly toward equality and, in many individual instances, gained ascendancy. These social transformations were attained either through conflict, in which women were victorious and thus dominant, or through recognition of important social contributions and thus eminent. The biological surmise that links with these social transformations and attainments is that women's T levels have risen too, or surged more frequently, thus historically changing the average T/E balance of women and (assuming the explanatory mechanisms of the Broverman hypothesis to be accurate) improving women's ability to perform spatial tasks.

How do we go about examining this hypothesis that links a social and historical transformation to physiological events? Admittedly, not easily (see, e.g., Beaumont 1987). It would help enormously were comparative endocrinological data available on the testosterone titers of women at different historical times, but this is not the case. Nor are adequate epidemiological hormonal data available today on either men or women (Dai et al. 1981). This is because there is as yet little appreciation of the possibility that social change can transform biological parameters over time.

However, there is an important instance of such change involving women; namely, change in the age of menarche, a phenomenon that does not require arcane or technical procedures such as radioimmunoassay to establish. In 1860, the mean age of menarche in the United States was sixteen to seventeen; in 1960 it was twelve to thirteen (Melges and Hamburg 1977:272; see also Frisch 1988). Now, some may argue that menarche is strictly a biological event whose age of onset is strictly biological as well, largely due to the amount of fat intake in the diet. Proximally speaking, this is true. But it is socially blind to think that fat intake is unrelated to income distribution, opportunities for social mobility, ideologies of mobility and social justice, exploitative control of underclass populations, the social valuation of women, cultural norms for attractiveness, and so on. One of the most poignant literary depictions of this confluence of the social and the biological is found in Émile Zola's ([1885] 1968) novel *Germinal.* In the novel a young woman (sixteen) who works in a coal mine experiences her first menses while engaged in a violent episode between soldiers and miners striking for better working conditions and pay. Returning home, she collapses from stress and fatigue. Her mother, seeing blood on the girl's dress, fears that she had been shot during the melee, but soon realizes that the blood is her daughter's first menstrual flow. The year is perhaps 1865, and the exhausting physical labor imposed on lower-class children and women was common. Nor did the wage rate provide for a high-calorie diet. Though menarche is obviously a biological event, it is also socially determined in a manner that is perhaps not yet fully appreciated.

Although menarche almost invariably occurs, despite the extremity of the social conditions—which is what gives it, in part, its appearance as a strictly biological variable—the three- to four-year historical variation in age of onset is socially determined and, in addition, has important consequences for such matters as the repression of sexuality and the enforcement of sex norms, the practice of courtship, and the conflict of biological and social pressure on both men and women. Just as age of menarche, a biological event, has social determinants, so, too, do other biological processes, such as health, illness, longevity, cause of death, and physical stature.

Further evidence of social determination of female biological function is found in Rossi and Rossi (1977), who charted menstrual periodicity in a sample of young women according to days of the week. Rossi and Rossi found that when menstruation or ovulation occurred on a weekend, it produced a significant increase in positive mood; but the mood was depressed when either of these phases of the cycle occurred during the week. Hence, the body was found to be responsive to "social time."

Here I frankly speculate that hormonal titers that putatively mediate a cognitive process are also susceptible to social determination. In extending the reach of the social in this way, I perhaps risk offending both biological and social scientists, the former because they may resent the imposition of a view so distant from their own on the results of the laboratory, and the latter because they may resent having to grant legitimacy to any form of biological explanation, when the social sciences developed in part to afford an alternative to such explanations. The effort here must, inevitably, complicate matters for both disciplines. Biologists must indeed come to recognize the social forces that affect and modify biological processes and to realize that they are as important to understand as the proximal biophysiochemical vectors (nutrition, disease, climate, toxic substances, and the like) that affect bodily structure and function. Social scientists, on the other hand, must acknowledge that social processes work through the bodies of individual organisms, as Collins (1981), Turner (1984), and Freund (1988) recognize, and that to ignore how the social translates its effects via the body is to miss how the antecedent social events actually create some of the consequent social effects.

Perper (1985) has intelligently dealt with this issue as a biologist, recognizing fully the important complementary, rather than preemptive, contributions of biologists and social scientists to the understanding of human sexuality (see also Hamburg 1974). Several candidly feminist analysts have taken the argument a step further, arguing that even at the level of brain anatomy and function, social experience makes a difference (Petersen and Hood 1980; Lowe 1983). Indeed, it is unlikely that any complex human process—whether ostensibly biological or social—can be fully understood without a bio and social approach, extended here to the socio-bio-social level.

To return now to the examination of how women's T level might have changed historically, I will examine the issue from three perspectives: female aggression and dominance, female sexuality, and female occupational involvement and attainment. I chose these because they are areas in which there are, to varying degrees, comparable data for males to provide benchmarks for our inferences from the data on females. The crucial question is whether T is related to these behavioral conditions in females as it is in males. If this proves to be the case, the next question is whether greater amounts of aggression and dominance, more assertive sexuality, and higher occupational involvement and attainment produce changes in T in females as we have reason to believe they do in males. The data are incomplete in regard to these questions, but enough is known to suggest that in certain though not all, social conditions, female biology works approximately the way it does for males. And, if this is the case, the Broverman hypothesis may have been transcended, not by an improved biological understanding, but by a social transformation of the conditions that made Broverman et al. (1968) possibly correct at one time and wrong at another.

Relatively little attention is given today to the Broverman hypothesis directly, but the notion that hormonal processes may underlie sex differences in spatial ability has not been abandoned. Indeed, a renewed attack on the problem in recent years has shifted from what is understood as the "activation" perspective to the "organization" perspective. In studies of brain function, activation signifies that whenever hormones or neurotransmitters are present in requisite amounts they set a particular process in motion. Organization, on the other hand, signifies that at a certain stage in (usually fetal) development, the brain has been structured by hormonal action so that it is capable of reacting in certain ways or of triggering certain processes at suitable points later in time. Where organization is necessary, failure to organize suitably will make it impossible for the brain to perform in the given way, even if all other conditions (usually hormonal) are right.

Clear examples of organization and activation can be seen in the following: If the fetal brain of a genetic (XY) male is not dosed with T at a given stage, it will not develop male external genital characteristics (Strand 1983; Martin 1988). No amount of T at a later date will activate these processes. Activation, on the other hand, may be seen in such results as the masculinizing of the behavior of female adult animals when they are dosed with testosterone (Bouissou 1983; Beach 1977:250ff.).

Broverman's is an activation hypothesis, and it depends implicitly on a balance between the amounts of T and E reaching the brain. Both males and females produce both T and E, although to different degrees. On average, male T levels are about ten times higher than T levels in females (Sherwin, Gelfand, and Brender 1985:342; Susman et al. 1987; Udry and Talbert 1988); and female E levels, which depend on the stage of the menstrual cycle, are for the most part many multiples higher than E in males. As with virtually all hormones, the absolute amounts present in the body are exceedingly small. T for example, is measure in such magnitudes as three to ten billionths of a gram per milliliter of blood serum, the normal range for human males (Nieschlag 1979). E is measured in such magnitudes as nine hundred trillionths of a gram per milliliter of blood serum, which is about the average E surge at the time of ovulation (Broverman et al. 1981). Any conditions that change the T/E balance are likely to change the effects that depend on either hormone separately or in combination.

I shall first treat the Broverman hypothesis and its possible historical and sociological modification from an activation perspective, on the assumption that changes in T, E, or the T/E balance will affect the distribution of spatial ability. In the last part of this chapter I will consider the issue from an organizational perspective, reflecting on how fetal brain development might be affected by changes in social patterns.

Spatial Ability and Testosterone

According to the Broverman hypothesis, spatial ability is superior in males because T activates the adrenergic system less than does E, hence the cholinergic system, which presumably allows for cognitive inhibition in problem solution, attains a relative dominance.[4] It should follow from this that the level of T in individuals is related to their ability to perform tasks requiring cognitive inhibition. Such a demonstration would at least support one element in the Broverman proposal. The actual results of investigations of T and spatial ability are, surprisingly, more supportive of the Broverman position in the case of females than in the case of males.

Keeping in mind that males have T titers on the order of ten times that of females, Klaiber, Broverman, and Kobayashi (1967) found that strong automatizers—who are weaker in spatial ability—displayed physiques that indicated higher T. Muscular development in both males and females is related to T, which is an anabolic steroid (Strand 1983). This is why steroids are sometimes given to athletes. Ferguson and Maccoby (in Maccoby 1966) also found the same negative relationship between indices of anatomical effects of T and spatial ability in boys. This means that boys with lower levels of T were better cognitive inhibitors. (This does not bear on the relation between T and E at the level of central adrenergic arousal, since even at relatively low levels of T, males still have grossly greater amounts of T than E.) Also using indices of physical development, Petersen (1976) found a curvilinear relationship between T and spatial abilty. Relatively high or low testosterone values were related to poorer spatial ability. Broverman et al. (1981) also have subscribed to the optimum level hypothesis. On the other hand, Christiansen and Knussman (1987b) have challenged the curvilinear thesis, arguing that physique and other features of sexual maturation, such as pubic hair, which the earlier investigators have used, are not determined by T, but by other androgens. Christiansen and Knussman found a direct relationship between spatial ability and blood serum level of T.

The pattern for females has shown, in all studies, a direct relationship between spatial ability and supposed indices of T. Ferguson and Maccoby (in Maccoby 1966) and Petersen (1976) found that spatial ability in females was related to higher body androgenization. An investigation of college basketball players (reported in Lederman 1989) found that female players were superior academically to male players. Although Lederman also found that the female players spent approximately five more hours per week on academic work, we may wonder whether or not their almost certainly more androgenized physique (compared with the female average) may also reflect an androgenization that would enhance their skill in mathematics, for example, and improve their grades. (It is tempting to wonder too whether such skills are related also to their ability to play basketball, a game that is dependent on accurate spatial judgment.) Waber (1981) found that girls who attained menarche relatively late were also superior in spatial ability. Age of menarche is affected by the pubertal E surge, with high amounts in early menarche girls. Thus, the Broverman hypothesis is again supported by hormonal evidence: females, who are ordinarily far lower in T than males, perform better on spatial tasks when their hormonal profile is more like that of males. Medical pathology also provides support for the Broverman hypothesis. Females with Turner's syndrome, which is marked by a lack of gonadal T, are particularly poor in tests of visuospatial ability (Hines 1982; Nyborg 1984). On the other hand, girls with androgenital syndrome, in which there was an excess of fetal T, have shown enhanced performance on spatial tasks (Resnick et al. 1986).

In light of these findings, some investigators (e.g., McGee 1982) believe that not the absolute, but rather the relative amount of each hormone—the androgen/estrogen balance—may provide an optimum hormonal foundation for spatial ability. Within the framework of the activation perspective, this would suggest that any factors or conditions that modify the balance would act to modify spatial task competence.

With regard to such modifications, it has been suggested (Geschwind and Galaburda 1985, pt. 1) that the lower the normal level of a particular hormone, the greater will be the effect of an increment, either by infusion or by natural secretion (see also Ellis 1982). For males, relatively large increases or decreases would be needed to change the hormonal effects; whereas for females relatively small changes in T level could produce relatively large effects. Numerous conditions are known to affect hormonal levels aside from the dominance/eminence—testosterone effects already discussed, and in some cases the effects vary by sex. For example, stress appears to affect male T levels adversely (Kreuz, Rose, and Jennings 1972), while it may increase T in females. This is because the major loci of T production are different in the two sexes. The main site in males is the testes. Adrenocorticotropic hormone (ACTH), produced by the pituitary in stressful conditions, inhibits gonadotropin-releasing hormone (GnRH), which is required for testicular T production (Ward 1974). A main site of T production in females is the adrenal cortex. ACTH induces the secretion of adrenal corticosteroids, including T.

Exercise, too, can affect T levels in both males and females. Shangold, Gatz, and Thysen (1981) found that moderate exercise elevated T levels in females between 12 and 61 percent. The effects were markedly different depending on stage of the menstrual cycle, with large increases occurring in the follicular (preovulatory) phase and minimal increases in the luteal (postovulatory) phase.

For present purposes it is enough to recognize that relatively large swings in the T titer of females can occur, although countervailing conditions, such as menstrual phase, may nullify some of the effects. If, according to the Broverman hypothesis, spatial ability is affected by the balance of sex hormones, then it should follow that conditions that modify the balance will also modify the ability. We turn now to some of those conditions in the social domain.

Female Aggression, Power, Dominance, and Testosterone

Social ideologies are designed to justify and legitimize existing social arrangements of power and status. Ordinarily, those with more power and more status preach the ideology to those who are lower on these hierarchies. The most successful ideologies are adopted as true by those they are designed to pacify; hence, social inferiors come to accept their inferiority as right, proper, just, natural, or otherwise legitimate (Kemper 1974). Yet, even where this occurs, rarely does an ideology succeed completely. There are always some who doubt and who resist the existing distribution of social benefits and the ideas that rationalize them. These exceptions are the creators of social change.

For a long time, although varying to some degree with shifting technologies and consequent patterns of social organization, the major ideology of male-female relations has specified male ascendance and female subordination. Only in very recent times has this ideology been subjected to institutional and public rejection. In most of the advanced societies of the West, both law and public policy proclaim the equality of the sexes. Actual practice, in many cases, has not yet caught up with the formal enactments, but the trend is clear despite the cultural lag. The new perspective legitimizes women as well as men as leaders of social hierarchies in government, business, the community and, while it has not been and perhaps cannot be legislated, in the home. However, until relatively recently, preeminence for women could not be seriously contemplated. Existing social arrangements of male dominance precluded preeminence for women, and the intensely mobilized ideology of that dominance forbade it as well. Not only were there ideological proscriptions against women assuming certain occupational positions and hierarchical ascendance, but there were, and we may assume that to a great extent there still remain, prescriptive models of the "normal," "natural," and desirable personality of women.

In a classic study that occasions no little irony, since it includes among its authors the selfsame Broverman whose hypothesis occupies us here, I. Broverman et al. (1970) examined the assumptions of psychotherapists about what constituted a healthy female personality. The results are instructive. Such traits as dependent, gentle, subjective, not competitive, and aware of the feelings of others were deemed by a sample of clinicians to characterize mentally healthy females. Significantly, the healthy traits do not include dominance, ascendance, or other power- or status-oriented characteristics that are attributed to males. Indeed, the psychotherapeutic ideology—not much different from that of the general population—relegated women to a subordinate position in relation to males.[5]

My point is that this does not accord with what we are increasingly coming to know about females. Across the spectrum of the social sciences, the results show that females are not essentially pacific, retiring, unaggressive, lacking in motives and psychological needs for power and dominance. While successful ideological socialization may persuade many women that this is true of themselves, it is not biologically true. Hrdy (1981), who has studied a number of animal species, states the case as firmly as anyone: It would be a mistake to think that the female of many species could afford to be unaggressive, especially in defense or her offspring, nor, as the evidence shows, is she unassertive in sexual relations.

> Throughout millions of years of evolution, mammalian mothers have differed from one another in two important ways: in their capacity to

> produce and care for offspring and in their ability to enlist the support of males, or at least to forestall them from damaging their infants. Female primates have differed from one another in their capacity to influence the reproductive careers of their descendants. Here is a sex wide open to natural selection and evolution has weighed heavily upon it. Those same forces which predisposed females to intelligence and assertiveness also selected the highly competitive individuals among them. This is the dark underside of the feminist dream. If it is shown—as I believe it will be—that there are no important differences between males and females in intelligence, initiative, or administrative and political capabilities, that women are no less qualified in these areas than men are, one has to accept also that these potentials did not appear gratuitously as a gift from Nature. Competition was the trial by fire from which these capacities emerged. The feminist ideal of a sex less egotistical, less competitive by nature, less interested in dominance . . . is a dream that may not be well founded.
>
> . . . There is also little to be gained from countermyths that emphasize women's natural innocence from lust for power. . . . Such a female never evolved among the other primates (189–190).

Reviewing a large body of literature on nonprimate species, Floody (1983) also concluded that females exhibit quite variable levels of aggression, depending on the species and the circumstances. Moyer (1974) set forth conditions that usually trigger female aggression. Thus, males are not universally the more aggressive sex. Shaw and Darling (1985) argued forcefully that across the broad spectrum of species females are often the more aggressive—perhaps assertive would be the more suitable term—sex in seeking sexual contact. As social norms concerning human sexuality change, female sexual assertiveness is more and more noted. Indeed, sex therapists now indicate a trend in which males are increasingly the sexually reluctant partners (*New York Times,* January 12, 1985, sec. I, 8.).

The advantages of aggressive behavior and dominance, as indicated by Hrdy, are sexual attention and the greater likelihood of survival of offspring. Keverne's (1979) study of talapoin monkeys confirmed these benefits. Like males, the females of this species form social hierarchies. Comparing the highest-ranking females with the lowest one, the former were more aggressive toward other animals and were clearly more attractive to males; while the latter received considerable amounts of aggression, particularly from other females, and was considerable less attractive to males, so had fewer offspring. Similar differences in reproductive success according to dominance rank have been noted among gelada baboons (Dunbar and Dunbar 1977).

Among humans, too, despite ideological proscriptions, female aggressiveness is widely manifest. Women and men are equal in rates of nonlethal family violence (Straus, Gelles, and Steinmetz 1980). Women are more abusive than men when it comes to children (Gelles 1972; Gil 1979). Although this has been explained by the fact that women spend more time with children than do men, the point of interest here is that women are abusive at all. Reviewing seventy-two experimental studies in which male and female aggression could be compared, Frodi, Macaulay, and Thome (1977) found that males did not exceed females in 61 percent of them. In a metaanalysis of sixty-nine studies, Hyde (1986) found that males exceeded females in aggression by about half a standard deviation. However, this varied by age (younger people were more aggressive than older people), setting (more aggression occurred in natural than in experimental settings), and type (physical aggression was greater than verbal aggression). Male superiority in aggression has thus been confirmed, but far from universally so.

Studies of male and female personality also show that females are as capable of high need for power as males (see, e.g., Stewart and Rubin 1976), nor is a high power role unfamiliar when females are asked to play it (Sadalla, Kenrick, and Vershure 1987). Gutmann (1977) has proposed that this is in keeping with a developmental trend in which women tend to rise in dominance with age while men tend to decline. This view is also consonant with the rising number of women who are attaining high political office (National Women's Political Caucus 1987), although the major explanation resides in the greater acceptance in American society of women as political leaders.

As presented in chapter 2, dominance and dominance-oriented aggression among males is associated with higher levels of T. Relatively little is known about the hormonal profile of dominant females, but the available data suggest that female dominance is also associated with elevated level of T. Working with a social group of *Macaca speciosa* monkeys, Kling and Dunne (1976) found that among females, social rank correlated with T level. In an experimental manipulation in which the highest-ranking female was reduced to low rank, her T level declined over time, while the levels of previously lower ranked animals rose. These results were also observed in males and reproduce the usual pattern of results in males, which show the relationship between social rank and T in periods of hierarchy formation or change (Mendoza 1984; Rose, Bernstein, and Gordon 1972). Injections of T into females of higher mammalian species also showed some relation between social rank and aggression (Bouissou 1983). Female rank tended to increase, apparently through a changed response to the aggression of other animals; the injected animals were less likely to yield or give ground when attacked.

Among humans, direct studies of the hormonal correlates of female aggression are extremely scarce. Some indirect evidence has been provided by "natural experiments" in which a physiological anomaly provided an opportunity to study an infrequently occurring phenomenon. In the condition of congenital adrenal hyperplasia (CAH), also known as adrenogenital syndrome or Cushing's syndrome (Ehrhardt and Baker 1974), an individual is unable to manufacture adequate amounts of cortisol in the adrenal glands. Due to the feedback nature of the adrenal system, the absence of cortisol means that the pituitary receives no signal to shut off adrenal stimulation. In females, the adrenal gland is the source of about 50 percent of total T (Abraham 1974); thus, the abnormal condition leads to excess production of this hormone. In some cases, CAH in females produces hirsutism and masculinization of the genitals; for example, enlargement of the clitoris. These effects are understood to result from excess androgens, including T. In a group of female victims of CAH, subjects were more energetic, more tomboyish, less "feminine" in orientation, and less interested in conventional female topics or goals than a control group of normal females and their normal siblings or mothers (Money and Ehrhardt 1972; Ehrhardt and Baker 1974). However, both Parsons (1980) and Martin (1988) have argued against interpreting a direct androgenic effect in the case of CAH females. They noted that the more masculine behavior syndrome may have resulted from differential treatment or from androgenically induced larger bone structure, which would have allowed these females to participate in the usually rougher sports engaged in by males.

In another study of a natural experiment, Reinisch (1981) compared children whose mothers had received progestin (an androgenic compound) treatments during pregnancy, with same-sex siblings whose gestation had no progestin involvement. Reinisch found that the exposed children (girls as well as boys) were significantly higher in physical aggression, although not in verbal aggression, than their siblings. These results are especially interesting since, unlike the CAH females (Money and Ehrhardt 1972), who were identified as "different" early in life, the children in the Reinisch study had never been identified as having a medical condition related to the mother's hormone treatment and were recruited into the sample from physicians' prescription records. It should be noted that the studies of both CAH and progestin children are organizational in nature, dealing with androgenic events in the fetal stage. Given the paucity of activation data, these are necessarily of interest.

No current T measures were obtained by Reinisch, so we do not know whether there was a dominance-T relationship among her subjects. Udry and Talbert (1988) found that, in a sample of teenage females, T was associated positively with a personality item labeled "dominance."

However, in a study of normal female adolescents, Susman et al. (1987) found no relationship between T level and personality or aggressive behavioral traits, although the usual positive pattern was found for boys. But this study was marked by an acknowledged methodological ambiguity because menarche-related hormonal variation was not controlled: 65 percent of subjects were premenarchal, hence were of uncertain hormonal status (Susman et al. 1987:1119). On the other hand, in a study of imprisoned adult females, Dabbs et al. (1988) more or less replicated the results of studies done with imprisoned males (Kreuz and Rose 1972; Ehrenkranz, Bliss, and Sheard 1974; Dabbs et al. 1987), in which a more aggressive or dominant pattern, either in biography or in current behavior was correlated with higher levels of T. Dabbs et al. (1988) found that women convicted of crimes of unprovoked violence had a higher T level than women who were imprisoned for theft or who had committed violence only after serious provocation, such as physical assault. T was also related positively to the number of previous criminal charges. In another study, which appears consonant with the results obtained by Dabbs et al. (1988), Ehlers, Rickler, and Hovey (1980) found that among women presenting a variety of neuropsychiatric complaints, higher T level was associated with a record of greater violence in social relations.

These few results provide some evidence that among females the pattern of endocrinology and dominance and aggression is similar to that usually found among human and infrahuman males. The results may be seen as more persuasive because serum T levels are heritable in males. Turner et al. (1986) found correlations of +.50 for fraternal twins and +.69 for identical twins. These results take on more meaning when it is noted that 61 percent of the variance in "social potency," a personality variable marked by frequent dominance and ascendancy in social interaction, is genetic in origin (Tellegen et al. 1988).

If a substantial part of the variance here is genetically based, it may seem as if the Broverman hypothesis, which depends on CNS modulation by T and E, can never be satisfied by women whose tonic levels of T are genetically limited and are normally low to begin with. Yet, it is not clear exactly what degree of T/E balance creates the effect that Broverman et al. (1968) claim is present in females and hinders their ability in the area of spatial relations. Indeed, only slight additions of T may be necessary to change the T/E ratio suficiently to enhance female spatial ability. In addition, although females have much less T than males, they are perhaps more sensitive to its effects (Parsons 1980; Nyborg 1984). Udry and Talber (1988) estimate that the magnitude of this greater sensitivity may be as much as five. Furthermore, although only a few studies (Kling and Dunne 1976; Ehlers, Rickler, and Hovey 1980) even comparatively show that female T level rises with social rank or with aggressive action, the results suggest that the social processes that lead to elevations of T in males do so also in females. If this is the case, there is ground for believing that a historical change in the social rank of women may achieve a sufficient transformation in the T/E balance to satisfy the requirements of the Broverman hypothesis for perceptual inhibition in the CNS.

Some part of the elevation of T that results from the transformation in women's social roles can be accounted for by greater involvement in occupational niches that allow for dominance in daily social encounters. I will deal with this below. Here I wish to address another ground for T elevation; namely, the emotional accompaniment of the emergence in the past two decades of a women's movement dedicated to change. Particularly in its mobilization phase, a social movement consists of both a pattern of social organization—individuals united in networks to engage in purposive action—and also, importantly, a reservoir of the emotions of its members. We may suppose that the dominant collective emotion of any social movement devoted to the liberation of its members from oppresssion is anger. Fed by the private resentments and ires of its members, the movement appropriates and legitimates these feelings, directing the underlying energy into instrumental activities—whether doorbell ringing, letter writing, picketing, or guerrilla warfare—to forward the group's agenda.

But anger is the emotion most closely associated with aggression (Berkowitz 1962) and a possible precursor of dominance when the aggression succeeds. In some respects, the women's movement has flourished on the energy of the anger—previously repressed or suppressed—that it has released. Both in the home and in the community, that energy has been a lever of social change. Propelled to a new self-regard by the very existence of the movement, many women have sought to direct their released emotion into constructive channels. For example, the widely available courses in assertiveness training have been taken mainly by women in the hundreds of thousands. In countless microinteractions, women have claimed and assumed rights and privileges previously reserved only for men. To attain equality is justly regarded as a victory by women. Out of such victories, I believe, has come an ascendant mood that is hormonally instigating.

Although individual women are more or less deeply touched by the emotions of liberation and by experiences of anger and triumph, the collective experience of women cannot fail to be transmitted to all women. A new pride, self-regard, and identification with a buoyant social force is women's heritage in recent years. Even minimal participation in the successes of the movement can, I believe, change the emotional, hence the endocrinological, profile of women. If defeat, as has been found for both males and females, reduces T level, then liberation from the tortures that follow defeat in daily life may affect T level as well. Even if it means only that the genetically set tonic level is maintained, as opposed to being depressed through subordination, it would, on average, provide for a higher level than was the case before the women's movement emerged.

Whether the higher T that we attribute to the emergence of a female consciousness and pattern of organization that rejects subordination is enough to change the hormonal balance in favor of improved spatial abilities is a matter of conjecture. But if Broverman et al. (1968) are right, and if women's rising social stature and assertiveness produces increased T, as the data suggest, then improvements in spatial ability should follow as well.

Female Sexuality and Testosterone

In a seminal article, Beach (1976) conceptualized the female contribution to intersex relations according to three aspects: *attractivity,* a female's stimulus value in evoking sexual responses from males; *proceptivity,* the degree to which a female assumes the initiative in sexual relations with males; and *receptivity,* the degree to which a female's responses are those that are necessary and sufficient for male intravaginal ejaculation. Based on the existing animal literature, Beach assigned an endocrinological locus for each of these aspects of female sexuality.

Attractivity is apparently most affected by ovarian hormones, of which the most prominent is E, although about half of female T also comes from the ovaries. E is related to a number of female stimulus characteristics that can have incentive value for males, including body fat, perspiration, and (for infrahuman species) vaginal odors that become prominent at estrus. Proceptivity, according to Beach, is also partly determined by E, but also by T or other androgens. Proceptivity is considered an analog of libido, or desire. Behaviorally, it is marked by affiliative or solicitational behavior, physical contact, and, in some species, "pseudoretreat," which entails alternating approach and withdrawal behavior—what we might anthropomorphically call "teasing." Finally, receptivity, which is highest during the period of highest E around ovulation, is also affected by T, which also tends to peak at midcycle.

Beach's important contribution was to permit a more careful examination of components of female sexuality, even in humans, in relation to hormone states, and a significant amount of research has ensued. Our greatest interest here is in the results involving T. In animal research, Everitt and Herbert (1971) and Michael et al. (1972) found female proceptivity to be enhanced when T levels were elevated pharmacologically. Keverne (1976) found that augmenting T level in female rhesus monkeys (a species whose sexual patterns are considered close to those of humans; see Luttge 1971) led to faster pressing of a lever for access to a male, while ceasing to augment T in these females led to a decline in this indicator of proceptivity.

In regard to humans, Money proposed that T affects female sexuality by sensitizing the clitoris (1961:1391). In a similar vein, Davidson, Kwan, and Greenleaf (1982) proposed that T agonizes sexual response in males by providing a pleasurable gonadal sensitivity to sexual thought and behavior. With higher levels or more frequent surges of T, one is likely to be more active in seeking sexual gratification. The same arousing property of T may hold also for females, and thus may explain the associations that Beach found in his review of the animal literature. Human studies have been done only relatively recently.

Persky et al. (1982) addressed a range of questions about women's sexuality in relation to both E and T. They postulated four stages of the sexual response cycle for females: sexual desire, sexual excitement or arousal, intercourse (with orgasm), and overall gratification. (The first and second phases appear to encompass proceptivity, while the third implies receptivity.) Persky et al. found that T was significantly related to each of these stages, though not with orgasmic frequency. By contrast, estradiol, the principal ovarian estrogen, did not correlate significantly with any of the four sexual stages.

These results have been confirmed to varying degrees, depending on the particular aspects of sexuality studied. Morris et al. (1987) found that married women with higher titers of T at midcycle also had the highest mean frequency of intercourse over the whole menstrual cycle. The data, based also on the husbands of the subjects, showed no evidence that higher T makes the wives more attractive or increases the husbands' motivation for intercourse. (I will come back to this point below.) The researchers also found that phasically higher T level was not associated with intercourse on the day, or plus or minus one day, of the elevated level. Thus, T does not necessarily lead to immediate behavioral effects, although it appears to have a much more rapid effect on sexual thoughts. Bancroft et al. (1983) sought to establish a variety of effects of the menstrual cycle on mood and sexuality, including the effects of variations in endocrine levels. Average T level was correlated with masturbation frequency (a proceptivity indicator when a male partner is not available), although it had a negative effect on frequency of intercourse.[6]

Studies of simple sexual arousal also support the enhancing role of T. Schreiner-Engel et al. (1981) found that both subjective and physiological indices of arousal from sexually stimulating materials were positively correlated with T level. But, as Bancroft et al. (1983) also reported, higher T was inversely associated with frequency of intercourse and with satisfying social relations in general. Myers and Morokoff (1986) also found that women with either naturally high levels of T or augmented T through replacement therapy experienced greater subjective physical sensations in response to erotic videotapes, as well as greater vaginal lubrication and breast sensations. Actual genital reactions showed a trend toward significant correlation with T.

Yet another body of research supports the enhancing effect of T on female sexuality. This involves therapeutic use of androgens when there are libidinal problems that are either psychologically or surgically induced. Carney, Bancroft, and Mathews (1978) and Bancroft and Skakkebaek (1979) found that women with anorgasmic or low-libido complaints significantly improved in their degree of arousal and pleasant feelings during sexual contact after treatment with T. In a more complex set of studies, Sherwin, Gelfand, and Brender (1985) studied the effects of different combinations of E and T as replacement therapy for women who were menopausal due to removal of ovaries in a complete hysterectomy. It will be recalled that the ovaries not only produce E, but also are one of the two major sources of T for women. The results showed that T was clearly related to increased sexual desire, arousal, and sexual fantasy, but, as in several other studies, E was not.

E was also found not to be related to vaginal atrophy—a condition in which vaginal elasticity, depth, lubrication, and other aspects have deteriorated from optimum—in postmenopausal women (Leiblum et al. 1983). However, T was an even better predictor of optimal vaginal condition than regular intercourse.

The relationship between female sexuality and T not only holds for adult women, but also helps to initiate sexuality in the immediate postpubertal stage. Udry, Talbert, and Morris (1986) investigated differential sexual involvement of teenage women and found that T and other androgens (dehydroepiandrosterone, or DHEA, and delta-4 androstenedione were positively related to thoughts about sex, expectations of future sexual involvement, masturbation, and other sexual experiences (excluding coitus). The proceptive and libido elements of arousal are clearly evident here.

Despite the trend of findings involving T in female sexual activity, some seemingly nonconfirmatory results have also appeared. Cutler et al. (1986) investigated the hormonal status of young adult women who had intercourse at least weekly, only sporadically, or not at all, and uncovered no relationship to T. Similarly, McCoy, Cutler, and Davidson (1985) found no association between T and sexual activity in a group of perimenopausal women. Although negative, neither of these results is as antagonistic to the T hypothesis as may first appear. As Cutler et al. (1986) acknowledged, no attempt was made to measure proceptive or "desire" components of sexual activity, to which T has been most definitively linked. Intercourse, the dependent variable in these studies, depends also on the interests and availabilty of a male partner. A number of factors, including social norms for who may legitimately initiate intercourse behavior, operate to modify purely hormonal effects. The same is not true for desire or libido, which can arise from internal hormonal activation independent of partner variables (see discussion in chapter 2 of similar issues involving males).

Another apparently contrary result showed no difference in T level between women suffering from inhibited sexual desire (ISD) and a group of otherwise comparable sexually normal women (Stuart, Hammond, and Pett 1987). The investigators did find important differences in sexual attitudes of parents and in the quality of the marital relationship. Anger at one's partner has been found to modify significantly sexual interest in one's partner (Rubin 1976; Kaplan 1974; Bozman and Beck 1988). Fear, too, is an emotional antagonist of sexual arousal (Kaplan 1974). Hence, the relationship between T and libido may be restricted to the condition where antagonistic social and autonomic conditions are not present.

Perhaps the most damaging evidence against the proposed role of T in enhancing sexual desire in females comes in research by Schreiner-Engel and her colleagues (1989). Comparing a small sample (N = 17) of low-libido women with normal controls (N = 13), they found no differences in T at any stage of the menstrual cycle, nor between the most impaired and least impaired low-libido women, or between those whose libido impairment was lifelong as opposed to more recently acquired. This is a carefully done study whose defect may be in its small sample sizes, which may have allowed a type II error, in which differences that are found, although real, are not large enough to reject the hypothesis that they might have occurred by chance alone. Yet another caveat converning these results is offered by the researchers themselves: A "significant portion" of the low-libido women "had positive histories of psychopathology, and in particular, affective disorders." The loss of libido was found to have occurred "during or after the first affective episode" (231). Thus, we are left with a somewhat ambiguous result. Like the prisoners in the original Kinsey data (see Gebhard et al. 1965, and discussion in chapter 2 above), the low-libido women suffering from affective disorders may represent a distinctly different population, with characteristics that override dispositions that would normally be activated by T.

In chapter 2 I proposed that the T that results from a successful dominance/eminence encounter can augment male sexual activity through a number of possible mechanisms. Given that T seems to augment sexual interest in females, it is at least possible that T in females has a further parallel with T effects in males: in sexual encounters, success also provokes a T surge. One kind of sexual success for a female would be to attract a desirable male who provides a satisfying sexual experience. Perper (1985) has helpfully shown that notions of a "natural" female reticence in matter of sexuality are not supported either biologically or socially. Rather, he suggests, females are selective in their proceptivity, willing to encourage some males, but not others. In recent years, the data suggest that at least in English-speaking countries, where many of the strongest effects of the women's movement and improved standing of women have been felt, there has also been an increase in sexual activity among young women.

This social and behavioral change must be factored into the present context to understand how it can affect present-day T levels in females. One of the most important of these is female participation in nonmarital sexual intercourse, whether prior to marriage or outside it. Numerous studies confirm that among unmarrried women, recent years have seen higher rates of intercourse than earlier in this century. Ford, Zelnick, and Kanter (1981) found that in 1971 some 27 percent of young women in the United States aged fifteen to nineteen had intercourse, but only a few years later, in 1976, the figure had risen to 35 percent (see also *New York Times,* October 7, 1987 sec. B, 7). A Canadian study found that intercourse rates among female college students rose from 32 percent in 1968 to 58 percent in 1978 (Barret 1980). Similar results were obtained in data from England (Anderson and McCance 1984).

Yet another indicator of the development of female sexual behavior in recent years is the increase in rates of extramarital coitus by women. Kinsey et al. (1953) found a rate of 26 percent by age forty. Hunt (1974) suggested that this figure was an overestimate because Kinsey included an unrepresentatively large proportion of divorced women. According to Hunt, a more accurate figure for the Kinsey data would be 20 percent. Hunt's own study found an overall rate of 18 percent.

Most revealing was that Kinsey et al. (1953) found only 8 percent of wives under twenty-four years had engaged in extramarital coitus, but Hunt found that 24 percent had done so. Bell and Peltz (1974) reported that 26 percent of their sample had had extramarital intercourse by age thirty-five, five years in advance of the same (uncorrected) rate for the Kinsey group. They estimated that by age forty, the rate would be 40 percent. Indeed, Tavris and Sadd (1975) found that 38 percent of women married ten years or more acknowledged extramarital relations, although the overall rate was 29 percent. In something of a reversion, Pietropinto and Simenauer (1979) reported an overall rate of 17 percent. But more striking results were in the offing, reported by Hite (1987): 70 percent of women married more than five years had had extramarital intercourse. Even if this figure is wildly off the mark for American women (Hite has been severely faulted for her sampling methods), it nonetheless suggests substantial evolution in sexuality by women since Broverman et al. published their work in 1968.

Not only have intercourse rates increased in recent years, the data also show that women are less inhibited than previously in sexual fantasy and in arousal to erotic stimuli (Brody 1986; Rubinsky et al. 1987). This indicates a general condition of greater sexual confidence and freedom, partly due to the availability of relatively reliable contraceptives, particularly the birth control pill. But it is due also to the independence women have gained through entry into the labor force. As they earn their living, they are also unshackled from traditional views of sexuality, especially the patriarchal forms in which women were a kind of chattel who were to be traded as *virginae intactae* for the purpose of procreation. A permissive sexuality in former times could not so easily have guaranteed female submissiveness and masculine ascendancy. Feminist authors (Firestone 1970; Greer 1970) point out that control of women's bodies by men is the deepest and strongest form of patriarchy. Hence the release of women's sexuality represents another domain in which dominance can be achieved. There is evidence, too, that dominance as a personality trait favors sexuality among females, just as it does among males. Keller, Elliott, and Gunberg (1982) found that sexually active young women manifested dominance as an important personality attribute, while virginal women did not.

Sexual liberation and social dominance are not unmixed blessings. I have deferred until now a discussion of some results, mentioned above, that show that just as social dominance may create problematic conditions for males, it may do so also for females. Both Schreiner-Engel et al. (1981) and Bancroft et al. (1983) found, somewhat surprisingly, that while women with higher levels of T had higher libidinal capacity, they had lower rates of intercourse. Bancroft et al. (1988) suggested, and with good reason, I believe, that the effects of higher T in women may complicate interpersonal relations so that intimacy is less often achieved. This may be for two reasons. One is that more career-oriented attitudes and activities may reduce both the time and interest available for pursuit of noncareer goals such as marriage and stable intimate relations. A corroborative finding is that women with more than twelve years of education begin marriage with lower rates of intercourse than less-educated women, and that rate declines more steeply than that of less-educated women after four years of marriage (Udry 1980).

An alternative explanation of higher-T women's lower rates of intercourse, despite apparently high levels of proceptivity, is that T's associated personality traits of disinhibition, autonomy, activity, and spontaneity (Daitzman, et al. 1978) may collide with male concepts of dominance and preeminence in intergender relations. If this is so, higher-T women may experience more difficulty in relations with men. This is consistent with the significant acceleration in the divorce rate around 1960, just as the women's movement got underway. Further, it is useful to understand that among the best predictors of divorce or a woman's considering divorce is that she holds, or has held a job (Huber and Spitze 1980; Booth and White 1980). Indeed, employment, as we will show below, is a domain for possible enhancement of female T.

Some additional support for the notion of more difficult intergender relations for higher-T women is available from data on the "marriage gradient" (Bernard 1972). Up to at least very recently, men have chosen women as mates who were inferior to them in important social dimensions, mainly having to do with power and status, and reflected in such attributes as income, education, and occupational prestige. The existence of the marriage gradient supports the idea that women who are higher in T (associated in some way with their greater attainment) will be precisely those who will tend to lose out in establishing permanent relations with men. Kelley, Pilchowicz, and Byrne (1981) provided some additional evidence concerning the negative effects of high levels of female proceptivity. Investigating male response to female-initiated dates, they found that while most males had a positive emotional response to such initiatives, 87 percent of the relationships that started through female initiative ended by the third date.[7] Thus, there is a possible pattern of improved social standing, employment in settings that allow for dominance or eminence, a freer sexuality, increased T, and greater conflict with males.

Although female sexuality appears dependent on T, and though American women's sexual activity has significantly increased in the period I am considering, the productive connection between increased sexuality and elevated T must still be made. The evidence on this point is nil. In chapter 2, I discussed the methodological and theoretical problems that have plagued the very few studies that bear on this question. There I also derived the proposition that male T ought to surge if the sexual encounter proved to be either a dominance or an eminence experience; that is, an expression of triumphant power or of elevated status. I believe it is at least as reasonable to assume the same for females. Hence, certain sexual interactions for females ought to produce elevated T. However, it may be conjectured that for females the most likely source of testosterone in a sexual interaction would come from sensing an elevation of status, or eminence (as opposed to power or dominance). Eminence can be obtained from a male's strong responsiveness to her attractivity or by his words conveying high status estimation, the most eloquent of which in this culture are, I love you. To what extent there is a biological basis for this supposed difference in male and female sources of self-enhancement is unknown.

A possible illumination comes from Waal's (1982) study of a large colony of chimpanzees in the zoo at Arnhem in the Netherlands. According to Waal, male apes appeared to be primarily concerned with their dominance standing, shifting immediately to power behavior when this was not recognized by another animal. The female animals enjoyed a more harmonious set of relations among themselves and with children. As Waal put it, "The female hierarchy . . . seems to be based on respect from below rather than intimidation and a show of strength from above" (186). This seems to express the concepts of status and of eminence, which are possibly the usual female modes in preference to power and dominance, without at the same time excluding power and dominance for females in given circumstances.

I necessarily recognize the web of intermixed data and conjecture that structures the argument at this point. But to weave a fabric that is, from the outset, a composite of what is solid and what is supposition is the nature of theory construction in science. The former is what we know empirically, and the latter is what is available to us through plausible inference. By themselves, the empirical facts are often insufficient to construct a theory of desirable scope and utility. Only by joining them to what is only supposed can the work of theory building be done.

Here it is at least plausible to think that women, too, can experience the rush of satisfaction that comes from either dominance or eminence and that this satisfaction is not simply cognitive, but rooted in the body as well, energizing and enhancing it. As a behavioral domain of central social and psychological significance, sexuality is as likely to arouse endocrinological responses as any other social encounter. It is highly unlikely that hormonal interests exhaust themselves in the acquisition of sexual partners and that the experience itself is barren of hormonal consequences. The parallels I have noted thus far between male and female T effects in aggression, dominance, and sexuality encourages me to conclude that, as for males, sexual interaction itself is capable not only of being instigated by T, but also, given the proper denouement, of producing it.

If this is the case, the recent liberation of women's sexuality, beginning almost coterminously with the publication of the Broverman et al. study in 1968, is another ground for the elevation of T in females; hence, a shift in the T/E balance; and, if the Broverman hypothesis is correct, an improvement in women's spatial ability.

In sum, many studies provide evidence for the importance of T as an instigator of female sexual interest and arousal. Just as in the areas of dominance and aggression, the hormonal underlay for female sexuality appears to be similar to that for males. This lends additional evidence for the notion that though T is found in much smaller concentrations in females, it operates in approximately the same ways. With respect to the Broverman hypothesis, it is possible to suppose that anything that increases T titers in females will bring them closer to males in the moderated adrenergic arousal that is putatively associated with spatial ability and with tasks requiring inhibition of immediate perceptual reponse.

Female Occupational Status and Testosterone

Earlier in this work I proposed that male social status, particularly in the occupational sphere, may affect T level. This is because, according to the major hypothesis of chapter 2, successful dominance/eminence encounters produce surges of T. In modern societies, the occupational arena is where many opportunities for dominance/eminence encounters occur for at least the upper middle class. Higher-status occupations, though often highly competitive and likely to engender losses as well as victories, are also, on average, more productive of success. Otherwise, they would not qualify as desirable occupations of high rank.

What is not clear is whether or not occupational status and its successes operate hormonally for women in the same way they may operate for men. Thus far I have shown that in two important arenas in which T has important correlates in males, dominance rank attainment and sexuality, females respond endocrinologically in parallel ways. The few results we have in the occupational domain are highly suggestive of a similar parallelism. Crucially, they raise the important question of causal priority; that is, whether occupational status precedes elevated T level, or T level precedes higher occupational status. There are no studies available to answer this question. Indeed, this is one of the most important research frontiers in this corner of the socio-bio-social field involving T.

Purifoy and Koopmans (1979) conducted the most complete occupational-hormonal study of females. Albeit they worked with a small sample spread over a considerable age span (twenty to eighty-seven years), they obtained the kind of results one would expect on the basis of the more extensive set of findings relating androgens to aggressive and dominant behavior. The researchers divided their sample into several occupational categories: professional, technical, and managerial; clerical and sales; service work; students; and (5) homemakers. Testosterone, free T, and androstenedione were the androgens investigated.

Dividing the sample according to age because T level appears to decline with age even in females, Purifoy and Koopmans found that in the twenty to thirty-four age group the professional, technical, and managerial group and the students had higher levels of the three androgens than homemakers or service personnel. In the thirty-five to fifty age group, all paid workers had higher androstenedione than homemakers. In the over-fifty age group, current or former workers had higher T and free T than homemakers. Of equal interest to the issue of how hormones relate to occupation were findings relating the androgens to substantive aspects of work. T and free T were significantly related to working with things; for example, in such occupations as engineering or architecture. Androstenedione and free T concentration were related to work involving people—teaching, nursing, and the like. Androstenedione was related to work bearing responsibility; for example, executive positions.

Purifoy and Koopmans were careful not to assume causal direction in those findings. They suggested that "increased relative [androgens] in early development and/or adulthood might lower one's threshold for learning masculine or androgynous behaviors and promote those aspects of personality related to career, rather than homemaking orientation in females" (1979:184). But they also noted, "Those careers which offer a greater degree of responsibility in dealing with other people and thus a higher level of positive social stimulation might stimulate adrenal androgen secretion" (185). The results show at least one important congruence with the Broverman hypothesis: the association of T with occupations in which the work is with things. In general, these results show that more active involvement in the social structure, especially in the professional and technical occupations in which there is opportunity to experience dominance/eminence, is associated with higher T. This would be fully expected in males. That it also appears to be true for females again narrows the possible differences in the social correlates of T for males and females, although the important question of causal direction is not answered by these results.

Other investigators have also found T in females to be related to their participation in the social structure. Bancroft et al. (1983) found a trend ($p < .10$) for higher T level in women who worked full time outside the home than in those who did not. In addition, they found that women who cohabited, rather than were married, had lower T level. The significance of this may be pondered, but it has been suggested that such women are less dominant by virtue of their failure to have achieved the legitimation of marriage (Risman et al. 1981).

Morris et al. (1987) found that graduate students in their sample of married women had higher levels of T than other women. Graduate training, of course, is preparation for upper-level professional, executive, and technical occupations. Such occupations may be seen to require certain personality characteristics; therefore, it is congruent with the occupational findings to discover that women with higher T see themselves as robust, resourceful, enterprising, sharp-witted, confident, spontaneous, and uninhibited (Baucom, Besch, and Callahan 1985). Daitzman et al. (1978) also discovered a trend ($p < .10$) for a positive relationship between T and "disinhibition," a characteristic that reflects spontaneity and an active orientation. These results are confirmed by Schindler (1979), who found that higher T concentration in a sample of working women was related positively to need for achievement and autonomy (although, interestingly, not to need for dominance or aggression).

Schindler also did the only purposeful comparative study of T in women in different occupations. She sampled urban law firm attorneys, professional team athletes, urban clinic nurses, and suburban elementary school teachers. Reasoning that the first pair were nontraditional occupations for women, while the latter pair were traditional, she hypothesized a T difference between the occupations on this basis. The results were somewhat surprising: the attorneys had significantly higher T than the other three occupations, which did not differ from each other. Although it was plausible to suppose that the athletes would have higher T, that they did not may be due to the rigor of their physical training, which depletes the body of fat, out of which T is synthesized (Strand 1983).

Although these are the only available data on the relationship between T and women's occupational positions, there are some cognate data that are consonant with these results. Based on the relationship between T level and libido and, in some studies, higher rates of intercourse, it can be argued that, to some extent, higher rates of sexual activity may reflect a higher level of T. This hypothesis is fraught with some difficulty (as described above) because intercourse, for example, involves a partner who may be required by cultural norms to be the major initiator. Notwithstanding this difficulty, it is useful to examine intercourse frequencies in different groups for their overall confirmation of the relationship between T and the occupational involvement of women.

Trussel and Westoff (1980) found that working women have a higher frequency of intercourse than nonworking women; and Stevens and Truss (1985) found that heterosexual activity in a sample of working women was correlated positively with number of jobs, job interest, and need for achievement. On the other hand, Udry (1980) has shown that the greatest decline in rate of intercourse over the first four years of marrriage occurs in women who have more than twelve years of education. That is to say that college or postgraduate schooling, orienting one to higher professional, managerial, and technical careers, reduces intercourse frequency even when there is an available partner. Given the previous findings, this is somewhat puzzling and hints again at the presence of different trends in the constellation of social and biological forces that may come into conflict with each other, as we noted earlier regarding the findings of Schreiner-Engel et al. (1980) and Bancroft et al. (1983).

In sum, the relationship between women's occupational involvements and T is complex. As among men, the higher the level of women's occupational prestige and the greater the opportunity for dominance/eminence in social encounters, the higher the level of T. Further, as among men, libido seems to be enhanced; higher libido may not translate automatically into more sexual intercourse. Instead, contrabiologically, women's higher T perhaps runs into a traditional male sanction against women who are "too" dominant or eminent. T possibly operates to fuel conflict between the sexes, creating hostility in males (Rubin 1976) and making females less likely to give way under attack (see, e.g., Bouissou 1983).

But that is not my direct concern with these data on women's occupational levels and sexuality. Rather, I am interested in how these elements affect women's spatial ability in light of the Broverman hypothesis. We may tentatively conclude that if women require more T to perform well in spatial relations tasks, higher occupational standing is associated with more T. It is not yet clear whether higher T is required at the outset to enter those occupations and perform successfully in them, or, once having entered, successful performance produces higher T. In either case, we would expect that women in higher-level occupations would have higher spatial ability.

The question of which is antecedent and which consequent in the relationship between occupational status and T among females leads us to examine a different approach to the Broverman hypothesis, one that depends not on behavioral conditions that enhance T, but rather on the initial creation of a CNS in females that can be responsive to T, as appears to be true of males. Although this approach will necessarily create a generational lag in the ability to perform well in spatial relations tasks, the major social determinants of augmented T—which goes into the making of such a nervous system in the course of fetal development—are the same as those that may have a role in changing the testosterone/estrogen activation conditions for females intragenerationally.

Organizational Effects

Thus far I have considered how the Broverman hypothesis may be modified according to transformations in women's sexuality and occupational involvement. These translate into opportunities for dominance/eminence in social encounters, which, on a daily or ongoing basis, enable a higher level of T. And if Broverman et al. (1968) are right, it would follow that today, and increasingly, as women gain a more equal foothold in the social structure, they will be able to perform better in tasks requiring spatial ability. I acknowledge that, corresponding to the hormonal transformation, there is also an ongoing transformation in the pattern and content of gender socialization. Doubtless there is an interaction here in which endocrinologically grounded readiness must be engaged by learning programs that take advantage of the readiness. If there is a biological basis for certain skills, failure to train in these skills will certainly not facilitate their manifestation.

We must also contemplate the possibility that even if Broverman et al. (1968) are right about the hormonal basis for spatial ability, they may be wrong about the way hormonal mechanisms operate to produce arousal or inhibition in the CNS. As described above, theirs is an activation approach. Alternatively, one may pose the organization hypothesis, which holds that arousal and inhibition do occur as Broverman et al. (1968) claim, but it is organization of the fetal brain at a critical stage that makes the effect possible, not simply currently circulating levels of T. This would seem to be a more unyielding condition with respect to a socio-bio-social analysis. Yet, there is some support for the view that even in utero the social may determine important outcomes for the gestating organism. If this is the case, then maternal activities at crucial fetal stages, especially activities that alter the mother's own testosterone level, will determine organizational outcomes of the fetal brain.

It is generally accepted that at the very earliest stages of fetal life there is no sexual differentation. However, in genetic males at about the seventh week, the developing testes begin to release T, which suffuses the male brain and changes it from the original undifferentiated state. The principal effect at this point is to ensure that the hypothalamus and pituitary of the male are organized to release various gonadotropic hormones, particularly LH and FSH, in a more or less continuous fashion, as required by the male genetic blueprint so that male sexual structures can be induced to grown as well as function in the male pattern (see Strand 1983 and Martin 1988 for details). Should this masculinization of the male brain fail to occur, primary male sexual characteristics will not develop. There are sufficient cases of such anomalies to ensure our understanding of the phenomenon (Money and Ehrhardt 1972). Once the normal flow of T has begun, it is possible that other structures and functions having to do with mental processes (particularly spatial ability) are differentiated as well. This is a highly conjectural issue, but there is some evidence for it. The major theoretical work here, as well as much of the empirical work, has been done by Geschwind and Galaburda (1985, pts. 1–3). These investigators have addressed the question that concerns us here from the perspective of cerebral dominance.

There is general agreement that the two hemispheres of the brain serve somewhat different mental functions: the left is devoted more to language, and the right to more integrative, emotional concerns. Studies of sex differences have shown that the two hemispheres of men's brains are ordinarily more segregated in function, while women's are more equally divided in function. Geschwind and Galaburda began their analysis with the point that while the left brain in humans is ordinarily larger in one spot than the right brain, and this spot is associated with language ability, among males the right hemisphere as a whole is usually larger than the left. Although size does not translate directly into cerebral dominance, it is also the case that right-hemisphere dominance produces left-handedness, which is more prevalent among males. Males are also more likely to suffer from dyslexia and from autoimmune diseases. Anatomically, dyslexics show more structural abnormalities of the left hemisphere. They are also found to have more active visual discrimination centers in the brain (Kolata 1987). Of special interest here is that left-handers, dyslexics, and victims of autoimmune diseases display greater spatial ability, as evidenced by their disproportionate presence in spatial ability–related fields such as architecture, engineering, mathematics, and musical composition. This appears to be true for females, too. Benbow's (1988) sample of highly gifted female math students had higher proportions of autoimmune disease and left-handedness than the general population. They were also four times more likely to be myopic, a condition thought to be associated with a higher intelligence quotient. A higher visual orientation has been suggested to account for both these characteristics (Teasdale, Fuchs, and Goldschmidt 1988).

Geschwind and Galaburda reasoned there may be some broad-sex linked basis for the association of these various characteristics that are particularly found in males. They hypothesized that the effects are due to the major differentiating hormone between the sexes at the fetal level, namely, T. They argued that T not only differentiates the fetus sexually, but also affects the brain by slowing the development of the left hemisphere. It does this by destroying neurons in at least some places in the left hemisphere. This enhances the development of the right hemisphere, which presumably explains the greater amount of male left-handedness and spatial skills (see also Wittelson and Swallow 1988).

At first glance, if Geschwind and Galaburda are correct about the effects of T, there would seem to be little reason to hope for female emergence in the domain of spatial abilities. But Geschwind and Galaburda are not locked into genetic determinism: "Our thesis is that while genes contribute importantly, many influences that lie outside the gene pool can alter [hemispheric] localization patterns. . . . Most powerful are variations in the chemical environment in fetal life and to a lesser extent in infancy and early childhood" (1985, pt. 1:431). This thesis opens up the possibility of environmentally determined variations around a genetic theme, particularly social determination of hormonal effects. Thus, even at the stage of brain organization, the socio-bio-social chain may come into play. If the Broverman hypothesis is shown to be neurochemically flawed at the activation level, it may yet be true, with a generational lag, at the organizational level. The major hormonal mechanism will still be T, as Broverman et al. (1968) claimed, but the decisive moment will be shifted from the current level of T to the fetal stage of brain organization.

According to Geschwind and Galaburda, "Both male and female

fetus are exposed to maternal and placental hormones" (1985, pt. 1:431). "The female zygote is also exposed to T . . . from the maternal ovaries, adrenals, and extragonadal structures such as fat. The [female] fetus is protected from much of this maternal T because aromatase [a chemical metabolizer] in the placenta converts it to estradiol, but the protection is not complete. . . . While male and female zygotes differ on the average in the degree of T effect to which they are subjected, there is no absolute difference between the sexes" (1985, pt. 2:524). Ellis (1982) estimated at least a 5 to 10 percent overlap between males and females in mean androgen levels at the crucial point of fetal nervous system formation. Furthermore, according to Geschwind and Galaburda, "It is clear that the placental barrier [to T for females] is far from complete. . . . It is likely there are individual variations in the aromatizing capacity of the placenta" (1985, pt. 2:533). Hence, under what can be understood as normal circumstances, there is no absolute difference between males and females in T at the time of brain organization.

The picture that Geschwind and Galaburda limn for us is that while genes will determine the general trend, in which males will be exposed to higher levels of T during brain development, the difference between the sexes is susceptible to narrowing due to the placental environment, which is a function of maternal T production. Althought most of the T present in the placental environment of the female fetus is neutralized by aromatization (chemical conversion to a form of E), not all effects are nullified. One indication of this is that female fetuses are susceptible to the effects of androgens externally administered to the mother (Geschwind and Galaburda 1985, pt. 2:524). For example, Reinisch (1977) found that children whose mothers received progestin (an androgenic compound) during pregnancy to prevent miscarriage were more independent, secure, self-sufficient, self-assured, and sensitive than those whose mothers received E therapy. In a later study, Reinisch (1981) found that progestin children were more physically aggressive than their untreated same-sex siblings.

What is most important about fetal androgens is that, if they have penetrated to the relevant neural sites, they "result in permanent changes in the responsiveness of the nervous system to androgens administered in adulthood" (Moyer 1974:348). Vande Wiele, too, has commented on the permanent changes that perinatal administration of androgens produces on an "animal's metabolism of T, Androstenedione, and cortisol" (in Levine and Doering 1974:78). There is the widely noted phenomenon in infrahuman species of the masculinizing or defeminizing effects on females who are in a litter with males and hence share a T-rich maternal environment with their male siblings.

One of the most striking instances of this is the freemartin, a female calf that shares a placental sac with a male sibling and is defeminized and usually sterile.[8] Among human twins, Geschwind and Galaburda suggested, "the females of opposite sex pairs should have . . . a higher rate of left-handedness because of exposure to T produced by the male cotwins" (1985, pt. 2:535). Left-handedness, in their view, is related to T, which enhances right-hemisphere dominance.

Geschwind and Galaburda also noted that T effects result not only from the amount of the hormone present, but also from the level of sensitivity of tissue (see also Nyborg 1984). Udry and Talbert (1988) pointed out that females are considerably more sensitive to T than males, thus a very little at a critical time can produce a large effect. In this regard, Geschwind and Galaburda offered what may be their most controversial proposal, which they frankly characterized as "Lamarckian," in which acquired characteristics are transmitted to a succeeding generation. They proposed that stress may be a mediator of possible intergenerational effects, producing "either structural alterations in the brain of the offspring and/or permanent metabolic alterations. . . . There is thus the increased possibility that the female who was subjected to increased stress in utero will herself show an increased tendency to hormonal masculinization that will in turn affect her offspring" (1985, pt. 2:533). Nyborg (1984) also supported a stress effect. This would convey the social effect to a second and succeeding generations.

Geschwind and Galaburda have offered a model of how social effects may operate even at the organizational, that is, fetal, stage of brain development; but as provocative as their theory may be, it has not been universally acclaimed. Martin (1988) raised a number of objections to brain-lateralization theories that purport to explain sex differences in behavior. Foremost among these, especially as it pertains to Geschwind and Galaburda, is that there has been no conclusive demonstration of the putative role of T in determining male specialization of the right hemisphere. Obler and Novoa (1988), although generally critical of lateralization as a source of sex differences, actually assumed a more neutral stance toward Geschwind and Galaburda. They noted also, somewhat in harmony with the Lamarckian aspects mentioned above, that "hormone levels, fetally, as well as in adolescence, are not purely 'genetically' determined. There is much interaction of environment in producing them" (1988:49). This theme was sounded also by Lowe: "There is no way to eliminate the possibility that brain differences may have resulted from behavior or environmental differences rather than the other way around" (1983:53). However, Lowe also added a general critique of lateralization studies, proposing that the way skills are supposedly divided between the two halves of the brain does not correspond to the way skills are divided between males and females. This leads to the general problem of how to identify the precise causal relationships among anatomical, physiological, and behavioral variables, a challenge that Beaumont (1987) specifically leveled against Geschwind and Galaburda's work.

Clearly this problem bedevils any investigator who tries to examine distal causes and effects of any focal phenomenon. It applies not only to the relatively narrow arena of brain, hormones, and behavior, but obviously also to the broad reach of the problems addressed in this book, in which social and historical trends are linked theoretically to hormones and brain. I pointed out above that perhaps the primary validating example of such an enterprise is the large decline in age of menarche since the middle of the last century. This shows that hormones and social change are not alien to each other. Although Geschwind and Galaburda may turn out to be in error about specifics, their general commitment to environmental effects on hormonal and brain processes encourages further examination of these possibilities. I turn to this now.

Because of the different loci of the source of androgens in males and females, stress can affect the sexes differently. Stress, which leads to pituitary secretion of ACTH, has the effect in males of reducing the gonadotropic hormones that create T. In several studies, stress produced a decline in T in males (e.g., Kreuz, Rose, and Jennings 1972; Ward 1974:14). By contrast, in females, ACTH activates the adrenal cortex, which is the source of about half the T in females. Thus, maternal stress can lead to increased production of T (Hubble 1963; Lloyd 1963; Gray and Gorzalka 1980).

Putting these elements together, we have at least one mechanism by which females in utero may receive more than a normal share of T. But what is the source of this maternal stress? There are, of course, numerous possibilities, but it is useful to conjecture about the increased stress of occupational involvement. In 1940 less than 30 percent of the female population sixteen years of age and older was in the labor force, as compared with more than 80 pecent of males. By 1986, 55 percent of females were in the labor force (U.S. Bureau of the Census 1987). The figure for women with preschool children was virtually the same—54 percent. The figure for women twenty to twenty-four years old is even higher, 72 percent. These last two categories are of special interest because both groups are among the most likely to conceive and carry a fetus to term. Hence, any endocrinological effects of mothers' occupation on the fetus are likely to fall within these groups.

It is entirely in keeping with the idea of the soci-bio-social chain to hypothesize that occupational stress in working women who are pregnant may release unusually high levels of T from the adrenal cortex. The hormone suffuses the placenta and, depending on the amount and timing of the stress, may perform certain unusual organizing functions on the brains of female fetuses. Males would generally be unaffected by increased level of placental T because they already have high levels due to its production by their own testes (Ellis 1982). There are many more women in the labor force today than in the past who are likely to be exposed to stress, even on a random basis, at critical phases of fetal development. Such exposure, with its consequent flow of T, may well effect a historical change in the spatial ability of female offspring.

The path from occupational stress to higher T in females is indirect, but there are some data to support it. Frankenhaeuser et al. (1978) and Rauste-von Wright, von Wright, and Frankenhaeuser (1981) found that achievement-oriented female students manifested higher levels of adrenaline, or epinephrine, during performance on achievement tests than students who were less interested in achievement. The latter group of females did not perform as well, but were more satisfied with themselves than the higher-achieving females, and they expressed sentiments that identified them with more traditional, nonachieveing female roles. These results prepare us to see the link between achievement stress and T via adrenaline. Axelrod and Reisine (1984) set down the conditions for the connection. Stress prepares a physiological pathway that connects epinephrine production to higher ACTH production, and ACTH in turn activates the adrenal cortex to secrete cortisol and adrenal steroids, including T. Heuristically, we may conclude that achievement stress in working women with high aspirations may instigate some extra adrenal T production. Pregnant women who work are likely to contribute more placental T to their in utero offspring.

Maternal occupational stress is but one possible ground for a T-based organizing effect on the brain of the female fetus. On the basis of the data cited above about the endocrine profiles of females in dominance relations or in occupations, such as law and medicine, where dominance/eminence opportunities are frequent and sharp increases of T are possible, we may hypothesize that the increasing numbers of women in more prestigious and authoritative occupations and in upper organizational strata (*New York Times,* March 19, 1986, sec. C, 1) disposes toward higher T among these women. Just as in the case of occupational stress, experiences of dominance/eminence among working women who are pregnant ought to elevate the placental testosterone concentration, with the possible effect of organizing the female fetus's brain toward spatial ability.

Another domain in which female dominance/eminence may have changed sufficiently to ensure increased T is in familial relations. Although patriarchal attitudes persist, and the family is perhaps the most difficult arena from which to eradicate them, the transformation of women's status has also affected family relations. Part of this is due to women's increased bargaining power based on their more prominent financial contributions to the family budget. Even if this means only that they are not as subdued as in the past, it would suggest that T reduction, which occurs after defeat is less likely. Furthermore, destabilization of modern relationships between spouses—a good deal more is negotiated today, rather than simply enacted as an expression of well-grooved, traditional roles—allows many more opportunities for female assertion and ascendancy in family relations than was previously the case. The net effect, again, is likely to be more frequent elevations of T in these women.

I want to emphasize the random aspect of the timing of increased T. This means that supranormal levels of T in the maternal placenta occur on an unpredictable timetable. Given that the organization of the brain to enable spatial ability occurs during a critical phase of fetal development, there is no way to know whether the increased amount of T actually is available at the critical point. Geschwind and Galaburda (1985, pt. 2) made a particular point about the timing of the excess T if it is to have the specified organizing effect on the brain. Hence, some frequently dominant women may miss providing the increased level of placental T in the critical phase for the female fetus they are carrying, while some women who are normally less often dominant may contribute the requisite amounts of T precisely at the critical time. Until we know more about the timing of the critical period for brain formation as it relates to spatial ability, we can expect more dominant women to produce female offspring with more spatial ability only stochastically.

If Geschwind and Galaburda's Lamarckian proposition is confirmed, it means that female improvements in spatial ability can be cumulative. In each generation that women occupy social positions and engage in social roles that enhance their T concentration, they will be producing female offspring whose endocrinological structure is altered and whose behavioral processes will make them more likely in turn to produce offspring who possess the T-related structures or processes that may underlie spatial ability. Thus, if Broverman et al. (1968) erred in attributing spatial ability to an activation process, the historical transformation of women's social structural position may guarantee improved spatial ability as a consequence of an organizational process on an intergenerational basis.

Finally, it is tempting to consider what hormonal-fetal outcomes might occur given different constellations of dominance between husband and wife in a marriage. We may suppose the following: women who are subordinated in their marriages, rarely winning victories in their familiar interactions and frequently defeated, will ordinarily have very low levels of T and, when pregnant, will contribute very little placental T by which to affect female offspring. Hence, male dominance in marriage is likely to be associated with relatively less dominant female offspring. At least these daughters are more likely to be more feminized, which would remove them from certain forms of aggression, competition, and spatial ability. On the other hand, if the wife achieves dominance often and her T level is high, she could contribute a masculinizing effect to female offspring. This question is susceptible to longitudinal research, although the caveats I mentioned about the timing of placental T still apply.

Conclusion

I began this chapter with the heuristic assumption that the Broverman hypothesis might be correct, and I conjectured what this might imply for female spatial ability if the hypothesis were viewed through a socio-bio-social lens. Although the data are far from complete, and in some cases are plainly unsatisfactory, they nonetheless permit us to postulate a network of connections between the social and the hormonal that conceivably frees the dependent variable, spatial ability, from biological determinism pure and simple. In three behavioral domains—aggression, sexuality, and occupation—the evidence shows some consistency with the findings obtained from males; namely, that T is related to these domains in similar, though not entirely identical, ways. The principal exception, and one that works in favor of females with respect to the central hypothesis of this chapter, is in the domain of occupational striving. Whereas this may cause some diminution in T among males, especially if the striving is unsuccessful, the stress of striving may actually increase female T. This results from the different major loci of T production in the two sexes.

In the sexual domain, not only do we mainly find that T is an agonist of sexual response in females, but it is also useful to speculate that successful sexual interaction also instigates T, as we have supposed earlier in this book for males. A more autonomous sexuality and spatial ability may thus be related. Indeed, some hint of this was adumbrated by Freud:

> You know, too, that women in general are said to suffer from "physiological feeble-mindedness"—that is, from lesser intelligence than men. The fact itself is disputable and its interpretation doubtful, but one argument in favor of this atrophy being of a secondary nature is that women labor under the harshness of an early prohibition against turning their thoughts to what would most have interested them—namely, the problems of sexual life. ([1927] 1961:55–56)

Indeed, the attainment of a more active sexuality both in thought and in fact is a historic development that may lead to augmentation of female T, hence to the manifestation of a truer level of spatial ability than repressed sexuality permits. Like men, women are capable of sexual arousal from erotic thought and fantasy (Griffitt 1987). It may benefit women even more than it does men to engage in such thought.

Although the scant evidence suggests that dominance/eminence experiences produce surges of T in females as in males, this is one of the least stable of our understandings. It raises the general question of what function might be served if T were related to dominance in females as it is in males. We may conjecture several phylogenetic possibilities. First, in dominance encounters with other females, the strongest will emerge, and by virtue of the positive effect of T on female proceptivity, these stronger females can preempt the stronger and more dominant males for themselves. Second, T would provide females with a red blood cell anabolist in the service of aggression to secure higher status in the female rank hierarchy or to protect offspring. Third, early demise of male consorts or their departure after mating—in groups where this is the practice—would require females to survive alone, to avoid becoming prey, and to protect their young. Fourth, although male dominance is the usual case, it does not come without some cost. That females can dominate males too, especially younger ones, rebalances some of the disparities of male-female relations. Admittedly, these are speculations based on very general principles that can be deduced from an evolutionary-adaptive perspective.

A final issue in the matter of female spatial ability is that even if (according to socio-bio-social analysis) female T levels are currently rising due to the transformation of women's roles, the effect on spatial ability is not likely to emerge very strongly if socialization and encouragement of females to enter spatial ability roles does not also proceed apace. This requirement need in no way diminish a heuristic commitment to a hormonal hypothesis. It would be idle to think that males could manifest their currently superior ability without assistance from socialization, which molds the biological clay into the shape that enables it to emerge as superior. Given that the biological matrix may be ripening, no less can be required of and for females.

5

VICARIOUS DOMINANCE/ EMINENCE: SPORTS, TESTOSTERONE, AND SOCIETY

In social organization the body is important because it is the vehicle of work, reproduction, patriotism, and, I shall develop now, certain aspects of social order. I will examine a social mechanism for vicarious dominance/eminence, which, I postulate, provides surges of testosterone (T) to an important group of males who might otherwise challenge social order. T is thus seen as a biological anchor that contributes to the stability of social systems.

My view is that males who experienced testosterone surges in sufficient number (how many that may be is not known) will be relatively contented with the existing social order. This theory fits with our understanding of testosterone as an energizer and libido enhancer (see chapter 2). Periodic surges are tonic and impart a sense of well-being, which is an agonist for success in subsequent interactions. Broadly speaking, success binds one more closely to the social status quo that is its setting. Conversely, lacking sufficient surges of T, males are more likely to become restive and alienated from the institutions that undergird the social order and to become available for experiences that negate that order, including withdrawal of commitment and motivation. Lack of success may disconnect one emotionally from existing social structures and make one ripe for social change.[1]

As developed in chapter 2, since T is related to socially demarcated opportunities for dominance/eminence, it is not simply a biological constant, but has a history. In earlier periods, survival through intense competition, either with nature of with other men, produced frequent contests for dominance, ergo victories for some, despite often great defeats for many. However, the then tougher, more violent relations within and between all social groups—men and women (despite much current abuse), parents and children (also despite current levels of abuse), slaves and masters, or workers and owners—led to a sorting out of individual dominance standing in a comprehensive pecking order, so that those who lost standing in an encounter with a stronger competitor might compensate in overcoming a weaker one. But with the psychologizing and softening of human relations in all institutional arenas in modern times, from work to home, and with the availability of a productive surplus to sustain the diminution of competitive rigor, the lot of those who had usually been dominated generally improved: women, children, workers, and minorities of all kinds. The result of this transformation in civil rights, which was of immense magnitude and achieved relatively peacefully, is that the starker, more direct confrontations of dominance have been curtailed. Despite elevated crime rates in recent decades and periodic social upheavals, if we aggregate individual experiences, society is still far more tranquil than perhaps at any time since the hunting and gathering stage (Graham and Gurr 1969; Wolf 1971; Brantingham and Brantingham 1984).

Though virtually all welcome this relative tranquility, it has come at a price; namely, a reduction in opportunities for direct, decisive dominance encounters as part of daily social life. Opportunities vary by social class, with somewhat greater opportunities afforded lower-class males in youth and early adulthood and higher-class males in later adulthood. This has meant a differential distribution of testosterone surges at different age and class levels, as I discussed in chapter 2. I want now to disaggregate the distribution of these experiences at the higher-class level.[2]

Although the higher social class does reap the biological rewards of its increased dominance/eminence opportunities in the prime of adulthood and later, not all members of this class are fortunate in this way. Indeed, the lower portion of the higher-class group is, in some ways, even worse off than the class below it. This is because it has neither the structural opportunities for dominance afforded the status echelons above, nor the freedom from civility that characterizes many of those in the class below (as described in chapter 2). The specific group in focus here is the lower white-collar subclass. Its dilemma is that it shares identity bonds with the higher social class, but is substantially denied its biological privileges. Yet it abhors the methods of the more violent groups below it, so it cannot seek its victories in the physical acting-out of impulse.

Failing a resolution of this dilemma, the lower white-collar group could become a problematic social entity—unreliable and politically troublesome. Though some have argued that this is an inevitable denouement for the lower white-collar group (e.g., Mills 1956), there is scant evidence of political testiness, even as the conditions that Mills thought would provoke this outcome have been exacerbated by increased hierarchy, formalization, and mechanization. Indeed, the evidence is that the lower white-collar group is virtually unproblematic from the point of view of social order.

My thesis is that while the structural opportunities for dominance/eminence and for testosterone surges are diminished for this group, a compensating social mechanism provides important opportunities for vicarious dominance and for testosterone. That mechanism is sports. As I will detail below, the emotional investment of the lower white-collar class in sports, to some extent as participants, but even more as spectators, provides not only entertainment, but also the occasion to compensate in some degree for the anemic opportunity structure for dominance/eminence. Indeed, in all historical periods sports are an ideal mechanism to provide vicarious dominance opportunities to groups who are otherwise deprived of dominance/eminence opportunities, but who might cause political trouble if not pacified.[3] I turn now to the application of this principle to the lower white-collar males in modern society.

Lower White-Collar Male Discontents

Despite intermittent wars (Korea, Vietnam) and severe economic dislocations (the oil price shocks of the 1970s, inflation, the decline of rustbelt industries and the surrender of considerable economic dominance to Japan and West Germany), the post–World War II United States remains the most prosperous nation in history. In the span of two generations it transformed itself into a middle-class society, stratified more like a diamond (with a big middle-class bulge) than a pyramid (bottom-heavy with an enormous lower class) (Levy 1987:19). GNP grew from $716 billion in 1939 to $3.71 trillion in 1986 (in 1982 constant dollars) (U. S. Department of Commerce 1987:58); and the United States changed from a society in the profound grip of capitalist crisis to one with a bipartisan consensus on the validity of the social welfare state. Indeed, the United States has flourished.

Due both to technological advance and to competitive adjustment, the tertiary service sector has overtaken the primary extraction and secondary production sectors of the economy. The United States now produces fewer things but offers more ancillary and subsidiary utilities: marketing, advertising, financing, insuring, educating, program planning, regulating, designing, high-tech equipment servicing, and the like. Managerial, professional, technical, and sales occupations (the white-collar jobs) steadily increase, while production, craft, assembly, transport, repair, laborer, and agricultural occupations (the blue-collar jobs) decline.

A significant part of the white-collar service sector includes the cadres of males who have until recently constituted the overwhelming numbers in the middle and lower levels of management and staff in government and the large corporations. This labor force group has grown faster in the years since 1950 than any other. In the corporations this is "political labor,"as opposed to "productive labor" (Collins 1979:50). Productive labor actually produces the material goods upon which wealth and standards of living depend. Political labor essentially controls how the wealth is distributed, either through direct decision making or through providing justifications upon which decisions can be made. According to Collins, political labor largely determines its own benefits, including those of pay and leisure. Indeed, many of these jobs are sinecures.

> We have elaborated a largely superfluous structure of more or less easy jobs, full of administrative make-work and featherbedding because modern technology allows it and because of political pressures from the populace wanting work. Thus we have the enormous structure of government employment (including education), the union sector protected by elaborate work regulations, and the huge work forces of our corporate oligopolies keeping themselves busy seeking new products to justify their jobs. (Collins 1979;55).

Although this group controls many of the conditions of its work and pay, and despite the built-in leisure that pads out the days and weeks, a substantial segment of it consists, in some sense, of white-collar menials. Their work is clean and they do it in well-lighted places, but for the most part they have reached the apex of their careers—and at a relatively young age. By contrast with the potential of an entrepreneurial class or of traditional professionals to ascend steeply in wealth and power, the broad lower-middle sector that works in organizations must conform to the kinds of opportunities that the large organizations make possible. First, the structure is hierarchical and pyramidal. Second, the "metabolic rate";[4] that is, movement through this system, is relatively slow. Third, the period of their most rapid mobility is over. For many of these men, the attainment of their current occupational niche will be their main mobility accomplishment. This means that the present group of white-collar males will experience only slow upward movement in the remainder of their career. Very few are on what is known as the fast track. Combine this with the make-work routines that these jobs frequently entail, and the stage is set for a significant degree of malaise.

In the American experience, discontent is difficult to detect and, where it exists, even more difficult to channel. It has been remarked often that the American working class has failed to mobilize itself on the model of European working classes to foster socialism. Marxists have attributed this to "false consciousness"; namely, identification with middle-class interests at the expense of one's own. Others attribute the relative passivity of the American working class to the more or less continuous improvement of living standards, the still robust opportunities for intergenerational if not intragenerational mobility, and to the demonstrated failure of rigorously socialist societies to provide outstanding amounts of either bread or freedom. The Eastern European events of 1989–1990 underscore this last point.

Middle-class discontent is perhaps more difficult to document or to understand. Occupational satisfaction ratings for this group are relatively high (Kahn 1974). After all, the group is relatively well situated economically, earning well above the median income. Considering only males, median annual income for the managerial and professional category in 1988 was approximately $35,000, as compared with median income for the total male labor force of $22,500 (U.S. Department of Labor 1988). Yet, within the middle class there is a considerable range, and we must disaggregate this group in order to understand its dynamics. For example, median income for sales occupations was approximately $25,000. While this also is above the male median for the total labor force, it is by no means munificent, as anyone who has lived in or visited a large American city in the early 1990s can attest. While the upper-income sectors of white-collar occupations ought obviously to be satisfied not only with what they are receiving, but also at their prospects for more, the middle and lower sectors of these occupations do not have reason for such gratitude.

Two additional features of many lower white-collar jobs are also important in understanding the prospects for discontent. First, they are less secure than the upper-sector jobs. Although white-collar employment is, in general, more secure than blue-collar employment, waves of dismissals pass through these ranks as the economy experiences its periodic vicissitudes. There was the famous engineers' recession of the early 1970s when the winding-down of the Vietnam War led to retrenchment in military procurement and development. Thousands were laid off as contracts ended or were terminated. Equally stark for white-collar employees were the layoffs in the industrial belt (autos, steel, manufacturing) in the early 1980s as both government economic policy to control inflation and import competition from Asia and West Germany prodded many companies to cut deeply into their salaried staff. Finally, the fiscal crises of the cities in the 1970s led to reductions not only in the uniformed forces, but across the whole array of white-collar service staff.

At the interactional level, a second difference between upper and lower white-collar workers is in the nature of dominance/eminence opportunities in the job. Collins (1975) analyzed large organizations as comprising principally order givers (the upper white-collar sector) and order takers (the blue-collar sector). But between the two is the lower white-collar group who both take and give orders. Although they outrank those they command, their orders are essentially transmissions from the true command posts above them, where policies are made and the very large gains to be reaped from those policies are mainly accrued. Of course, there are opportunities for dominance or eminence in organizational encounters and struggles at all levels, or in pitting oneself against competitors in other organizations, or against impersonal market forces. But, preponderantly, such opportunities accrue to those at the order-giving level of organizations. That is the plateau of inclusion, where one's opinions and decisions become relevant to decisive moves and to significant dominance/eminence results.

By contrast, the lower white-collar sector implements and supervises conformity to decisions from above. Little of substantial organizational interest hinges on what is done here. Personnel are largely interchangeable, since there are few opportunities for unique, creative contribution, although status symbols distinguish this group from the lower echelons to whom it transmits the commands from above. Lower white-collar employees often have desks in private offices or cubicles; receive three or four, not two, weeks of vacation; have access to some secretarial services; and punch no time-cards. But the critical fact about such work is that it provides few opportunities for true individuation, for the bold stroke, coup, or distinguishing act of self-assertion from which dominance or eminence arises.

In addition to the structural disadvantages of lower white-collar status, recent years have seen the introduction of an unsettling new element: women. With the rise of the women's movement in the 1960s, increasing numbers of women have entered the white-collar work force. Although still clearly present in miniscule numbers in some professions (see chapter 3), women have found a solid place in at least the lower managerial, professional, technical, and sales occupations. In fact, women now slightly exceed males in professional occupations (*New York Times,* March 19, 1986, sec. C, 1). This is due in large part to the several professions, such as teaching and nursing, that are overwhelmingly female. But even in the more restricted executive, administrative, and managerial category, the number of women has grown.

In 1972 (the earliest year for which annual comparisons are available for the occupational category at issue), men occupied more than 80 percent of the positions. In 1982 (the latest year for which direct annual comparisons are available), men occupied less than 68 percent of the positions (Klein 1984). By 1988, males had declined to under 59 percent in the executive, administrative, and managerial positions.[5]

Notwithstanding the large influx of women, they have been assigned relatively low status in the white-collar category. Few women have emerged at the higher executive levels (Klein 1984). Clustered in the lower white-collar positions, they have rendered the work setting somewhat sexier, providing more tonic ambience for men. According to studies by Mortimer Feinberg and Aaron Levenstein and by Robert A. Quinn (reported in Westoff 1985:19–20), between 60 percent and 80 percent of samples of white-collar corporate personnel knew of at least one office romance. Unlike the traditional office affairs between bosses and their secretaries or handmaiden administrative assistants, the romances of today are often between equals (Westoff 1985:13). But there are other, less gratifying, ramifications for the men. In general, discrimination tends to distort a labor force in such a way that the group that is discriminated against is not only disproportionately present at the lower echelons, but is also, due to the lack of dilution upward, more able on average than those at the lower echelon who are from the majority group. Clearly, the majority group is more likely to be sorted according to true ability than will be the case for the minority group.[6]

In the present context, this means that the lower white-collar sector males are increasingly confronting a group of females who are, on average, more able than they are. In the daily routines of office discourse, exchange of ideas, supervision of subordinates, and communication with superiors, the women are more likely to excel. This can come as no small discomfort to men who are already lacking both in status and in significant status attainment opportunities.

Despite the overall cultural endorsement of equal opportunity for women and the virtual acceptance of this principle at least verbally, in practice considerable antagonism greets the entry of women into labor market preserves that were once almost exclusively male. In a somewhat disturbing study, Dubin (1985) found that male M.B.A. candidates' negative attitudes toward women managers remained unexpectedly stable over the period 1975 to 1983. In a study of a single newspaper organization in which there was an almost equal distribution of male and female employees (nonsupervisory in this case) the two sexes essentially operated in sex-segregated networks (Brass 1985). Women were excluded from the male networks, and especially from the dominant coalition from which most promotions were made. Other research confirms the pattern of sex-segregated association (Kaufman 1978; Larwood and Blackmore 1978). The inference from these studies seems quite clear: males are experiencing status threat from females and act to preserve their privileged position. The threat should be most acute for those whose status is least secure and whose prospects are least promising. The lower white-collar sector, where most of the women are concentrated, is the most likely structural site for status uncertainty, and the males within it are more likely than the females to feel ill at ease about their position and its prospects. Under the circumstances—income only moderately above the national median, limited opportunity for dominance/eminence or for further mobility, and an increasing threat to existing status from women—we might expect some discontent among lower white-collar males.

Some general societal developments also contribute to the putative malaise of the lower white-collar group. Over a relatively long historical period, Western societies have experienced what Elias called a "civilizing process" ([1939] 1978; Elias and Dunning 1986). This development, effecting societal structural changes, manifests itself most plainly in the individual sphere. The civilizing process is marked by increasing differentiation of roles, which enhances individuality by providing a larger number of unique niches for individuals to fill, but also limits the scope of each individual to a specific, well-defined domain of responsibility that ordinarily fits within a clearly demarcated organizational hierarchy. Civil society is also transformed in that the means of violence become more concentrated in the state. This removes from individuals the ability to seek quick, direct remedies to real and imagined grievances, and reserves for the state the power to enforce both laws and contracts concluded between private individuals. The effect is to moderate violent emotions, because individuals are constrained from acting on their immediate feelings. The further effect is to restrict opportunities for dominance.

The civilizing process brings about emotional control in other ways, too. A democratization of manners occurs in which all classes are expected to conform to a single code of etiquette that, importantly, concerns the body: circumspection with regard to what parts of the body are exposed and in what circumstances; the reduction of alimentary displays of too much gusto, whether in smacking the lips or in passing wind; a privatization of toilet functions, with a consequent extension of the domain of disgust when the code here is not fully observed; an equal privatization of sexual activity, architecturally marked by the separation of rooms in living quarters, with one specifically reserved both for sleeping and for sex. In general, the civilizing process distances individuals from nature, intervening with socially determined codes of preferred behavior. Elias and Dunning (1986) argue that a high level of civilization, as they describe it, commits a society to a state of blandness that leaves individuals yearning biogenetically for excitement.

Notably, some sectors of society are less in the grip of the civilizing process than others. The upper classes, who are the leaders of fashion, can ignore most social codes if they choose, even sometimes the law. Wealth protects them from the costs of most errors they may commit. The lower classes, too, are freer from the social controls of etiquette and manners. They have less to lose from nonconformity (Homans 1961).

The brunt of the civilizing process, as it affects the social control of the body, falls most heavily on the middle class, for whom, as Elias ([1939] 1978) pointed out, the code represents one route to acceptance by the class above it. In the upper class, a solecism is simply a sign of willfulness; in the middle class it suggests poor training, hence inadequacy. As with many social stringencies, the lower sector of the middle class is more likely than the upper to feel the need to conform in order to maintain the boundary between itself and the working class, which is adjacent to it in the social hierarchy. Taking a broad, historical perspective, the civilizing process is an additional feature of modern social life that weighs upon the lower sector of the middle class.

Males, too, are more likely to suffer from the civilizing process. They are ordinarily more physically aggressive than females (Maccoby and Jacklin 1974; Hyde 1986), and the civilizing process is particularly restrictive on this kind of conduct. Hence, males are more likely to seek opportunities for excitement (Zuckerman 1984). Given the social deficits thus imposed by a too "nice" society in the realm of manners and an increasingly competitive and unpromising set of prospects at work, we might expect the lower white-collar males to be disgruntled and somewhat alienated. Yet there are few signs of this in the form of political activity or radical social or economic views. Although, if organized, this group might act effectively as a political force, it does not pursue any such route. In the true white-collar tradition, it is highly individualistic, shunning collective organization, as, for example, in unions. That approach reeks too much of the lower-class group from which it is important to differentiate itself.

Indeed, in one depiction (by Ralph Whitehead, Jr., University of Massachusetts) lower white-collar males are "new collar voters . . . middle Americans under the age of 45 [with] annual income of $20–$40,000. [They are] workhorses of the service economy . . . politically independent and ideologically fickle. They voted overwhelmingly for President Reagan in 1984. They are heavy television viewers whose favorite programs are 'Saturday Night Live,' 'Entertainment Tonight,' and 'Monday Night Football' " (quoted in Gailey 1985: sec. A, 10). The portrait is unsurprising, given the demographics discussed earlier. But in one respect it is very interesting; namely, the taste for televised football. As I will develop below, sports are a more powerful social and biological mechanism than observers have yet noted. Although commentators on the political Left take sports very seriously, I believe that they miss the true basis of the political efficacy of sports spectatorship.

From the perspective of many on the political Left, sports perform ideological functions to mollify and pacify otherwise discontented populations and to foster capitalist values. Notwithstanding whatever truth this analysis may have, the questions remain as to why certain sectors of the population choose sports over other possible activities and why certain sports—particularly football in the past two decades—over others. These issues will concern us here, not only in order to understand how different elements of social organization fit together, but also to learn how social variables produce bodily effects that feed forward into new conditions of social organization in accordance with the model of the socio-bio-social chain. I hypothesize that as the lower white-collar sector has evolved, so have the sports institutions of society, to the point that sports play a major role in the political passivity of the lower white-collar sector. They pacify this group through providing opportunities for vicarious dominance/eminence through identification with winning players or teams. Whether real or vicarious, dominance/eminence produces elevations in T, and after bread, should provide a bodily locus of social stability.

The Appeal of Sports

Sports are a form of play, and play is universal. Oddly, though we are usually able to recognize play when we see it, we find it difficult to say exactly what it is that makes it play—perhaps its spontaneity, lack of obvious functionality, ability to evoke both intense concentration and pleasure, and its unhamperedness as one thing leads to another without normative guidance (Huizinga [1939] 1970; Guttman 1978).

Those are some elements of play before it becomes socialized. Once subjected to social control, play loses some of its spontaneity and develops into specific forms, including highly ritual ones, and also into rule-governed games and contests in which outcomes are unpredictable. When organized play in game form relies at least in part on strength, fleetness, deftness of movement, or keenness of vision, we are approaching the kind of activity we call sport. These attributes also characterize premodern activities of a play nature—Roman games such as chariot racing and gladiatorial contests. The distinguishing feature of modern sports is that they are played according to standard rules that are intended to provide equal opportunities for competitors and to limit violence, when this is a possibility (Dunning 1983; Guttman 1978).

Viewed through the lens of the civilizing process, sports release a specific form of pleasurable excitement in which certain deeply rooted emotions can find expression in relatively safe contexts. The safety derives from the force of the rules, their wide public support, and the power of the state to uphold them (Elias and Dunning 1986).

Sports have always involved contests for dominance or eminence. In the former type, competitors try to best each other directly by means of strength and skill, as in wrestling, boxing, baseball, or football. In the latter type, competitors try to outperform each other in respect to a standard, as in gymnastics, running, shot put, or ski jumping. Thus, sports outcomes are intimately linked to stratification in that individuals or teams are awarded social credit and standing in proportion to their wins and losses.

According to Elias and Dunning (1986), sports evoke primitive emotions that have relatively little chance for expression in modern societies in the forefront of the civilizing process. These are the openly expressed delight in vanquishing a foe, which announces one's dominance and power, and the equal delight of gaining the kudos of the crowd, which bespeaks eminence and status. In societies well advanced in the civilizing process, what Elias and Denning call "unexciting societies" (1986:71), individuals must ordinarily moderate their glee as well as their despair. In sports, the social control of emotions is partially suspended, and some asocial feeling is permitted to emerge. From this perspective, sports can be viewed as a mechanism of social control, allowing people to let off some steam that might otherwise burst out in unpredictable ways (Parsons 1951). Sports are thus quasi-ritual opportunities to become emotional in societies where emotions are closely circumscribed. Lasch (1979) focused on the dullness of most modern jobs to explain the appeal of sports. Bureaucratized work routines provide little in the way of challenge and excitement;

hence, sports spectacles are a relief from cognitive and emotional monotony.

My primary interest here is in sports as viewed by spectators, for despite a large number of players, there are many more viewers. Although radio and television have enormously increased sports spectatorship in the twentieth century, spectatorship is no new development. In Greece and Rome, sports were performed for spectators, as evidenced by the great stadiums built for their presentation, and at no time were sports intended to be played with no audience.

In some ways like dramatic art, sports convey certain ideal possibilities of social life. In art the outcome is determinate, never varying in a given work. In sports the outcome is always in doubt; yet, in the end, it is as irrevocable as the denouement of any drama. The suspense heightens the pleasure for many, but there is more to it than that. In daily social life, where the "game" is for real stakes, winning and losing are often determined to a large extent in advance, mainly by the ascriptive qualities that determine one's limits and opportunities. Historically, caste, race, gender, age, and social class have been so telling that in many societies little is left to personal qualities to create a fate that differs from that of one's ascriptive peers. In more open societies, ascriptive attributes have an increasingly attenuated hold on personal fortune. Nevertheless, race and social class are still meaningful determinants of the fate of many, restricting them from becoming major competitors in the social struggle. And among those who do manage to engage in the struggle with the hope of winning, victory is often denied.

By contrast, sports constitute a symbolic arena in which the contending forces are theoretically unhampered by social ascription, where merit is ostensibly the main criterion of success, where the shoddier politics of organizations—whom one knows, who owes whom a favor, what coalition one belongs to—are suspended. Sports are a pure form of social life (see Simmel 1951) in a society where individuals are expected to strive against one another for status. (Although the concern here is with the symbolism of sports as a paradigm of ideal competition between social competitors, sports can also symbolize other competitions; for example, the individual against nature, as in mountain climbing, or even, as Barendse (1983) put it, against a mechanistic technology, as in auto racing.) When sports scandals occur, they are considered shocking, in a manner that business or government corruption is not, because sports are supposed to be cleaner and fairer than real life.

This leveling of the playing field so that all parties have an equal opportunity to win makes sports particularly appealing to those who may feel either disadvantaged or threatened in society. The disadvantaged can obtain in sports, at least symbolically, the ideal opportunity they are denied because of race, class, or other condition. On the other hand, the threatened can obtain in sports the symbolic confirmation of their merit. For them the message of sports is that they have won because they deserved to win. Thus, although serving different and competing interests of different sectors of society, sports accommodate and integrate those interests into a common quasi-ritual model. Sports harmonize the interests of groups that are otherwise in conflict with each other. Thus, sports conversation is meaningful at virtually all but the very top levels of society, where theodicies of good fortune (Weber 1946:276) are not required.

As the paradigm of an ideal competitive society, sports, and, as I shall detail below, perhaps especially football, compel more than average attention from lower white-collar males. The interest is evident from patterns of spectatorship. Frank and Greenberg's 1980 study of television viewing found that white-collar workers were second only to students in watching sports programs, while professionals and managers were the occupational group least likely to watch them. The latter, of course, are the upper white-collar group. When they do choose to watch sports, tennis is more likely than football (Levine 1988). Tennis is also a highly competitive sport, but it conforms to the structural requirements of higher-class social life (for example, personal excellence) and since tennis is a highly cerebral sport, it demands a very quiet, unemotional spectatorship (Bourdieu 1978; Chandler 1985). The grounds on which football makes its claim on the lower white-collar male sector resonate with the social and occupational conditions of this group. They are the features that provide spectators with simulacra to real life, thus allowing for identification. These features include organizational teamwork, idealized competition, individuation, masculine assertion, and vicarious dominance.

Organizational Teamwork

Most work in modern societies is done in organizations with defined roles, or jobs, that are linked to each other according to the technology and division of labor of the industry. This is by way of contrast with earlier forms of work in which the individual craft or entrepreneurial activity played a more prominent part. Although there would seem to be no necessary link between these historical developments in the economy, on the one hand, and the structure of sports, on the other, there is evidence of how sports reflect the developments of the society that contain them. In a content analysis of sports coverage in the *Chicago Tribune* from 1900 to 1975, Lever and

Wheeler (1984) found that coverage had shifted over the years from amateur to professional, from local to national, and—importantly for present purposes—from individual to team activity. The division of labor in society thus ramifies even into sports.

In the modern division of labor, the given pattern of job links is supposedly arrayed to provide an optimum outcome. But organizational tables, which are task directed, usually consider neither the people who perform them, nor the social relations between those people. Here the ideal pattern of job linkages often breaks down. It is common knowledge that bureaucratically programmed links between jobs cannot program relations between the people who are in the jobs. Personal characteristics and styles sometimes mix well and augment each other, but often do not. One reason is that all jobs are foci of competition for control over the conditions of work (Collins 1975). Each point of linkage with another job requires some modification in autonomy. Linked jobs are dependent on each other, either bilaterally or unilaterally in a sequential flow. Normally, job occupants jealously guard the perimeters of their autonomous territory, resisting incursions from others, trying, however, to foist responsibilities in the other direction. This leads to more than a few disputes and disgruntlements and to a lack of the wholehearted cooperation programmed by the table of organization. The division of labor may be perfect on paper, but in actuality is often badly warped, as hurt feelings, barely suppressed animosities, and other emotional barriers prevent the realization of the ideal pattern.

In a compelling analysis, Keidel (1987) proposed that team sports closely model certain organizational formats. Three sports in particular are useful analogs of organizational variability: "Baseball is a metaphor for the autonomy of organizational parts, football, for the hierarchical control over the parts, and basketball for voluntary cooperation among the parts" (592). Given the particular relevance of football for lower white-collar males, it is useful to understand that it follows most closely the organizational conditions that are most likely to contain this group. Even more to the point is that the organizational structure and style of football are power oriented: hierarchial and authoritarian respectively, with the head coach as chief dictator of policy, strategy, and plays (Keidel 1987:592). Teamwork is scripted, and the whole, though depersonalized, assembles formidable power. It is precisely the organizational terrain with which many lower white-collar males are familiar, but with a difference. Unlike nonsports organizations, in which the festering relations between job occupants may go on indefinitely, in football teams, particularly, the concentration on victory is so central that personal rivalries and animosities are severely repressed.[7] The winning team is said to function, in the words of the popular cliche, like a well-oiled machine; that is, with a minimum of friction between its parts, the players. Each player is chosen for excellence in a particular position. Each player is trained to harmonize his efforts with those of the other players. Players who cannot do this are ordinarily benched or bumped from the team. Personal animus within teams is severely discouraged, and hostility is funneled outward toward other teams.

Well-functioning teams evoke an almost aesthetic pleasure in which form elegantly fits function.[8] To those who work in organizations, there is perhaps a special pleasure in watching the smooth performance of a team that has mastered the grittier elements of the human equation. Each player performs exactly as required, facilitating the team effort instead of hindering it through demands for personal autonomy or in trying to encroach on others. How different from the way real organizations operate. The pleasure of this organizational perfection is reserved more for spectators than for participants because participants, mainly amateurs who play for recreation, cannot devote the hours to drill and practice that make teams that perform optimally.

To lower white-collar males there may be something especially appealing in this idealized depiction of teamwork. They are not necessarily more victimized by defects of the organizational milieu than others, but they are perhaps less able to do anything about them. Unlike lower-level workers, who are often unionized and hence have a collective strength and voice that they lack individually (see, e.g., Kohn 1969), the lower white-collar echelon is individuated, isolated, and without much autonomous clout. Unlike its superiors, this echelon cannot change policies, reassign personnel, or bring organizational force to bear against recalcitrants or overconformists who refuse to play by the rules. The reality of organizational life for this group may be far from ideal, and the ideal representation of it in sports—football particularly—argues for its appeal to this group.

Idealized Competition

The premise of modern sports is that teams in a given league are approximately at the same level of skill and training. In certain respects this assumption is untrue. Even within given leagues, teams differ in their ability to recruit players and to provide facilities for them. Sometimes this is because nothing succeeds like success; winning teams tend to generate more resources and more attractive opportunities for better players, whether in salary (in professional sports) or in other perquisites (in collegiate sports). Notwithstanding these inequities, there are counterbalancing mechanisms to equilibrate the system, such as the manner in which new players are drafted into professional sports like football and basketball: the lowest-ranking team gets first pick from among the pool of eligibles (draft choices), and the highest-ranking team recruits last, thus assuring that the teams with the poorest records are able to recruit from among the best new players. An additional mechanism is the trade, which allows teams to dispose of and acquire players according to their theory of what combination of talents the team needs to win.

The general effect of these league practices is to create a field for competition that is close to ideal. One can see here an effort to appropriate the competitive model of an ideal capitalism, as envisioned by Adam Smith ([1776] 1937); that is, one in which a set of evenly matched competitors confront each other in the marketplace. What ultimately distinguishes them (that is, who wins and who loses) is who has the better product in that market. The better product means quality of construction, sensitivity to need, and diligence in the pursuit of these. Among equally balanced sports teams, the desideratum is diligently pursued competition vis-à-vis opposing teams.

In the real world of competitive striving among economic entities or in the murkier competition between agencies and branches of government, players are very often unevenly matched, or the players are so large that it is extremely difficult to overcome an existing pattern of market shares. Competition thus exists as a vague premise, but is often vitiated in a manner that nullifies superior effort. And, in this, sports teams differ. Clearly, competition is the focal concern in sports, and the object is to overcome the opposition. This motive is reduced to a simple and idealized formula, carried out nakedly and without pretense, which is not the case among economic competitors, who often becloud the issue with spurious claims of performing a public service. Not only are the motives and activities in sports starkly clear, but the results have an immediate consequence for the simple ranking of teams in a league. The top-ranked team is there by virtue of having won the most contests. There is a clarity here that is often absent in the competitions of real life.[9]

In personal life, too, competition often plays an important role. One strives for rank among colleagues and associates, and one hopes for good opinions of one's ideas and contributions, whether in solving problems on the job or in noninstrumental conversations. Yet, usually, unless one is at or near either the top or the bottom of the social-rank order, it is very difficult to tell exactly where one stands. So much is told by nuance or implication. One's social standing with superiors and peers is often ambiguous, and the significance of one's actions for one's rank are often unclear for a long time. By contrast, a game is of finite duration. When it ends, so does the suspense of how the teams stand. Except in the rare case of a tie, there is a definite winner and a definite loser. In an ambiguous world, this clarity can be highly satisfying. In the lower white-collar organizational world the competition is fierce, but the results are also frequently uncertain. Salary reviews are often only semiannual, if not less often, and promotions rarer still. In sports the clarity, frequency, and certainty of the outcome are satisfyingly not in doubt.

Individuation

In most organizations with a strictly hierarchical arrangement, credit for organizational accomplishment mainly accrues to the chief officer or head. Only he or she is aware of the specific contributions of individuals, and ordinarily, when judgment is rendered, the chief or head of the organization is given credit for the performance of the unit.[10] Individual elements are now merged into a coherent pattern with those of others in order to obtain the benefits of the synergy provided by the division of labor.[11] Yet the division of labor also robs the individual of the full gratification of attainment by burying it in the composite product to which all other individuals have contributed. At its worst the division of labor leads to mindless, brutalizing alienation, contrary to species needs as Marx (1964) put it and as Tocqueville ([1835] 1945:169) saw even earlier). At best, the individuated task that is only a part contribution to a whole blurs the grounds of the individual's claim to status for that contribution.

Here, again, sports provide a very satisfying model of how the division of labor and individuation can be combined (see, e.g., Lipsky 1985). Although teamwork is vital, most sports allow a crystalline view of the contributions of individual players. Each play in a game is ultimately the work of specific players, who hit, catch, throw, run, block, kick, tackle, or score. Ordinarily, a play centers on the contribution of a particular individual or on a visible sequence of moves by specific players. There is virtually no doubt, when a play is concluded, about who did what and how well. That player receives the credit or blame for outstanding play or for error.

Although sports teams approximate the organizational pattern of many nonsports groups, there is a striking difference in one respect. The team captain is relatively unimportant when compared with organizational leaders in nonsport groups. This role has scant functional duties, and when the team performs well, the captain receives virtually no credit. Replacing the captain is the coach, who dictates strategy and, in football, usually calls the plays (Keidel 1987). This grants the coach special status in the performance of the team, but the coach, by virtue of his or her nonplaying role, cannot be the star, cannot deliver the crucial, visible performance, cannot "win" the game. Only the individual players become noteworthy; under the eyes of thousands, perhaps millions of spectators, no superior contribution is lost or fails to be acknowledged by the roar of the crowd. Even the quarterback in football cannot eclipse the performance of other players, although he has a special status in managing play (as will be described below).

There is an elemental quality to this direct relationship between performance and its result that is rare in social life, especially in advanced societies. Contributions are often submerged with those of others, or it may take years before their implications are understood, or, given the small orbit in which the meaning of the contribution can be evaluated, envy and other careerist motives among co-workers may rob some of the approval they deserve.

In the sports arena, the clarity of contributions is augmented by the presence of relatively impartial spectators (more on this below) who are not rivals for fame with the players, but can judge a player's merits clearly. Spectators thus contribute to the direct relationship between performance and reward. They can also benefit from it on a deeper level. Many are organizational functionaries, and the reduced complexity of relating individual performance to reward can be highly satisfying. For most of them, who depend for approval in real life on the very supervisors and bosses who often receive credit for the aggregate of individual performances, the stark rendering of direct and immediate approval of what is done on the playing field has the intuitive appeal of fundamental justice.

Masculine Assertion

Physicality is central to sports as a distinctive form of social conduct. Whatever qualities of mind may be needed in a given sport—shrewdness, judgment, analytic intelligence—the state of the body is preeminent. This usually goes beyond simply strength, speed, and endurance to include agility, flexibility, visuospatial perceptual accuracy, and emotional poise under stress. This combination of attributes has a distinctly masculine feel. Furthermore, by all traditional accounts (D. Broverman et al. 1964; I. Broverman et al. 1970), in athletes these attributes are honed to a level of rarely attained perfection. They are also the qualities that most approximate male physical status at its developmental peak, in his twenties.

Though many sports participants are also counted among the most faithful spectators (Guttman 1986), the reverse is not true. Thus many, perhaps most, spectators are not active participants in the sports they watch, although many currently inactive spectators once did play the games they view others playing now. In fact, this is likely, given the usual pattern of male childhood and adolescence in the last half-century; increasing numbers of young males are able to prolong their schooling and delay entering the work force until at least age eighteen or after graduation from high school. An extended period of free time for sports is available to them up to that age. By contrast, at the turn of the century, most young males were long since working full time by age eighteen due to the obligation to assist with family finances. Indeed, American productivity in this century has been spent in part in providing all youths an extended adolescence in which sports ordinarily take an important and socially sanctioned part.

One important reason for the social endorsement of sports was the Victorian belief that sports participation could supplant male gonadal interests (Guttman 1978). The self-discipline, the time consumed in play, and the physical exhaustion of sports were believed to deter young males from sexual pursuits. (Little thought was given to the testosterone surges of sports victors, which made them more likely to be interested in sex than if they had not played.)

Although critics seeking to obtain a social reorganization of sports have attacked modern sports as a masculine preserve that presents and extols macho attributes (e.g., Meggysey 1970; Scott 1971), precisely these qualities may provide some of the strongest inducements to sports spectators. Dunning (1986) described sports as an arena where traditional masculine activities are practiced in relatively pure form. Masculine physicality, so carefully delimited and refined for ordinary daily conduct, is allowed a relatively free reign. Bodies colliding with bodies is encouraged, and strength and speed are nurtured to compete with strength and speed. This is atavistic, ontogenetically, phylogenetically, and culturally. On all three counts, it is a reversion to a more brute form of masculine assertion that is not usually permitted to express itself.

For many men, sports represent an almost pure arena of traditional male activity, undiluted by female interests. With an increasing number of women in the labor force and in the white-collar echelons, a more toned-down masculinity is required—crudeness of manner, gender jokes, and sexual harassment of female subordinates are proscribed (see Westoff 1985:10–11). There are few remaining social arenas in which out-and-out traditional, rough-and-tumble masculinity is encouraged. However, on the playing field, the new social constraints on males are inoperative. Indeed, the rougher the play, the more appreciated it may be (Bryant, Comisky, and Zillman 1981).

Dunning (1986) also argued that sports represent a rejection of homosexuality, which many consider sissyish and unmasculine. With the increasing liberality of sexual morality in recent decades and the emergence of homosexuals from the penumbra, the dominance of heterosexual males is threatened from this quarter as well. The outright dedication of sports to traditional masculine values and physicality provides an important value support and source of satisfaction to those males who confront serious competitive challenges from women or have some concern about the emergence of the homosexual minority.

Vicarious Dominance

Earlier in this book I reported the results of experiments showing that winners of sports encounters displayed elevated levels of testosterone (Mazur and Lamb 1980; Elias 1981; Booth et al. 1989). It is difficult to resist the hypothesis that those who identify with the winners, even as spectators, also experience a sense of dominance—vicariously—and, in consequence, receive a surge of testosterone with all the attendant benefits, including buoyant feelings of energy, concentration, and increased libido.

Although sports are not real life, they are real life in an ideal form. All the elements of reality are present, but sharpened and more concentrated. Sports also take on an importance in the life plan that shows they are not a minor matter. Time is programmed to include participation or spectatorship. The news media are scanned carefully for the sports results. The quasi-sacredness of certain sports occasions is widely acknowledged—the World Series, the Super Bowl—and a national ritual is enacted in the watching of these. The president of the United States ordinarily inaugurates the District of Columbia baseball season by throwing the first ball to start the first game. Weekly and seasonal cycles of sports and of particular games affect the way sociability is planned and with whom. Hence, sports are not merely incidental to modern American social life.

Vicarious dominance is arguably an important aspect of why sports have so strong a hold on the American interest. As symbolic enactments of major components of reality, sports give both the winners and losers in the social class system a second chance, so to speak. Losers, those who lack position and opportunities for dominance/eminence, have an opportunity to gain symbolic victories through the teams and players they support. These surrogate contests absorb attention and concern, and, even if one's own life chances are poor or only middling, the victory of one's team is an emotional surrogate for one's own symbolic victory. Cialdini et al. (1976:366) found that college students "basked in reflected glory." Their identification with a winning football team elevated their own self-esteem, a possible psychological precursor of a testosterone surge (Mazur and Lamb 1980). It is arguably the case that the satisfactions that ensue from these symbolic victories are as real as in true victories. In this sense there are no fake emotions. Symbolic dominance may thus have all the effects of real dominance so far as the body is concerned. Of course, this is conjecturable, since empirical evidence for the direct tie between vicarious dominance and testosterone is absent. But the case for the hypothesis is persuasive.

Grounds for Vicarious Dominance

The pivotal idea of this book is that social encounters that end in either dominance or eminence produce elevations in T. The issue now is whether experiences of vicarious dominance, particularly those derived from sports outcomes (although not limited to them), can also elevate T. If one has not actually contested and won, but only identified with the eventual winner, is there a testosterone effect? There is no direct evidence on this question, but as a matter of logical surmise, a T effect is a plausible outcome in those who strongly identify with winners. The effect ought not be as strong as in the actual winners, but it may be strong enough to bear on the stability of the entire social structure, as will be discussed below. This is a heuristic conjecture that has not been offered before. Indeed, other explanations for the relative stability of social structures have been proposed, but if vicarious dominance is possible, and if it leads to T, then an additional, perhaps more cogent, understanding of social structures is available.

There are several reasons to suppose that vicarious dominance derived from sports victories is real and should, therefore, have a physiological effect. Each of them supports the idea that the spectators of sports events, whether present at the actual event or as media onlookers, are actively involved in the contest, emotionally aroused by it, and physiologically reactive to it.

Identification with Team

Identification means that an individual's responses are shaped by the experience of another person. In some readings, self and other are assimilated, so that there is no distinction between the two. This has raised a question about whether spectators actually identify with players or performers (or characters in drama) or whether another mechanism is operating. Zillman (1980) challenged the notion of identification as the source of personal involvement in drama. He proposed that "the illusion lies in the fact that the respondent behaves as if he or she were there—as a *witness to real happenings*. Such behavior suggests that suspense-induced empathic distress . . . can be dealt with as the affective reaction of a concerned 'third party' who vehemently deplores impending outcomes" (1980:143; emphasis in original).

Although Zillman argued for a narrow construction of identification and opposed it as an explanation of viewers' emotions, his position is consonant with the one espoused here: that dramatic and sports events elicit spectators' emotions because the events have the power to draw observers sufficiently into the action so that they react *as if* to real events. But, according to Zillman, an additional feature of the ability, and perhaps desire, to put oneself into the setting (that is, the identification) depends on whether one likes the protagonist of the action. Zillman proposed that audiences "feel for" a protagonist in situations of peril, as if they were themselves present to experience what the protagonist does, only if they like him or her. If this is true for drama, a fortiori ought it to be true for sports, in which live performers engage their fans' attention, interest, and affections, not only by what they do on the playing field, but also by the glamour that often marks their private lives.

Taking a somewhat different stance from that of Zillman, Tannenbaum (1980) endorsed the idea that observers of sports and drama derive their satisfactions vicariously. He saw this as an extension of the species ability to learn about events not only through actual participation, but also from communications about them. "Just as a communication capacity allows us to learn vicariously, so too can we become emotionally involved vicariously. One of the powerful attractions of . . . television is that [it] provides so many with so much emotional experience at so little personal cost" (110).

According to Tannenbaum, "Most of the time for most people the arousal produced by TV entertainment is a low-level or modest dosage (enough to titillate without really exciting)" (111). Here we need to distinguish between fictive drama, where action, plot, and characters are composed beforehand, and sports events, where the elements of action and plot unfold before the spectator just as they happen in reality. Indeed, from the displayed emotions of spectators, one must conclude that arousal is often very intense. Partly this must result from the reality of the event and the real, not manufactured, uncertainty of the outcome. But it is reasonable to surmise that there is also strong identification with one or another team or player(s). This is manifested, according to Goldstein (1982), when fans' arousal that leads to violence varies in proportion to the hostility of the players they are watching. Spectator aggression after viewing player aggression may be explained by a theory of allegiance. Spectators are fans, which means they are partisans of a side. When the contest heats up, fans are implicated too. It is as if they themselves were winning or losing. The players' fate is the spectators' own, if they identify with the players, as there is reason to believe fans do.

These notions have been subjected to some empirical examination. In an ingenious study to test the effects of winning and losing on fans, Cramer and Ellins (1986) found that fans of the winning team assisted individuals who were ostensibly fans of the losing team (but were actually confederates of the experimenters), while fans of the losing team were unlikely to do so when they were asked for assistance by ostensible fans of the winning team. At issue? A mere ten cents.

In a series of studies, Sloan (1979) specifically examined evidence for a number of theories of the impact of sports on fans. In the sense already discussed here, fans identified with the teams whose play they watched. Crucial for present purposes were the differences in emotional outcome between winning and losing occasions and between fans and nonfans. Basketball and football fans (in the college setting where the data were collected) experienced significant emotional uplift when their team won and significant discouragement, anger, and sadness when their team lost. (Supporting the idea of the emotional uplift to be gained from the victory of one's team, Dervin proposed in 1985 that "regenerative energy" (297) is a sequel of such experience.) Confirming the identification hypothesis, Sloan stated that "fans do believe themselves to be a part along with the team, of a meaningful group in their lives" (1979:252). By contrast, a sample of students who observed a series of bouts between amateur boxers on the same campus showed no similar positive or negative emotional consequences, even though they were quite involved in the event (frequently shouting and jumping to their feet). The crucial difference between the basketball and football contests, on the one hand, and the boxing events, on the other, was the lack of the student spectators' identification with any of the boxers. Obviously, the difference is not that boxing is unable to evoke identification.

Guttman (1986) described the ecstatic reaction of the black community to the lightning victory of Joe Louis over German boxer Max Schmeling in their 1938 rematch (see also LaPointe 1988). Among blacks, Louis was seen as the representative of his race; and even more than among whites, Louis carried the flag for the United States against Nazi Germany. For a black to do so at that time was doubly ironic: Nazi racial theories held blacks in contempt; and in the United States blacks were still virtually everywhere an abused and disadvantaged minority. Indeed, a great deal was riding on Louis's performance so far as blacks were concerned, both in giving the lie to Nazi racial ideology and shaming the American conscience. The joyous outbursts in black communities that greeted Louis's victory were a warrant of the strong identification that existed there.[12] The ethnic direction of identification with teams or players is not limited to boxing, although that sport is likely to focus partisanship very clearly along these lines due to the undiluted ethnic identity of the contestants. College football, too, has been viewed as an arena for status contests between rival ethnic groups (Collins 1975).

While it may seem entirely plausible for blacks to identify with Joe Louis, or students with their college team, or alumni with their alma mater's team, does it make sense that New Yorkers identify with the Jets or Mets, Los Angelenos with the Dodgers or Rams, Bostonians with the Celtics or Patriots, and so on? These are merely franchise teams that can be, and occasionally are, moved elsewhere by their owners; nor are the players usually local personalities, indigenous to the area, with friends and family rooted in the community. There is virtually no organic relationship between team and territory, yet the community is usually hotly partisan in the team's behalf, and the winning of a pennant or World Series or Super Bowl can unleash considerable emotional arousal (Guttman 1986). What explains this identification? I propose that modern social life provides differential opportunities for dominance/eminence, ordered in part by social class. In every community there are sectors that have only moderate chances for dominance or eminence in their major involvements. Sports make available an alternative arena in which to obtain a dominance "high." Intersecting these interests, sports teams are geographically labeled and identified. Despite the waning strength of community ties, sectors of the population with a local outlook—precisely those toward the lower reaches of the class system—can nonetheless derive considerable enhancement of dominance from local achievements. British soccer fans, with their frenzy and occasionally deadly violence, are perhaps the ultimate in this kind of vicarious dominance attainment (Rule 1989; Whitney 1989). In keeping with other forms of differentiation between and within classes, the upper echelons are more cosmopolitan in both interaction networks and outlooks (Collins 1981). Of course, they can be, since they have less need of vicarious victories won by the local teams.

Strategizing Outcomes

A second basis of vicarious dominance may be found in the potential of certain sports to evoke a high level of interactive involvement between spectators and the ongoing flow of the game. One of the most important developments in American sports since the 1950s has been the emergence of football as the dominant spectator sport. Although horse racing and baseball attract more attendance, this is due in part to differences in frequency of play. For example, professional baseball teams play 154 games in a season, compared with 20 played by professional football teams. Guttman denoted the emergence of football by the number of covers devoted to it by *Sports Illustrated,* the premier sports magazine in the United States. In the period 1955–1958, forty-one covers were devoted to baseball and twenty-two to football. By the period 1971–1974, baseball had declined to thirty-eight and football had risen to fifty-three (Guttman 1978:141). Equally telling is the shift in job absenteeism in the Detroit auto plants from the traditional postweekend Monday peak to a Tuesday peak, which is attributed to "Monday Night Football" on television (Guttman 1986:140): Process servers are advised that Monday night is the best time to find those named in subpoenas at home (Gunther and Carter 1988). Nielsen (1978, 1980) and Gallup (1986) reported that football has been the top spectator sport of males since 1963.

Why has football emerged to dominate sports consciousness? Bourdieu (1978) proposed that sports serve different functions for different social classes. Thus, upper-class interest in sports is focused on how sports train future leaders for command. This idea is well conveyed by the old saw, attributed to the duke of Wellington, that the battle of Waterloo was won on the playing fields of Eton. It is probably not accidental that the greatest growth in sports involvement, whether as participant or as spectator, and in sports media coincided with the great expansion of the white-collar labor force during the 1950s to 1970s. Instructive here is the emergence in 1955 of *Sports Illustrated,* one of the most popular special interest magazines and an astounding success by any publishing criterion, although it took extraordinary faith, or prescience, on the part of publisher Henry Luce to sustain it through eleven years of losses.[13] The success of *Sports Illustrated* indicates the growth in the social importance of sports in the 1950s and 1960s. The availability of televised games widely augmented the spectator audience and reverberated in other media. The sports audience grew most during the great corporate-growth breakout period.[14]

Indeed, we have here a rare insight into the integration of a number of societal elements: a changing labor force, more and more sequestered in offices, with relatively low opportunities for individual dominance/eminence; the availability of the technology of television and satellite communications, with the ability to transmit live-action broadcasts from almost anywhere in the world; and the exploitation of sports, particularly football, as one of the most significant items on the television menu.[15] I contend that this confluence did not occur by chance, but is rather an instance of how diverse forces in society are activated or emphasized to accommodate emerging interests and groups with special needs. The male lower white-collar sector was a ready client for a form of play that would provide for its special needs. Sports grew at about the same pace as the group that needed such outlets.

Data on sports spectatorship in the United States show that baseball fans are older and less well off socioeconomically, while football fans are younger and somewhat better off (A. Guttman 1986; Gallop 1986; Levine 1988). There is a reason for this: football is more likely to be the preferred sport of those who attended college, where the game is overwhelmingly more popular than baseball, and from which many star players graduate to professional teams. Football also manifests a number of characteristics that are attractive to a middle-class group that is relatively well placed compared with the American average, but may be confronted with mobility problems. Having reached a moderate level of attainment, many lower white-collar males recognize that they will not achieve much more except through seniority, which is far different from dominance/eminence, where one's advancement depends on the recognition of one's excellence. Football is an ideal sport for this group because it allows observers to participate actively in the strategizing of play.

Football ordinarily allows about forty plays per game. Each play is preceded by an interim period in which the results of the previous play can be considered and the goals and logic of the next play determined. Although the quarterback ostensibly decides the play, more often he is preempted by the coach (Keidel 1987). Regardless of who actually calls the plays, spectators, too, can "play" quarterback. Given the circumstances on the field, spectators can strategize the next play; whether to run, pass, kick, or shift formation on offense, and how to place linebackers and ends on defense. Does the quarterback choose the same strategy? Did the strategy succeed or fail? The evidence is available almost immediately.

In lending itself to spectator strategizing, football involves viewers in a more intense manner than either baseball or basketball. As Guttman (1978) pointed out, basketball, hockey, and soccer move too fast to strategize play easily, although there are some opportunities in regard to whom to put in the lineup and how to make plays after crucial timeouts. Baseball, too, allows for less strategizing than football. But, crucially, baseball strategies generally focus on single players—what the batter should do, what the pitcher should do—while football strategies involve the whole team (Keidel 1987). To strategize football is, to make only a modestly hyperbolic claim, akin to directing a military campaign. The quarterback (or coach), whether on the field or as spectator, is, in this respect, a general who determines the disposition of his forces against the enemy. For male lower white-collar cadres, this is an inviting role to play, even if only vicariously. Although in organizational life their powers are limited and the consequences of their decisions highly circumscribed, in the vicarious world of the game they can plan a complete strategy upon which depends an outcome that often millions will cheer. Football, in particular, affords those who lack executive status the opportunity to play the leader role vicariously and often to receive immediate feedback on the validity of their decisions.

Strategizing the play of a winning team—perhaps especially if one has called the plays much like the quarterback (or coach) did—is a tribute to one's own sagacity. Under the circumstances, the team victory cannot fail to stir in oneself a sense of one's own deserts as victor. Indeed, the effect here may go beyond vicarious dominance, which so largely depends on identification. Successful generalship requires no such condition. To choose the right strategy for victory is self-validating independently of whether one has an emotional attachment to those who carry it out. Indeed, to have one's strategy confirmed as correct is a victory even if the team loses.

Ritual Arousal

A third ground for vicarious dominance involves the visceral emotions that are mobilized by the spectacle of play. Durkheim ([1915] 1965) was perhaps the first to propose that collective rituals evoke emotional arousal and sentiments of solidarity among participants. Although Durkheim focused on relatively small tribal groups in close physical proximity, we may extend the scope of his insight to include extremely large groups so long as all members are participating simultaneously in the same activity. One has only to think of the mass Nazi rallies in the stadium at Nuremberg in the 1930s or the mass television audience during the four days following the assassination of President John F. Kennedy in 1963 to understand that similarity and simultaneity, not size, are the main constituents of ritual arousal.

Quite like any other mass phenomenon manifesting similarity and simultaneity, sports arouse emotions even in spectators who are not present at the actual game. There is the sense of participation with perhaps millions of others, all focused on precisely the same action at precisely the same moment. There is even a specific intention to create such arousal on the part of the several groups that decide what the game spectacle should be, including the teams, the television broadcasters, and advertisers. Harris pointed to such elements as "band music, computerized stadium signs and instant replay devices, play-by-play accounts blaring from portable radios, team colors" (1983: 184). These all foster intense ritual arousal in the crowds to whom they are directed.

Guttman (1978), who is otherwise quite sensitive to spectatorship phenomena, does not share this view. On the contrary, "watching a physical contest is not really very much like engaging in a physical contest" (1978:184). In one important sense this is true. The spectator does not hit the line, take the punch, or receive the body check; thus the somatic component is missing. But, except in cases of serious injury, and sometimes not even then, players may not experience their body in the heat of the action. On the other hand, spectators report exhaustion after watching hard-fought matches or games (Sloan 1979). This is due in large part to the emotional roller coaster created by suspense and to the metabolism of glycogens and the wracking of the body with spurts of catecholamines and cortisol as one's team encounters the vicissitudes of play.

To add to the physiological involvement of spectators, there is also the shouting, exacerbated by the din created by the shouts of others, and the jumping to one's feet to get a better view of critical plays or sequences of action. At least anecdotally, there is evidence that similar responses take place even in front of the television screen, where the same potential exists for emotional investment in the fortunes of one's favorites. Importantly, crowd noise from the stadium or arena is also transmitted, almost instantaneously providing a second channel for the communication of what is important about the current or just completed play. Home viewers, too, are exposed to the moment-by-moment voice-over analysis and emotions of sports commentators.

Even if alone, the home viewer is not remote from the social orbit in which similar, simultaneous response with others, leading to ritual arousal, is possible. Multiple channels of stimuli continuously impinge on even the so-called passive spectator to involve him or her in the action. Aside from the actual play itself, which puts the spectator into the scene as a third party confronting the same perils and incentives, the remaining elements that result from the sensed copresence of a large, perhaps global, crowd of fellow spectators, act powerfully to involve the spectator. The score by which the favored team is victorious is no mere cold statistic. It has been earned emotionally by spectators in their play-by-play arousal and bodily investments.

Meadian Role Taking

The emotional grounds of vicarious dominance just discussed depend in part on cognitive-symbolic processes that entrain the body's rhythms to that of the play on the field, enabling the obliteration of some of the distinction between participation and observation. Differences between players and spectators have been stressed frequently, often to the detriment of the spectator (see Guttman 1978:184). Although there are obvious effects on players that no amount of excited watching can deliver, it is erroneous to think that watching play is passive in a simple sense. Knecht and Zenger (1985) found that spectator involvement in a basketball game varied curvilinearly with knowledge of the rules of the game. Those with moderate knowledge displayed more involvement than those with very little or substantial knowledge. On the assumption of a normal distribution of knowledge, we may assume that most spectators fall somewhere in the middle category, hence can become quite involved in the play. But the experience of the social is involving in a sense not yet mentioned.

First, even to be an observer requires an active participation. The meaning of a scene is not inherent in the perception of it, but rather in the conception. As detailed by Mead (1934) and also by Weber (1947), this is accomplished by an empathic introduction of the self into the place of the other, thereby cognitively invoking in oneself the meaning of what is taking place. To keep up with the fast-breaking action of sports play, the spectator is necessarily putting him or herself into the place (or taking the role) of what Mead called "the generalized other," a symbolic construct that comprehends the interests of all the parties involved in the game, including not only one's own favored team, but the opposition as well. Through role taking, one gets the meaning of the action at the cognitive level.

Role taking is not merely a cognitive process, but includes also involuntary muscular empathies that accompany all social interaction. In calling up in oneself the stance of the other, the investment of self is somatic as well as cognitive, even if only observation is involved. Role taking initiates somatic micromovements of the very musculature whose actions in the other are being viewed. Precisely there, one's own body flexes as part of the role-taking process. McPhail and Rexroat (1979) reviewed experiments in which observers were found to contract muscles upon viewing the movement of the same muscles by another actor. To observe a game or contest of physical movement must evoke a continuing series of somatic resonances. Given the frequently violent movements, whole body actions, and sustained efforts that mark much sports play, the role-taking observer is subjected to a somatic workout at the microlevel that exceeds the normal in most respects.

By role taking the physical moves of the players, there is also the possibility of the entrainment of bodily rhythms with those of players (McClelland 1985). The spectator who rises from his seat after viewing a successful run by a swivel-hipped quarterback is more likely to swivel his own hips even in walking the distance from the television screen to the refrigerator and back; this should be especially true when the quarterback has danced and twisted his way to significant gain of yardage. Indeed, successful models are more likely to be imitated (Bandura 1977). These postplay somatic elicitations are assisted by the immediate playback, sometimes in slow motion, of what just occurred. Role taking, both cognitive and somatic, augments the intensity of investment by fans in the action of their teams, creating additional ground for the experience of vicarious dominance when the team wins.

Helping the Home Team

Another form of personal investment in sports, even as a spectator, can emerge in active efforts to enhance team morale on one's own side and depress it for the opposition. It is well known that spectator passivity can result from a dull game or a lopsided one in which, despite automatic, somatic role taking, there is too little suspense or significance to the ongoing play to arouse the viewer. Dull games are a damper on excitement generally. But they are not the norm, otherwise attendance would sag and home viewing dwindle. Indeed, when teams are in slumps or are going through a disastrous season, attendance usually plunges. Even ardent fans feel there is little to be gained from watching another drubbing. Tannenbaum (1980) reported that when experimental subjects were given an opportunity to watch a game they had never seen before or the rerun of a game in which their team won, they chose the latter. Significantly, if their team had lost the earlier game, they chose to watch the new one.

An exciting game is often a close one, in which uncertainty of outcome is a marked feature. At such contests spectators are especially aroused, apparently to good purpose. A number of researchers have recognized what is called the "home-team advantage." The team tends to win more when it plays at home than when it plays away. For example, Snyder and Purdy (1985) found that the basketball teams they followed won 66 percent of their home games. A number of reasons have been advanced for this, including visiting players' relative unfamiliarity with the facilities and the fatigue of traveling. Although these may contribute to the home-team advantage, there is also evidence that home-team spectators provide assistance to their players.

Snyder and Purdy (1985) analyzed the home-team advantage phenomenon from a Durkheimian perspective. According to Durkheim ([1915] 1965), groups create symbolic representations of themselves (totems) and often apotheosize these so that they attain sacred status. Sports teams with an avid cadre of followers—who are more likely to be present on home grounds—take on a certain sacred, totemic status. The paraphernalia of the team—colorful uniforms and equipment, bands playing music, attractive cheerleaders in rhythmic performance—lend the players an unnatural status, removed, as Durkheim required for the sacred, from the ordinary. The ritual nature of the presentation of teams, under special lights, in a special setting, often with music (the team song), all contribute to the extraordinary nature of the occasion. With an overwhelming majority of spectators cheering them on during home games, players are aware of the special bond between them and the fans. The cheers for their good plays and moans of disappointment over failed plays contribute to unite fans and players, impressing on the players their representative role in symbolizing the collectivity's aspirations. This is then seen to energize and motivate the players to perform better than they would without spectator support.

Other analysts take these notions a step further. Zillman, Bryant, and Sapolsky (1979) found that ardent fans are not simply devotees of sport, but only of the winning sport of the team with which they identify. Hence, despite the canons of good sportsmanship, these fans do not applaud the good plays made by the opposition team. They reserve their approval for their own side. Greer (1983) found that spectator booing of the visiting team at basketball games helped to depress the visitors' performance, and cheering the home team tended to elevate its performance. Although only spectators who are present at the game can affect its outcome through their biased spectatorship, and while it is likely that the most passionate fans are the ones who attend games, this can hardly exhaust the corps of fans with the most intense feelings for the team. Regardless of where they are, many spectators are active exponents of their team; they are just as likely to boo the opposition and cheer for the home team from screenside. What is indicated is that, as in ancient Rome, where spectators could render verdicts of life or death on gladiators, the watchers of sports and games are not mere observers, but are active participants in support of their favorites. Hence, when their team wins, so do they, as cocontributors to some extent to team victory.

Conversational Resource

For sports spectators, the game ramifies and has consequences that appear in settings far removed from the arena of play or the site of the television screen on which it was seen. Across a very broad spectrum of the American male population, except in ultra-high culture circles, sports are perhaps the basic common denominator of conversation and the most common topic (Guttman 1986:180).[16] The American agreement to avoid discussion of politics and religion as perhaps too serious to be talked about leaves an important gap. But virtually everyone can participate in sports talk. Among males in many walks of life, last night's game is an inevitable if not primary topic of conversation. This obligates many males to know what happened to the various teams and sports that are followed in their circle. Failing this, the individual must necessarily surrender participation to others who are knowledgeable. It behooves males, then, to attend to the raw materials of tomorrow's discourse: the details of play; the strategies, both successful and failed; the opportunities that were missed; and the prospects for players and teams for the remainder of the season.

Spectatorship is not simply passive watching. Even apart from the emotional challenges of the game interaction, there is the impact of how spectatorship fits into other parts of social life. At least among males, the fact of having watched a particular sports event suits one to participate in subsequent social interactions in which the event is a singularly important topic of conversation. One's spectator experiences became raw material for one's sociability participation. The novelty of one's insight into what happened and why, the intensity of one's emotional commitment, and the wisdom of one's judgment about strategy, both past and future, are the substantive grounds on which one makes a status claim in the postevent sociability. Ignorance of nuance, error of interpretation, or a commonplace view condemns one to the social periphery. Others do not heed one's assertions, and to speak at all in the group becomes difficult, except when no one is paying attention. This bespeaks low status. Indeed, spectatorship is a rehearsal for later interaction, in which the sports event is the topic that allows one to claim distinction. This in itself can be a source of T. Under the circumstances, one's involvement is likely to be enhanced, for one can participate later on the basis of vivid impressions and a distinctive sense of what happened. Identification with a team, a player, a strategy defines one's own position more clearly.

The subsequent verbal reprise of play requires some concentration of attention during it. For example, it means reserving viewing time free of distraction from family, domestic chores, and community obligations. One way to accomplish this is to watch the game in the company of like-minded males, who then constitute themselves as a male society in active session for the period of the game. Guests are understandably free of domestic responsibility, and the host is similarly liberated by virtue of the dignity conferred by his status as host. Spouse and children are usually well tutored in what this involves. In their aggregation for purposes of simultaneous and similar activity, the watchers conform also to the requirements of Durkheimian ritual arousal (Collins 1981). Thus, whatever factors of arousal are transmitted through the screen from the field of play are enhanced by the copresence of a group in front of the screen.

Yet, the effect of the presence of others is to sharpen one's concentration and subsequent understanding of the play as it proceeds (Zajonc 1965). Comments, explanations, and creative analysis are elements in a synthesis of comprehension and the formation of sentiments about the play and its outcomes that becomes the conversational resource of the morrow. Coffee breaks and lunch hours are prime occasions for replaying the game. But one does not replay it very well unless one has engaged in it seriously, even as a spectator. The need to make use of the game in subsequent interaction binds spectators more closely to it, thus making it all the more likely that they will experience the outcome more personally and, as argued here, physiologically.

Male Territory

Finally, although women have increasingly become sports fans, and women's sports and sports figures are increasingly prominent, the dominant sports and sports figures are male for a large sector of the population. This mystique of maleness in sports has been deplored by some (Hoch 1972; Scott 1971; Meggysey 1970) and treated analytically by others (e.g., Dunning 1986). Whatever the ideological implications, there is general agreement that male images and masculine values dominate the major sports presently commanding the most media attention.

In the service of vicarious dominance the male roster of performers allows for an unmixed identification in gender terms. If an important constituent of the audience for these male displays is a group that is already under status threat from women (as discussed above), the sex homogeneity of performers and spectators can only serve to augment the tie to winners and to a shared experience of dominance. Indeed, Redekop (1984) reported that men prefer competitive sports while women prefer noncompetitive sports. This accords with the pronounced male interest in winning and in attaining the benefits of dominance.

Sports, Testosterone, and Social Stability

To this point I have proposed that sports, mainly football, provide an important source of vicarious dominance for lower white-collar males, and that it is plausible to think that this leads to periodic enhancements or surges of T, which these men usually cannot obtain from their daily work involvements. These surges make their recipients feel good, and this, I contend, has consequences for social stability and the maintenance of social order.

One of the central problems of sociological analysis is that of social order. How are the often stable and predictable patterns of social life maintained? With society prey both to the random impulses of individuals and to organized disruption by groups unhappy with their share of the collective benefits of production and control, why isn't there more social chaos? The two most important theories here are consensus and conflict.

The consensus view is that societies are organized according to certain functionally desirable patterns that benefit the group as a whole, and that they socialize their members to accept and believe in these patterns as just, to feel guilt if they should violate them, and to court punishment if the guilt mechanism should fail.

By contrast, the conflict view is that social order is maintained because dominant groups enforce conformity on those who are weaker and cannot resist. Control consists of superior force, when necessary, but more often only the threat of it. Repressed groups have ideologies foisted upon them that rationalize existing social relations and rules that the powerful endorse. One of the most important effects of ideology, according to this view, is false consciousness; for example, workers who vote in line with upper-class interests and not their own.

Another instance of possible false consciousness is that of lower white-collar workers who identify with their superiors in the mistaken belief that they too will someday be superiors. Although some will rise to much higher levels of organizational power, overwhelmingly most will not, due to the pyramidal shape of the hierarchy. Each succeeding step up becomes more difficult, as fewer and fewer opportunities are available at each higher level. Yet despite this clear knowledge, there is little evidence that this stirs discontent among the large number of lower white-collar workers to whom it must become apparent, relatively young, that they will not rise very far. And this is something of a puzzle.

Given that this is an educated group with some insight into organizational processes, it poses a problem in the theory of politics. Why does this group not act in its own interests? Why does it not express its discontent in movements for organizational democratization, for example, or in some form of resistance through collective effort, such as unionization? Indeed, instead of confronting the organizational system that sentences most of this group to only very moderate levels of career attainment, it reacts by conservative voting preferences (Gailey 1985) or in resenting newly arrived competitors such as women managers (Dubin 1985).

Fundamentally, we need to explain why those who lose or are only small winners in the contests that sort out one's status in society relative to others do not either rebel or withdraw commitment to productivity and to playing the game. The particular group that concerns us here, lower white-collar males, could be particularly troublesome were it to turn against the system that effectively denies it very much status. This group is the mechanism through which the upper white-collar ranks insulate themselves from the lower echelons of the work force. They do what might be called the dirty work of hierarchy, imparting and justifying decisions they have not made to groups below them who will not necessarily desire to obey. Yet their loyalty is virtually never in doubt. Several theories have been offered to explain this.

One theory, touched on above, involves false consciousness. It refers to ideas and beliefs about reality that presumably make sense of the world, but which from an "interest" point of view do not make sense because they deprive a group of its rightful benefits. Although employed mainly by Marxist theorists (Lukacs 1971) to explain working-class quiescence in capitalist societies, the concept may be applied in the present case. Instead of perceiving themselves as minions and tools of the more powerful, lower white-collar workers are imbued with the notion that they will someday also attain power and that mobility opportunities are sufficient to guarantee their success, thus realizing the American dream. All this despite a readily apparent reality that denies this likelihood for most of them.

Another explanation of the pacification of discontent in industrial societies involves false needs. Marcuse (1964) argued that a central fact of industrial societies is their ability to produce enormous amounts of goods and services. Also a feature of the present time is the drive to commodify human interests. In capitalist society this means that objects and services that might serve human needs are created and packaged for sale. One can, then, buy anything. Advertising and marketing forces step in to create needs for the goods and services that are produced specifically to satisfy these needs. According to Marcuse, the pacification of potentially discontented groups in capitalist and (but not as well) in socialist societies is accomplished through the manufacture of false needs for these goods and services. The needs are false because, in Marcuse's view, the commodities that satisfy them do not liberate their consumers to move to higher levels of human consciousness or relatedness with others; rather, the commodities simply occupy attention for a time, as a toy diverts a child from annoying its parents with demands for attention. In like manner, those who are stimulated by false needs are equally diverted from confronting the barrenness of their lives, their entrapment in a system that does not permit their truly human interests to emerge. The logic of such a system, according to Marcuse, is to continue to create new products and the needs that the products are available to serve.

The position taken here is that neither false consciousness nor false material need is sufficient to accomplish the task of pacification of the discontented. False consciousness would be insufficient by itself to attain its object. The mind is too weak to withstand emotions; the will collapses if the body refuses its cooperation. Hence, if false consciousness is viable, it is only because the body has consented. The Marcusean theory of false needs cedes too much power to the satisfaction of highly transient needs that the theory itself derides as unfulfilling. Furthermore, neither false consciousness nor false need is rooted in social relationships, which are the bedrock upon which individuals and collectivities establish their sense of worth and the measure of their attainment of what is just and deserving. False consciousness projects relational benefits into the future, and false need is barren of relationship entirely, except in the sense of keeping up with one's neighbors.

Without rejecting completely the validity of the false consciousness and false needs hypotheses, I wish to offer as an additional explanation of the underlying source of social stability among populations that might otherwise be discontented the concept of *false potency.* False potency is the feeling that one is dominant (and there is the biological substrate to prove it), but the feeling issues not from true relational attainment, where one has combated and won, but from vicarious dominance, obtained through identification with surrogate winners. Vicarious dominance, according to the theory presented earlier, results in a surge of T, and this is the proximal source of false potency. It provides males with an extra physiological push that releases energy, a sense of well-being, and perhaps some feistiness that is admired by male friends and by females, including one's spouse, and may lead, by a longer route, to increased libido. These are no small benefits. They are grounded in the body, the ultimate repository of contentment, and they derive from a sense of one's standing vis-à-vis others. Although that standing is inauthentic—vicarious victories are not true victories—it nonetheless unlocks the mood and the physiological elements that accompany true victory, and the effect of this is a striking social denouement. Those who are contented in the body are not likely to seek social upheaval.

Several body languages can directly mediate participation in politics. One is drugs. Another is sex (Birenbaum 1970). A third is exercise. In the first, the body is tricked into good feeling. In the second, sexual freedom becomes a surrogate for all other types of freedom, and if it provides a T surge, so much the better. In the third, personal effort against physical inertia can also lead to elevation of T. Each of these works directly on the body to make it feel good, and the general hypothesis relating contentment and political stability is expected to hold for them. Another source of bodily good feeling is vicarious dominance. The history of sports from its very beginning reveals the capacity to satisfy human needs for dominance vicariously. I have hypothesized that while actual participants derive direct bodily satisfaction from their contests if they win, they provide their partisans satisfaction that is also physical and that this explains some of the frenzied popularity of sports for spectators. The hope of experiencing the win of a favorite is a powerful incentive, one that explains the roar of the crowd in both Roman colosseums and modern stadiums. The players are not merely entertainers, they are also substitute contestants in battles that many of the spectators are not able or permitted to enter. In this sense, they are psychic extensions of the onlookers, highly paid to fight one's battles because one is not positioned to fight them oneself.

Geertz (1972) analyzed the cockfight in Bali as a contest that symbolizes the status structure of the society through the display of "social passions . . . the thrill of risk, the despair of loss, and the pleasure of triumph" (27). The Balinese, said Geertz, "go to cockfights to find out what a man usually composed, aloof . . . feels like when attacked, tormented, challenged, insulted, and driven in result to extremes of fury, he has totally triumphed or been brought low" (27). Of course, triumphed only vicariously, since, as Geertz contended, the real social structure remains unaffected.

Virtually every sporting age from classical Greece to the present has been marked by intense arousal and partisanship among spectators (Guttman 1986). Indeed, the civilizing process has greatly moderated the intensity of spectator involvement.[17] The role of sports in the maintenance of social stability has been argued most forcibly by Marxists, but, in my view, on the wrong grounds. As Marxists conceive the problem, sports operate in some way to prevent the occurrence of revolution, mainly by the working class, which can become aware of its class interests and rise against its oppressors. Sports presumably interfere with the coming to consciousness of the working class by arousing contrary impulses. Keil (1984) has argued that the structure of sports attainment via competition is an implicit endorsement of bourgeois self-oriented achievement and thus discredits collective action. Other critics link sports presentations to the dominant ideology of American society (Harris 1983), including patriotism (Kennard and Hofstetter 1983), the validity of the political system (Lipsky 1985), the desirability of United States global dominance (Galtung 1982), the legitimacy of the dominant class's hegemony (Ingham and Hardy 1984), and outright racism and sexism (Kennard and Hofstedter 1983; Hoch 1972; Scott 1971; and Meggysey 1970). Sports are also supposed to act as a modern opiate, much as Marx considered religion to do in his day (Gruneau 1975).

These attacks on sports depend largely on cognitive elements and the manipulation of belief systems. Not so the attack by another Marxist-oriented group of critics (see Guttman 1986: 147–150) who see in sports a process of binding up excess sexual energy (libido) that is not needed in capitalist production, but which might otherwise be available for revolutionary politics. For these theorists, sports, even spectatorship, are cathartic because they channel the rages and resentments that might be felt against the capitalist system toward the opposing team. Emotionally exhausted by the game, spectators lack energy for political interests and activity. Sports thus serve as a negative mechanism, robbing the populace of the ability to act in its own behalf.

In contrast, my argument is that the primary emotional result of spectatorship when one's team wins is positive by virtue of vicarious dominance and a surge of sexual energy via testosterone. It is fair to ask how long the benefits of the enhanced mood last. Although this question must be addressed by extensive research, some data suggest that the mood can last for a few days. Cialdini et al. (1976) found that college students were more likely to wear school insignia and garments displaying school colors on the Monday after a Saturday afternoon football victory than if the team lost. This suggests that vicarious dominance has a carry-over effect and is not immediately dissipated.

However, it may be argued that adult males are less likely to be affected so strongly given their maturity, more serious outlook, greater responsibilities, and the like. Indeed, this may be true, although at least anecdotally the animation manifested in Monday morning quarterbacking would belie any significant difference between the college students and the older cohort. In addition, the carry-over of mood in vicarious dominance should not be thought of according to a simple hydraulic model in which pressure in one part of the system translates immediately into movement in another part. A surge of T from a dominance experience does not translate, for humans at least, into an immediate sexual paroxysm. The modulation of biological patterns by culture is both established and exceedingly functional in most respects. And to this extent constructionists such as Gagnon and Simon (1973) are correct. But all a T surge need do is lead to a modification of behavior that would not otherwise have occurred. For example, for males it may be no more than a slightly heightened awareness of a woman's walk or perception of the curve of a breast. This is the differentia that would not have occurred without the additional T surge, but it is also the first step on a path that may culminate in coitus even days later. In the intervening period, hundreds of small goal-directed behaviors may be required to consummate what was initiated by the T surge. Of course, since social life is ongoing, the sequence can either be enhanced or accelerated through further dominance/eminence experiences and T or deflected and reversed by subsequent loss and defeat. Today's great victory can be canceled by tomorrow's great defeat. Vicarious dominance should operate in the same way. Although vicarious dominance initiates a behavior sequence, the sequence does not inevitably culminate in a sexual consummation.

It may be useful to think of a dominance/eminence–testosterone economy. Some personal economies are rich in dominance/eminence and testosterone, with a plethora of social opportunities to gain them. Other personal economies may be relatively poor. For the rich, the marginal utility of another win is probably very small. There may even be danger of ennui, the result not of too much good experience, but too much of the same experience (Berlyne 1971). But at moderate and lower dominance/eminence–T economic levels, the marginal utility of each victory or defeat may carry a larger weight.

For the male lower white-collar group, with its relatively scant opportunities for workplace dominance/eminence, each enhancement, whether real or vicarious, may be just enough to initiate a chain of actions that produce further small dominances or eminences and their associated testosterone enhancement, as Mazur (1985) has suggested. The process may occur in postgame conversation in which a particularly astute analysis settles a contested issue, or it may instigate a particularly assertive address to one's spouse, which may settle an issue between them, or it may instigate a sexual appraisal that leads to intercourse, and so on. The layered pattern of the many elements of the social and the biological allows for quite complex sequences of effects.

6

CONCLUSION

A theorist bears a heavy responsibility. With no data of his or her own to rely upon, hence no laboratory or field experience from which to get the feel of the phenomenon, the theorist must intuit plausible links between the multifarious and often disparate results obtained by others. Yet, if the theorist has grasped the thing right, a sensible pattern becomes apparent that integrates all of the elements into a coherence previously lacking. More than mere coherence, theory provides a heuristic structure that reveals the missing links in observation; thus, it projects a future not previously available to a body of thought. Theory directs attention to new conclusions and the work that needs to be done to establish their validity. Thus, even when wrong, theory can serve to extend knowledge.

In the previous chapters I have theorized several topics that logically and empirically connect with the dominance/eminence–testosterone (T) relationship. In each case, I have extrapolated from the known to the unknown, taking the existing data as my text and considering their implications. I was guided mainly by sociological understandings, but also partly by what I have experienced as a social actor. In the latter instance, I stand to err greatly about the central tendency if I am not close to it myself. Yet, in areas as socially sensitive as sexuality and intimacy—it is widely known that researchers of these topics often use themselves as subjects—there is reason to include oneself as a datum and to reflect both on one's own experience and on the reported experience of one's circle of acquaintances. Although this has its pitfalls, it does not ipso facto produce erroneous results and conclusions.

In this final chapter, I wish to point out a few additional areas in which the dominance/eminence–T model may provide some enlightenment. These reflections are somewhat freer in form than what has preceded, where every effort was made to tie assertions to the bedrock of empirical verification. Here the observations are frankly more speculative, although they follow logically from what was developed earlier.

Dominance/Eminence and the Self

At the core of this book is a model in which social relations determine biological parameters, with further consequences for the social—in brief, the socio-bio-social chain. One of the contributions I have hoped to make is the specification of the social across a broad spectrum of encounters, from the intimate context of sexuality to the anonymous settings of mass media spectatorship. These encounters illustrate possible sources of dominance/eminence experience and should lead to further explorations of social contexts in which the outcomes may have biosocial relevance.

Here I wish to extend the concept of the social to perhaps its ultimate lodging: the self. One of the problems of establishing the conceptual reality of the social is that as human organisms we are imprisoned within the self. All references to the world must finally be filtered through the self both as sensorium and as intellect that conceives of what the senses provide by way of raw material. In consequence of this distancing of self from the reality that is present but must be sensed and conceived, Kant distinguished between phenomena, which we apprehend, and noumena, which the phenomena represent but which, in the presumed nature of things, we cannot apprehend (see Wilkerson 1976:180ff). Reality, whatever that may be, is thus forever hidden from us because we are imprisoned within our self. This situation raises the question of solipsism. How is it that we do not all live in totally private worlds, unconnected with each other? How is it that we are able to make sense of what others are doing, that we often know what they mean, what they are thinking, and what they feel? Although imperfectly, much of the time we can locate others in social and psychological space quite well. And, when we err, we usually get a chance to revise our understanding and get it closer to what the other thinks, feels, or means. An important link between the organism as private entity and the external world to which it must adapt is the self. As currently understood, the self is an arena in which we can explore the structure and process of the external world symbolically, using the tools of thought to arrive at hypotheses that we test in real interaction.

A well-rooted tradition in sociological theory, through the work of G. H. Mead, C. H. Cooley, and W. James, identifies the self as a product of social interaction, acquired in the course of relating to others. In the crucial formulation by Mead (1934), the self emerges when the individual can regard him/herself from the perspective of another person, looking at oneself as if one were an object in the other person's perceptual field. Only through this process of role taking—we imagine how the other would think about and act toward us—do we acquire a self.

Indeed, according to William James, the self is a social arena in its very structure: "A man has as many . . . selves as there are individuals who recognize him and carry an image of him in their mind. . . . But as the individuals form naturally into classes, we may practically say that he has as many different social selves as there are distinct groups about whose opinions he cares. . . . From this there results what practically is a division of the man into several selves" ([1890] 1981:280–281).

In light of this social division and the grounding of the self, we can say that the individual is continually interacting with the self; that is, we frequently seek to know the stance of the other toward us, so we put ourself in the other's place and see our self. In Mead's (1934) provocative formulation, an internal dialogue can take place between the other, as conceived by us, and other others who also reside in the self. When we take the stance of any given other, we are temporarily transformed into that other. This is what enables us to treat ourselves as if we were an object. Underlying this idea of internal dialogue is that a social domain resides within us. It also seems consistent with these ideas that from the stance of any individual self (as James put it) the remainder of the self is a social field, even though the whole field is inside.

From the perspective of any one part of the self, one can struggle with the rest—indeed, challenge it, oppose it, and, overcome it. For example, we know that we should exercise, but family responsibilities, work, and so on stand in the way. Weeks pass without even a brisk walk. Then one day we decide to exercise. But unaccustomed to exercise, we feel enervated even at the thought of exertion. It would be so much easier to postpone the effort to another day; yet we persist, with difficulty at first, but then with increasing motivation and élan. As we come to realize that we have overcome the resistance, we may become exultant. We have dominated an opponent who was perhaps all the more formidable for being oneself.[1] Overcoming any resistance from the self—which is always accomplished from another part of the self—is crucially a social victory, not merely an individual event. This is because the part of the self that is overcome is the constellation of others who are opposing the part of the self that desires to overcome. It does not matter that one may not be aware of who those others actually are. They may be, as Mead put it, a "generalized other" (154) representing a particular tendency in society at large or in the subgroups to which one belongs.

One may take this social perspective on the self yet another step, into the domain of creativity. It can be argued that creativity is very much an outcome of the dialogue between different parts of the self. Mead conceived of the self in terms of an "I" and a "me" (173). The me represents the existing structure of the self, the configuration of others and their particular outlooks of which the self is, at any moment, constituted. But the self exists in an environment that demands response, even if it is only to adjust one's physical position better to accommodate to the light available for reading. Of course, social demands are paramount. Others are always wanting something of us. Or we want something from others, who have the power to grant or deny what we desire. How are we to act? Mead postulated the role-taking process described above as the way of figuring out what to do, how to proceed.

Internally, a dialogue takes place between different parts of the self that are already present, which constitute the me. However, the outcome of the dialogue is unpredictable. The internal process may be imagined as the analogue of what might occur if actual others—those represented in the me—were to gather for a real exchange of views. Nothing new may come of it, as these others simply state their position and, by some process of social influence that we need not spell out here, arrive at a conclusion that is the previously known opinion of one of them. It is the case of one of the others having his or her own way. Similarly, our internal dialogue between these others may also conclude conventionally, with our taking the stance of one of them and simply offering that in our behavior.

However, there is another possibility. In the real gathering of others a new position may emerge, perhaps initiated by a slight deviation in the way a customary view is stated; this may be picked up and elaborated by another member of the group, and this elaboration further elaborated, until there is true novelty, a solution far from the conventional position of any of the participants. Similarly, the internal dialogue may take an utterly new direction, one that was never previously represented in the self by any of the internalized others. Something new has been conceived. This, says Mead, is the I.[2]

The creative act, expressed as the I, can be seen to partake of a certain harmony that is not far from the harmony of love. The parallel between aesthetic and romantic pleasure has been remarked (see Kemper 1978). Authors, artists, scientists, among others in creative endeavors, report what seems to be a cry of victory when they have solved a particularly difficult problem or have been graced by an especially creative vision of how to proceed in their work. But the creative resolution of a literary, artistic, or scientific problem is a social outcome in the sense that it results from a dialogue between different parts of the self. Indeed, it is a social victory, since it required going beyond the existing margins imposed by the others represented by the me.

It is easy to see this in the case of scientific advance. We are taught the canons of conventional knowledge, the theories of great thinkers. These are now elements of the me, and we arrive thereby at the boundaries of what is known. The me has taken us to that point. But how to move on? How to step across into the unknown and claim it for ourself. In the Meadian model there is often a need to adapt to new circumstances (for example, the existing theory does not cover certain phenomena); hence, the elements of the me, containing all of the existing theory, are forced into a dialogue that, when productive, pass on to novelty and the I. But the I is even more essentially our self than the me, for the me is but the representative of the incorporated others, while the I is the form of our transcendence of that circle. Indeed, once we have a glimmer of an opening, just the hint of emergence into the I, we tend to exploit it relentlessly. For with the first appearance of novelty in the internal dialogue between different sources of the me, the I has come to life and is now a stance that we can take over against the panoply of the selves in the me—indeed, what is already for us mere convention, though those selvse may represent great thinkers and teachers. But we have surprised them in the discourse taking place in our head. We started out by pitting them against each other in an internal dialogue, and have won a new definition of reality. As all know who have had this good fortune, the emergence of the I in the creative moment is a major victory, for it means we have dared to oppose the reigning definers of reality and have bested them. In a less militant metaphor, but equally productive from the present viewpoint, we have collaborated in a common project with them and have made a contribution of such scope and importance as to deserve eminence.

That there can be victories over the self that are essentially social in form and that creativity results from an internal dialogue between others whose stance we are able to take allow the conjecture that the internal social domain is homologous to the external social world where there are literally two or more actors contesting for dominance or seeking eminence. If this supposition is true, then a crucial conclusion follows: at least some elements of the socio-bio-social chain can be applied to the individual organism. If victory over self or the eminence accorded to self by the others who populate the self is sufficiently great, a T elevation should result.

Victories over the self are immediate and require no further confirmation, but in the creative domain the pleasure of the creative moment is often the only recompense the author, artist, or scientist receives in a long while. Other struggles must still be won: to realize the creative vision in the pertinent medium (art form, experiment, and so on); and, finally, to win the attention, understanding, and allegiance of the audience for such productions. These structures are also usually social. Attainment here should produce a normal testosterone surge.

Testosterone and Political Opinion

In chapter 2, I argued that working-class and higher-class life provide their male members with preponderant opportunities for victory and testosterone at different life stages—earlier for the former class and later for the latter. This suggests discontent that may instigate political interest should be different in these groups at different ages. I assume that the personal becomes political when it needs to do so, but not, in American culture, otherwise. This has something to do with the American ethos of individualism, personal responsibility for one's status in society, and the lack of legitimacy of avenues of political expression outside the two major parties.

In the particular case at hand, I hypothesize as follows: (1) younger lower-class males are likely to be politically conservative; (2) younger higher-class males are likely to be politically liberal; (3) older lower-class males are likely to be politically liberal; and (4) older higher-class males are likely to be politically conservative. The terms *liberal* and *conservative* are relative, so they do not signify extremes, but rather tendencies that may in a given instance (such as an election) indicate the choice of one candidate over another.

I propose that T is an intervening condition. Those whose cultural and structural positions allow them dominance/eminence opportunities are those most likely to be satisfied with their lives and least likely to endorse changes associated with a broadly liberal agenda. This means younger lower-class and older higher-class males, for they have a relative advantage in dominance/eminence opportunities.

On the other hand, younger higher-class and older lower-class males experience a relative deficit of dominance/eminence opportunities. They should be more likely to sanction changes that would create a more egalitarian social structure in which either their dominance/eminence opportunities would rise, or the opportunities of the current elite would be reduced.

This hypothesis counters the somewhat poignantly expressed dictum, Who is not liberal when young has no heart; and who is still liberal when old has no head. This "wisdom" assumes that age and experience are indivisible. But from the perspective of the age–social class interaction with respect to dominance/eminence and testosterone, we can see that the saying errs in two respects. First, it seems only to speak to a limited subject, the higher-class member, since the politics described would seem to fit only that class. The assumption is that regardless of status when young, in later years the individual is well off. Second, the implied basis for the reversal of political judgment is cognitive, a rational apprehension of things as they are, rather than the (implied) emotional idealism of youth. Yet, on the basis of the dominance/eminence–T relationship, I would argue that not only the mind, but also the gonads may be important in the transformation of political sentiment.[3]

Alternatives for Vicarious Dominance

In chapter 5 I presented a theoretical analysis of false potency in which sports, as a central feature of advanced societies, provide important opportunities for vicarious dominance for some sectors of the male population for whom real dominance/eminence opportunities are relatively limited. I concentrated on sports because of their emergence to prominence in just the period that marked an important transformation of the American occupational structure—the extreme bureaucratization of the sphere of work and the consequent creation there of large numbers of positions with limited scope for dominance or eminence.

In sports, the main mechanism for vicarious dominance is identification with the fortunes of certain teams and players. Identification is aided by the media's heavy concentration on them. Teams and players have continuity over time, and they experience important vicissitudes in fortune, or are threatened with such, and periodically confront opportunities for dominance as they battle their opponents on the playing field.

Other cultural icons are also available for identification and for vicarious dominance experiences in their audiences. Cultural icons can include media heroes and stars of movies or continuing series on television. The Rambo figure in the series of movies featuring that character has been well received as a paradigm of the macho man who single-handedly confronts foreign villains and decisively defeats them. He avenges insults and injuries to American honor and falls well within the American fantasy tradition of male heroism. The films are very popular, even after the fourth in the series. Without pressing the analogue too far, one can see in the Rambo character a species that has a more classic incarnation in James Fenimore Cooper's Natty Bumpo, the archetypal woodsman and hero of the American frontier period. Though exceedingly violent and bloody, Rambo atavistically returns the American psyche to that earlier period of innocence and victory. Natty Bumpo is us when the land was young; Rambo is Natty transmogrified, changed mainly in firepower and in the elegance of his inarticulateness.

Indeed, from the perspective developed here, it is not accidental that the denouements of the Rambo epics are violent, nor that his victories are as decisive as an adolescent fantasy might wish for. I hypothesize that male fans of the Rambo films are emotionally animated by them and that there is a hormonal accompaniment to the vicarious dominance experienced—a surge of T.

A second domain of vicarious dominance that is periodically available is national politics. Presidential elections appear to release a tremendous surge of emotion in the partisans of the candidates. This has always been true, but recent elections in the United States have featured a new element that is particularly pertinent to the issue of vicarious dominance; that is, whether the personality of the candidate is sufficiently manly. Indeed, the worst pejorative of the 1984 campaign was that Democrat Walter Mondale was a wimp. Following sequentially, the early reading of the Republican George Bush was that he was a wimp. Indeed, one can read his successful campaign strategy as a text in which he established that he was tough and even mean, when necessary, in the service of the United States. The opposing Democratic candidate, Michael Dukakis, was depicted as weak on crime and weak on national defense. It is no surprise that, with these appeals in play, a gender gap opened up: males rejected Dukakis by giving him only 41 percent of their votes; while women gave him 48 percent of their votes. Indeed, the political campaign—regarded as extraordinarily banal by other measures—was a competition for definition of the candidates' personal qualifications to serve as president. The axis along which the decision was made was that of who could appear more personally and substantively dominant.

Although the political war is fought passionately only every four years, it allows for a considerable period of identification with a candidate—as much as a year or more in some cases. The final months of the campaign are frenized, not only for the candidates, but for their passionate supporters. For one group, there is a tremendous coup of vicarious dominance on election night. Picking the winner early and going to the wire with him reflects also on one's good sense and political acuity. These, doubtless engaged and challenged by partisans of the other candidate during the campaign, are now vindicated. I hypothesize a T surge under such circumstances. This does not mean that everyone who supports a strong leader does so because of that leader's strength. Some may do so because it serves their material interests directly; but others, whose interests are not served in this way, may do so because identification with the leader provides vicarious dominance and, in the leader's victory, a bodily satisfaction that is otherwise unattainable.

Magnitude of the Effect

Even assuming the validity of the empirical generalization that dominance/eminence attainment elevates T and, further, that social sequelae can be traced to this, it is fair to ask about the magnitude of the effects being discussed here. How much dominance is required to obtain a testosterone effect? How much eminence? How large a social effect is there likely to be? And, crucially, how often are we likely to see such effects?

Although I have argued for the validity of the socio-bio-social chain in the dominance/eminence–T domain, I believe that we are dealing here with a relatively infrequent event in modern societies. There is a reason Thoreau wrote, in an age that perhaps lent itself even more than our's to dramatic shifts of fortune, that most people lived "lives of quiet desperation," I take this phrase to mean that the victories were few and that opportunities for eminence were limited. Even in the most dynamic ages, the victors are relatively few in number. Probably in much of history, the overwhelming majority of persons were what we bluntly call "losers"; at least most were certainly not storybook winners. Accidents of birth affect social standing or outstanding physical stature (which, in earlier times, might have assured one's dominance) precluded most people from rising much above the level of their neighbors. With the emergence of capitalism, a broader base of dominance/eminence potential emerged. But we must consider how few of those who tried actually succeeded. Most did not try, and most of those who did failed. Today the postindustrial welfare state assures that opportunity is more widely available, and that absolute deprivation is significantly reduced, even if relative deprivation still thrives.[4] The overall effect of the welfare state must be to flatten the potential for major dominance/eminence attainment.

Any period of economic growth, especially where large sums of money can be made, augurs for dominance/eminence. But only insignificantly small sectors of the population are involved in this high-stakes play, hence likely to be experiencing frequent surges of T—or declines, for that matter. This means that if we look at most lives, we are not likely to find strong evidence of the dominance/eminence–T effect. This would almost seem to discount the importance of the phenomenon that has occupied our attention here. But it should be apparent that what is at issue is not the frequency of the event, but understanding the underlying principle of its occurrence. Indeed, as suggested most strongly in the discussion of the Broverman hypothesis (chapter 3), occurrence is historically conditioned. Hence, what may be a relatively rare event under one set of social and historical circumstances may become more prevalent in another set of circumstances. Indeed, we have the opportunity to see that the socio-bio-social chain is itself nested in a social and historical context. Large-scale social circumstances may not permit many individuals, or even classes of individual, to experience significant amounts of dominance/eminence. Thus, the frequency of occurrence of the phenomenon in such circumstances would be low. Obviously, when the large-scale circumstances change, so will the frequency of dominance/eminence occasions.

Opportunities for dominance/eminence are variable across the span of social organizational contexts, from the interpersonal primary group to impersonal bureaucratic settings. The interpersonal primary group may afford plentiful opportunities, since roles and rules of conduct are less rigid and afford greater scope to individual temperament and momentary mood. The bureaucratic context may sharply limit the range of allowable moves that may gain dominance/eminence. Societal politics also determine the chances for dominance/eminence. An apartheid society such as South Africa bars such opportunities for the majority of its population in virtually all but the interpersonal and family spheres. Culture too plays a part. Social-class norms that inhibit violence and provide detailed codes of etiquette to avoid conflict also minimize dominance opportunities in the interpersonal sphere.[5] Considerations of this kind underlie the analysis of the difference in dominance/eminence opportunities of the different classes at different ages, as discussed in chapter 2. By virtue of its particular structure and culture, each society prepares a specific menu of dominance/eminence opportunities for its members—and, of course, for subsets of members denominated into social classes, genders, races, and the like.

Another factor that will tend to diminish the rate of dominance/eminence is the stability of social interaction. As Mendoza (1984) found in animal studies, the T surge occurred at the time of dominance attainment, but subsequently, T levels were not correlated with position in the social hierarchy. Hence, in the conventional work settings of our time, usually large bureaucracies where social locations are well defined, there should be a muting of the dominance/eminence–T relationship in comparison, say, with frontier conditions, where each day may bring a new constellation of possibilities to the fore.

Testosterone, Status Perception, and Narcissism

High absolute levels of T have been associated with strongly focused, perhaps rigid, perception.[6] As discussed in chapter 4, visuospatial skills in males were related curvilinearly to T by at least some investigators. Extremely high and extremely low levels were related to poor visuospatial ability. A possible reason for the failure of the extremely high types is that T, which is related to perceptual style, may foster too great a concentration on the existing perceptual field, thus preventing the restructuring that visuospatial skills require.

I suggest that concentration on the existing perceptual field and the relative inflexibility that prevents restructuring the field also bear on interpersonal style. I mean by this that high-T individuals are limited in their interactional flexibility by a kind of perceptual tightness. This can be manifested by an extreme concentration on the self—perhaps shading into narcissism. The narcissistic stance creates numerous problems in interaction, among them an inability to participate sympathetically in the thought processes of others. The failure is marked by excessive concentration on one's own needs, while those of others are blocked from view. A high level of T may prevent the kind of shift in perspective that allows an individual to accommodate others and to recognize the validity of their claims and interests.

Blocked or rigid perspective would make interaction difficult, not immediately for the individual with high T, but for his or her interactional companions. They are hard put to cope with someone who cannot easily shift at least empathically to their perspective, who indeed seems impervious to doing so. But this rigidity may also foster certain advantages to both parties. Because the high-T individual is relatively impervious to messages from others, this applies also to messages of deprecation. Hence, high-T individuals may be difficult to insult, difficult to affect through ignoring them, difficult to bring to angry arousal. They are, as it were, receiving only small amounts of the message that is sent, because their flaw is precisely in being unable to receive messages from others. When such persons hold authority in organizations—as well they may for a variety of reasons having to do with their elevated levels of T—they may be indefatigable in their demands on subordinates, even on peers, but may be oblivious of the resistance that their demands evoke. Depreciatory remarks, failure to comply with requests, and other signs of status withdrawal may not register; hence, the perpetrators of these acts may be able to do so with relative impunity. The problem is with the overly rigid lock of the high-T individual on the perceptual field of the moment. This may even affect recall, so that yesterday's clash of personalities or interests leaves behind only a dim trace today.

The perceptual rigidity of the high-T person may be especially focused because his or her attainments may be gained mainly through dominance and not through eminence. Dominance is particularly given to blindness to the interests of others, who are seen as inferior or as victims to be exploited, and whose opinions are not worthy of consideration. Since high T may actually facilitate dominance (this is only a conjecture, as the discussion in chapter 2 makes clear), it feeds its perceptual rigidity directly into the attainment of dominance, and afterward into the style of relations between dominants and their inferiors. Since eminence is rarely sought or at issue, its absence, loss, or the failure of others to accord it in the first place is of little account.

Social Structure, Socialization, and the Socio-Bio-Social Chain

In *Civilization and Its Discontents,* Freud ([1930] 1951) in effect postulated the socio-bio-social chain, but from a pessimistic point of view. It was necessary to control sexual and aggressive impulses, he said, lest they lead to social destruction. Hence, the mechanisms of social control, mainly the development of the superego, but also external controls (e.g., police), were designed to regulate otherwise unruly instincts.

Notwithstanding Freud's pessimism, the regulative question can be looked at optimistically. That is, social regulation of biological processes can foster beneficial outcomes that do not bear the kind of costs of instinctual repression that Freud lamented. Indeed, the consideration of women's T/E balance in chapter 4 is an example of this sort of social modification of biology that can lead to a socially positive outcome. Actually, not all may agree with this judgment, since some believe that the release of women into the higher reaches of the labor force creates incentives, motives, and drives that conflict with nature's intent for females; namely, that females relegate their attention to nurturant roles in the domestic sphere, especially, but not exclusively, focused on children. In part this is a value question, but it touches also on empirical issues, such as the degree of harmony between men and women, the effects of reduced family size—an inevitable consequence of women's involvement in the modern labor force—on societal stability and global position, the effects of small families on children's character and their disposition as adults, the effects of surrogate mothering (as in child care) on the personalities and development of children, and so on. Clearly, social modification of biology to achieve other social effects is a complex matter, carrying not only manifest, but also latent costs and benefits.

In regard to such social manipulations, two major modes are possible: one is the manipulation of social structures; the other is socialization. In the first approach, the broad structures of power and status within which opportunities for dominance/eminence are either facilitated or denied are themselves changed. By democratizing higher education and making it available to a very broad sector of youth, we have changed the parameters by which dominance/eminence opportunities are available to lower-class youth. By instituting equal-opportunity commissions and procedures, we have afforded previously rejected minorities more chance to compete on a level playing field that does not favor some competitors over others from the start. Clearly, in regard to women's participation in certain labor force positions that require high visuospatial skills, it would not have mattered what level of skill women displayed if the discriminatory hiring patterns of the years prior to the late 1960s and early 1970s were not outlawed. Thus, social structural changes helped pave the way for the emergence of women in roles where they could manifest and experience dominance/eminence, and, if the surmises drawn here are correct, T elevation too.

In socialization, the second mode of large scale social effort to promote a modified biology, active effort at tuition is directed toward particular population segments where social policy deems it necessary. To continue the example of visuospatial activity in women, it is not sufficient simply to provide opportunity to compete more fairly with males. In addition, women must be given the same kind of socialization with respect to the domain of visuospatially related activities, from learning to orient themselves in neighborhood and community space to learning how to read maps and other symbolic materials connoting spatial relations. It would be a specious gain if the structural opportunities that have opened up the labor force to women were squandered because women had not been provided with the necessary socialization of the skills that they may now have in greater abundance, but nonetheless require shaping and honing through specific kinds of training that have traditionally been available to males.

From Power to Status, from Dominance to Eminence

I have referred in this book to historical transformations of several kinds—in relation to women's opportunities and to changes in the structure of the United States labor force and how they have affected work and the settings in which work is done. Here I wish to broach a final historical consideration. Over a long time span, it may be possible to see a transformation of social relations from power to status and, correlatively, from dominance to eminence, as the major modes of attaining social standing. Tocqueville ([1835] 1945) seems to have had something like this in mind in his view of Western history since the Middle Ages; he asserted that there had been for nearly a thousand years a continual press for "freedom." Mainly political, but, in broadening ripples, social as well, the movement toward liberation from the controls of authority resulted, in Tocqueville's time, in two great revolutions—in the United States in 1776 and in France in 1789. Without belaboring the point, it can be seen that freedom is the antonym of domination.

Durkheim ([1933] 1964) too, commented somewhat in this vein when he proposed that earlier forms of society were marked by laws with repressive sanctions, by which violent punishment was meted out to those who violated the fundamental moral precepts. By contrast, as societies became more complex, the tendency was toward law with restitutive sanctions: recompense for damages done and restoration of the original state of things as much as possible. Money payment is the most widespread method. I note, too, the number of societies that have abandoned the death penalty, whereas this was pandemic until virtually the present century.

The "unexciting" quality of advanced societies is also a part of this spectrum of reduced violence, in which the state is most firmly ensconced as the only legitimate executor of violence (Elias [1939] 1978:139, 202–203). Power is reserved to the state, and the only other legal method to acquire what one wants is through consensus and contract—an exchange of equal values—or through manifesting qualities that earn status. This long-term trend, which becomes even more pronounced as occupations demand higher and higher amounts of education, has some bearing on the societal flow of T. In the previous chapter I proposed that a certain sector of the male white-collar labor force may resort to vicarious opportunities for dominance precisely because real dominance/eminence opportunities are lacking in their occupational milieu. Here I want to suggest that not only are the opportunities diminished in bureaucratically organized settings, but they are also restricted by virtue of the elimination, to all intents and purposes, of many pure dominance activities, leaving only eminence by and large. Yet the slowing down of the rate of personal ascent may go hand in hand with greater longevity. There is simply more biological time available in which to attain social elevation. Social organization too has accommodated to the elongated timetables by providing the means through education for eminence attainment. If eminence has a fault, it is that it often takes longer to attain than dominance. Happily, according to the present body of evidence, the shift from dominance to eminence need not be at the expense of reduced T. This is very encouraging for those who seek a more peaceful society.

Coda

Although my explicit intention in this book was to examine inductively and deductively the implications of the socio-bio-social chain in a number of areas that are presently accessible from this vantage point, it will not have escaped the reader that some questions considered here are value-laden. For example, to offer hypotheses about how males might best approach females in coitus is a question of this sort. Clearly, I have a value preference for an egalitarian relationship between the sexes, perhaps nowhere more so than in the archetypal exemplar of male dominance over females—in sexual intercourse (cf. Dworkin 1987 for a polemic on this account). If nature has so designed us that the penetrating and thrusting must be done by males, and if nature or culture constructs these actions to fulfill the dominance paradigm, then this is but half the tale as told from a socio-bio-social perspective. Indeed, by taking the socio-bio-social stance, I believe we enlarge our understanding about what is possible when the social and the biological converge in the context of human sexual intimacy. Likewise, a consideration of the social-historical transformation of women's roles and the effects of this on women's dominance/eminence and T allows us to envision a more reasoned social structure based on a better understanding of bodily processes. When racist and sexist ideologies sanction certain hierarchical social arrangements on the basis of biology, the biology is usually false. Viewing the relations between males and females from a biologically more adequate position, it may be possible to bring body and society into better alignment, at the same time creating more egalitarian social arrangements. Biology and social justice have sometimes been set against each other in a way to limit our best hopes and aspirations. A better understanding of the interaction of biology and the social holds out a better prospect.

Notes

Chapter One: Introduction

1. Kaye has argued that, contrary to widespread belief, neither Spencer nor Sumner promoted the notion of the survival of the fittest in the sense of individuals struggling against each other: "They did not advocate the application of Darwin's theory of natural selection, 'the law of the jungle,' to human society" (1986:34). In addition, Kaye pointed to a revisionist view of Hofstadter's 1955 analysis: "The ideological use of Darwinism to support previously held social and political views has not been limited to the apologists for laissez-faire capitalism" (1986:24).

2. The important issues can best be focused by examining the polar cases of the triad, sociology and biology; therefore, a discussion of the standing of psychology as a theoretical discipline is omitted here. As an intermediate case, psychology shares some of the problems and advantages of the other two disciplines.

3. Consider the following examples of frank speculation: "Despite these caveats, several speculative conclusions are suggested by the data (Floody 1983:58); "Marler (1956) speculated . . ." (Archer 1988:2); "Speculation on the mode of action of a hormone-sensitive brain system . . . leads to the conclusion that . . ." (Hutchison 1978:285); and "What is sensitivity? At this point only speculation can be offered" (Gandelman 1980:135).

4. My experience is that many biological scientists are oblivious to the invidious relations that prevail between them and social scientists. A physician who directs a prominent professional society once assured me, "I treat everyone alike," yet his preceding remarks reflected his appreciation of a nicely differentiated set of status ranks.

5. Durkheim ([1915] 1965) was himself no mean hand at preempting other disciplines. Consider, for example, his sociological explanation of Kant's a priori mental categories.

6. Culture may train us to experience pain somewhat differently at a subjective level and to cope with it more or less well (Zborowski 1952; Zola 1966), but the basic experience of a sharp blow to the face is pain, and that this is so is not culturally mediated.

Chapter Two: Social Structure, Testosterone, and Male Sexuality

1. Animal studies are useful if they offer insight into possible hypotheses about humans, or if they confirm results obtained with humans (Hinde 1974).

Although widely used, comparative results are not universally approved. Benton (1983) objected on the grounds that human cognitive and cultural capacities are so far beyond that of animals that animal studies are of doubtful value.

2. Although not all primate species have clear dominance hierarchies, a substantial number do (Jolly 1972; Rowell 1974; Manning 1979). What counts here is whether T fluctuates according to dominance attainment or loss. This has been found in numerous animal socieites and also among human males.

3. The sexual sadists studied by Langevin et al. (1988) may fall into a different social category, one with purely aggressive, as opposed to dominance, motives. According to Mazur (1983), only dominance motives may be related to T.

4. Manning (1979) makes a clear case for this in most animal societies. But it is also useful to take note of the position taken by Popp and DeVore who point out that "dominance hierarchies are . . . time and resource specific" (1979:331). This means that even if sexual precedence and access by dominant animals is usual, it will not necessarily always be the case, due to different and competing appetites at different times.

5. In what must be accepted as evidence only with caution, Blotnick (1987:237–238) reported finding that men who received significant pay raises or promotions translated these marks of eminence into higher frequency of coitus with their spouse. Conversely, status setbacks, such as a demotion or severe criticism from their boss significantly reduced sexual desire. These results remarkably parallel those of Mazur and Lamb (1980) with tennis players who experienced a surge of T after decisive victories while badly beaten losers' T declined. Although Blotnick's findings strongly support the present analysis, Blotnick's methods of data collection—which may not be at issue here—have been seriously challenged (see Jones 1987).

6. This pattern seems to conform to that of the longer refractory period after multiple orgasms reported by Masters and Johnson (1966).

7. There is some ambiguity in the several reports authored by Raboch and his colleagues. Raboch and Starka (1972) reported that normal males with relatively high levels of T exceeded males who were deficient in T in coital frequency. In Raboch and Starka (1973), normal males (between twenty-one and thirty years of age) again exceeded several, but not all, categories of males who were deficient in T, but the analysis obscured this. In Raboch, Mellan and Starka (1975), what was omitted in 1973 was reported as having been found only in 1975. Raboch's attention was apparently focused on findings that showed that within the normal and within the deficient groups, quite varying amounts of coitus occurred. In the latter group, some males reported quite elevated rates of coitus. Raboch and Starka proposed a "favorable social environment," along with "adequate responsivity of peripheral tissue to the effect of T," as an explanation (1973:309).

8. Hospital personnel are also more likely to be skilled in techniques for drawing blood samples at required intervals.

9. This was suggested by C. Norma Baiocco.

10. Although the stimulating hypothesis put forth by Davidson and his colleagues complements very nicely, on the physiological side, the sociological perspective of this work, I am not committed specifically to it. Quite other mechanisms may be at work, including the more cognitively-oriented one of Bancroft and Wu (1983), the energizing notions of McAdoo et al. (1978), the attractiveness-to-females hypothesis of Keverne (1979), and the strutting,

confident-posture view of Mazur (1985). Perhaps these mechanisms are not independent of each other, acting with not only additive but also interactive effects.

11. A new study, comparable in scope and ambition to Kinsey's but incontrovertibly superior in method, has been announced (Booth 1989), but funding status is uncertain owing to resistance by conservatives to undertaking such surveys (see *San Francisco Chronicle,* July 26, 1989, Sec. A, 9).

12. I conclude this as a fact that is intended neither to support a stereotype nor to "blame the victim" (Ryan 1971).

13. Jacob (1974) found that in lower-class families, adolescent males gained status in the family at the expense of the father.

14. This would perhaps explain why some studies have found no social class differences in sexual behavior among adolescents and young adults using parent's education or family income as a class indicator (e.g., Delamater and MacCorquodale 1979; Knoth, Boyd, and Singer 1988; Coles and Stokes 1985; Billy et al. 1988). However, other researchers have found social class differences in adolescence (e.g., Weinberg and Williams 1980; Chilman 1983; Harris and Associates 1986; Miller and Olson 1988; Furstenberg et al. 1987; and Udry 1988).

15. The recent national craze for tennis notwithstanding, this game was not considered entirely manly in past years. Chester reported: "My brother and I had a tennis court just off the tracks of the Canarsie Shuttle, a trolley car [in Brooklyn, N.Y.]. On weekends we had to endure the taunts and jeers or merrymakers on their way to the Canarsie Shore [a nearby beach]. Back in the Twenties, tennis was not regarded as a masculine sport" (1985:14). Obviously, too, there was a social class element in this scene: upper-middle-class owners of land being heckled by lower-class riders of public transportation.

16. The work on this issue is scant. In a comparison among small samples drawn from different occupations, LaRue and Dabbs (1989) found that professional actors and members of a National Football League team had significantly higher T than church ministers. Occupying the middle of the spectrum, and not significantly different either from each other or from the extreme categories, were physicians, college professors, firemen, and salesmen, descending in that order. From these data there is no way to detect whether there was self-selection by T into different occupations, or whether the interactional and relational conditions of the different occupations produce different frequencies of surges and, as a consequence, perhaps different average levels of circulating T.

Chapter Three: Infidelity and Sexual Intimacy

1. Ralph Turner (1976) has captured some of the tension between self and collectivity in his analysis of the recent shift from a self that is anchored in institutional, ergo socially controlling, contexts to a "real" self that is oriented toward its own elaboration and satisfaction indifferent to institutional constraints.

2. There may also be an area of the brain where the sexual and the bonding mechanism can be distinguished. Goy reported that "a lesion in the preoptic-anterior hypothalamic region of the brain in [adult rhesus monkeys] greatly reduced heterosexual copulation to ejaculation. But lesioned males did not stop masturbating, and they masturbated as regularly as before the

brain lesion. This could mean that this particular lesion produces a deficiency in heterophilic bonding behavior. . . . This brain area appears to be important to bonding" (1979: 255).

3. I exclude here the pathological category of narcissists, for whom no amount of getting can be enough and for whom giving is an unknown mode of response to others.

4. There is a tantalizing hint about T sex in Kilman et al. (1984). Husbands of anorgasmic women reported higher sexual pleasure than husbands of orgasmic women. They were also less perceptive about their wife's preferences for sexual activity. These may well be males whose approach stems from dominance and who are in the taking mode, thus are more or less indifferent to their spouse, not catering to her needs, and not delaying their own satisfaction.

5. The dynamics of satisfaction in this case can only be conjectured. On the one hand, there is the possibility of a T surge from a decisive victory over the resistant partner; on the other hand, victory may be hard won, with no T surge (Mazur and Lamb 1980).

Chapter Four: Social Structure, Testosterone, and Women's Spatial Ability

1. A possible reason for the seeming adamancy of the biological argument is that it is likely to be more accurate when the issue is genetic. Genes change only very slowly and apparently randomly. But biology is much less an immutable category at the hormonal level. Although hormones generally serve genetic masters and their programs, they also have wide latitude in doing so and are subject to considerable determination by environmental factors, including the social.

2. Linn and Petersen's (1985) tripartite breakdown of spatial ability is a refined version of the two dimensions proposed by McGee, spatial visualization and spatial orientation: "Spatial visualization is an ability to mentally manipulate, rotate, or twist, or invert pictorially presented visual stimuli. . . . Spatial orientation involves the comprehension of the arrangement of elements within a visual stimulus pattern, the aptitude for remaining unconfused by the changing orientations in which a configuration may be presented, and the ability to determine spatial relations in which the body orientation of the observer is an essential part of the problem" (1979:3–4). Linn and Peterson's mental rotation and spatial visualization are included in McGee's spatial visualization, while their concept spatial perception is more or less equivalent to McGee's spatial orientation. Differences between the two categorizations are based on derivation of concepts from cognitive or psychometric perspectives (Linn and Peterson 1985).

3. Yen's categories are essentially the same as McGee's (1979), thus do not correspond exactly with Linn and Petersen's model of spatial relations ability. Yen found heritability for what he called "spatial orientation," which appears to be about the same as Linn and Petersen's spatial perception. He found little evidence for heritability for what he called "spatial vizualization," which includes Linn and Petersen's spatial visualization and mental rotation. Thus, heritability was found for one area in which sex differences have been shown (spatial perception) and not for another (mental rotation). Also, only certain aspects of Yen's spatial orientation have produced sex differences: rod and frame tests have, while embedded figures have not (Linn and Petersen 1985).

4. Whether this occurs because of direct effects of the gonadal steroid

hormones on both NE and ACh, as Broverman et al. (1968) originally supposed, or only on NE, via modulation of MAO as Broverman et al. (1980) affirmed, is unimportant for the present argument. Both T and E retain their role in the determination of spatial ability. Even the adrenergic and cholinergic reciprocity structure of the original Broverman hypothesis can remain in place, since any event that affects one system may affect the relative dominance of the other.

5. Widiger and Settle (1987) contend that the Broverman et al. (1970) results stem from a methodological artifact; namely, an imbalance of male-valued and female-valued items. However this may be, the Broverman et al. findings conform to widespread stereotypes about suitable roles and characteristics for women (see Goffman 1979).

6. These odd results may be due to some kind of social state effects that influence intercourse rates among males of different levels of T, as discussed in chapter 2.

7. Regrettably, there are no data showing termination rates of male-initiated relationships after the third date.

8. The term *freemartin* means "sterile cow" in old Scottish (Ellis 1982:176).

Chapter Five: Vicarious Dominance/Eminence

1. This is not intended as a theory of revolution. Rather it is an assertion about the bodily dispositions of males who may be more or less susceptible to appeals for social change. If hunger and other somatic effects of poverty make sense as grounds for movements of social transformation, hormonal poverty may also create incentives for change.

2. I will not examine the upper lower-class level, since it benefits from standing on the top of its social ladder.

3. Indeed, sports as a form of play may have evolved as an important mimic of the competitive aspects of social life, serving through participation as a training ground for competition and through spectatorship to afford losers in the competitive struggle of social life a symbolic second chance with attenuated but real effects.

4. I wish to thank Edgar M. Mills, Jr., for this felicitous metaphor of organizational process.

5. The comparisons between 1988 and the 1972–1982 figures are not strictly accurate, since all counts since 1983 are based on the 1980 census designations of occupations, which differ importantly from those used in estimates from 1982 and earlier. The 1972–1982 comparisons are based on conversion factors estimated by Klein (1984) in order to show the historical trend in occupations. Despite these methodological disjunctions between different data series, it should be apparent that the trend to include women in the executive, administrative, and managerial occupations has continued.

6. A similar argument with respect to ethnicity and mental health suggests that minorities that suffer occupational discriminations will have a higher proportion of mentally healthy individuals in its lowest socioeconomic category than groups that are not discriminated against. This is because many able, mentally healthy individuals in the former group will be held back by virtue of discrimination (see Dohrenwend and Dohrenwend 1969).

7. Jordan (1989) claimed that "clubhouse harmony" isn't necessary for winning—but only in baseball because of the more individualistic nature of

the sport, where performance is less dependent on one's teammates. Although football is less individualistic in this sense, the great control of coaches over play determination and the subsequent close analysis of play via video playback are likely to minimize the interference of personal vendettas on the field.

8. Some Marxist critics have excoriated modern sports for this ultimate division of labor, charging that it is a sign of the way capitalist political economy intrudes on sports: reducing players to the status of machinelike automatons in the style of industrial workers for the sake of more efficient production, hence profits. Without disputing the possible dollar motives for the fine honing of talents and the differentiation of specialties in modern sports, the fact remains that a well-functioning team does provide an aesthetic satisfaction, at least for a while. If it becomes too dominant as a result and wins too often, the lack of suspense and of somewhat fairly matched opponents decreases satisfaction among spectators. Ultimately, as in all human systems, the "perfect" team loses its touch.

9. Although luck as well as skill may play a part in determining the outcome of team contests, this is not ordinarily a large part of the sport, despite Will's (1988) contentions.

10. In this, modern hierarchical organizations conform to a military model that has ancient roots. Alexander the Great, Caesar, and Vercingetorix are the names recorded by posterity, as are Washington, Grant, Foch, Pershing, Eisenhower, and MacArthur, though their victories were constituted by the small devotions and heroisms of thousands and even millions of individuals.

11. Durkheim ([1933] 1964) argued that the division of labor also promotes individuation, and in at least one important respect this is true. By providing an individual niche for instrumental achievement, the division of labor allows individuals to seek to do tasks that are more compatible with their unique self. In addition, the different task helps to etch sharply distinctive contours of the one who does it.

12. Rudman (1986) reported data suggesting that identification with teams and performers is stronger among blacks that among whites. It is tempting to see this as confirming the vicarious dominance hypothesis, in as much as blacks, who severely lack occupational dominance/evidence opportunities, would therefore seek them vicariously through identification with the many black sports celebrities.

13. Readers should know that when *Sports Illustrated* first appeared in 1955, I predicted its demise within the year. I felt that while there were many cheap sports magazines, usually printed on "butcher paper" stock and oriented toward working-class interests, there was no chance for a slick, high-quality sports publication that was clearly directed to the middle class. In this I gravely erred—so much for my skills as prognosticator of social trends—but I was sociologically untutored at the time and had no idea of the occupational trendline of which publisher Henry Luce's market researchers were obviously aware. But it is also instructive to learn that Luce lost money on *Sports Illustrated* for 11 years before it turned its first profit (Fabrikant 1985). This is an inordinately long time to back an unprofitable magazine venture. But more than faith went into the stubbornness here. Year by year, the profile of the labor force was changing into the kind that *Sports Illustrated* was designed to attract.

14. In all accuracy, the period of the late 1950s and early 1960s was also

when the enormous baby boom cohorts were reaching the stage of avid adolescent sports participants and spectators.

15. This contrasts with working-class reliance on collective strength and representation through unions and leaves the lower white-collar worker in a relatively isolated position vis-à-vis the power structure of the modern organization. This may encourage even greater conformity than is required by the technical requirements of the job.

16. Sports also appear to be a conversational resource in the Soviet Union (Ponomariev 1980).

17. I am not considering spectator violence here. Elements other than vicarious dominance seem to be involved in this, although it is not entirely excluded.

Chapter Six: Conclusion

1. As we know, victories of this sort are not empty, but, rather, change the social equation in interaction with real others, where we are in consequence more masterful, better able to dominate when challenged, and better able to strive for eminence.

2. The analogue between a set of real others in dialogue and the same set as internalized in a self can be carried only so far. For one thing, the self can only carry on an internal dialogue based on what it knows of the others. This is necessarily much less than what each of the others actually consists of. Hence, the internal dialogue starts out much poorer in content. But this is compensated for in other ways. First, it is sometimes impossible for the given set of others to meet face to face to conduct the real dialogue. Geographical dispersion is the least of the problems such an assembly might face. A crucial stumbling block is that some, perhaps even all of them, may be dead. The internal conversation among these others is not hindered by the usual constraints of real time. Second, the internal dialogue has an immediancy that requires no observation of the customary rules of turn taking in conversation, deference to those of higher status, and the like. This allows for a condensation of the process, perhaps assisting in linking one perspective to another.

3. Teasing out the evidence for these hypotheses is complicated by the possible confounding of age and cohort or historical effects. Five combinations are possible: age has an effect, while cohort is irrelevant; cohort has an effect, while age is irrelevant; age and cohort have additive effects; age and cohort have interaction effects; and, finally, neither age nor cohort have an effect. In light of these possibilities, we must treat very charily such supportive evidence as that provided by Seagull (1977) detailing the age-class interactions in political party identification in the 1972 presidential elections. As I have hypothesized, eighteen- to twenty-four-year-old working-class youths were more conservative than middle-class youths of that age, while middle-class voters thirty-five and over were more conservative than working-class voters of that age (116). This is a rare case in which the age-class interaction with respect to political attitudes is available to us and, notwithstanding the support provided to the proposed hypotheses, must be seen as anything but conclusive.

4. Although the welfare state has placed a floor under the poorest segments of the population, thus reducing absolute deprivation, the relative distribution of income to quintiles of the population has remained stable for more than forty years. For example, the bottom quintile receives about 5

percent of income, while the highest quintile receives about 40 percent (U.S. Bureau of Census 1988: 428; Levy 1987).

5. How much leakage there may be through the barrier is another matter. How much is relegated to vicarious opportunities is an additional question. If Elias and Dunning's (1986) point about the special need for emotional arousal in "unexciting societies" is valid, sport is a ready-made mechanism for providing hormonal fillips that social life otherwise precludes.

6. Andrew (1978) found this to be the case in chickens.

References

Abraham, G. E. 1974. "Ovarian and Adrenal Contribution to Peripheral Androgens during the Menstrual Cycle." *Journal of Clinical Endocrinology and Metabolism* 39:340–346.

Abrahams, R. D. 1962. "Playing the Dozens." *Journal of American Folklore* 75:209–220.

Alexander, R. D. 1979. "Sexuality and Sociality in Humans and Other Primates." In *Human Sexuality: A Comparative and Developmental Perspective,* ed. H. A. Katchadourian, 81–112. Berkeley and Los Angeles: University of California Press.

Anderson, P. and C. McCance. 1984. "Sexual Behavior and Contraceptive Practice at Oxford and Aberdeen Universities." *Journal of Biosocial Science* 16:287–290.

Andrew, R. J. 1978. "Increased Persistence of Attention Produced by Testosterone, and Its Implications for the Study of Sexual Behaviour." In *Biological Determinants of Sexual Behaviour,* ed. J. B. Hutchison, 255–275. Chicester, England: Wiley.

Archer, J. 1988. *The Behavioral Biology of Aggression.* New York: Cambridge University Press.

Arnetz, B. B., T. Theorell, L. Levi, A. Kallner, and P. Eneroth. 1983. "An Experimental Study of Social Isolation of Elderly People: Psychoendocrine and Metabolic Effects." *Psychosomatic Medicine* 45:395–406.

Arque, J. M., M. Unzeta, and R. Torrubia. 1988. "Neurotransmitter Systems and Personality Measurements: A Study in Psychosomatic Patients and Healthy Subjects." *Neuropsychobiology* 19:149–157.

Axelrod, J. and T. D. Reisine. 1984. "Stress Hormones: Their Interaction and Regulation." *Science* 224:452–459.

Axelrod, J. and R. Weinshilboum. 1972. "Catecholamines." *New England Journal of Medicine* 287:237–242.

Baier, H., G. Biro, and K. F. Weinger. 1974. "Serum Levels of FSH, LH, and Testosterone in Human Males." *Hormone and Metabolism Research* 6:514–516.

Baker, S. W. 1980. "Biological Influences on Human Sex and Gender." In *Women: Sex and Sexuality,* ed. C. R. Stimson and E. S. Person, 175–191. Chicago: University of Chicago Press.

Bancroft, J. 1984. "Hormones and Human Sexual Behavior." *Journal of Sex and Marital Therapy* 10:3–21.

Bancroft, J., D. Sanders, D. Davidson, and P. Warner. 1983. "Mood,

Sexuality, Hormones, and the Menstrual Cycle." Part 3, "Sexuality and the Role of Androgens." *Psychosomatic Medicine* 45:509–516.

Bancroft, J. and N. E. Skakkebaek. 1979. "Androgens and Human Sexual Behavior." In *Symposium on Sex, Hormones, and Behaviour, London, 1978,* 209–226. Ciba Foundation Symposium, n.s. 62. Amsterdam: Excerpta Medica.

Bancroft, J. and F.C.W. Wu. 1983. "Changes in Erectile Responsiveness during Androgen Replacement Therapy." *Archives of Sexual Behavior* 12:59–66.

Bandura, A. H. 1977. *Social Learning.* Englewood Cliffs, N.J.: Prentice-Hall.

Barchas, P. 1976. "Physiological Sociology: Interface of Sociological and Physiological Processes." *Annual Review of Sociology* 2:297–333.

———, ed. 1984. *Social Hierarchies: Essays Toward a Sociophysiological Perspective.* Westport, Conn.: Greenwood.

Barchas, P., and S. Mendoza, eds. 1984. *Social Cohesion: Essays Toward a Sociophysiological Perspective.* Westport, Conn.: Greenwood.

Barclay, A. M. 1969. "The Effects of Hostility on Physiological and Fantasy Responses." *Journal of Personality* 37:651–667.

Berendse, M. A. 1983. "Individualism, Technology, and Sport: The Speedway Nexus." *Journal of Sport and Social Issues* 7:15–23.

Barrett, F. M. 1980. "Sexual Experience, Birth Control Usage, and Sex Education of Unmarried Canadian University Students: Changes between 1968 and 1978." *Archives of Sexual Behavior* 9:367–390.

Baucom, D. H., P. K. Besch, and S. Callahan. 1985. "Relation between Testosterone Concentration, Sex Role Identity, and Personality among Females." *Journal of Personality and Social Psychology* 48:1218–1226.

Beach, F. A. 1957. "Characteristics of Masculine 'Sex Drive'." In *Nebraska Symposium on Motivation 1956,* ed. M. R. Jones, 1–32. Lincoln: University of Nebraska Press.

———. 1976. "Sexual Attractivity, Proceptivity, and Receptivity in Female Mammals." *Hormones and Behavior* 7:105–138.

———. 1977. "Hormonal Control of Sex Related Behavior." In *Human Sexuality in Four Perspectives,* ed. F. A. Beach, 247–268. Baltimore: Johns Hopkins University Press.

Beatty, W. W. 1979. "Gonadal Hormones and Sex Differences in Nonreproductive Behaviors in Rodents." *Hormones and Behavior* 12:112–163.

Beaumont, J. G. 1987. *Cerebral Lateralization: Biological Mechanisms, Associations, and Pathology,* by N. Geschwind and A. M. Galaburda. *Biological Psychology* 24:100–102.

Beck, J. G., D. H. Barlow, D. K. Sakheim, and D. J. Abrahamson. 1987. "Shock Threat and Sexual Arousal: The Role of Selective Attention, Thought Content, and Affective States." *Psychophysiology* 24:165–172.

Becker, B. J., and L. V. Hedges. 1984. "Meta-Analysis of Cognitive Gender Differences: A Comment on an Analysis by Rosenthal and Rubin." *Journal of Educational Psychology* 76:583–587.

Becker, G. 1984. "The Social Regulation of Sexuality." In *Current Perspectives in Social Theory: A Research Annual,* ed. by S. G. McNall, 5:45–69. Greenwich, Conn.: JAI.

Becker, H. 1953. "Becoming a Marihuana User." *American Journal of Sociology* 59:235–242.

———. 1963. *Outsiders: Studies in the Sociology of Deviance.* New York: Free Press.

Bell, R. R., and D. Peltz. 1974. "Extramarital Sex among Women." *Medical Aspects of Human Sexuality* 5:10–31.

Beller, A. H., and K. K. Han. 1984. "Occupational Sex Segregation: Prospects for the 1980s." In *Sex Segregation in the Workplace: Trends, Explanations, and Remedies.* ed. B. Reskin, 91–114. Washington, D.C.: National Academy Press.

Benbow, C. P. 1988. "Sex Differences in Mathematical Reasoning Ability in Intellectually Talented Preadolescents: Their Nature, Effects, and Possible Causes." *Behavioral and Brain Sciences* 11:169–232.

Benbow, C. P. and J. C. Stanley. 1980. "Sex Differences in Mathematical Ability: Fact or Artifact?" *Science* 210:1262–1264.

Benderley, B. L. 1989. "Don't Believe Everything You Read: A Case Study of How the Politics of Sex-Difference Research Turned a Small Finding into a Major Media Flap. *Psychology Today,* November, 67–69.

Benton, D. 1983. "Do Animal Studies Tell Us Anything about the Relationships between Testosterone and Human Aggression?" In *Animal Models of Human Behavior,* ed. G.C.L. Davey, 281–298. Chicester, England: Wiley.

Berkenbosch, F. 1983. *The Role of Catecholamines in the Control of the Secretion of Pro-Opiomelanocortin Derived Peptides from the Rat Pituitary Gland, and Its Implications in the Response to Stress.* Amsterdam: Rodopi.

Berkowitz, L. 1962. *Aggression: A Social Psychological Analysis.* New York: McGraw-Hill.

Berlyne, D. E. 1971. *Aesthetics and Psychobiology.* New York: Appleton-Century-Crofts.

Bernard, J. 1972. *The Future of Marriage.* New York: World.

Berstein, I. S., R. M. Rose, and T. P. Gordon. 1977. "Behavioral and Hormonal Responses of Male Rhesus Monkeys Introduced to Females in the Breeding and Non-Breeding Seasons. *Animal Behavior* 25:609–614.

Bielby, D. 1978. "Career Sex-Atypicality and Career Involvement of College Educated Women: Baseline Evidence from the 1960's." *Sociology of Education* 51:7–28.

Bielby, W. T., and J. N. Baron. 1986. "Men and Women at Work: Sex Segregation and Statistical Discrimination." *American Journal of Sociology* 91: 759–799.

Billy, J.O.G., N. S. Lansdale, W. R. Grady, and D. M. Zimmerle. 1988. "Effects of Sexual Activity on Adolescent Social and Psychological Development." *Social Psychology Quarterly* 51:190–212.

Birenbaum, A. 1970. "Revolution without the Revolution: Sex in Contemporary America." *Journal of Sex Research* 6:257–267.

Blakeslee, S. 1989. "Female Sex Hormone Is Tied to Ability to Perform Tasks." *New York Times,* November 18, Sec. A, 1.

Bleier, R. 1979. "Social and Political Bias in Science: An Examination of Animal Studies and Their Generalizations to Human Behavior and Evolution." In *Genes and Gender.* Vol. 2, *Pitfalls in Research on Sex and Gender,* ed. R. Hubbard and M. Lowe 49–69. New York: Gordian.

Block, J. and J. Block. 1982. "Cognitive Development from Childhood and Adolescence." NIMH Research Grant MH16080. Typescript.

Blossfeld, H.-P. 1987. "Labor Market Entry and Sexual Segregation of Careers in the Federal Republic of Germany." *American Journal of Sociology* 93:89–118.

Blotnick, S. 1987. *Ambitious Men: Their Dreams, Drives, and Delusions.* New York: Viking.

Blume, S. S. 1974. *Toward a Political Sociology of Science.* New York: Free Press.

Blumstein, P. and P. Schwartz. 1983. *American Couples: Money, Work, Sex.* New York: William Morrow.

Bock, R. D., and D. Kolakowski. 1973. "Further Evidence of Sex-linked Major-Gene Influence on Human Spatial Visualizing Ability." *American Journal of Human Genetics* 25:1–14.

Booth, A., G. Shelley, A. Mazur, G. Tharp, and R. Kittock. 1989. "Testosterone and Winning and Losing in Human Competition." *Hormones and Behavior* 23:556–571.

Booth, A, and L. K. White. 1980. "Thinking about Divorce." *Journal of Marriage and the Family* 42:605–616.

Booth, W. 1989. "Asking America about Its Sex Life." *Science* 243:304.

Botwin, C. 1988. *Men Who Can't Be Faithful.* New York: Warner.

Bouissou, M. 1983. "Androgens, Aggressive Behavior, and Social Relationships in Higher Mammals." *Hormone Research* 18:43–61.

Bourdieu, P. 1978. "Sport and Social Class." *Social Science Information* 17:819–840.

———. [1979] 1984. *Distinction: A Social Critique of the Judgment of Taste.* Reprint. Cambridge, Mass.: Harvard University Press.

Boyle, R., R. Dykman, and P. Ackerman. 1965. "Relationship of Resting Autonomic Activity, Motor Impulsivity, and EEG Tracings in Children." *Archives of General Psychiatry* 12:314–323.

Bozman, A. W., and J. G. Beck. 1988. "Psychological Factors in Inhibited Sexual Desire: A Test of Kaplan's Model." Poster presented at meetings of the American Psychological Association, August 12, Atlanta, Ga.

Bradford, J.M.W. 1988. "Organic Treatment for the Male Sexual Offender." In *Annals of the New York Academy of Sciences,* ed. R. A. Prentky and V. L. Quinsey, 528:193–202. New York: NYAS.

Bradford, J.M.W., and D. McLean. 1984. "Sexual Offenders, Violence, and Testosterone: A Clinical Study." *Canadian Journal of Psychiatry* 29:335–343.

Brantingham, P., and P. Brantingham. 1984. *Patterns in Crime.* New York: Macmillan.

Brass, D. J. 1985. "Men's and Women's Networks: A Study of Interaction Patterns and Influence in an Organization." *Academy of Management Journal* 28:327–343.

Bremer, J. 1959. *Asexualization: A Follow-up of 244 Cases.* New York: Macmillan.

Bremner, W. J., A. E. Karpas, A. M. Matsumoto, R. A. Steiner, D. K. Clifton, and D. M. Dorsa. 1983. "Reproductive Neuroendocrinology in the Ageing Male." In *Neuroendocrine Aspects of Reproduction,* ed. R. L. Norman, 379–393. New York: Academic Press.

Brim, O. G. 1960. "Personality Development and Role Learning." In *Personality Development in Children,* ed. I. Iscoe and H. Stevenson, 127–159. Austin: University of Texas Press.

Brinkmann, E. H. 1966. "Programmed Instruction as a Technique for Improving Spatial Visualization." *Journal of Applied Psychology* 50:179–184.

Brody, J. 1986. "Researchers Say Sex Fantasy is almost Universal." *New York Times,* August 27, C8.

Broverman, D. M., I. K. Broverman, E. L. Klaiber. 1966. "Ability to Automatize and Automatization Cognitive Style: A Validation Study." *Perceptual and Motor Skills* 23:419–437.

Broverman, D. M., I. K. Broverman, W. Vogel, R. D. Palmer, and E. L. Klaiber. 1964. "The Automatization Cognitive Style and Physical Development." *Child Develpment* 35:1343–1359.

Broverman, D. M., E. L. Klaiber, Y. Kobayashi, and W. Vogel. 1968. "Roles of Activation and Inhibition in Sex Differences in Cognitive Abilities." *Psychological Review* 75:23–50.

———. 1969. Reply to the Comment by Singer and Montgomery on "Roles of Activation and Inhibition in Sex Differences in Cognitive Abilities." *Psychological Review* 76:328–331.

Broverman, D. M., E. L. Klaiber, and W. Vogel. 1980. "Gonadal Hormones and Cognitive Functioning." In *The Psychobiology of Sex Differences and Sex Roles,* ed. J. E. Parsons, 57–80. Washington, D.C.: Hemisphere.

Broverman, D. M., W. Vogel, E. L. Klaiber, D. Mayrher, D. Shea, and V. Paul. 1981. "Changes in Cognitive Task Performance Across the Menstrual Cycle." *Journal of Comparative and Physiological Psychology* 95:646–654.

Broverman, I. K., D. M. Broverman, F. E. Clarkson, P. S. Rosenkrantz, and S. R. Vogel. 1970. "Sex-role Stereotypes and Clinical Judgments of Mental Health." *Journal of Consulting and Clinical Psychology* 34:1–7.

Brown, N. O. 1959. *Life against Death: The Psychoanalytic Meaning of History.* Middletown, Conn.: Wesleyan University Press.

Bryant, J., P. Comisky, and D. Zillman. 1981. "The Appeal of Rough-and-tumble Play in Televised Professional Football." *Communication Quarterly* 29:256–262.

Bunge, M. 1968. "The Maturation of Science." In *Problems in the Philosophy of Science,* ed. I. Latakos and A. Musgrove, 120–138. Amsterdam: North Holland.

Burn, J. H. 1975. *The Autonomic Nervous System for Students of Physiology and Pharmacology.* 5th ed. Oxford: Blackwell.

Butterfield, F. 1987. "Hite's New Book Is under Rising Attack." *New York Times,* November 13, sec. B, 4.

Buss, D. H. 1989. "Sex Differences in Human Mate Preferences: Evolutionary Hypotheses Tested in Thirty-seven Cultures. *Behavioral and Brain Sciences* 12:1–49.

Cannon, W. B. 1929. *Bodily Changes in Pain, Hunger, Fear, and Rage.* 2d ed. New York: Ronald.

Carney, A., J. Bancroft, and A. Mathews. 1978. "Combination of Hormonal and Psychological Treatment for Female Sexual Unresponsiveness: A Comparative Study." *British Journal of Psychiatry* 133:339–346.

Carns, D. E. 1973. "Talking about Sex: Notes on First Coitus and the Double Sexual Standard." *Journal of Marriage and the Family* 35:677–688.

Carver, C. S., and D. C. Glass. 1978. "Coronary-prone Behavior Pattern and Interpersonal Aggression." *Journal of Personality and Social Psychology* 36:361–366.

Catania, J. A., and C. B. White. 1982. "Sexuality in an Aged Sample: Cognitive Determinants of Masturbation." *Archives of Sexual Behavior* 11:237–245.

Centers, R. 1971. "Evaluating the Loved One: The Motivational Congruency Factor." *Journal of Personality* 39:308–318.

Chambers, K. C., and C. H. Phoenix. 1982. "Sexual Behavior in Old Male

Rhesus Monkeys: Influence of Familiarity and Age of Female Partners." *Archives of Sexual Behavior* 11:299–308.

Chance, M.R.A., and C. J. Jolly. 1970. *Social Groups of Monkeys, Apes, and Men.* London: Thames and Hudson.

Chandler, J. 1985. "American Televised Sport: Business as Usual." In *American Sport Culture: The Humanistic Dimension,* ed. W. L. Umphlett, 83–97. Lewisburg, Pa.: Bucknell University Press.

Chester, G. W. 1985. "Another View of Brooklyn." *TWA Ambassador* 18, no. 11:14.

Chilman, C. S. 1983. *Adolescent Sexuality in a Changing American Society: Social and Psychological Perspectives for the Human Service Professions.* New York: Wiley.

Christiansen, K., and R. Knussmann. 1987a. "Androgen Levels and Components of Aggressive Behavior in Men." *Hormones and Behavior* 21:170–180.

———. 1987b. "Sex Hormones and Cognitive Functioning in Men." *Neuropsychobiology* 18:27–36.

Christiansen, K., R. Knussman, and C. Couwenbergs. 1985. "Sex Hormones and Stress in the Human Male." *Hormones and Behavior* 19:426–440.

Cialdini, R. B., R. J. Borden, A. Thorne, M. R. Walker, S. Freeman, and L. R. Sloan. 1976. "Basking in Reflected Glory: Three (Football) Field Studies." *Journal of Personality and Social Psychology* 34:366–375.

Clement, U. 1989. "Profile Analysis as a Method of Comparing Intergenerational Differences in Sexual Behavior." *Archives of Sexual Behavior* 18:229–237.

Cochran, W. G., F. Mosteller, and J. W. Tukey. 1955. *Statistical Problems of the Kinsey Report.* Washington, D.C.: American Statistical Association.

Coe, C. I., and L. A. Rosenblum. 1984. "Male Dominance in the Bonnet Macaque: A Malleable Relationship." In *Social Cohesion: Essays toward a Sociophysiological Perspective,* ed. P. R. Barchas and S. Mendoza, 31–63. Westport, Conn.: Greenwood.

Cohen, A. K. 1955. *Delinquent Boys.* New York: Free Press.

Coles, R., and J. Stokes. 1985. *Sex and the American Teenager.* New York: Harper and Row.

Collins, A., P. Eneroth, and B. Landgren. 1985. "Psychoneuroendocrine Stress Responses and Mood as Related to the Menstrual Cycle." *Psychosomatic Medicine* 47:512–527.

Collins, R. 1975. *Conflict Sociology.* New York: Academic Press.

———. 1979. *The Credential Society.* New York: Academic Press.

———. 1981. "On the Microfoundations of Macrosociology." *American Journal of Sociology* 86:984–1014.

———. 1990. "Stratification, Emotional Energy, and the Transient Emotions." In *Research Agendas in the Sociology of Emotions,* ed. T. D. Kemper, 27–57. Albany, N.Y.: SUNY Press.

Connor, J. M., L. A. Serbin, and M. Schackman. 1977. "Sex-related Differences in Response to Practice on a Visuo-spatial Test and Generalization to Another Test." *Developmental Psychology* 13:293–294.

Coser, L. 1971. *Masters of Sociological Thought.* New York: Harcourt Brace Jovanovich.

Cramer, R. E., and S. R. Ellins. 1986. "Sport Fan Generosity: A Test of Mood, Similarity, and Equity Hypotheses." *Journal of Sport Behavior* 9:31–37.

Cutler, W. B., C.-R. Garcia, G. R. Huggins, and G. Preti. 1986. "Sexual Behavior and Steroid Levels among Gynecologically Mature Premenopausal Women." *Fertility and Sterility* 45:496–502.

Dabbs. J. M., Jr. 1988. "Summary of Saliva Testosterone Research Projects." Department of Psychology, Georgia State University. Typescript.

Dabbs., J. M., Jr., R. L. Frady, T. S. Carr, and N. F. Besch. 1987. "Saliva Testosterone and Criminal Violence in Young Adult Prison Inmates." *Psychosomatic Medicine* 49:174–182.

Dabbs, J. M., Jr., and R. Morris. 1989. "Testosterone and Antisocial Behavior in a Large Sample of Normal Men." Department of Psychology, Georgia State University. Typscript.

Dabbs, J. M., Jr., R. B. Ruback, and N. F. Besch. 1987. "Males' Saliva Testosterone following Conversations with Male and Female Partners." American Psychological Association Poster Session, August 30, New York, N.Y.

Dabbs, J. M., Jr., R. B. Ruback, C. H. Hopper, and D. S. Sgoutas. 1988. "Saliva Testosterone and Criminal Violence Among Women." *Personality and Individual Differences* 9:269–275.

Dai, W. S., L. H. Kuller, R. E. LaPorte, J. P. Gutai, L. Falvo-Gerard, and A. Caggiula. 1981. "The Epidemiology of Plasma Testosterone in Middle-aged Men." *American Journal of Epidemiology* 114:804–816.

Dailey, D. M., and J. Rosenzweig. 1988. "Variations in Men's Psychological Sex Role Self-perception as a Function of Work, Social, and Sexual Life Roles." *Journal of Sex and Marital Therapy* 14:225–240.

Daitzman, R. J., M. Zuckerman, P. Sammelwitz, and V. Ganjam. 1978. "Sensation Seeking and Gonadal Hormones." *Journal of Biosocial Science* 10:401–408.

Darwin, C. 1873. *The Expression of Emotions in Man and Animals.* New York: Appleton.

Davidson, J. 1980. "The Psychobiology of Sexual Experience." In *The Psychobiology of Consciousness,* ed. J. Davidson and R. J. Davidson, 271–332. New York: Plenum.

Davidson, J., J. J. Chen, L. Crapo, G. D. Gray, W. Greenleaf, and J. A. Catania. 1983. "Hormonal Changes and Sexual Functioning in Aging Men." *Journal of Clinical Endocrinology and Metabolism* 57:71–77.

Davidson, J. M., M. Kwan, and W. J. Greenleaf. 1982. "Hormonal Replacement and Sexuality in Men." *Clinics in Endocrinology and Metabolism* 11: 599–623.

Davidson, J., E. R. Smith, and S. Levine. 1978. "Testosterone." In *Psychobiology of Stress: A Study of Coping Men,* ed. H. Ursin, E. Baade, and S. Levine, 57–62. New York: Academic Press.

Dawkins, R. 1976. *The Selfish Gene.* New York: Oxford University Press.

DeAllende, I.L.C. 1956. "Anovulatory Cycles in Women." *American Journal of Anatomy* 98:293–305.

Dean, C. 1988. "Study Links Intelligence and Myopia." *New York Times,* December 20, C3.

DeLacerda, L., A. Kowarski, and A. J. Johanson. 1973. "Integrated Concentration and Circadian Variation of Plasma Testosterone in Normal Men." *Journal of Clinical Endocrinology and Metabolism* 37:366–371.

DeLamater, J. 1981. "The Social Control of Sexuality." In *Annual Review of Sociology,* ed. A. Inkeles et al., 263–290. Menlo Park, Calif.: Annual Reviews.

DeLamater, J., and P. MacCorquodale. 1979. *Premarital Sexuality: Attitudes, Relations, and Behavior.* Madison, Wis.: University of Wisconsin Press.

Dervin, D. 1985. "A Psychoanalysis of Sports." *The Psychoanalytic Review* 72:277–299.

Diamond, M. C. 1984. "Age, Sex, and Environmental Influence." In *Cerebral*

Dominance: The Biological Foundations, ed. N. Geschwind and A. M. Galaburda, 134–146. Cambridge, Mass.: Harvard University Press.

Doering, C. H., K. H. Brodie, H. C. Kraemer, H. B. Becker, and D. A. Hamburg. 1974. "Plasma Testosterone Levels and Psychologic Measures in Men over a Two-Month Period." In *Sex Differences in Behavior,* ed. R. C. Friedman, R. M. Richart, and R. L. Vande Wiele, 413–431. New York: Wiley.

Doering, C. H., K. H. Brodie, H. C. Kraemer, R. H. Moos, H. B. Becker, and D. A. Hamburg. 1975. "Negative Affect and Plasma Testosterone: A Longitudinal Human Study." *Psychosomatic Medicine* 37:484–491.

Dohrenwend, B. P. 1967. "Toward the Development of Theoretical Models." *Milbank Memorial Fund Quarterly* 45 (2): 155–162.

Dohrenwend, B. P., and B. S. Dohrenwend. 1969. *Social Status and Psychological Disorders.* New York: Wiley.

Doty, R. L. 1978. "Gender and Reproductive State Correlates of Taste Perception in Humans." In *Sex and Behavior: Status and Prospects,* ed. T. E. McGill, D. A. Dewsbury, and B. D. Sachs, 337–362. New York: Plenum.

Doty, R. L., P. A. Green, C. Ram, and S. L. Yankell. 1982. "Communication of Gender from Human Breath Odors: Relationship to Perceived Intensity and Pleasantness." *Hormones and Behavior* 16:13–22.

Dubin, P. 1985. "Attitudes toward Women Executives: A Longitudinal Approach." *Academy of Management Journal* 28:235–239.

Dunbar, R.I.M., and E. P. Dunbar. 1977. "Dominance and Reproductive Success among Female Gelada Baboons." *Nature* 266:351–352.

Dunning, E. 1983. "Social Bonding and Violence in Sport: A Theoretical-Empirical Analysis." In *Sports Violence,* ed. J. H. Goldstein, 129–146. New York: Springer-Verlag.

———. 1986. "Sports as a Male Preserve: Notes on the Social Sources of Masculine Identity and Its Transformations." *Theory, Culture, and Society* 3:79–90.

Durkheim, E. [1895] 1966. *The Rules of Sociological Method.* Reprint. New York: Free Press.

———. [1933] 1964. *The Division of Labor in Society.* Trans. G. Simpson, Reprint. New York: Free Press.

———. [1897]. 1951. *Suicide.* Reprint. New York: Free Press.

———. [1915]. 1965. *The Elementary Forms of the Religious Life.* Trans. J. W. Swain. Reprint. New York: Free Press.

Dworkin, A. 1987. *Intercourse.* New York: Free Press.

Eaton, G. G. 1978. "Longitudinal Studies of Sexual Behavior in the Oregon Troop of Japanese Cacaques." In *Sex and Behavior: Status and Prospects,* ed. T. E. McGill, D. A. Dewsbury, and B. D. Sachs, 35–59. New York: Plenum.

Eberhart, J. A., U. Yodyingyuad, and E. B. Keverne. 1985. "Subordination in Male Talapoin Monkeys Lowers Sexual Behaviour in the Absence of Dominants." *Physiology and Behavior* 35:673–677.

Eccles, J. S. 1987. "Gender Roles and Achievement Patterns: An Expectancy Value Perspective." In *Masculinity and Femininity: Basic Perspectives,* ed. J. M. Reinisch, L. A. Rosenblum, and S. A. Sanders, 240–280. New York: Oxford University Press.

Edwards, J. N., and A. Booth. 1976. "Sexual Behavior in and out of Marriage: An Assessment of Correlates." *Journal of Marriage and the Family* 38:73–81.

Ehlers, C. L., K. C. Rickler, and J. E. Hovey. 1980. "A Possible Relationship between Plasma Testosterone and Aggressive Behavior in a Female Outpatient Population." In *Limbic Epilepsy and the Dyscontrol Syndrome,* ed. M. Girgis and L. G. Kiloh, 183–194. New York: Elsevier.

Ehrenkranz, J., E. Bliss, and M. H. Sheard. 1974. "Plasma Testosterone: Correlation with Aggressive Behavior and Social Dominance in Man." *Psychosomatic Medicine* 36:469–475.

Ehrenreich, B. 1983. *Hearts of Men: American Dreams and the Flight from Commitment.* Garden City, N.Y.: Doubleday.

Ehrhardt, A. A., and S. W. Baker. 1974. "Fetal Androgens, Human Central Nervous System Differentiation, and Behavior Sex Differences." In *Sex Differences in Behavior,* ed. R. C. Friedman, R. M. Richart, and R. L. Vande Wiele, 33–51. New York: Wiley.

Ehrhardt, A. A., and H.F.L. Meyer-Bahlburg. 1979. "Psychosexual Development: An Examination of the Role of Prenatal Hormones." In *Symposium on Sex, Hormones, and Behaviour, London, 1978,* 41–57. Ciba Foundation Symposium, n.s. 62. Amsterdam: Excerpta Medica.

Ekman, P. 1984. "Expression and the Nature of Emotion." In *Approaches to Emotion,* ed. K. R. Scherer and P. Ekman, 319–343. Hillsdale, N.J.: Erlbaum.

Elias, M. 1981. "Serum Cortisol, Testosterone, and Testosterone Binding Globulin Responses to Competitive Fighting in Human Males." *Aggressive Behavior* 7:215–224.

Elias, N. [1939] 1978. *The Civilizing Process: The History of Manners.* Reprint. New York: Urizen.

Elias, N., and E. Dunning. 1986. "The Quest for Excitement in Leisure." In *Quest for Excitement: Sport and Leisure in the Civilizing Process,* ed. N. Elias and E. Dunning, 63–90. Oxford: Basil Blackwell.

Ellertsen, B., T. B. Johnsen, and H. Ursin. 1978. "Relationship between the Hormonal Responses to Activation and Coping." In *Psychobiology of Stress: A Study of Coping Men,* ed. H. Ursin, E. Baade, and S. Levine, 105–122. New York: Academic Press.

Ellis, L. 1982. "Developmental Androgen Fluctuations and the Five Dimensions of Mammalian Sex (with Emphasis upon the Behavioral Dimension and the Human Species)." *Ethology and Sociobiology* 3:171–197.

———. 1986. "Evidence of Neuroandrogenic Etiology of Sex Roles from a Combined Analysis of Human, Nonhuman Primate, and Nonprimate Mammalian Studies." *Personality and Individual Differences* 7:519–552.

Ellis, L., and M. A. Ames. 1987. "Neurohormonal Functioning and Sexual Orientation." *Psychological Bulletin* 101:233–258.

Elmadjian, F., J. M. Hope, and E. T. Lamson. 1958. "Excretion and Epinephrine in Various Emotional States." *Journal of Clinical Endocrinology* 17:608–620.

Erlanger, H. S. 1974. "Social Class and Corporal Punishment in Childrearing: A Reassessment." *American Sociological Review* 39:68–85.

Everitt, B. J. 1979. "Monoamines and Sexual Behavior in Non-Human Primates." In *Symposium on Sex, Hormones, and Behaviour, London, 1978,* 329–358. Ciba Foundation Symposium, n.s. 62. Amsterdam: Excerpta Medica.

Everitt, B. J., and J. Herbert. 1971. "The Effects of Dexamethasone and Androgens on Sexual Receptivity of Female Rhesus Monkeys." *Journal of Endocrinology* 51:575–588.

Eysenck, H. 1975. *Sex and Personality.* Austin: University of Texas Press.

Fabrikant, G. 1985. "A Media Giant Loses Its Swagger." *New York Times,* December 1, sec. 3, 1, 29.

Fausto-Sterling, A. 1985. *Myths of Gender: Biological Theories about Women and Men.* New York: Basic.

Firestone, S. 1970. *The Dialectic of Sex.* New York: William Morrow.

Flaubert, G. [1857] 1977. *Madame Bovary.* Trans. J. L. May. Reprint. New York: Hart.

Flood, A. B., and W. R. Scott. 1978. "Professional Power and Professional Effectiveness: The Power of the Surgical Staff and the Quality of Surgical Care." *Journal of Health and Social Behavior* 19:240–53.

Floody, O. R. 1983. "Hormones and Aggression in Female Mammals." In *Hormones and Aggressive Behavior,* ed. B. B. Svare, 39–89. New York: Plenum.

Ford, C. S., and F. A. Beach. 1951. *Patterns of Sexual Behavior.* New York: Harper and Row.

Ford, K, M. Zelnick, and J. F. Kanter. 1981. "Sexual Behavior and Contraception Use among Socioeconomic Groups of Young Women." *Journal of Biosocial Science* 13:31–45.

Forsman, L. 1980. "Habitual Catecholamine Excretion and Its Relation to Habitual Stress." *Biological Psychology* 11:83–97.

Forte, F. L., D. Mandato, and W. A. Kayson. 1981. "Effect of Sex of Subject on Recall of Gender-Stereotypes Magazine Advertisements." *Psychological Reports* 49:619–622.

Foucault, M. 1977. *Discipline and Punish.* New York: Pantheon.

———. 1980. *History of Sexuality.* Vol. 1. New York: Pantheon.

Fox, C. A., A. A. Ismail, D. N. Love, K. E. Kirkham, and J. A. Loraine. 1972. "Studies on the Relationship between Plasma Testosterone Levels and Human Sexual Activity." *Journal of Endocrinology* 52:51–58.

Frank, R., and M. Greenberg. 1980. *The Public's Use of Television: Who Watches and Why.* Beverly Hills, Calif.: Sage.

Frankenhaeuser, M. 1976. "Experimental Approaches of Catecholamines and Emotions." In *Emotions: Their Parameters and Measurement.* ed. L. Levi, 209–234. New York: Raven.

Frankenhaeuser, M, M. Rauste von Wright, A. Collins, J. von Wright, G. Sedvall, and C.-G. Swahn. 1978. "Sex Differences in Psychoneuroendocrine Reactions to Examination Stress." *Psychosomatic Medicine* 40:334–343.

Freese, L. 1988. "Evolution and Sociogenesis. Part 1, Ecological Origins." In *Advances in Group Processes,* ed. E. J. Lawler and B. Markowsky, 5:51–89. Greenwich, Conn.: JAI.

Freud, S. [1905] 1938. "The Transformations of Puberty." In *The Basic Writings of Sigmund Freud,* ed. A. A. Brill, 604–629. New York: Random House.

———. [1905] 1949. "Three Essays on the Theory of Sexuality." In *Standard Edition of the Complete Psychological Works of Sigmund Freud,* ed. J. Strachey, 7:123–143. London: Hogarth.

———. [1905] 1959. "Civilized Sexual Morality and Modern Nervous Illness." In *Standard Edition of the Complete Psychological Works of Sigmund Freud,* ed. J. Strachey, 9:179–204. London: Hogarth.

———. [1910] 1957. "The Psychoanalytic View of Psychogenic Disturbance of Vision." In *Standard Edition of the Complete Psychological Works of Sigmund Freud,* ed. J. Strachey, 11:209–218. London: Hogarth.

———. [1927] 1961. "The Future of an Illusion." In *Standard Edition of the*

Complete Psychological Works of Sigmund Freud, ed. J. Strachey, 21:5–56. London: Hogarth.

———. [1930] 1951. *Civilization and Its Discontents,* tran. J. Riviere. London: Hogarth and Institute for Psycho-analysis.

———. [1933] 1964. "New Introductory Lectures in Psychoanalysis." In *Standard Edition of the Complete Psychological Works of Sigmund Freud,* ed. J. Strachey, 22:3–182. London: Hogarth.

Freund, P.E.S. 1988. "Bringing Society into the Human Body: Understanding Socialized Human Nature." *Theory and Society* 17:839–864.

Frisch, R. 1988. "Fatness and Fertility." *Scientific American* 258:88–95.

Frodi, A., J. Macaulay, and P. R. Thome. 1977. "Are Women Always Less Aggressive than Men? A Review of the Experimental Literature." *Psychological Bulletin* 84:634–660.

Funkenstein, D. 1955. "The Physiology of Fear and Anger." *Scientific American* 192:74–80.

Funkenstein, D., S. H. King, and M. E. Drolette. 1957. *Mastery of Stress.* Cambridge, Mass.: Harvard University Press.

Furstenberg, F. H., Jr., S. P. Morgan, K. A. Moore, and J. L. Peterson. 1987. "Race Differences in the Timing of Adolescent Intercourse." *American Sociological Review* 52:511–518.

Gagnon, J. H. 1973. "Scripts and the Coordination of Sexual Conduct." In *Nebraska Symposium on Motivation, 1973,* ed. J. K. Cole and R. Dienstbier, 27–59. Lincoln: University of Nebraska Press.

Gagnon, J. H., and W. Simon. 1973. *Sexual Conduct.* Chicago: Aldine.

Gailey, P. 1985. "Politics: Yuppie Is Dead, Long Live the 'New Collar' Voter." *New York Times,* July 19, sec. A, 10.

Gallop, G. W., Jr. 1986. *The Gallop Poll: Public Opinion 1985. Wilmington, Del.: Scholarly Research.*

Galtung, J. 1982. "Sport as Carrier of Culture and Deep Structure."*Current Research on Peace and Violence* 5:133–143.

Gandelman, R. 1980. "Gonadal Hormones and the Induction of Intraspecific Fighting in Mice." *Neuroscience and Biobehavioral Reviews* 4:133–140.

Gans, H. 1962. *The Urban Villagers.* New York: Free Press.

Garbarino, J. 1981. "An Ecological Approach to Child Maltreatment." In *The Social Context of Child Abuse and Neglect,* ed. L. H. Pelton, 124–132. New York: Human Sciences.

Garcia, L. T., K. Brennan, M. DeCarlo, R. McGlennon, and S. Tait. 1984. "Sex Differences in Sexual Arousal to Different Erotic Stories." *Journal of Sex Research* 20:391–402.

Gebhard, P. H., J. H. Gagnon, W. B. Pomeroy, and C. Christenson. 1965. *Sex Offenders: An Analysis of Types.* New York: Harper-Hoeber.

Gebhard, P. H., and A. B. Johnson. 1979. *The Kinsey Data: Marginal Tabulations of the 1938–1963 Interviews Conducted by the Institute for Sex Research.* Philadelphia: W. B. Saunders.

Geertz, C. 1972. "Deep Play: Notes on the Balinese Cockfight." *Daedalus* 101:1–37.

Gelles, R. T. 1972. *The Violent Home.* Beverly Hills, Calif.: Sage.

Gelles, R. T., and M. A. Straus. 1988. *Intimate Violence.* New York: Simon and Schuster.

Gellhorn, E. 1967. *Principles of Autonomic-Somatic Integrations.* Minneapolis: University of Minnesota Press.

———. 1968. "Attempts at a Synthesis: Contribution to a Theory of Emotion." In *Biological Foundations of Emotion: Research and Commentary,* ed. E. Gellhorn, 144–153. Glenview, Ill.: Scott Foresman.

Gellhorn, E., and G. N. Loofbourrow. 1963. *Emotions and Emotional Disorders.* New York: Harper and Row.

Geschwind, N, and A. Galaburda. 1985. "Cerebral Lateralization: Biological Mechanisms, Associations, and Pathology: A Hypothesis and a Program for Research." Parts 1–3. *Archives of Neurology* 42:428–459, 521–552, 634–654.

Gil, D. G. 1979. *Child Abuse and Violence.* New York: AMS Press.

Gittelson, N. 1979. *Dominus: A Woman Looks at Men's Lives.* New York: Harcourt Brace.

Glick, S. 1983. "Heritable Determinants of Left-Right Bias in the Rat." *Life Sciences* 32:2215–2221.

E. Goffman. 1967. *Interaction Ritual.* Garden City, NY: Doubelday.

———. 1979. *Gender Advertisements.* Cambridge, Mass.: Harvard University Press.

Goldfoot, D. A., and D. A. Neff. 1987. "Assessment of Behavioral Sex Differences in Social Contexts: Perspectives from Primatology." In *Masculinity and Femininity: Basic Perspectives,* ed. J. M. Reinisch, L. A. Rosenblum, and S. A. Sanders, 179–195. New York: Oxford University Press.

Goldstein, A. G., and J. E. Chance. 1965. "Effects of Practice on Sex-related Differences in Performance on Embedded Figures." *Psychonomic Science* 3:361–362.

Goldstein, J. H. 1982. "Sports Violence." *National Forum* 62:9–11.

Goleman, D. 1986. "Major Personality Study Finds That Traits Are Mostly Inherited." *New York Times,* December 12, sec. C, 1.

———. 1989a. "Study Defines Major Sources of Conflict between the Sexes."*New York Times,* June 13, sec. C, 1.

———. 1989b. "Subtle but Intriguing Differences Found in the Brain Anatomy of Men and Women." *New York Times,* April 11, sec. C, 1.

Gordon, H. W. 1985. "A Relationship between Gonadotropins and Visuospatial Function." *Neuropsychologia* 24:563–576.

Gordon, H. W., E. D. Corbin, and P. A. Lee. 1986. "Changes in Specialized Cognitive Functions Following Changes in Hormone Level." *Cortex* 22: 399–415.

Gould, S. J. 1980. "Sociobiology and Human Nature." In *Sociobiology Examined,* ed. A. Montague, 283–290. Oxford: Oxford University Press.

Gould, S. J., and R. C. Lewontin. 1978. "The Spandrels of San Marco and the Panglossian Paradigm: A Critique of the Adaptationist Programme." *Proceedings of the Royal Society of London* 105:581–598.

Goy, R. W. 1968. "Organizing Effects of Androgens on the Behavior of Rhesus Monkeys." In *Endocrinology and Human Behavior,* ed. R. P. Michael, 12–31. London: Oxford University Press.

———. 1979. "Sexual Compatibility in Rhesus Monkeys: Predicting Sexual Performance of Oppositely-sexed Pairs of Adults." In *Symposium on Sex, Hormones, and Behaviour, London, 1978,* 227–249. Ciba Foundation Symposium, n.s. 62. Amsterdam: Excerpta Medica.

Goy, R. W., and B. S. McEwen. 1981. *Sexual Differentiation of the Brain.* Cambridge, Mass.: MIT Press.

Graham, H. D., and T. R. Gurr. 1969. *Violence in America: Historical and Comparative Perspectives.* Washington, D.C.: GPO.

Graham, L. A., S. I. Cohen, and B. M. Shmavonian. 1967. "Some Methodological Approaches to the Psychophysiological Correlates of Behavior." In *Emotional Stress: Physiological and Psychological Reactions; Medical, Industrial, and Military Applications*, ed. L. Levi, 178–191. New York: Elsevier.

Gray, D. S., and B. B. Gorzalka. 1980. "Adrenal Steroid Interactions in Female Sexual Behavior." *Psychoneuroendocrinology* 5:157–175.

Greene, B. L., R. R. Lee, and N. Lustig. 1974. "Conscious and Unconscious Factors in Marital Infidelity." *Medical Aspects of Human Sexuality* 8:86–115.

Greer, D. L. 1983. "Spectator Booing and the Home Advantage." *Social Psychology Quarterly* 46:252–260.

Greer, G. 1970. *The Female Eunuch*. London: McGibbon and Kee.

Griffitt, W. 1987. "Females, Males, and Sexual Responses." In *Females, Males, and Sexuality: Theories and Research*, ed. K. Kelley, 141–173. Albany: State University of New York Press.

Gruneau, R. 1975. "Sports, Social Differentiation, and Social Inequality." In *Sport and Social Order*, ed. D. Ball and J. W. Loy, 117–184. Reading, Mass.: Addison-Wesley.

———. 1983. *Class, Sports, and Social Development*. Amherst: University of Massachusetts Press.

Gumplowicz, L. [1899] 1977. *The Outlines of Sociology*, ed. I. L. Horowitz, Reprint. New York: Arno.

Gunther, M., and B. Carter. 1988. *Monday Night Mayhem: The Inside Story of ABC's Monday Night Football*. New York: Beech Tree/William Morrow.

Gutmann, D. 1977. "The Cross-cultural Perspective: Notes toward a Comparative Psychology of Aging." In *Handbook of the Psychology of Aging*, ed. J. E. Birren and K. W. Schaie, 302–326. New York: Van Nostrand Reinhold.

Gutman, A. 1978. *From Ritual to Record: The Nature of Modern Sports*. New York: Columbia University Press.

———. 1986. *Sports Spectators*. New York: Columbia University Press.

Hacker, A. 1983. *U.S.: A Statistical Portrait of the American People*. New York: Viking.

Hamburg, B. A. 1974. "The Psychobiology of Sexual Differences: An Evolutionary Perspective." In *Sex Differences in Behavior*, ed. R. C. Friedman, R. M. Richart, and R. L. Vande Wiele, 373–392. New York: Wiley.

Hammond, G. L., J. A. Nisker, L. A. Jones, and P. K. Siiteri. 1980. "Estimation of the Percentage of Free Steroid in Undiluted Serum by Centrifugal Ultrafiltration-Dyalysis." *Journal of Biological Chemistry* 255:5023–5026.

Hammond, M. 1988. "The Shadow Man Paradigm in Paleoanthropology, 1911–1945." In *The History of Anthropology*, ed. G. Stocking, 5:117–137. Madison: University of Wisconsin Press.

Hampson, E., and D. Kimura. 1988. "Reciprocal Effects of Hormonal Fluctuations on Human Motor and Perceptual-Spatial Skills." *Behavioral Neuroscience* 102:456–459.

Harburg, E., E. H. Blakelock, Jr., and P. J. Roeper. 1979. "Resentful and Reflective Coping with Arbitrary Authority and Blood Pressure: Detroit." *Psychosomatic Medicine* 41:189–201.

Hariton, B. E., and F. L. Singer. 1974. "Women's Fantasies during Sexual Intercourse: Normative and Theoretical Implications." *Journal of Consulting and Clinical Psychology* 42:313–322.

Harman, S. M., and P. D. Tsitouras. 1980. "Reproductive Hormones in Aging Men: I. Measurement of Sex Steroids, Basal LH, and Leydig Cell

Response to HcG." *Journal of Clinical Endocrinology and Metabolism* 51: 35–40.

Harper, L. V., and K. M. Sanders. 1978. "Sex Differences in Preschool Children's Social Interaction and Use of Space: An Evolutionary Perspective." In *Sex and Behavior: Status and Prospects,* ed. T. E. McGill, D. A. Dewsbury, and B. D. Sachs, 61–81. New York: Plenum.

Harris, J. C. 1983. "Sports and Ritual: A Macroscopic Comparison of Form." In *Play, Games, and Sports in Cultural Contexts,* ed. J. C. Harris and R. J. Park, 177–189. Champaign, Ill.: Human Kinetics.

Harris, L. J. 1981. "Sex-related Variations in Spatial Skill." In *Spatial Representation and Behavior across the Life Span,* ed. L. S. Liben, A. H. Patterson, and N. Newcombe, 83–125. New York: Academic Press.

Harris. L, and Associates. 1986. *American Teenagers Speak: Sexual Myths, TV, and Birth Control.* New York: Planned Parenthood.

Haupt, H. A., and G. D. Rovere. 1984. "Anabolic Steroids: A Review of the Literature." *American Journal of Sports Medicine* 12:469–484.

Heiman, J. R. 1980. "Female Sexual Response Patterns: Interaction of Physiological, Affective, and Contextual Cues." *Archives of General Psychiatry* 37:1311–1316.

Heiman, J. R., and D. L. Rowland. 1983. "Affective and Physiological Sexual Response Patterns: The Effects of Instructions on Sexually Functional and Dysfunctional Men." *Journal of Psychosomatic Research* 27:105–116.

Hellhammer, D. H., W. Hubert, and T. Schurmeyer. 1985. "Changes in Saliva Testosterone after Psychological Stimulation in Men." *Psychoneuroendocrinology* 10:77–81.

Henry, J. P. 1980. "Present Concept of Stress Theory." In *Catecholamines and Stress: Recent Advances,* ed. E. Usdin, R. Kvetnansky, and I. J. Kopin, 557–571. Amsterdam: North Holland/Elsevier.

Henry, J. P., and P. M. Stephens. 1977. *Stress, Health, and the Social Environment: A Sociobiologic Approach to Medicine.* New York: Springer-Verlag.

Herbert, J. 1978. "Neuro-hormonal Integration of Sexual Behavior in Female Primates." In *Biological Determinants of Sexual Behaviour,* ed. J. B. Hutchison, 467–493. Wiley. Chichester, England.

Hess, W. R. 1954. *Diencephalon, Autonomic, and Extra Pyramidal Functions.* New York: Grune and Stratton.

Hest. A. V., F. V. Haaren, and N.E.V.D. Poll. 1989. "Perseveration Responses in Male and Female Wistar Rats: Effects of Gonadal Hormones." *Hormones and Behavior* 23:57–67.

Hinde, R. A. 1974. *Biological Bases of Human Behavior.* New York: Mcgraw-Hill.

———. 1979. "The Nature of Social Structure." In *The Great Apes: Perspectives on Human Evolution,* ed. D. Hamburger and E. McGowan, 5:295–315. Menlo Park, Calif.: Benjamin-Cummings.

Hindelang. M. J., T. Hirschi, and J. Weis. 1979. "Correlates of Delinquency: The Illusion of Discrepancy between Self-report and Official Measures." *American Sociological Review* 44:995–1014.

Hines, M. 1982. "Prenatal Hormones and Human Sex Differences." *Psychological Bulletin* 92:56–80.

Hite, S. 1981. *The Hite Report on Male Sexuality.* New York: Knopf.

———. 1987. *Women and Love: A Cultural Revolution in Progress.* New York: Knopf.

Hoch, P. 1972. *Rip Off the Big Game: The Exploitation of Sports by the Power Elite.* Garden City, N.Y.: Doubleday.

Hofstadter, R. 1955. *Social Darwinism in American Thought.* rev. ed. Boston: Beacon.

Hollister, L. H., K. L. Davis, and B. M. Davis. 1980. "Hormones in the Treatment of Psychiatric Disorders." In *Neuroendocrinology,* ed. D. T. Kreiger and J. C. Hughes, 167–175. Sunderland, Mass.: Sinauer Associates.

Homans, G. 1961. *Social Behavior: Its Elementary Forms.* New York: Harcourt Brace, World.

Hornung, C. A., B. C. McCullough, and T. Sugimoto. 1981. "Status Relationships in Marriage: Risk Factors in Spouse Abuse." *Journal of Marriage and the Family* 43:675–692.

Hrdy, S. B. 1981. *The Woman That Never Evolved.* Cambridge, Mass.: Harvard University Press.

Hubble, D. 1963. "The Psyche and the Endocrine System." *Lancet* 2: 209–214.

Huber, J, and G. Spitze. 1980. "Considering Divorce: An Expansion of Becker's Theory of Marital Instability." *American Journal of Sociology* 86: 75–89.

Hudson, J. W., and L. F. Henze. 1969. "Campus Values in Mate Selection: A Replication." *Journal of Marriage and the Family* 31:772–775.

Huesman, L. R., M. Lefkowitz, L. Eron, and L. O. Walder. 1984. "Stability of Aggression over Time and Generations." *Developmental Psychology* 20: 1120–1134.

Huizinga, J. [1938] 1970. *Homo Ludens: A Study of the Play Element in Culture.* London: Temple Smith.

Hunt, M. 1974. *Sexual Behavior in the 1970s.* Chicago: Playboy Press.

Hutchison, J. B. 1978. "Hypothalamic Regulation of Male Sexual Responsiveness to Androgen." In *Biological Determinants of Sexual Behaviour,* ed. J. B. Hutchison, 277–317. Chicester, England: Wiley.

Hutt, S. J., G. Frank, N. Mychalkiw, and M. Hughes. 1980. "Perceptual-Motor Performance during the Menstrual Cycle." *Hormones and Behavior* 14:116–125.

Hyde, J. S. 1986. "Gender Differences in Aggression." In *The Psychology of Gender: Advances through Meta-Analysis,* ed. J. S. Hyde and M. C. Linn, 51–66. Baltimore: Johns Hopkins University Press.

Ingham, A, and S. Hardy. 1984. "Sports: Structuration, Subjugation, and Hegemony." *Theory, Culture, and Society* 2:85–103.

Isen, A. M., and P. F. Levin. 1972. "The Effects of Feeling Good on Helping: Cookies and Kindness." *Journal of Personality and Social Psychology* 21:384–388.

Izard, C. E. 1977. *Human Emotions.* New York: Plenum.

Jackson, M. 1984. "Sex Research and the Construction of Sexuality: A Toll of Male Supremacy?" *Women's Studies International Forum* 7:43–51.

Jacob, T. 1974. "Pattern of Family Conflict and Dominance as a Function of Child Age and Social Class." *Developmental Psychology* 10:1–12.

James, W. [1890] 1981. *Principles of Psychology.* Reprint. Cambridge, Mass.: Harvard University Press.

———. 1983. "Decline in Coital Rates with Spouses' Ages and Duration of Marriage." *Journal of Biosocial Science* 15:83–87.

Jasso, G. 1985. "Marital Coital Frequency and the Passage of Time: Estimating the Separate Effects of Spouses' Ages and Marital Duration, Birth and Marriage Cohorts, and Period Influences." *American Sociological Review* 50:224–243.

Jeffcoate, W, N. Lincoln, C. Selby, and M. Herbert. 1986. "Correlation between Anxiety and Serum Prolactin in Humans." *Journal of Psychosomatic Research* 29:217–222.

Jenkins, C. D., R. H. Rosenman, and S. J. Zyzanski. 1974. "Prediction of Clinical Coronary Disease by a Test for the Coronary-prone Behavior Pattern." *New England Journal of Medicine* 290:1271–1275.

Jensen, G. D. 1976. "Adolescent Sexuality." In *The Sexual Experience,* ed. B. J. Sadock, H. I. Kaplan, and A. M. Freedman, 142–155. Baltimore: Williams and Wilkins.

Jolly, A. 1972. *The Evolution of Primate Behavior.* New York: Macmillan.

Jones, A. S. 1987. "Forbes Column Ended as Research Is Doubted." *New York Times,* July 21, sec. B, 3.

Jordan, P. 1989. "A Team Divided Can Still Win." *New York Times,* March 19, sec. S, 10.

Juraska, J. M., C. Henderson, and J. Muller. 1984. "Differential Rearing Experience, Gender, and Radial Maze Performance." *Developmental Psychobiology* 17:209–215.

Kahn, R. L. 1974. "The Work Module: A Proposal for the Humanization of Work." In *Work and the Quality of Life,* ed. J. O'Toole, 199–226. Cambridge, Mass.: MIT Press.

Kail, R., P. Carter, and J. Pellegrino. 1979. "The Locus of Sex Differences in Spatial Ability." *Perception and Psychophysics* 26:182–186.

Kallen, D. J., and A. Doughty. 1984. "The Relationship of Weight, the Self-Perception of Weight, and Self-esteem with Courtship Behavior." *Marriage and Family Review* 7:93–114.

Kaplan, A. 1964. *The Conduct of Inquiry.* San Francisco: Chandler.

Kaplan, H. S. 1974. *The New Sex Therapy.* New York: Brunner/Mazel.

Kaplan, H. B., and S. W. Bloom. 1960. "The Use of Sociological and Social Psychological Concepts in Physiological Research: A Review of Selected Experimental Studies." *Journal of Nervous and Mental Disease* 131:128–134.

Kaufman, D. R. 1978. "Associational Ties in Academe: Some Male and Female Differences." *Sex Roles* 4:9–21.

Kaye, H. L. 1986. *The Social Meaning of Modern Biology: From Social Darwinism to Sociobiology.* New Haven, Conn.: Yale University Press.

Kedenburg, H. D. 1977. "Androgen and Aggressive Behavior in Man." Ph.D. diss., Department of Anthropology, Rutgers University, New Brunswick.

Keidel, R. W. 1987. "Team Sports as a Generic Organizational Framework." *Human Relations* 40:591–612.

Keil, T. 1984. "Sport in Advanced Capitalism." *Arena Review* 8:15–39.

Keller, J. F., S. S. Elliott, and E. Gunberg. 1982. "Premarital Sexual Intercourse among Single College Students: A Discriminant Analysis." *Sex Roles* 8:21–32.

Kelley, K, C. T. Miller, D. Byrne, and P. A. Bell. 1983. "Facilitating Sexual Arousal via Anger, Aggression, or Dominance." *Motivation and Emotion* 7:191–202.

Kelley, K, E. Pilchowicz, and D. Byrne. 1981. "Response of Males to Female-initiated Dates." *Bulletin of the Psychonomic Society* 17:195–196.

Kemper, T. D. 1974. "On the Nature and Purpose of Ascription." *American Sociological Review* 39:844–853.

———. 1978. *A Social Interactional Theory of Emotions.* New York: Wiley.

———. 1987. "How Many Emotions Are There? Wedding the Social and the Autonomic Components." *American Journal of Sociology* 93:263–289.

Kemper, T. D., and R. W. Bologh. 1980. "The Ideal Love Object: Structural and Family Sources." *Journal of Youth and Adolescence* 9:33–48.

Kemper, T. D., and R. Collins. 1990. "Dimensions of Microinteraction." *American Journal of Sociology* 96:32–68.

Kennard, J., and E. O. Hofstetter. 1983. "Sports and Television: A Bibliography." *Arena Review* 7:28–38.

Kety, S. S. 1972. "Norepinephrine in the CNS and Its Correlation with Behavior." In *Brain and Human Behavior,* ed. A. G. Karczmar and J. C. Eccles, 115–128. New York: Springer-Verlag.

Keverne, E. B. 1976. "Sexual Receptivity and Attractiveness in the Female Rhesus Monkey." In *Advances in the Study of Behavior,* ed. J. S. Rosenblatt, R. A. Hinde, E. Shaw, and C. Beer, 7:155–200. New York: Academic Press.

———. 1979. Sexual and Aggressive Behaviour in Social Groups of Talapoin Monkeys." In *Symposim on Sex, Hormones, and Behaviour, London, 1978,* 271–297. Ciba Foundation Symposium, n.s. 62. Amsterdam: Excerpta Medica.

Kilman, P. R., K. H. Mills, C. Caid, B. Bella, E. Davidson, and R. Wanlass. 1984. "The Sexual Interaction of Women with Secondary Orgasmic Dysfunction and Their Partners." *Archives of Sexual Behavior* 13:41–49.

Kimura, D., and E. Hampson. 1988. "Sex Differences and Hormonal Influences on Cognitive Brain Function." Seminar presented to meetings of Society for Neuroscience, Toronto, Canada, November 16.

Kinsey, A. C., W. B. Pomeroy, and C. E. Martin. 1948. *Sexual Behavior in the Human Male.* Philadelphia: W. B. Saunders.

Kinsey, A. C., W. B. Pomeroy, C. E. Martin, and P. H. Gebhard. 1953. *Sexual Behavior in the Human Female.* Philadelphia: W. B. Saunders.

Klaiber, E. L., D. M. Broverman, and Y. Kobayashi. 1967. "The Automatization Cognitive Style, Androgens, and Monoamine Oxidase." *Psychopharmacologia* 11:320–336.

Klaiber, E. L., D. M. Broverman, and W. Vogel. 1971. "Effects of Infused Testosterone on Mental Performances and Serum LH." *Journal of Clinical Endocrinology and Metabolism* 32:341–349.

Klaiber, E. L., D. M. Broverman, W. Vogel, and Y. Kobayashi. 1979. "Estrogen Therapy for Severe Persistent Depressions in Women." *Archives of General Psychiatry* 36:550–554.

Klaiber, E. L., Y. Kobayashi, D. M. Broverman, and F. Hall. 1971. "Plasma Monoamine Oxidase Activity in Rgularly Ménstruating Women and in Amenorheic Women Receiving Cyclic Treatment with Estrogens and a Progestin." *Journal of Clinical Endocrinology and Metabolism* 33:630–638.

Klein, D. P. 1984. "Occupational Employment Statistics for 1972–82." *Employment and Earnings* 31:13–17.

Kling, A., and K. Dunne. 1976. "Social Environmental Factors Affecting Behavior and Plasma Testosterone in Normal and Amygdala Lesioned *M. Speciosa.*" *Primates* 17:23–42.

Klinteberg, B. af, S. E. Levander, L. Oreland, M. Asberg, and D. Schalling. 1987. "Neuropsychological Correlates of Platelet Monoamine Oxidase (MAO) Activity in Female and Male Subjects." *Biological Psychology* 24:237–252.

Knecht, R. S., and B. R. Zenger. 1985. "Sport Spectator Knowledge as a

Predictor of Spectator Behavior." *International Journal of Sports Psychology* 16:270–279.

Knoth, R., K. Boyd, and B. Singer. 1988. "Empirical Tests of Sexual Selection Theory: Predictions of Sex Differences in Onset, Intensity, and Time Course of Sexual Arousal." *Journal of Sex Research* 24:73–89.

Knussman, R. K. Christiansen, and C. Couwenbergs. 1986. "Relations between Sex Hormone Levels and Sexual Behavior in Men." *Archives of Sexual Behavior* 15:429–445.

Kobayashi, T., T. Kobayashi, J. Kato, and H. Minaguchi. 1966. "Cholinergic and Adrenergic Mechanisms in the Female Rat Hypothalamus with Special Reference to Feedback of Ovarian Steroid Hormones." In *Steroid Dynamics,* ed. G. Pincus, T. Nakao, and J. Tait, 305–307. New York: Academic Press.

Kohn, M. 1969, *Class and Conformity.* Homewood, Ill.: Dorsey.

———. 1983. *Work and Authority.* Norwood, N.J.: Ablex.

Kolata, G. 1987. "New Clues to Complex Biology of Dyslexia." *New York Times,* December 8, sec. C, 7.

———. 1989. "Gender Gap in Aptitude Tests Is Narrowing, Experts Find." *New York Times,* July 1, sec. A, 8.

Komarovsky, M. 1940. *The Unemployed Man and His Family.* New York: Dryden.

———. 1976. *Dilemmas of Masculinity: A Study of College Youth.* New York: Norton.

Kommenich, P., D. M. Lane, R. P. Dickey, and S. C. Stone. 1978. "Gonadal Hormones and Cognitive Performance." *Physiological Psychology* 6:115–120.

Koss, M. P., and T. Dinero. 1988. "Predictors of Sexual Aggression among a National Sample of Male College Students." In *Annals of the New York Academy of Sciences,* ed. R. A. Prentky and V. L. Quinsey, 528: 133–147. New York: NYAS.

Kraemer, H. C., H. B. Becker, H. K. Brodie, C. H. Doering, R. H. Moos, and D. A. Hamburg. 1976. "Orgasmic Frequency and Plasma Testosterone Levels in Normal Human Males." *Archives of Sexual Behavior* 2:125–132.

Kreuz, L., and R. M. Rose. 1972. "Assessment of Aggressive Behavior and Plasma Testosterone in Young Criminal Population." *Psychosomatic Medicine* 34:470–471.

Kreuz, L., R. M. Rose, and R. Jennings. 1972. "Suppression of Plasma Testosterone Levels and Psychological Stress." *Archives of General Psychiatry* 26:479–482.

Kruse, J. A., and J. Gottman. 1982. "Time Series Methodology in the Study of Sexual Hormonal and Behavioral Cycles." *Archives of Sexual Behavior* 11:405–415.

Kuhn, T. 1962. *The Structure of Scientific Revolutions.* Chicago: University of Chicago Press.

Kwan, M., W. J. Greenleaf, J. Mann, L. Crapo, J. M. Davidson. 1983. "The Nature of Androgen Action on Male Sexuality: A Combined Laboratory–Self-Report Study on Hypogonadal Men." *Journal of Clinical Endocrinology and Metabolism* 57:557–562.

LaFerla, J. J., D. M. Anderson, and D. S. Schlach. 1978. "Psychoendocrine Response to Sexual Arousal in Human Males." *Psychosomatic Medicine* 40: 166–172.

Lancaster, J. B. 1979. "Sex and Gender in Evolutionary Perspective." In

Human Sexuality: A Comparative and Developmental Perspective, ed. H. A. Katchadourian, 51–80. Berkeley and Los Angeles: University of California Press.

Langevin, R., J. Bain, G. Wortzman, S. Hucker, R. Dickey, and P. Wright. 1988. "Sexual Sadism: Brain, Blood, and Behavior." In *Annals of the New York Academy of Sciences,* ed. R. A. Prentky and V. L. Quinsey, 528:163–171. New York: NYAS.

Langhorne, M. C., and P. F. Secord. 1955. "Variations in Marital Needs with Age, Sex, Marital Status, and Regional Location." *Journal of Social Psychology* 41:19–37.

LaPointe, J. 1988. "The Championship Fight That Went beyond Boxing." *New York Times,* June 19, sec. 8, 1.

LaRue, D. de, and J. M. Dabbs, Jr. 1989. "Vocational Differences in Saliva Testosterone among Men." Department of Psychology, Georgia State University. Typescript.

Larwood, L., and J. Blackmore. 1978. "Sex Discrimination in Manager Selection: Testing Predictions of the Vertical Dyad Linkage Model." *Sex Roles* 4:359–367.

Lasch, C. 1979. *The Culture of Narcissism.* New York: Norton.

Laye, J. D. 1981. "Effects of Demand for Performance, Self-monitoring of Arousal, and Increased SNS Activity on Male Erectile Tissue." *Archives of Sexual Behavior* 10:443–464.

Lederman, D. 1989. "Female Basketball Players Outperform Their Male Counterparts in the Classroom." *Chronicle of Higher Education* (August 16):1.

Lee, P. A., R. B. Jaffe, and A. R. Midgley, Jr. 1974. "Lack of Alteration of Serum Gonadotropins in Men and Women following Sexual Intercourse." *American Journal of Obstetrics and Gynecology* 120:985–987.

Leiblum, S., G. Bachmann, E. Kemmann, D. Colburn, and L. Swartzman. 1983. "Vaginal Atrophy in Postmenopausal Women: The Importance of Sexual Activity and Hormones." *Journal of the American Medical Association* 249:2195–2198.

LeMasters, E. E. 1975. *Blue Collar Aristocrats: Life Styles at a Working Class Tavern.* Madison: University of Wisconsin Press.

Leventman, P. 1981. *Professionals Out of Work.* New York: Free Press.

Lever, J., and S. Wheeler. 1984. "The *Chicago Tribune* Sports Page, 1900–1975." *Sociology of Sports Journal* 1:299–313.

Levi, L. 1972. "Sympathoadrenomedullary Responses to 'Pleasant' and 'Unpleasant' Psychosocial Stimuli." In *Stress and Distress in Response to Psychosocial Stimuli: Laboratory and Real Life Studies in Sympathoadrenomedullary and Related Reactions,* ed. L. Levi, 35–73. Acta Medica Scandanavica, suppl. 528. Stockholm: Almquist and Wiksell.

Levine, J. 1988. "Sports Sponsorships: Maximizing the Potential." *Incentive –162:30–37.*

Levine, S., and C. H. Doering. 1974. "Discussion: Effects of Hormones on the Development of Behavior." In *Sex Differences in Behavior,* ed. R. C. Friedman, R. M. Richart, and R. L. Vande Wiele, 77–84. New York: Wiley.

Levy, F. 1987. *Dollars and Dreams: The Changing American Income Distribution.* New York: Russell Sage Foundation.

Lewontin, R. 1977. "Sociobiology—A Caricature of Darwinism." In *Proceedings of the 1976 Biennial Meeting of the Philosophy of Science Association,* ed.

F. Suppe and P. O. Asquith, 2:22–31. East Lansing, Mich.: Philosophy of Science Association.

Liben, L. S., and S. L. Golbeck. 1980. "Sex Differences in Performance on Piagetian Spatial Tasks: Differences in Competence or Performance." *Child Development* 51:594–597.

Lincoln, G. A. 1974. "Luteinizing Hormone and Testosterone in Man." *Nature* 252:232–233.

Linn, M. C., and A. C. Petersen. 1985. "Emergence and Characterization of Sex Differences in Spatial Ability: A Meta-Analysis." *Child Development* 56:1479–1498.

———. 1986. "A Meta-Analysis of Gender Differences in Spatial Ability: Implications of Mathematics and Science Achievement." In *The Psychology of Gender: Advances through Meta-Analysis,* J. S. Hyde and M. C. Linn, 67–101. Baltimore: Johns Hopkins University Press.

Linnankoski, J. 1981. "Determinants of Sexual Behavior of *Macaca arctoides* in a Laboratory Colony." *Archives of Sexual Behavior* 10:207–222.

Lipsky, R. 1985. "The Political and Social Dimensions of Sports." In *American Sport Culture: The Humanistic Dimension,* ed. W. L. Umphlett, 70–75. Lewisburg, Pa.: Bucknell University Press.

Lisak, D., and S. Roth. 1988. "Motivational Factors in Nonincarcerated Sexually Aggressive Men." *Journal of Personality and Social Psychology* 55:795–802.

Lloyd, C. W. 1963. "Central Nervous System Regulation of Endocrine Function in the Human." In *Advances in Neuroendocrinology,* ed. A. Z. Nalbandov, 460–510. Urbana: University of Illinois Press.

Lorenz, K. 1966. *On Aggression.* New York: Harcourt, Brace, and World.

Lowe, M. 1983. "The Dialectic of Biology and Nature." In *Woman's Nature: Rationalizations of Inequality,* ed. M. Lowe and R. Hubbard, 39–62. New York: Pergamon.

Lowe, M, and R. Hubbard. 1979. "Sociobiology and Biosociology: Can Science Prove the Biological Basis of Sex Differences in Behavior?" In *Genes and Gender.* Vol. 2, *Pitfalls in Research on Sex and Gender,* ed. R. Hubbard and M. Lowe, 9–112. New York: Gordian.

Lukacs, G., 1971. *History and Class Consciousness.* Cambridge, Mass.: MIT Press.

Lumsden, C. J., and E. O. Wilson. 1981. *Genes, Mind, and Culture: The Coevolutionary Process.* Cambridge, Mass.: Harvard University Press.

Luria, Z. 1982. "Sexual Fantasy and Pornography: Two Cases of Girls Brought Up with Pornography." *Archives of Sexual Behavior* 11:395–404.

Luttge, W. 1971. "The Role of Gonadal Hormones in the Sexual Behavior of the Rhesus Monkey and the Human: A Literature Survey." *Archives of Sexual Behavior* 1:61–88.

Lynn, D. B. 1966. "The Process of Learning Parental and Sex Role Identification." *Journal of Marriage and the Family* 28:466–470.

———. 1969. "Curvilinear Relationship between Cognitive Functioning and Distance of Child from Parent of the Same Sex." *Psychological Review* 76:236–240.

McAdoo, B. C., C. H. Doering, H. C. Kraemer, N. Dessert, H.K.H. Brodie, and D. A. Hamburg. 1978. "A Study of the Effects of Gonadotropin-releasing Hormone on Human Mood and Behavior." *Psychosomatic Medicine* 40:199–209.

McCabe, M. P., and J. K. Collins. 1983. "The Sexual and Affectional Attitudes and Experiences of Australian Adolescents during Dating: The Effects of Age, Church Attendance, Type of School, and Socioeconomic Class." *Archives of Sexual Behavior* 12:525–539.

McCall, R. B., and J. Kagan. 1967. "Stimulus-Schema Discrepancy and Attention in the Infant. *Journal of Experimental Child Psychology* 5:381–390.

McCarthy, B. W. 1984. "Strategies and Techniques for the Treatment of Inhibited Sexual Desire." *Journal of Sex and Marital Therapy* 10:97–104.

McClelland, K. 1985. "On the Social Significance of Interactional Synchrony." Department of Sociology, Grinnell College. Typescript.

Maccoby, E. E. 1966. "Sex Differences in Intellectual Functioning." In *The Development of Sex Differences,* ed. E. E. Maccoby, 25–55. Standord: Stanford University Press.

Maccoby, E. E., and C. N. Jacklin. 1974. *The Psychology of Sex Differences.* Stanford, Calif.: Stanford University Press.

McCoy, N., W. Cutler, and J. M. Davidson. 1985. "Relationship among Sexual Behavior, Hot Flashes, and Hormonal Levels in Perimenopausal Women." *Archives of Sexual Behavior* 14:385–394.

McGee, M. G. 1979. *Human Spatial Abilities: Sources of Sex Differences.* New York: Praeger.

———. 1982. "Spatial Abilities: The Influence of Genetic Factors." In *Spatial Abilities: Developmental and Physiological Foundation,* ed. M. Potegal, 199–222. New York: Academic Press.

McGuiness, D. 1976. "Sex Differences in the Organization of Perception and Cognition." In *Exploring Sex Differences,* ed. B. Lloyd and J. Archer, 123–156. New York: Academic Press.

McPhail, C., and C. Rexroat. 1979. "Mead vs. Blumer: The Divergent Methodological Perspectives of Social Behaviorism and Symbolic Interactionism." *American Sociological Review* 44:449–467.

MacPhillamy, D. J., and P. M. Lewinsohn. 1974. "Depression as a Function of Desired and Obtained Pleasure." *Journal of Abnormal Psychology* 83:651–657.

Majeres, R. L. 1977. "Sex Differences in Clerical Speed: Perceptual Speed versus Comparison and Decision Speed." *Perceptual and Motor Skills* 45: 1287–1290.

Malamuth, N. M. 1986. "Predictors of Naturalistic Sexual Aggression." *Journal of Personality and Social Psychology* 50:953–962.

Malamuth, N. M., and J.V.P. Check. 1983. "Sexual Arousal to Rape Depictions: Individual Differences." *Journal of Abnormal Psychology* 92:55–67.

Malamuth, N. M., S. Feshback, and Y. Jaffe. 1977. "Sexual Arousal and Aggression: Recent Experiments and Theoretical Issues." *Journal of Social Issues* 33:110–133.

Manning, A. 1979. *An Introduction to Animal Behavior.* 3d ed. Reading, Mass.: Addison-Wesley.

Marcuse, H. 1955. *Eros and Civilization.* Boston: Beacon.

———. 1964. *One-Dimensional Man.* Boston: Beacon.

Marini, M. 1980. "Sex Differences in the Process of Occupational Attainment: A Closer Look." *Social Science Research* 9:307–361.

Marler, P. 1956. "Studies of Proximity in Chaffinches, 3. Proximity as a Cause of Aggression." *Animal Behavior* 4:23–30.

Maroulis, G. B. 1981. "Evaluation of Hirsutism and Hyperandrogenemia." *Fertility and Sterility* 36:273–305.

Marshall, R. H. 1973. *Class, Citizenship, and Social Development.* Westport, Conn.: Greenwood.

Martin, C. E. 1981. "Factors Affecting Sexual Functioning in 60–79 Year Old Married Males." *Archives of Sexual Behavior* 10:399–420.

Martin, C. 1985. *Endocrine Physiology*. New York: Oxford University Press.

———. 1988. "Brain Differences: Facts and Myths." In *Genes and Gender.* Vol. 5, *Women at Work: Socialization toward Inequality*, ed. G. Vroman, D. Burnham, and S. G. Gordon, 11–36. New York: Gordian.

Marx, K. 1964. *Early Writings*. Trans. and ed. T. B. Bottomore. New York: McGraw-Hill.

Mascie-Taylor, C.G.N., and J. L. Boldsen. 1984. "Assortative Mating for IQ: A Multivariate Approach." *Journal of Biosocial Science* 16:109–117.

Mason, J. 1968. " 'Overall' Hormone Balance as a Key to Endocrine Organization." *Psychosomatic Medicine* 30:791–807.

Masters, W. H., and V. E. Johnson. 1966. *Human Sexual Response*. Boston: Little, Brown.

———. 1970. *Human Sexual Inadequacy*. Boston: Little, Brown.

———. 1976. *The Pleasure Bond: A New Look at Sexuality and Commitment.* Boston: Little, Brown.

Matras, J. 1975. *Social Inequality, Stratification, Mobility*. Englewood Cliffs, N.J.: Prentice-Hall.

May, J. L., and M. Bobele. 1988. "Sexual Dysfunction and the Unemployed Male Professional." *Journal of Sex and Marital Therapy* 14:253–262.

Mazur, A. 1983. "Hormones, Aggression, and Dominance in Humans." In *Hormones and Aggressive Behavior*, ed. B. B. Svare, 563–576. New York: Plenum.

———. 1985. "A Biosocial Model of Status in Face-to-Face Primate Groups." *Social Forces* 64:377–402.

Mazur, A., and T. A. Lamb. 1980. "Testosterone, Status, and Mood in Human Males." *Hormones and Behavior* 14:236–46.

Mead, G. H. 1934. *Mind, Self, and Society*. Chicago: University of Chicago Press.

Mechanic, D. 1978. *Medical Sociology*. 2d ed. New York: Free Press.

Meehan, A. M. 1984. "A Meta-Analysis of Sex Differences in Formal Operational Thought." *Child Development* 55:1110–1124.

Meggysey, D. 1970. *Out of Their League*. Berkeley, Calif.: Ramparts.

Melges, F., and D. A. Hamburg. 1977. "Psychological Effects of Hormonal Changes in Women." In *Human Sexuality in Four Perspectives*, ed. F. A. Beach, 269–295. Baltimore: Johns Hopkins University Press.

Mendoza, S. P. 1984. "The Psychobiology of Social Relationships." In *Social Cohesion: Essays toward a Sociophysiological Perspective*, ed. P. R. Barchas and S. P. Mendoza, 3–29. Westport, Conn.: Greenwood.

Mendoza, S. P., E. L. Lowe, J. J. Davidson, and S. Levine. 1979. "The Physiological Response to Group Formation in Adult Male Squirrel Monkeys." *Psychoneuroendocrinology* 3:221–229.

Meyer-Bahlburg, H.H.L., R. Nat, and D. A. Boon. 1974. "Aggressiveness and Testosterone Measures in Man." *Psychosomatic Medicine* 36: 269–274.

Michael, R. P. 1972. "Determinants of Primate Reproductive Behavior." *Acta Endocrinologica Supplementum* 166:322–361.

Michael, R. P., D. Zumpe, E. G. Keverne, amd R. W. Bonsall. 1972. "Neuroendocrine Factors in the Control of Primate Behavior." *Recent Progress in Hormone Research* 28:665–706.

Miller, B. C., and T. D. Olson. 1988. "Sexual Attitudes and Behavior of

High School Students in Relation to Background and Contextual Factors." *Journal of Sex Research* 24:194–200.

Miller, C. T., and D. Byrne. 1981. "Effects of Dominance Cues on Attributions of Sexual Behavior." *Journal of Research in Personality* 15:135–146.

Miller, D., and G. E. Swanson. 1960. *Inner Conflict and Defense.* New York: Holt.

Miller, P. Y., and M. R. Fowlkes. 1980. "Social and Behavioral Constructions of Female Sexuality." In *Women: Sex and Sexuality,* ed. C. R. Stimson and E. S. Person, 256–273. Chicago: University of Chicago Press.

Miller, P. Y., and W. Simon. 1974. "Adolescent Sexual Behavior: Context and Change." *Social Problems* 22:58–76.

Miller, S. M., and F. Reissman. 1961. "The Working Class Subculture: A New View." *Social Problems* 9:86–97.

Miller, W. B. 1958. "Lower Class Culture as a Generating Milieu of Gang Delinquency." *Journal of Social Issues* 14:5–19.

Mills, C. W. 1956. *White Collar: The American Middle Classes.* New York: Oxford University Press.

Money, J. 1961. "Sex Hormones and Other Variables in Human Eroticism." In *Sex and Internal Secretions,* 3d ed., ed. W. C. Young, 1383–1400. Baltimore: Williams and Wilkins.

———. 1973. "Pornography in the Home: A Topic in Sex Education." In *Contemporary Sexual Behavior: Critical Issues in the 1970s,* ed. J. Zubin and J. Money, 409–440. Baltimore: Johns Hopkins University Press.

Money, J., and A. A. Ehrhardt. 1972. *Man and Woman: Boy and Girl.* Baltimore: Johns Hopkins University Press.

Montague, A., ed. 1980. *Sociobiology Examined.* Oxford: Oxford University Press.

Monti, P. M., W. A. Brown, and D. D. Corriveau. 1977. "Testosterone and Components of Aggressive and Sexual Behavior in Man." *American Journal of Psychiatry* 134:692–694.

Morris, D. 1967. *The Naked Ape.* McGraw-Hill

Morris, N. M., J. R. Udry, F. Khan-Dawood, and M. Y. Dawood. 1987. "Marital Sex Frequency and Midcycle Female T." *Archives of Sexual Behavior* 16:27–37.

Moss, G. 1973. *Illness, Immunity, and Social Interaction.* New York: Wiley.

Moyer, K. E. 1974. "Sex Differences in Aggression." In *Sex Differences in Behavior,* ed. R. C. Friedman, R. M. Richart, and R. L. Vande Wiele, 335–372. New York: Wiley.

Muelenhard, C. E., and S. W. Cook. 1988. "Men's Self-Reports of Unwanted Sexual Activity." *Journal of Sex Research* 24:58–72.

Munjack, D. J., and P. H. Kanno. 1979. "Retarded Ejaculation: A Review." *Archives of Sexual Behavior* 8:139–150.

Murphy, J. P., and E. Gellhorn. 1968. "Commentary." In *Biological Foundations of Emotion: Research and Commentary,* ed. E. Gellhorn, 46–55. Glenview, Ill.: Scott Foresman.

Murray, M.A.F., and C. S. Corker. 1973. "Levels of Testosterone and Luteinizing Hormone in Plasma Samples Taken at Ten-Minute Intervals in Normal Men." *Journal of Endocrinology* 56:157–159.

Myers, L. S., and P. J. Morokoff. 1986. "Physiological and Subjective Sexual Arousal in Pre- and Postmenopausal Women Taking Replacement Therapy." *Psychophysiology* 23:283–292.

Nadi, N. S., J. I. Nurnberger, Jr., and E. S. Gershon. 1984. "Muscarinic Cholinergic Receptors on Skin Fibroblasts in Familial Affective Disorder." *New England Journal of Medicine* 311:225–230.

National Center for Health Statistics. 1983. "Americans Assess Their Health: United States, 1978." Report prepared by P. W. Ries. *Vital and Health Statistics*, Ser. 10, no. 142. DHHS Pub. No. (PHS) 83-1570. Washingon, D.C.: GPO.

National Science Foundation. 1982. *Women and Minorities in Science and Engineering*. Washington, D.C.: GPO.

National Women's Political Caucus. 1987. *National Directory of Women Elected Officials*. Washington, D.C.: National Women's Political Caucas.

Nature. 1970. "Effects of Sexual Activity on Beard Growth in Man." *Nature* 226:869–870.

Neilsen, A. C. 1978. *Sports 1977*. Northbrook, Ill.: A. C. Neilson.

———. 1980. *Sports 1980*. Northbrook, Ill.: A. C. Neilson.

Newcombe, N. 1982. "Sex-related Differences in Spatial Ability: Problems and Gaps in Current Approaches." In *Spatial Abilities: Developmental and Physiological Foundation*, ed. M. Potegal, 223–250. New York: Academic Press.

Nieschlag, E. 1979. "The Endocrine Function of the Human Testis with Regard to Sexuality." In *Symposium on Sex, Hormones and Behaviour, London, 1978*, 183–208. Ciba Foundation Symposium, n.s. 62. Amsterdam: Excerpta Medica.

Nyborg, H. 1984. "Performance and Intelligence in Hormonally Different Groups." *Progress in Brain Research* 61:491–508.

Obler, L. K., and L. M. Novoa. 1988. "Gender Similarities and Differences in Brain Lateralization." In *Genes and Gender*. Vol. 5, *Women at Work: Socialization toward Inequality*, ed. G. Vroman, D. Burnham, and S. G. Gordon, 37–51. New York: Gordian.

O'Carroll, R., and J. Bancroft. 1984. "Testosterone Therapy for Low Sexual Interest and Erectile Dysfunction in Men: A Controlled Study." *British Journal of Psychiatry* 145:146–151.

O'Carroll, R., C. Shapiro, and J. Bancroft. 1985. "Androgens, Behavior, and Nocturnal Erection of Hypogonadal Men: The Effect of Varying Replacement Dose." *Clinical Endocrinology* 23:527:538.

Olweus, D, A. Mattsson, D. Schalling, and H. Low. 1980. "Testosterone, Aggression, Physical, and Personality Dimensions in Normal Adolescent Males." *Psychosomatic Medicine* 42:253–269.

———. 1988. "Circulating Testosterone Levels and Aggression in Adolescent Males: A Causal Analysis." *Psychosomatic Medicine* 50:261–272.

O'Neill, N., and G. O'Neill. 1972. *Open Marriage: A New Life Style for Couples*. New York: Evans.

Parlee, M. B. 1972. Comments on "Roles of Activation and Inhibition in Sex Differences in Cognitive Abilities," by D. M. Broverman, E. L. Klaiber, Y. Kobayashi, and W. Vogel. *Psychological Review* 79:180–184.

Parsons, J. E. 1980. "Psychosexual Neutrality: Is Anatomy Destiny?" In *The Psychobiology of Sex Differences and Sex Roles*, ed. J. E. Parsons, 3–29. Washington, D.C.: Hemisphere.

Parsons, T. 1951. *The Social System*. Glencoe, Ill.: Free Press.

Pearce, J., and S. Newton. 1963. *The Conditions of Normal Growth*. Secaucus, N.J.: Citadel.

Pelton, L. H. 1978. "The Myth of Classlessness in Child Abuse Cases." *American Journal of Orthopsychiatry* 48:56–79.

Perper, T. 1985. *Sex Signals: The Biology of Love.* Philadelphia: ISI Press.

Persky, H., L. Dreisbach, W. R. Miller, C. P. O'Brien, M. A. Khan, H. I. Lief, N. Charney, and D. Strauss. 1982. "The Relation of Plasma Androgen Levels to Sexual Behaviors and Attitudes of Women." *Psychosomatic Medicine* 44:305–319.

Persky, H, H. I. Lief, D. Strauss, W. R. Miller, and C. P. O'Brien. 1978. "Plasma Testosterone Level and Sexual Behavior of Couples." *Archives of Sexual Behavior* 7:157–173.

Persky, H., K. D. Smith, and G. K. Basu. 1971. "Relation of Psychologic Measures of Aggression and Hostility to Testosterone Production in Man. *Psychosomatic Medicine* 33:265–277.

Person, E. S. 1980. "Sexuality as the Mainstay of Identities: Psychoanalytic Perspectives." *Signs* 5:605–630.

Persson, G., I. V. Nilsson, and A. Svanborg. 1983. "Personality and Sexuality in Relation to an Index of Gonadal Steroid Hormone Balance in a Seventy-year-old Population." *Journal of Psychosomatic Research* 27:469–477.

Petersen, A. C. 1976. "Physical Androgeny and Cognitive Functioning in Adolescence." *Developmental Psychology* 12:524–233.

———. 1980. "Biopsychosocial Processes in the Development of Sex-related Differences." In *The Psychobiology of Sex Differences and Sex Roles,* ed. J. E. Parsons, 31–55. Washington, D.C.: Hemisphere.

Petersen, A. C., and K. E. Hood. 1988. "The Role of Experience in Cognitive Performance and Brain Development." In *Genes and Gender:* Vol. 5, Women at Work: Socialization toward Inequality, ed. G. Vroman, D. Burnham, and S. G. Gordon, 52–77. New York: Gordian.

Pfeiffer, E., and G. C. Davis. 1972. "Determinants of Sexual Behavior in Middle and Old Age." *Journal of the American Geriatric Society* 20:151–158.

Phoenix, C. H. 1980. "Copulation, Dominance, and Plasma Androgen Levels in Adult Rhesus Males Born and Reared in the Laboratory." *Archives of Sexual Behavior* 9:149–167.

Phoenix, C. H., and K. C. Chambers. 1984. "Sexual Deprivation and Its Influence on Testosterone Levels and Sexual Behavior of Old and Middle-aged Rhesus Monkeys." *Biology of Reproduction* 31:480–486.

Phoenix, C. H., A. K. Slob, and R. W. Goy. 1973. "Effects of Castration and Replacement Therapy on Sexual Behavior of Adult Male Rhesuses." *Journal of Comparative and Physiological Psychology* 84:472–481.

Pietropinto, A., and J. Simenauer. 1977. *Beyond the Male Myth.* New York: New York Times.

———. 1979. *Husbands and Wives.* New York: New York Times.

Pirke, K. M., G. Kockott, and F. Dittmar. 1974. "Psychosexual Stimulation and Plasma Testosterone in Man." *Archives of Sexual Behavior* 3:577–584.

Plutchik, R. 1980. *Emotion: A Psychoevolutionary Synthesis.* New York: Harper and Row.

Ponomariev, N. I. 1980. "Sport as a Show." *International Review of Sport Sociology* 15:73–79.

Popp, J., and I. DeVore. 1979. "Aggressive Competition and Social Dominance Theory: Synopsis." In *The Great Apes: Perspéctives on Human Evolution,* ed. D. Hamburger and E. McGowan, 5:317–338. Menlo Park, Calif.: Benjamin-Cummings.

Porges, S. W. 1976. "Peripheral and Neurochemical Parallels to Psychopathology: A Psychophysiological Model Relating Autonomic Imbalance to

Hyperactivity Pathology and Autism." In *Advances in Child Development and Behavior,* ed. H. W. Reese, 2:35–65. New York: Academic Press.

Provost, G. L. 1981. "Teaching Strategies, Modes of Evaluation, and Field-Dependence Factor." *Perceptual and Motor Skills* 52:163–173.

Purifoy, F. E., and L. H. Koopmans. 1979. "Androstenedione, Testosterone, and Free Testosterone Concentrations in Women of Various Occupations." *Social Biology* 26:179–188.

Purvis, K., B. M. Landgren, Z. Cekan, and E. Diczfalusy. 1976. "Endocrine Effects of Masturbation in Men." *Journal of Endocrinology* 70:439–444.

Raboch, J., J. Mellan, and L. Starka. 1975. "Plasma Testosterone in Male Patients with Sexual Dysfunction." *Archives of Sexual Behavior* 4:541–545.

Raboch, J., and L. Starka. 1972. "Coital Activity of Men and the Levels of Plasmatic Testosterone." *Journal of Sex Research* 8:219–224.

———. 1973. "Reported Coital Activity and Levels of Plasma Testosterone." *Archives of Sexual Behavior* 2:309–315.

Rada, R. T., D. R. Laws, and R. Kellner. 1976. "Plasma Testosterone in the Rapist." *Psychosomatic Medicine* 38:257–268.

Rainwater, L. 1964. "Marital Sexuality in Four Cultures of Poverty." *Journal of Marriage and the Family* 26:457–464.

Rauste-von Wright, M., J. von Wright, and M. Frankenhaeuser. 1981. "Relationships between Sex-related Psychological Characteristics during Adolescence and Catecholamine Excretion during Achievement Stress." *Psychophysiology* 18:362–370.

Reading. A. E., and W. M. Wiest. 1984. "An Analysis of Self-reported Sexual Behavior in a Sample of Normal Males." *Archives of Sexual Behavior* 13:69–83.

Redekop, P. 1984. "Sports and the Masculine Ethos: Some Implications for Family Interaction." *International Journal of Comparative Sociology* 25:262–269.

Redmond, D. E. Jr., J. Baulu, D. L. Murphy, D. L. Loriaux, M. G. Ziegler, and C. R. Lake. 1976. "The Effect of Testosterone on Plasma and Platelet Monoamine Oxidase (MAO) and Plasma Dopamine-Hydroxylase (DHB) Activities in the Male Rhesus Monkey." *Psychosomatic Medicine* 38:315–326.

Redmond, D. E., Jr., D. L. Murphy, and J. Baulu. 1979. "Platelet MAO Activity Correlates with Social Affiliative and Agonistic Behaviors in Normal Rhesus Monkeys." *Psychosomatic Medicine* 41:87–100.

Reed, D., and M. S. Weinberg. 1984. "Premarital Coitus: Developing and Established Sexual Scripts." *Social Psychology Quarterly* 47:129–138.

Reese, H. W., and S. W. Porges. 1976. "Development of Learning Processes." In *The Development of Cognitive Processes,* ed. V. Hamilton and M. Vernon, 413–451. New York: Academic Press.

Reich, W. [1965] 1976. *Character Analysis.* Reprint. New York: Pocket Books.

Reinisch, J. M. 1977. "Prenatal Exposure of Human Foetuses to Synthetic Progestin and Oestrogen Affects Personality." *Nature* 226: 561–62.

———. 1981. "Prenatal Exposure to Synthetic Progestines Increases Potential for Aggression in Humans." *Science* 211:1171–1172.

Reiss, I. L. 1967. *The Social Context of Premarital Permissiveness.* New York: Holt, Rinehart and Winston.

Remoff, H. T. 1985. *Female Choice.* New York: Lewis.

Resnick, S. M., S. A. Berenbaum, I. I. Gottesman, and T. J. Bouchard. 1986. "Early Hormonal Influences on Cognitive Functioning in Congenital Adrenal Hyperplasia." *Developmental Psychology* 22:191–198.

Ridgeway, C. and D. Diekema. 1989. "Dominance and Collective Hierarchy Formation in Male and Female Task Groups." *American Sociological Review* 54:79–93.

Risman, B. J., C. T. Hill, Z. Rubin, and L. Peplau. 1981. "Living Together in College: Implications for Courtship." *Journal of Marriage and the Family* 43:77–83.

Rose, R. M., I. S. Bernstein, and T. P. Gordon. 1972. "Plasma Testosterone Levels in Male Rhesus: Influences of Sexual and Social Stimuli." *Science* 178:643–645.

———. 1975. "Consequences of Social Conflict on Plasma Testosterone Levels in Rhesus Monkeys." *Psychosomatic Medicine* 37:50–61.

Rose, R. M., I. S. Bernstein, T. P. Gordon, and S. F. Catlin. 1974. "Androgens and Aggression: A Review of Recent Findings in Primates." In *Primate Aggression, Territoriality, and Xenophobia,* ed. R. L. Holloway, 275–304. New York: Academic Press.

Rose, R. M., I. S. Bernstein, T. P. Gordon, and J. G. Lindsley. 1978. "Changes in Testosterone and Behavior during Adolescence in the Male Rhesus Monkey." *Psychosomatic Medicine* 40:60–70.

Rosen, R., and S. R. Leiblum. 1987. "Current Approaches to the Evaluation of Sex Desire Disorders." *Journal of Sex Research* 23:141–162.

Rosenthal, R., and D. B. Rubin. 1982. "Further Meta-Analytic Procedures for Assessing Cognitive Gender Differences." *Journal of Educational Psychology* 74:708–712.

Rossi, A. S. 1973. "Maternalism, Sexuality, and the New Feminism." In *Contemporary Sexual Behavior: Critical Issues in the 1970s,* ed. J. Zubin and J. Money, 145–173. Baltimore: Johns Hopkins University Press.

Rossi, A. S., and P. E. Rossi. 1977. "Body Time and Social Time: Mood Patterns by Menstrual Cycle Phase and Day of the Week." *Social Science Research* 6:273–308.

Rowell, T. E. 1974. "The Concept of Social Dominance." *Behavioral Biology* 11:131–154.

Rowland, D. L., J. R. Heiman, B. A. Gladue, J. P. Hatch, C. H. Doering, and S. J. Weiller. 1987. "Endocrine, Psychological, and Genital Responses to Sexual Arousal in Man." *Psychoneuroendocrinology* 12:149–158.

Rubin, H. B., D. E. Hensen, R. E. Falvo, and R. W. High. 1984. "The Relationship between Men's Endogenous Levels of Testosterone and Penile Responses to Erotic Stimuli." *Behavior Research and Therapy* 17:305–312.

Rubin, L. B. 1976. *Worlds of Pain.* New York: Basic Books.

Rubin, R. T., R. E. Poland, B. B. Tower, P. A. Hart, A. L. Blodgett, B. Nelson, and B. Forster. 1981. "Hypothalamo-Pituitary-Gonadal Function in Primary Endogenously Depressed Men: Preliminary Findings." In *Proceedings of the Wenner-Gren Symposium on Steroid Hormone Regulation of the Brain,* ed. K. Fuxe, J. A. Gustafsson, and L. Witterberg, 387–396. Oxford: Pergamon.

Rubinsky, H. J., D. A. Eckerman, E. W. Rubinsky, and C. R. Hoover. 1987. "Early-phase Physiological Response Patterns to Psychosexual Stimuli: Comparison of Male and Female Patterns." *Archives of Sexual Behavior* 16:45–56.

Rudman, W. J. 1986. "The Sports Mystique in Black Culture." *Sociology of Sports Journal* 3:305–319.

Rule, S. 1989. "There's Comfort in Loving the Team." *New York Times,* April 22, sec. A, 4.

Ryan, W. 1971. *Blaming the Victim.* New York: Pantheon.

Sachar, E. J., F. S. Halpern, R. Rosenfeld, T. Gallagher, and L. Hellman. 1973. "Plasma and Urinary Testosterone in Depressed Men." *Archives of General Psychiatry* 28:15–18.

Sadalla, E. K., D. T. Kenrick, and B. Vershure. 1987. "Dominance and Heterosexual Attraction." *Journal of Personality and Social Psychology* 52: 730–738.

Sadock, B. J., and V. A. Sadock. 1976. "Techniques of Coitus." In *The Sexual Experience*, ed. B. J. Sadock, H. I. Kaplan, and A. M. Freedman, 206–216. Baltimore: Williams and Wilkins.

Sadock, V. A., and B. J. Sadock, 1976. "Dual-Sex Therapy." In *The Sexual Experience*, ed. B. J. Sadock, H. I. Kaplan, and A. M. Freedman, 464–478. Baltimore: Williams and Wilkins.

Salmimies, P., G. Kockott, K. M. Pirke, H. J. Vogt, and W. B. Schill. 1982. "Effects of Testosterone Replacement on Sexual Behavior in Hypogonadal Men. *Archives of Sexual Behavior* 11:345–354.

Sanders, D., P. Warner, T. Backstrom, and J. Bancroft. 1983. "Mood, Sexuality, Hormones, and Menstrual Cycle, I. Changes in Mood and Physical State: Description of Subjects and Method." *Psychosomatic Medicine* 45:487–516.

Scaramella, T. J., and W. A. Brown. 1978. "Serum Testosterone and Aggressiveness in Hockey Players." *Psychosomatic Medicine* 40:262–265.

Schenk, J., and H. Pfrang. 1986. "Extroversion, Neuroticism, and Sexual Behavior: Interrelationships in a Sample of Young Men." *Archives of Sexual Behavior* 15:449–455.

Schenk, J., H. Pfrang, and A. Rausche. 1983. "Personality Traits versus the Quality of the Marital Relationship as the Determinant of Marital Sexuality." *Archives of Sexual Behavior* 12:31–42.

Schiavi, R. C., C. Fisher, D. White, P. Beers, M. Fogel, and R. Szechter. 1982. "Hormonal Variations during Sleep in Men with Erectile Dysfunction and Normal Controls." *Archives of Sexual Behavior* 11:189–200.

Schiavi, R. C., C. Fisher, D. White, P. Beers, and R. Szechter. 1984a. "Pituitary-Gonadal Function during Sleep in Men with Erectile Impotence and Normal Controls." *Psychosomatic Medicine* 46:239–254.

Schiavi, R. C., D. Owen, M. Fogel, D. White, and R. Szechter. 1978. "Pituitary-Gonadal Function in XYY and XXY Men Identified in a Population Survey." *Clinical Endocrinology* 9:233–239.

Schiavi, R. C., P. Schreiner-Engel, D. White, and J. Mandeli. 1988. "Pituitary-Gonadal Function during Sleep in Men with Hypoactive Sexual Desire and in Normal Controls." *Psychosomatic Medicine* 50:304–318.

Schiavi, R. C., A. Thielgaard, D. Owen, and D. White. 1984b. "Sex Chromosome Anomalies, Hormones, and Aggressivity." *Archives of General Psychiatry* 41:93–99.

Schindler, G. L. 1979. "Testosterone Concentration, Personality Patterns, and Occupational Choice in Women." Ph.D. diss., Department of Psychology, University of Houston.

Schmock, J. C. 1971. "The Relation of Autonomic Balance to Selected Measures of Achievement and Affective Behavior in Young Children." Ph.D. diss., Department of Psychology, University of California, Los Angeles.

Schneider, J. P. 1988. *Back from Betrayal.* New York: Harper/Hazelden.

Schreiner-Engel, P., R. C. Schiavi, H. Smith, and D. White. 1981. "Sexual Arousability and the Menstrual Cycle." *Psychosomatic Medicine* 43:199–214.

Schreiner-Engel, P., R. C. Schiavi, A. White, and A. Ghizzani. 1989. "Low

Sexual Desire in Women: The Role of Reproductive Hormones." *Hormones and Behavior* 23:221–234.

Schwartz, M. F., R. C. Kolodny, and W. H. Masters. 1980. "Plasma Testosterone Levels of Sexually Functional and Dysfunctional Men." *Archives of Sexual Behavior* 5:355–366.

Scott, J. 1971. *The Athletic Revolution.* New York: Free Press.

Seagull, L. M. 1977. *Youth and Change in American Politics.* New York: New Viewpoints.

Seidenberg, R. 1973. *Corporate Wives—Corporate Casualties.* New York: AMACOM.

Shakespeare, W. 1923. *The Complete Works of William Shakespeare.* London: Selfridge.

Shamos, M. H. 1959. *Great Experiments in Physics.* New York: Holt, Rinehart, and Winston.

Shangold, M. M., M. L. Gatz, and B. Thysen. 1981. "Acute Effects of Exercise on Plasma Concentrations of Prolactin and Testosterone in Recreational Women Runners." *Fertility and Sterility* 35:699–702.

Shaw, E. and J. Darling. 1985. *Female Strategies.* New York: Walker and Company.

Sherwin, B. B., and M. M. Gelfand. 1985. "Sex Steroids and Affect in the Surgical Menopause: A Double Blind Crossover Study." *Psychoneuroendocrinology* 10:325–335.

Sherwin, B. B., M. M. Gelfand, and W. Brender. 1985. "Androgen Enhances Sexual Motivation in Females: A Prospective Crossover Study of Sex Steroid Administration in the Surgical Menopause." *Psychosomatic Medicine* 47:339–351.

Simmel, G. 1950. *The Sociology of George Simmel.* Trans. and ed. K. H. Wolff. Glencoe, Ill.: Free Press.

Simon, W. 1974. "The Social, the Erotic, and the Sexual: The Complexities of Sexual Scripts." In *Nebraska Symposium on Motivation 1973,* ed. J. K. Cole and R. Dienstbier, 61–82. Lincoln: University of Nebraska Press.

Singer, G., and R. B. Montgomery, 1969. Comment on "Roles of Activation and Inhibition in Sex Differences in Cognitive Abilities," by D. M. Broverman, E. L. Klaiber, Y. Kobayashi, and W. Vogel. *Psychological Review* 76:325–327.

Sinyor, D., S. G. Schwartz, F. Peronnet, G. Brisson, and P. Seraganian. 1983. "Aerobic Fitness Level and Reactivity to Psychosocial Stress: Physiological, Biochemical, and Subjective Measures." *Psychosomatic Medicine* 45:205–217.

Sloan, L. R. 1979. "The Function and Impact of Sports for Fans." In *Sports, Games, and Play: Social and Psychological Viewpoints,* ed. J. H. Goldstein, 219–262. Hillsdale, N.J.: Erlbaum.

Smith, A. [1776] 1937. *The Wealth of Nations.* Reprint. New York: Random House.

Smith, E., J. R. Udry, and N. M. Morris. 1985. "Pubertal Development and Friends: Biosocial Explanation of Adolescent Sexual Behavior." *Journal of Health and Social Behavior* 26:183–192.

Smith, P., and E. Midlarsky. 1985. "Empirically Derived Conceptions of Femaleness and Maleness: A Current Review." *Sex Roles* 12:313–328.

Snyder, E. E., and D. A. Purdy. 1985. "The Home Advantage in Collegiate Basketball." *Sociology of Sport Journal* 2:352–356.

Spencer, H. [1862] 1958. *First Principles of a New System of Philosophy.* Reprint. New York: DeWitt Revolving Fund.

Sprecher, S., K. McKinney, and T. Orbuch. 1987. "Has the Double Standard Disappeared? An Experimental Test." *Social Psychology Quarterly* 50:24–31.

Stanley, J., and C. P. Benbow. 1982. "Huge Sex Ratios at Upper End." *American Psychologist* 37:972.

Stearns, E. L., J.S.D. Winter, and C. Faiman. 1973. "Effects of Coitus on Gonadotropin, Prolactin, and Sex Steroid Levels in Man." *Journal of Clinical Endocrinology and Metabolism* 37:687–691.

Stevens, D. P., and C. V. Truss. 1985. "Stability and Change in Adult Personality over Twelve and Twenty Years." *Developmental Psychology* 21:568–584.

Stewart, A. J., and Z. Rubin. 1976. "The Power Motive in Dating Couples." *Journal of Personality and Social Psychology* 34:305–309.

Stoller, R. J. 1976. "Sexual Excitement." *Archives of General Psychiatry* 33:899–909.

Storr, A. 1968. *Human Aggression.* New York: Atheneum.

Stouffer, S., E. A. Suchman, L. C. DeVinney, S. A. Star, and R. H. Williams. 1949. *The American Soldier: Adjustment during Army Life.* Vol. 1, Princeton: Princeton University Press.

Strand, F. 1983. *Physiology: A Regulatory Systems Approach.* 2d ed. New York: Macmillan.

Straus, M., R. Gelles, and S. Steinmetz. 1980. *Behind Closed Doors: Violence in the American Family.* New York: Doubleday.

Stuart, F. M., D. C. Hammond, and M. A. Pett. 1987. "Inhibited Sexual Desire." *Archives of Sexual Behavior* 16:91–106.

Sullivan, T. J., and K. S. Thompson. 1988. *Introduction to Urban Problems.* New York: Macmillan.

Sumner, W. G. [1906] 1959. *Folkways.* Reprint. New York: Dover.

Susman, E. J., G. Innoff-Germain, E. D. Nottelmann, D. L. Loriaux, G. B. Cutler, Jr., and G. P. Chrousos. 1987. "Hormones, Emotional Dispositions, and Aggressive Attributes in Young Adolescents." *Child Development* 58:1114–1134.

Tannenbaum, P. H. 1980. "Entertainment as Vicarious Experience." In *The Entertainment Functions of Television,* ed. P. H. Tannenbaum, 107–132. Hillsdale, N.J.: Erlbaum.

Tavris, C., and S. Sadd. 1975. *The Redbook Report on Female Sexuality.* New York: Dell.

Taylor, G. T., J. Haller, R. Rupich, and J. Weiss. 1984. "Testicular Hormones and Intermale Aggressive Behavior in the Presence of a Female Rat." *Journal of Endocrinology* 100:315–321.

Taylor, G. T., J. Weiss, and D. Komitowski. 1983. "Reproductive Physiology and Penile Papillae Morphology of Rats after Sexual Experience." *Journal of Endocrinology* 98:155–163.

Teasdale, T. W., J. Fuchs, and E. Goldschmidt. 1988. "Degree of Myopia in Relation to Intelligence and Educational Level." *Lancet,* no. 8624 (December 10): 1351–1354.

Tellegen, A., D. T. Lykken, T. J. Bouchard, Jr., K. J. Wilcox, N. L. Segal, and S. Rich. 1988. "Personality Similarity in Twins Reared Apart and Together." *Journal of Personality and Social Psychology* 54:1031–1039.

Thornberry, T. P., and M. Farnsworth. 1982. "Social Correlates of Criminal Involvement: Further Evidence on the Relationship between Social Status and Criminal Behavior." *American Sociological Review* 47:505–518.

Tiefer, L. 1978. "The Context and Consequences of Contemporary Sex

Research: A Feminist Perspective." In *Sex and Behavior: Status and Prospects,* ed. T. E. McGill, D. A. Dewsbury, and B. D. Sachs, 363–385. New York: Plenum.

———. 1987. "Social Constructionism and the Study of Human Sexuality." In *Review of Personality and Social Psychology,* ed. P. Shaver and C. Hendrick, 7:70–94. Newbury Park, Calif.: Sage.

———. 1988. "A Feminist Perspective on Sexology and Sexuality." In *Feminist Thought and the Structure of Knowledge,* ed. M. M. Gergen, 16–26. New York: New York University Press.

Tittle, C. R., W. J. Villemez, and D. A. Smith. 1978. "The Myth of Social Class and Criminality: An Empirical Assessment of the Empirical Evidence." *American Sociological Review* 43:643–656.

Tocqueville, A. de. [1835] 1945. *Democracy in America.* Vol. 1. Reprint. New York: Vintage.

Trivers. R. L. 1971. "The Evolution of Reciprocal Altruism." *Quarterly Review of Biology* 46:35–57.

Troyer, R. J., and G. E. Markle. 1982. "Creating Deviance Rules: A Macroscopic Model." *Sociological Quarterly* 23:157–169.

Trussell, J., and C. F. Westoff. 1980. "Contraceptive Practice and Trends in Coital Frequency." *Family Planning Perspectives* 12:246–249.

Tsitouras, P. D., C. E. Martin, and S. M. Harman. 1982. "Relationship of Serum Testosterone to Sexual Activity in Healthy Elderly Men." *Journal of Gerontology* 37:288–293.

Turner, B. 1984. *The Body and Society.* London: Basil Blackwell.

Turner, C. W., M. H. Ford, D. W. West, and A. W. Meikle. 1986. "Genetic Influences on Testosterone, Hostility, and Type A Behavior in Adult Male Twins." Poster presented at the meetings of the American Psychological Association, August 23, Washington, D.C.

Turner, R. H. 1976. "The Real Self: From Institution to Impulse." *American Journal of Sociology* 81:989–1016.

Turow, S. 1977. *L-One.* New York: Putnam.

Udry, J. R. 1970. *The Social Context of Marriage,* 2d ed. Philadelphia: Lippincott.

———. 1980. "Changes in the Frequency of Marital Intercourse from Panel Data." *Archives of Sexual Behavior* 9:319–325.

———. 1988. "Biological Predispositions and Social Control in Adolescent Sexual Behavior." *American Sociological Review* 53:709–722.

Udry, J. R., and J.O.G. Billy. 1987. "Initiation of Coitus in Early Adolescence." *American Sociological Review* 52:841–855.

Udry, J. R., J.O.G. Billy, N. M. Morris, T. R. Groff, and M. H. Raj. 1985. "Serum Androgenic Hormones Motivate Sexual Behavior in Adolescent Boys." *Fertility and Sterility* 43:90–94.

Udry, J. R., F. R. Deven, and S. J. Coleman. 1982. "A Cross-National Comparison of the Relative Influence of Male and Female Age on the Frequency of Marital Intercourse." *Journal of Biosocial Science* 14:1–6.

Udry, J. R., and L. M. Talbert. 1988. "Sex Hormone Effects on Personality at Puberty." *Journal of Personality and Social Psychology* 54:291–295.

Udry, J. R., L. M. Talbert, and N. M. Morris. 1986. "Biosocial Foundations of Adolescent Female Sexuality." *Demography* 23:217–228.

U.S. Bureau of the Census. 1988. *Statistical Abstracts of the United States.* Washington, D.C.: GPO.

U. S. Department of Commerce. 1987. *Survey of Current Business*. September. Washington, D.C.: GPO.

U.S. Department of Health and Human Services. 1982. *National Study of the Incidence and Severity of Child Abuse and Neglect*. Washington, D.C.: National Center on Child Abuse and Neglect.

U.S. Department of Labor. 1988. *Median Weekly Earnings*. USDL no. 88-219. Washington, D.C.: GPO.

Vance, C. S. 1984. "Pleasure and Danger: Toward a Politics of Sexuality." In *Pleasure and Danger: Exploring Female Sexuality*, ed. C. S. Vance, 1–27. Boston: Routledge and Kegan Paul.

Vandenburgh, J. G. 1973. "Endocrine Coordination in Monkeys: Male Sexual Response to the Female." *Physiology and Behavior* 4:261–264.

Vander, A. J., J. H. Sherman, and D. S. Luciano. 1975. *Human Physiology: The Mechanisms of Body Function*. 2d ed. New York: McGraw-Hill.

Vener, A. M., and C. S. Stewart. 1974. "Adolescent Sexual Behavior in Middle America Revisited: 1970–73." *Journal of Marriage and the Family* 36:728–735.

Vogel, W., E. L. Klaiber, and D. R. Broverman. 1978. "Roles of Gonadal Steroid Hormones in Psychiatric Depression in Men and Women." *Progress in Neuropharmacology* 2:487–503.

———. 1985. "A Comparison of the Antidepressant Effects of a Synthetic Androgen (Mesterolone) and Amitriptyline in Depressed Men." *Journal of Clinical Psychiatry* 46:6–8.

Waal, F.B.M. de. 1982. *Chimpanzee Politics*. London: Jonathan Cape.

Waber, D. P. 1977a. "Biological Substrates of Field Dependence: Implications of the Sex Difference." *Psychological Bulletin* 84:1076–1087.

———. 1977b. "Sex Differences in Mental Abilities, Hemispheric Lateralization, and Rate of Physical Growth at Adolescence." *Developmental Psychology* 13:29–38.

———. 1981. "Environmental Influences on Brain and Behavior." In *Sex Differences in Dyslexia* ed. A. Ansara, N. Geschwind, A. Galaburda, and N. Gartrell, 73–79. Towson, Md.: Orton Dyslexia Society.

Wang, C., S. Plymate, E. Neischlag, and C. A. Paulsen. 1981. "Salivary Testosterone in Men: Further Evidence of Direct Correlation with Free Serum Testosterone." *Journal of Clinical Endocrinology and Metabolism* 53:1021–1024.

Warburton, D. M. 1983. "Extrapolation in the Neurochemistry of Behavior." In *Animal Models of Human Behavior*, ed. G.C.L. Davey, 339–353. New York: Wiley.

Ward, I. L. 1974. "Sexual Environmental Differentiation: Prenatal Hormonal and Environmental Control." In *Sex Differences in Behavior*, ed. R. C. Friedman, R. M. Richart, and R. L. Vande Wiele, 3–18. New York: Wiley.

Warner, P., and J. Bancroft. 1988. "Mood, Sexuality, Oral Contraceptives, and the Menstrual Cycle." *Journal of Psychosomatic Research* 32:417–427.

Wasilewska, E., E. Kobus, and Z. Bargiel. 1980. "Urinary Catecholamine Excretion and Plasma Dopamine-Beta-Hydroxylase Activity in Mental Work Performed in Two Periods of the Menstrual Cycle in Women." In *Catecholamines and Stress: Recent Advances*, ed. E. Usdin, R. Kvetnansky, and I. J. Kopin, 34–39. Amsterdam: North Holland/Elsevier.

Weber, M. 1946. *From Max Weber: Essays in Sociology*. Trans. and ed. H. H. Gerth and C. W. Mills. New York: Oxford University Press.

———. 1947. *Theory of Social and Economic Organization.* Trans. A. M. Henderson and T. Parsons. New York: Oxford University Press.

———. [1904–1905] 1958. *The Protestant Ethic and the Spirit of Capitalism.* Trans. T. Parsons. New York: Scribner.

Weinberg, M. S., and C. J. Williams. 1980. "Sexual Embourgeoisement? Social Class and Sexual Activity, 1938–1970." *American Sociological Review* 45:33–48.

———. 1988. "Black Sexuality: A Test of Two Theories." *Journal of Sex Research* 25:197–218.

Weiss, H. D. 1972. "The Physiology of Human Penile Erection." *Annals of Internal Medicine* 76:793–799.

Wenger, M. A., and T. D. Cullen. 1972. "Studies of Autonomic Balance in Children and Adults." In *Handbook of Psychophysiology,* ed. N. S. Greenfield and R. A. Sternbach, 955–975. New York: Holt, Rinehart and Winston.

Westoff, C. F., and N. Ryder. 1977. *The Contraceptive Revolution.* Princeton: Princeton University Press.

Westoff, L. A. 1985. *Corporate Romance.* New York: Times Books.

Whalen, R. E. 1984. "Multiple Actions of Steroids and the Antagonists." *Archives of Sexual Behavior* 13:497–502.

Whitehurst, R. N. 1969. "Extra-marital Sex: Alienation or Extension of Normal Behavior." In *Extra-marital Relations,* ed. G. Neubeck, 129–144. Englewood Cliffs, N.J.: Prentice-Hall.

Whitney, C. 1989. "The Rage That Is Unleashed in the Soccer Stadium." *New York Times,* April 23, sec. E, 3.

Whyte, W. F. 1943. *Street Corner Society: Social Structure of an Italian Slum.* Chicago: University of Chicago Press.

Widiger, T. A., and S. A. Settle. 1987. "Broverman et al. Revisited: An Artifactual Sex Bias." *Journal of Personality and Social Psychology* 53:463–469.

Wiedeking, C., C. R. Lake, M. Siegler, A. A. Kowarski, and J. Money. 1977. "Plasma Noradrenaline and Dopamine-Beta-Hydroxylase during Sexual Activity." *Psychosomatic Medicine* 39:143–148.

Wilkerson, T. E. 1976. *Kant's Critique of Pure Reason: A Commentary for Students.* Oxford: Clarendon.

Will, G. 1988. "Revenge of the Ectomorphs." *Newsweek,* October 10, 84.

Williams, R. B., J. D. Lane, C. M. Kuhn, W. Melosh, A. White, and S. M. Schanberg. 1982. "Type A Behavior and Elevated Physiological and Neuro-Endocrine Responses to Cognitive Tasks." *Science* 218:483–485.

Wilson, A. P., and S. H. Vessey. 1968. "Behaviour of Free-ranging Castrated Rhesus Monkeys." *Folia Primatologica* 9:1–14.

Wilson, E. O. 1975. *Sociobiology: The New Synthesis.* Cambridge, Mass.: Harvard University Press.

Wilson, W. J. 1978. *The Declining Significance of Race.* Chicago: University of Chicago Press.

Winter, D. G. 1973. *The Power Motive.* New York: Free Press.

Witkin, H. A., and D. R. Goodenough. 1977. "Field Dependence and Interpersonal Behavior." *Psychological Bulletin* 84:661–689.

Wittelson, S. F., and J. A. Swallow. 1988. "Neuropsychological Study of the Development of Spatial Cognition." In *Spatial Cognition: Brain Bases and Development,* ed. J. Stiles-Davis, M. Kritchevsky, and U. Bellugi, 373–409. Hillsdale, N.J.: Erlbaum.

Wolf, P. 1971. "Crime and Development: An International Comparison of Crime Rates." *Scandinavian Studies in Criminology* 3:107–120.

Wolfgang, M. E., R. M. Figlio, and T. Sellin. 1972. *Delinquency in a Birth Cohort.* Chicago: University of Chicago Press.

Wrong, D. 1961. "The Oversocialized Conception of Man in Modern Sociology." *American Sociological Review* 26:184–193.

Wurtman, R. J., and J. Axelrod. 1963. "Sex Steroids, Cardiac 3H-Norepinephrine, and Tissue Monoamine Oxidase Levels in the Rat." *Biochemical Pharmacology* 12:1417–1419.

Yablonsky, L. 1979. *The Extra-Sex Factor.* New York: Times Books.

Yen, W. M. 1975. "Sex-linked Major-Gene Influences in Selected Types of Spatial Performance." *Behavior Genetics* 5:281–298.

Yesavage, J. M., J. Davidson, L. Widrow, and P. A. Berger. 1985. "Plasma Testosterone Levels, Depression, Sexuality, and Age." *Biological Psychiatry* 20:222–225.

Young, A. M., and A. H. Ismail. 1978. "Ability of Biochemical and Personality Variables in Discriminating between High and Low Physical Fitness Levels." *Journal of Psychosomatic Research* 22:193–199.

Young, T. R. 1984. "The Sociology of Sport: A Critical Overview." *Arena Review* 8:1–14.

Zajonc. R. B. 1965. "Social Facilitation." *Science* 149:269–274.

Zborowski, M. 1952. "Cultural Components in Response to Pain." *Journal of Social Issues* 8:16–30.

Zillman, D. 1980. "Anatomy of Suspense." In *The Entertainment Functions of Television,* ed. P. H. Tannenbaum, 133–163. Hillsdale, N.J.: Erlbaum.

———. 1984. *Connections between Sex and Aggression.* Hillsdale, N.J.: Erlbaum.

———. 1986. "Coition as Emotion." In *Alternative Approaches to the Study of Sexual Behavior,* ed. D. Byrnne and K. Kelley, 173–199. Hillsdale, N.J.: Erlbaum.

Zillman, D., J. Bryant, and B. S. Sapolsky. 1979. "The Enjoyment of Watching Sports Contests." In *Sports, Games, and Play: Social and Psychological Viewpoints,* ed. J. H. Goldstein, 297–335. Hillsdale, N.J.: Erlbaum.

Zola, É. [1885] 1968. *Germinal.* Trans. H. Ellis. Reprint. Gloucester, Mass.: Peter Smith.

Zola, I. K. 1966. "Culture and Symptoms: An Analysis of Patients Presenting Complaints." *American Sociological Review* 31:615–630.

Zuckerman, M. 1971. "Physiological Measures of Sexual Arousal in the Human." *Psychological Bulletin* 75:297–329.

———. 1984. "Sensation Seeking: A Comparative Approach to a Human Trait." *Behavioral and Brain Sciences* 7:43–71.

Zumoff, B., R. S. Rosenfeld, M. Friedman, S. Byers, R. H. Rosenman, and L. Hellman. 1984. "Elevated Daytime Urinary Excretion of Testosterone Glucuronide in Men with Type A Behavior Pattern." *Psychosomatic Medicine* 46:223–225.

INDEX

acetylcholine (ACh), 98; role in spatial ability, 124, 128–129, 226–227n4
Acquired Immune Deficiency Disease (AIDS), 108
activation hypothesis, 134, 156, 158
adrenal cortex, as source of T, 25, 49, 111, 161–162
adrenergic system, 123, 128–131, 135. *See also* autonomic nervous system
adrenocorticotropic hormone (ACTH), 98, 137, 161–162
age, and social class and sexual activity (male), 10, 40, 66–67, 79
aggression: dominance and, 74–76, 79; female, 137–144; male, in presence of females, 30; sexual activity and, 34–35, 53, 224n3; social class and, 71–76; T and female, 133–134, 140–142; T and male, 30–34, 53, 74
aging, sexual activity and, 69–70
alienation, 183
androgens. *See* testosterone; androstenedione; etc.
androstenedione, 153
anger. *See* aggression
anomie, dominance/eminence and, 87–90
attractivity, T and, 144, 151
autoimmune disease, spatial ability and, 158
automatization cognitive style, 121–122, 125
autonomic balance, 126
autonomic nervous system, 31–32, 34, 92, 98, 107, 123, 126, 128

biology: influence on sexuality, 10, 15, 18, 47, 83, 93; political use of, 2, 4, 112; social effects on, 1–2, 12–14, 133, 226n1; social justice and, 112, 221; sociology and, 1–6, 12, 133; transformation of women's, 13–14, 132, 143–144, 148–149, 152, 161
"blaming the victim," 73, 225n12
body, society and the, 2, 5
bridging disciplines, ix
Broverman hypothesis, 121–127, 131–135, 152, 155–156, 158, 163–164, 226–227n4; activation aspects, 134, 142; critique of, 125, 127–135; evidence for, 125–126, 128–130, 154; historical validity of, 11, 131, 134, 216

castration, 38, 49, 52
central nervous system (CNS), 32, 55, 60, 123–124, 129, 156
cerebral dominance: effects of, 157–158, 160–161; spatial ability and, 157; T and, 158
cholinergic system, 123, 128–129, 131. *See also* autonomic nervous system
Civilization and Its Discontents (Freud), 108, 218
civilizing process, 174–175, 177

coitus, female: increasing rates of, 148–149; marriage and, 67–68, 70–71, 155; T and, 145–147, 155
coitus, male, 33, 39, 41–43, 58, 66–69, 82–83, 106, 109; dominance/eminence and, 36, 49, 52, 105–106, 221, 224n5; extramarital, 17, 66–67, 84–93, 148–149 (*see also* infidelity); marital, 67–68, 70–71, 155; premarital, 17, 66–67, 148–149; T and, 44, 52, 55–57, 224n7, 227n6
comparative data, objections to, 48, 124, 223–224n1
corticosteroids, stress and, 98–99, 137, 161–162
cortisol, 99, 162
culture: effect on sexuality, 10, 15, 17–20; as explanatory, 4, 10, 20–22, 223n6; social class differences of, 78–79; social structural determinants, 21. *See also* norms

Darwin, Charles, 2
defeat (subordination), T and, 23, 28–29, 50, 54, 56–58, 61–63, 79–80
defeminization, fetal, 159
dehydroepiandrosterone (DHEA), 146
delta-4 androstenedione, 146
depression: norepinephrine and, 129; sexual activity and, 40; T and, 32–33, 100
divorce, 150
dominance, female, 138–142, 149–150; gonadal pathology and, 141; T and, 140–143
dominance, male; aggression and, 29, 34–35, 53–54, 74–76; over females, 137–138; females attracted by, 35, 47; personality and, 6, 28; as power, 6–8, 20, 97; progestin and, 141; sexuality and, 28, 49, 54, 226n4; T and, 6–7, 27–29, 47, 55, 103. *See also* dominance/eminence
dominance, vicarious. *See* vicarious dominance
dominance/eminence: as alternatives, 218–221; bureaucratization and, 26, 220; creativity and, 90, 210–211; definition of, 7–8, 27; female attainment of, 219; female competition for, 61, 172–174; females attracted by, 36, 50; female sexuality and, 61, 149–151; historical opportunities for, 167–168, 215–216, 220–221; interpersonal relations and, 61; libido and, 47, 61, 100–101, 106; loss of in sexual interaction, 57–58; lower white-collar opportunities for, 172, 200–201, 205; marginal utility of, 205–206; politics and, 229n3; problems of females high in, 149–150; 155; self and, 208–212; sexual activity and, 35–38, 47, 50, 57, 60, 86–90, 96, 101–110; sexual satisfaction and, 11, 109–110; social class and, 76–80, 190; T in females and, 11, 111, 133, 137–144, 148, 151–156, 161–164; T in males and, 61, 63, 77–78, 87, 99, 100, 137, 205–206, 213, 215–217, 224n5; T/E balance in women and, 11
dominance hierarchies, 28, 224n2, 224n4
Durkheim, Emile, 3, 15, 80, 87, 193, 199, 223n5

ejaculation, 39, 42–43, 45–47, 52, 57, 58, 225–226n2
eminence: definition of, 8; female bias toward, 151; longer timetable to attain, 220–221; as status, 8, 20, 97–98; T and, 6–7, 27–29, 30, 50. *See also* dominance/eminence
emotions, 98–99
endocrine system, 25
endocrino-logic, 65
epinephrine (adrenalin), 98–99, 162
erection, 39, 42–43, 47, 53, 58. *See also* sexual arousal
ergotropic system, 123, 128. *See also* autonomic nervous system
erythrocyte production, 62
estrogen (E), 49; sexual arousal and, 144–145; spatial ability and, 124–127, 130, 134
evolution, 4, 63–64

false consciousness, 11, 137, 171, 200–204
false needs, 201–202
false potency, 202–203
family violence, 73–75, 139–140
follicle-stimulating hormone (FSH), 125, 157
football, 177, 180, 189, 191–192, 227–228n7; division of labor in, 180–181; as idealized competition, 181–183; lower white-collar males and, 179–187, 200
free T, 29, 46, 153
Funkenstein hypothesis, 31–32

gender gap, 214
"generalized other," 195, 209
giving. See tenderness
gonadotropin-releasing hormone (GnRH), 31, 137

homosexuality, 17, 186
hormonal poverty, 227n1
hormones. *See specific names of hormones*
hypogonadism. *See* sexual dysfunction

individualism, aspects in football, 183–184
inferiority, 97, 100–101, 103–104, 108
infidelity, 79, 85–93, 173; compensatory, 90–92, 100–102; dominance/eminence and, 86–93; motives for, 85–86; occupational rates of, 89–90; overflow, 86–90; underflow, 92–93, 102. *See also* coitus, male: extramarital
inhibited sexual desire (ISD), 147
intercourse, sexual. *See* coitus, male; coitus, female
intimacy. *See* sexual intimacy

James, William, 209

Kant, Immanuel, 208, 223n5
Kinsey studies, defects of, 65, 67

labeling theory, 15
labor force, women in, 152–156, 161, 185
Lamarckian hypothesis, 160, 163
libido, 17–20, 32, 34, 38, 42–43, 87, 204; dominance/eminence and, 47, 53, 88–89, 100–101, 103, 186; T and female, 146–147, 155; T and male, 6, 24, 39, 47, 64, 100, 186
love, 97, 110
luteinizing hormone (LH), 55, 125, 157

males, lower white-collar: antagonism toward women, 173–174; competition from women, 172–174, 200; discontents of, 169–176, 201; significance of sports for, 167–206
Marcuse, Herbert, 87, 108, 201–202
marriage, coitus and, 67–68, 70–71, 155
marriage gradient, 150
Marx, Karl, 3, 183, 204
Marxists, 5, 171, 201, 204, 228n8
masculine assertion, football and, 184–186, 199–200
masculinization, fetal, 159–160
masturbation, 17–18, 33, 39–40, 43, 49, 66, 82–83, 93, 101, 104–105, 107–108, 225–226n2; T and female, 145–146; T and male, 45–46, 50, 55, 59–60
mathematical ability. *See* spatial ability
Mead, George H., 195, 208–209
menarche, age of, 132, 136, 161
menstrual cycle, as evidence for Broverman hypothesis, 124–126, 130–133, 137
mental rotation, 114, 226n2, 226n3
"Monday Night Football," 176, 191
monoamine oxidase, 32–33, 129–130, 226–227n4
monoamine oxidase inhibitor (MAO), 124
mores. See norms

narcissism, T and, 217–218
new collar voters, 176
norepinephrine (NE), 98–99, 107; aggression and, 31–34; spatial ability and, 123–124, 128–130; T and, 31–34

norms, sexual activity and, 10, 15–16, 19, 77–78, 80, 88. *See also* culture

occupational attainment (female), T and, 133–134, 152–156
occupational differences, T and, 79–80, 89, 153–155, 225n16
occupational discrimination, gender and, 61, 120–121, 173–174, 227n6
occupational involvement stress, 161
order givers, 172
order takers, 172, 181
organizational teamwork, football as model of, 179–181
organization hypothesis, 134, 156–164
orgasm, 33, 40, 45, 53, 56–57, 107, 224n6
ovaries, 25, 111

parasympathetic nervous system (PNS). *See* autonomic nervous system
perceptual restructuring, 121–123
pheremones, 47
"playing the dozens," 78
political labor, 170
pornography, 37–38, 60
postsexual satisfaction, 94–95, 105–108
power. *See* dominance, female; dominance, male
power and status; interaction outcomes of, 96–97; interaction partners and, 99–101; as model of social relations, 7–8, 20, 95, 98, 137; neurotransmitters of, 99; T and, 99
premarital sex, 17, 66–67, 148–149
proceptivity, T and, 144–146, 148, 150, 165
productive labor, 170
professional occupations, women in, 173, 227n5
progestin, 159
prostitution, 17, 50
psychosexual stimulation, T and, 39, 106

Rambo, as male hero, 213–214
rape, 30, 34, 37, 50–51, 56, 90, 224n3
receptivity, 47, 56; T and, 144–145
relative deprivation, 92
resentment, 97, 99, 100–105, 107
resistance, 97, 99–105, 107
role-taking, 195–196

science: gender aspects, 94–95, 111; hierarchy in, ix, 9, 12–13; specialization and, ix; speculation in, 9–10, 223n3
self: I and me aspects, 210–211; as social arena, 209–210, 229n2
sensation seeking, T and, 33, 150, 154
sex hormone binding globulin (SHBG), 26
sex hormones. *See specific names of sex hormones*
sex offenders, 30, 67–68
sexual activity: aggression and, 34–35; aging and, 69–70; defeat (subordination) and, 49, 54–55, 80; as dominance encounter, 48, 101–103, 105–106, 109–110; as eminence encounter, 102–103, 106, 109–110; female, and T, 133–134, 144–152; health and, 69–70; initiation of, 19–20, 41–43; laboratory studies of, 82–83, 110; male, and social class and age, 10, 40, 65–71, 79; marital, 66–68; novelty and, 58, 70–71, 91–92; of prisoners, 67–68; T and, 19, 38–65, 86–90. *See also* coitus; masturbation
sexual aggression, 30. *See also* rape
sexual arousal: inhibited by hostility, 34, 147; T and female, 146–147; T and male, 103. *See also* erection
sexual assertiveness (female), 139
sexual behavior. See sexual activity
sexual confidence, 63
sexual desire. *See* libido
sexual deviance, 16–18
sexual dysfunction, T and, 39, 41, 147–148
sexual double standard, 17

sexual experience, social determinants of, 94–98
sexual fantasies, 37, 48, 58–60, 93, 104, 106, 165
sexual interaction: defeat in, 57–58; as dominance/eminence encounter, 50–55, 100, 102, 110; T and, 51, 86–87, 90–92, 106; taking in, 101–103, 105–106; tenderness (giving) in, 102–103, 106, 109–110
sexual intercourse. *See* coitus
sexual intimacy, dominance/eminence and, 11, 51, 97–98, 101–103; taking in, 101–102, 105–106, 109–110, 226n4; tenderness (giving) in, 102, 106, 109–110
sexuality: biological elements in, 15–16, 18, 20, 83; biosocial elements in, 19–20, 83; cultural elements in, 15, 17–18; social elements in, 13, 14–22; social construction and, 14–20
sexual performance, 24, 34, 38, 40
sexual pleasure, T and, 11, 64, 226n5
sexual practice(s). *See* sexual activity
sexual satisfaction, dominance/eminence and, 11, 105–106
Smith, Adam, 182
social class: age and sexual activity and, 10, 40, 66–67, 79; aggression and, 71–76; and crime rates, 74, 168; dominance/eminence and, 76–80, 89, 168; male sexual activity and, 10, 15, 65–71, 77, 89, 225n14; politics and, 212–213; stereotypes of, 72–73; T and, 40, 71, 74–80, 89
social construction: critique of, 5, 14–22; of sexuality, 14–22, 42, 205
social Darwinism, 2, 15, 223n1
social hierarchy, 21
social mobility, 17, 170–171
social order: and T, 167; theories of, 200–202, 204
social structure, 10, 20–22, 65–71, 223n6. *See also* social class
social time, 133
sociobiology, 2, 35–36, 47
socio-bio-social chain, 2, 6, 10, 14, 38, 81, 121, 133, 176, 218–219, 223n1
sociology: and biology, 1–6, 11–12, 15, 133, 158, 223n1, 223n4
sociophysiology, 24
sociopsychoendocrinology, ix, 24
spatial ability: ACh and, 124, 129, 226–227n4; careers dependent on, 112, 117–121; components of, 112, 114, 117, 226n2, 226n3; E and, 124, 127, 130, 226–227n4; family effects on, 116–117, 164; female sexuality and, 152, 164–165; gender differences in, 112–117, 122, 127, 158, 226n3; genetic explanation of, 113, 115, 117, 226n3; gonadal pathology and, 127, 136; hormonal explanation of, 113, 115, 123, 129–130; ideology and, 112, 115; intergenerational female improvement in, 163–164; and left-handedness, 157–158; socialization explanation of, 113, 115–117, 122, 156, 165–166, 219; T and, 113, 123–127, 130, 152–156, 158, 217, 226–227n4; women in careers requiring, 119–121
spatial orientation, 226n3
spatial perception, 114, 118, 226n2, 226n3
spatial visualization, 114, 117, 226n2, 226n3
sports: appeal of, 176–187, 227n3; baseball, 177, 180, 191–193, 227–228n7; basketball, 177, 180, 189, 192–193, 195, 197; boxing, 74, 177, 189–190; as conversational resource, 179, 198–199, 229n16; division of labor in, 183, 228n3, 228n11; emotional catharsis in, 177, 204; hockey, 192–193; home-team advantage in, 196–198; as idealized social organization, 178–179, 182, 227n3; impact on fans, 188–189, 203–204; Left's view of, 176, 204, 228n8; local identification with, 189–190; male attributes and, 185–186, 199–200;

sports (*continued*)
physiological arousal and, 189, 194, 196, 199, 203–204; as play, 176–177, 227n3; politics and, 176, 204, 228n8; as ritual occasion, 172, 186, 193–195, 197, 199; role-taking and, 195–196; soccer, 190, 192–193; social class and, 179, 181, 186, 190–192, 198, 225n15; spectators and, 187–200, 227n3; strategizing outcomes of, 191–193; stratification and, 177, 186; tennis, 23, 28, 63, 78, 179, 225n15; TV spectators and, 179, 188; "unexciting societies" and, 177, 230n5; Victorians' view of, 185; violence in, 190. *See also* football
Sports Illustrated, 191, 228n13
status. See eminence
stress: occupational cause of, 161–162; spatial ability and, 161–162
submission, 97, 99, 101, 103, 105, 107
"surplus repression," 5, 87, 108
"survival of the fittest," 2, 4, 223n1
sympathetic nervous system (SNS). See autonomic nervous system

taking: in sexual intimacy, 101–102, 105–106, 109–110, 226n4
tenderness (giving): in sexual intimacy, 102, 106, 109–110
testosterone (T): aggression and, 30–34, 53, 74; aging and, 26, 40, 79; coitus and, 44, 52, 55–57, 224n7, 227n6; critical timing of (female), 163; defeat (subordination) and, 23, 28–29, 50, 54, 56–58, 61–63, 79–80; depression and, 32–33, 147–148; dominance and, 23–24, 27–29, 61, 137, 163, 186, 198, 216, 218; eminence and, 23–24, 27–29, 61, 137, 198, 216; erections and, 53; evolution (female) and, 165; exercise and, 137, 155; family relations and, 163; female sensitivity to, 142, 160; genetic determination of, 159; heritability of, 142; historical change in (female), 113, 131, 134, 142, 162–163; libido and, 6, 24, 150; in males, 25–26, 134; MAO and, 124; masturbation and, 45–46; maternal level of, 157, 159–160, 163; measurement of, 24–26, 39–40, 43–44, 46, 224n8; menstural cycle and, 144–145, 147; mental concentration and, 47, 186, 217, 230n6; narcissism and, 217–218; NE and, 31–34; personality and, 33, 150, 154, 217–218; political opinion and, 176, 202–206, 212–213; positive effects of, 6, 62, 167, 186, 224–225n10; problems when higher (female), 150–151; psychosexual stimuli and, 39, 53–54, 60, 106–107; replacement therapy and, 6, 39, 146; sex, 105–106; sex differences in, 113, 122, 127, 130, 158; sexual aggression and, 30; sexual differentiation and, 25; sexuality (female) and, 19, 133–134, 144–152; sexuality (male) and, 19, 24, 38–65; sexual pleasure and, 64, 145, 224–225n10; social class and, 40, 71, 74–77, 79; spatial ability and, 135–137, 156; stress and, 136–137, 160–162; variation in level of, 25–26, 38; vicarious dominance and, 186–187, 200, 203–204; well-being and, 62, 167
testosterone/estrogen (T/E) balance, 126, 131, 134–137, 142–143, 152, 218
testosterone sex, 105–106
testosterone surge: sexual consequences of, 205; social class and, 71, 77–80; of sports victors, 185
theory: as method, 8–10
Tocqueville, Alexis de, 183, 220
trophotropic system, 123, 128–129. *See also* autonomic nervous system
type A personality, 32
type B personality, 32

vicarious dominance: alternative modes of, 213–215; duration of mood of, 204–205; identification and, 187–190, 228n12; movie heroes and, 213–214; political

vicarious dominance (*continued*)
figures and, 214–215; social class and, 186, 228n12; sports and, 186–200, 203–204, 214, 228n12; T and, 186–187, 200, 203–204, 214
vicarious dominance/eminence, 11, 202–203; and national politics, 214
victory. *See* dominance, female; dominance, male
violence, 30, 73–75, 139–140, 168. *See also* aggression
visuospatial ability. *See* spatial ability

Weber, Max, 3
white-collar service sector, 169–170
women: change in structural position of, 131–132, 134, 142, 227n5; T and working women, 152–156
women's movement, 143–144